Modern Western Society

To Sony,
With all good wishes,
Peter Sidun

Modern Western Society

A Geographical Perspective on Work, Home and Well-Being

Peter Dicken and Peter E. Lloyd
University of Manchester

HARPER & ROW, PUBLISHERS
LONDON

Cambridge
Hagerstown
Philadelphia
New York

San Francisco
Mexico City
Sao Paolo
Sydney

First published 1981
Harper & Row Ltd
28 Tavistock Street
London WC2E 7PN

British Library Cataloguing in Publication Data
Dicken, Peter
  Modern Western Society.
  1. Anthropo-geography
  I. Title   II. Lloyd, Peter
  909   GF41

ISBN 0-06-318030-8
ISBN 0-06-318048-0 Pbk

Typeset by Inforum Ltd, Portsmouth
Printed and bound by the Pitman Press, Bath

CONTENTS

Preface

The seeds from which this book has grown were planted more years ago than we care to remember. The fact that they have taken so long to germinate is due to a number of causes. Some of the seeds were clearly of the slow-growing variety, taking far longer to bring forth fruit than we had expected. Other seeds from the initial sowing were dug up in the course of cultivation as our ideas changed and were replaced by other, hardier strains. Lastly, it has to be admitted that the cultivators themselves from time to time had their energies diverted to other academic tasks. In the event, however, we feel that the longer-than-expected growing period has produced a healthier and more satisfactory plant, though one which, undoubtedly, still has its weaknesses.

Our starting point was the feeling that many of the topics dealt with separately in different branches of human geography should be looked at together because the connections between them are stronger than the differences in their subject matter. The aim, therefore, is to provide a logical and coherent framework within which many of the topics studied separately by social, urban, economic and political geographers (and by some other social sciences) can be treated. Our focus is modern Western society and, especially, the ways in which people live out their daily lives in what is a complex and rapidly changing society. In particular, we examine the efforts of individuals and social groups to make a living, find a home and generally enhance their levels of well-being against the larger-scale social, economic and political processes operating at the present time. Our interest, then, is in the geography of what some writers call 'post-industrial' society, though we prefer not to use this term.

Given the constraints of time and space, our approach is inevitably selective and not everybody will agree with our judgement. Some topics are dealt with at great length, others get little more than a passing nod. However, we have tried to indicate where most, if not all, of the pieces fit. Hence, there is considerable scope for users of the book to expand particular topics to suit their own needs. Although this is a fairly lengthy book the number of chapters is small, a reflection of the highly interconnected nature of the subject matter. Long chapters can pose problems, but we decided that the merits of more, but shorter, chapters were more than offset by their fragmenting effect. To guide readers through each of the long chapters, therefore, each one begins with a detailed listing of its contents. The broad scope of the material included suggests that the book may have some appeal beyond the rather fuzzy boundaries of human geography. We believe it has relevance not only for courses in urban, social, economic and political geography but also for courses in urban studies, public administration, government and a variety of interdisciplinary courses concerned with modern society.

As always in books of this kind enormous debts (generally non-financial) are incurred by the authors. Inevitably, our respective wives and children have taken most of the strain. They, more than anybody except the authors themselves, will be relieved to see this book finally appear. Two other people deserve special thanks. Michael Forster of Harper & Row has displayed tolerance and patience beyond the bounds of duty. To him and to the production team in London we express our thanks. Nearer to home, Denise Horrocks has been a secretary of unequalled skill and industry. We are amazed that she managed to remain so cheerful as she fought her way through the innumerable drafts of the manuscript. Thanks are also due to the staff of the Drawing Office in the Department of Geography at the University of Manchester, especially Nick Scarle. The undergraduate members of the Department deserve our thanks in two senses – the one for their tolerance of our preoccupations, the other for their liveliness in debating the issues which form the substance of this book. Teaching remains both the stimulus and the testbed for writing. Lastly, we thank those colleagues on both sides of the Atlantic who reviewed an earlier version of the manuscript and made a number of very helpful suggestions. We have incorporated a good many into the final version and we hope that they will feel that their efforts were worthwhile. At the end, of course, only we are to blame for the errors and inadequacies which may remain.

Peter Dicken
Peter E. Lloyd

Manchester, January 1981.

Chapter One

Points of view

CHANGING VIEWPOINTS

During the past twenty-five years, human geography has experienced such a series of changes – in method and technique, in philosophy and outlook, even, to some extent, in its objects of study – that, to some, it is no longer recognizable.* Such changes contrasted very markedly with the many decades of apparent stability in geographical philosophy, the period in which the regional focus prevailed as the central core of the subject. Geography was about places – particular places – and the highest goal was to seek to identify the essence of place or region.

The so-called revolution which occurred in the late 1950s and early 1960s overthrew the rule of the 'particular place' school, replacing it with a régime based upon the search for theory and abstraction. The focus of attention became space in general rather than place in particular. From a position of relative isolation within the broader intellectual and social climate, human geography became imbued with the values and methods of science and with the tools of modern technology, especially the computer. At the time, the developments of the 1960s were seen as marking a major, even a revolutionary, change in geographical thinking. Peter Gould, for example, saw the 1960s as

> one of the greatest periods of intellectual ferment in the whole history of geography . . . involving in virtually every instance, the substitution of quantitative approaches to problems formerly treated in descriptive, verbal terms . . . if we are willing to accept that 'the past is prologue' then the actions of the players in the years ahead will be exciting to watch.
> *Gould (1969), p.3.*

The emphasis of the 1960s in human geography, then, was strongly mathematical and theoretical, a self-conscious attempt to emulate the physical sciences and to build scientific laws concerning the spatial arrangement of human activities.

In many ways, the revolution in human geography in the 1960s was the parallel of the British Prime Minister's, Harold Wilson's, 'white-hot technological revolution'. Both were seen at the time as heralding the millennium. But as we moved through the 1970s, as the economic climate cooled, as some geographers began to re-evaluate the not inconsiderable achievements of the previous decade, it became clear that the millennium had not arrived. Indeed, many of the storm-troopers of the 1960s' methodological revolution became highly critical. Brian Berry wrote, in 1973, of the

> mindless use of conventional inference statistics and measures of association in geographic research without regard for the validity of their assumptions.
> *Berry (1973), p.3.*

David Harvey pronounced that

> the quantitative revolution has run its course and diminishing marginal returns are apparently setting in. . . . There is a clear disparity between the

---

*Johnston (1979) provides an extremely useful survey of the various strands of development in Anglo-American human geography since 1945, while Chisholm (1975) exlores the extent to which the developments have been revolutionary or evolutionary.

sophisticated theoretical and methodological framework which we are using and our ability to say anything really meaningful about events as they unfold around us.
Harvey (1973), pp.128–129.

In the particular cases of economic and urban geography, in which many of the developments had been centred, Leslie King argued that

> it is already clear that the so-called quantitative revolution changed mainly the research techniques employed by economic and urban geographers and did little, at least directly, to channel their attention away from a traditional concern for the static location patterns of economic activities and the flows of people, goods and services in economic settings which were sterile in respect of any acknowledgement, let alone analysis, of the prevailing value systems, be they political, societal or individual. To the extent that there was a 'revolution' in the sixties it was a revolution in techniques and not in the main thrusts of intellectual enquiry in economic and urban geography.
> *King (1976), p.293.*

Thus, the research atmosphere of the early 1980s is substantially different from that of the 1960s. Quite apart from the marked shift of emphasis away from mathematical techniques as ends in themselves, there is a concern for a much deeper understanding of the *processes* which create the human geography of the world in which we live. There is, too, a greater concern with the social, economic and political *problems* which such processes generate. Indeed, much of the criticism of the work of the 1960s relates to its tendency to abstract from reality and to be overly concerned with trivial, rather than 'socially relevant', problems.

These issues are discussed more fully later in this chapter. Here, we should pause to identify the viewpoint of this book. Despite all the changes that have occurred in human geography, despite the tendency for geographers of one generation to jettison the work of previous generations – and often, in so doing, to throw out the baby with the bathwater – there is a thread of continuity in human geographical thought. This thread may have been given different labels at different times but it is, essentially, a concern with the location and spatial organization of human activities on the earth's surface, with the similarities and differences between places as the habitat of mankind.

The ways in which people, groups, institutions, organizations and their activities are distributed spatially and how they use space to meet their requirements are of considerable interest in their own right. But location in geographical space has a deeper significance than merely satisfying academic curiosity. A moment's thought should reveal how critical a person's location is to the kind of life he or she is able to lead, to the range of opportunities available, to the quality of 'life-chances'. Each of us is born into a particular place at a particular time. Some places are much more favoured than others – in terms of physical amenities, of work opportunities, of cultural and recreational facilities. *Where* we are born, then, will have a major influence on the kind of life we are able to lead, even in the extreme case as to whether we can survive at all. Obviously, geographical location is not the only influence but it is undoubtedly a very important one. It is sufficiently important to make geographical study worthwhile, to make human geography an important member of the social sciences because no other academic discipline places *space* at the centre of its inquiries. However, in adopting a spatial viewpoint we have to be very careful not to adopt a naïve view of space. Space cannot be isolated as a totally separate object of study. It is neither merely a 'stage' on which the human drama is acted out nor a 'container' within which human activities occur. It is a basic dimension of human existence but one whose properties and influence are extremely difficult to disentangle. It is a dimension which cannot be understood in isolation from the social, economic, political and cultural processes at work in the world at different scales. At the same time, we would argue, our knowledge of such processes is incomplete without an understanding of the spatial dimension of human existence.

PATTERNS AND PROCESSES

In adopting a spatial viewpoint, human geographers ask two basic questions:

1 In what ways do human activities vary spatially on the earth's surface and how do such *spatial patterns* change over time?

2 Why are human activities patterned spatially in the ways we observe, that is, what are the *underlying processes* which generate them?

At first sight answering such questions would seem to be a disarmingly simple task. In fact, it is exceptionally difficult because the relationships between the spatial distribution of human activities and the processes generating them are extremely complex. In the first place, the relationship between process and pattern is not simply one way:

$$\text{process} \longrightarrow \text{pattern.}$$

Processes obviously do produce patterns. Indeed, one way of thinking of spatial patterns is to regard them as a snapshot of a continuing process at a single point in time. In this sense, observed patterns – for example, maps of population distribution, of the location of economic activities, of variations in income – are 'frozen processes' in which the action has been stopped (similar to the action replay of a football game on television). But the patterns produced at any one time themselves influence and modify subsequent processes. In Kenneth Boulding's terms,

> growth creates form but form limits growth
> *Boulding (1953), p.337.*

The relationship, then, is circular rather than one way:*

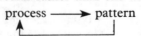

---

*An obvious example to illustrate this point is the city. Cities built in the nineteenth century were the product of the economic, political and social processes operating at that time. Their built form reflected both the social order of nineteenth-century society and also the prevailing technology, particularly the technology of industrial production and of transport. The nineteenth-century city was, spatially, very compact; it had a high-density central core on which most transport routes focused. Cities tend to last for a very long time (at least in terms of human time-spans). Their physical structure tends to change more slowly than the activities which are contained within them. Twentieth-century industrial and transport technologies differ considerably from those of the nineteenth century. Industrial processes tend to need more space, preferably on a single level; transportation is predominantly private (the automobile) rather than public. Twentieth-century industrial development has, for the most part, had to take place outside the city centres partly because of the constraints imposed by their inherited form. People have had to try to find places to live which are accessible to their places of work. As a result, twentieth-century urban development has been mostly *peripheral* to the nineteenth-century cores; *sub*urban rather than urban. The new urban form, in turn, modifies ongoing processes. Growth in the periphery has tended to generate decline at the centre. The economic and social geography of the city is changed further.

A second complication arises from the nature of the processes themselves. A common practice among geographers has been to seek the explanation of one spatial pattern in terms of other spatial patterns; in other words, to look for spatial associations or correlations. But mere association, whether spatial or otherwise, need not signify a causal relationship or, indeed, any functional relationship at all. More generally, many, if not most, of the processes which generate spatial patterns are not, themselves, spatial in origin. They arise from processes operating in the social, economic, political or cultural spheres. Hence, although human geographers ask predominantly *spatial questions* they need to seek *aspatial answers* as well as spatial ones. This is why geographers need to have some considerable understanding of other relevant disciplines. But we would also argue that other academic disciplines should be more aware of the influence of geographical processes – of the influence of location – on the phenomena they study. Many of them seem to proceed in the belief that we all live on the head of a pin; that the world is somehow spaceless.

But once we accept that spatial patterns are the outcome of both spatial and *a*spatial processes then we face the problem of trying to disentangle one from the other. In statistical terminology, which is the dependent, and which is the independent, variable? There is, in Harvey's terminology, a 'problem of confounding' in which it is difficult to separate out the influence of geographical space and the influence of other variables. The example he gives to illustrate this problem concerns the process of diffusion. The topic of spatial diffusion has become a substantial research area in human geography. One of its major bases is that locational proximity is the primary variable in the diffusion process: ideas, information, innovations diffuse most readily, it is suggested, between people who live in close geographical proximity. As geographical distance increases, the likelihood of contact decreases, an effect commonly known as distance decay.

Other academic disciplines interested in the diffusion of ideas and information, for example, sociology and social anthropology, tend to focus on different variables. In particular, they would suggest, people tend to communicate most readily with others most like themselves, whether in terms of certain personality attributes or of social class. The problem is that people of similar social class tend to live close to each other geographically. Which, then, is the more important influence on the diffusion process, 'geographical' distance or 'social' distance? What may, from one viewpoint, be regarded as a predominantly geographical phenomenon may, in fact, be a social phenomenon, or vice versa.

This problem of confounding is present in most situations which interest human geographers. We need to be wary not only of making simple cause-and-effect inferences but also, in asking spatial questions, we must expect to search for answers in broader *a*spatial processes. With such reservations in mind, however, we can accept the view that human geographers characteristically look at the world through spatial 'spectacles'. But what is actually seen depends very much upon the nature of the lenses in the frames. In particular, it depends upon the geographical scale of analysis and upon the value-system of the observer. Let us look briefly at each of these.

Geographical scales and 'levels of resolution'

The spatial scale we adopt very much influences both what we are able to observe and also our understanding and interpretation of what we see. If we adopt an inappropriate spatial scale – either voluntarily or because data are available only at particular scales – then we may well get a totally misleading impression of what is actually happening. Two examples will illustrate the effect of using different spatial scales.

The first example is concerned with the spatial distribution of family poverty in the United States. Figure 1.1a maps family poverty using a 'state size' spatial lens. At the state level the incidence of family poverty is seen to be highest in the block of southern states with high levels also in the Dakotas. At this level of resolution, it would seem that between 27.6 and 35.7 percent of all families in North Dakota were suffering from poverty. But if we refocus the spatial lens and alter the scale to that of the county, the view changes considerably. Figure 1.1b shows the pattern of family poverty *within* North Dakota. Quite clearly, the spatial pattern was far from regular. Large areas in the east of the state, especially, but also elsewhere had extremely low levels of family poverty; levels similar to those observable at the state level for the 'wealthy' states of California, Nevada, Utah in Figure 1.1a. Conversely, several counties in the south and west of North Dakota had very much higher percentage poverty levels. Thus if we use a large-scale lens we miss a great deal of the real-world variation. If we were to focus on the pattern *within counties* we would find further detailed differences.

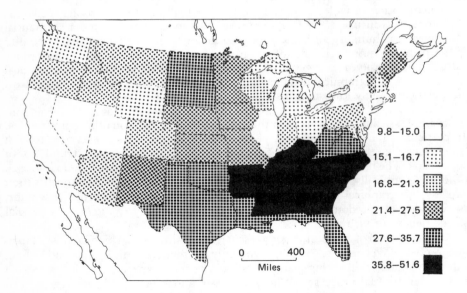

9.8–15.0	
15.1–16.7	
16.8–21.3	
21.4–27.5	
27.6–35.7	
35.8–51.6	

Figure 1.1a   Family poverty in the United States at different spatial scales. Variations in family poverty by state, 1959

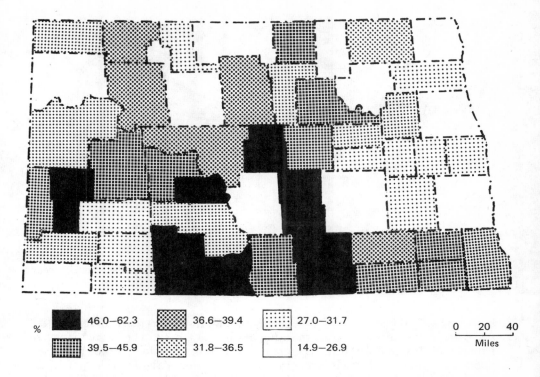

<figure>

%

- ■ 46.0–62.3
- ▓ 39.5–45.9
- ▨ 36.6–39.4
- ▨ 31.8–36.5
- ▨ 27.0–31.7
- □ 14.9–26.9

0   20   40
Miles

Figure 1.1b Family poverty in the United States at different spatial scales. Variations in family poverty by county, North Dakota, 1959

</figure>

Source: R.L. Morrill & E.H. Wohlenberg (1971) *The Geography of Poverty in the United States*, New York: McGraw Hill, figures 2.9 and 3.1a. With permission of McGraw Hill Book Company.

Our second example is at the scale of the individual city. Merseyside, in northwestern England is an area with major economic problems. But our view of the nature of these problems depends on our scale of observation. In the case of employment change, for example, Merseyside as a whole suffered a net loss of roughly 1500 manufacturing jobs between 1966 and 1975 (Figure 1.2a). In percentage terms, this was less than 1 percent of its total stock of manufacturing employment in 1966. But the level and direction of employment change varied dramatically within Merseyside (Figure 1.2b). For example, employment in inner Merseyside *fell* by 20,000 (26 percent of the 1966 total). In stark contrast, employment in outer Merseyside *increased* by 18,500 (an increase of 20 percent). Clearly our view of the nature of Merseyside's economic problems and, therefore, our understanding of their possible causes will be greatly determined by the scale of analysis.

Thus the level of spatial resolution adopted has a very profound effect on what we are able to observe and on the kind of explanation we are likely to adopt. But this is not simply a technical issue. There may be a *functional* relationship between different spatial scales. This is shown diagrammatically in Figure 1.3. The diagram is

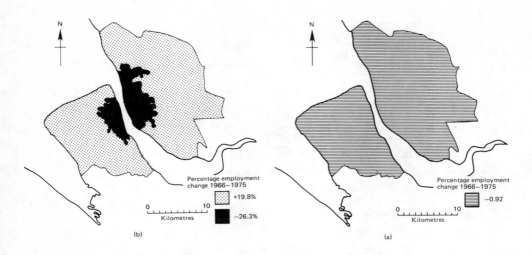

Figure 1.2   Employment change in Merseyside, Northwest England, viewed at different spatial scales

based on Stafford Beer's idea of 'cones of resolution'. It suggests that different spatial scales are 'nested' one within another. For example, we need to be aware that what happens in Britain – say to its economy – is only partly a function of processes operating within Britain itself. Economic forces operating at a larger scale – the EEC, the world economy as a whole – may be the major forces to be considered. This idea of *interdependence* between events at different geographical scales is a theme which recurs at several places in the following chapters.

Values

There is a fairly widespread belief that academic study, particularly scientific study, is a process of detached, objective observation and analysis. By this interpretation, the views, attitudes, prejudices and general values of the scholar should not be allowed to distort the objective pursuit of knowledge. In human geography, at least until recently, it is probably fair to say that either most practitioners gave little thought to the question or, especially during the white-hot quantitative revolution of the 1950s and 1960s, self-consciously adopted the role of the detached scientist. Within the last few years, however, human geographers have increasingly come to realize that – like all social scientists – we cannot view the world in a totally objective and unbiased way. No matter how 'scientifically objective' we may claim to be, in reality we display our values and attitudes in the things we choose to study and in how we choose to study them. During the 1970s, in particular, there emerged a growing concern among geographers with the *problems* which face people in modern society. This is reflected both in the kinds of things studied – the distribution of poverty, disease, crime, spatial injustice, for example – and in the direction of the studies. At the extreme, it is even argued by some that not only must we be actively engaged in solving specific problems but also in changing society in a revolutionary manner.

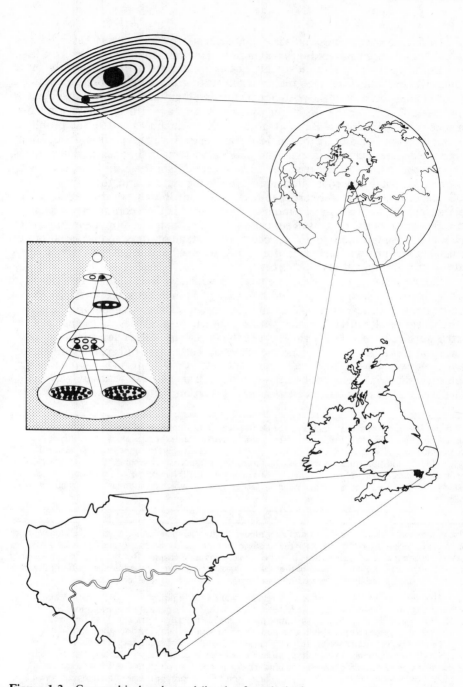

Figure 1.3 Geographical scales and 'levels of resolution'

Source: adapted from S. Beer (1968) *Management Science*, New York: Doubleday & Co., p.114.

The debate over values and viewpoints, ideals and ideologies* has produced much that is thought-provoking. It is forcing many human geographers to at least consider the philosophical and ideological basis of their work. But some of the more vituperative exchanges between the protagonists of different viewpoints seem more akin to blood sports, with the participants hurling their jargon-ridden ideologies at each other. There can be no doubt that we live in a world of many problems, injustices and inequalities. But a great deal can be done to alleviate the problems without necessarily manning the barricades and engaging in revolution. Inequalities of varying degrees exist in *all* social and political systems in the present day; there is no guarantee that a new order would be any better than the old. What is certain, however, is that we need to understand both the nature and the causes of the problems of today's world in order to be able to contribute towards their solution, whether through direct involvement in policy-making or community action or indirectly through the process of education. We need to make more people aware of how social, economic and political processes operate to produce spatial variations in human activity and well-being. In doing this, we need to draw extensively on ideas and theories from a variety of sources.†

One thing is very clear about the world in which we live: there is a pronounced *spatial unevenness* in the nature and intensity of human activities and in levels of well-being. Such unevenness is evident at a number of different geographical scales: at the world level, within nations, within regions, within cities. Some parts of the earth's surface have a very high level of human activity – high densities of population, large concentrations of economic activities – others are but sparsely inhabited. Some 'pathways' are in heavy and constant use – certain air and shipping routes, highways, railroads, telephone lines – others are little used. In terms of 'well-being' there are areas of abundance and areas of deprivation. Often such areas exist cheek

---

*Johnston (1979, chapter 6) summarizes the debate very well. Examples of specific 'exchanges' can be found in various issues of the *Professional Geographer* and *Area*, while the radical journal *Antipode* projects the revolutionary view in many of its articles. (A selection of articles from *Antipode* has been edited by Peet, 1978.) In addition, there is an emerging 'humanist' perspective in geography, as demonstrated in Ley and Samuels (1978). More specifically, David Smith (1977) has proposed that human geography should be restructured around the theme of *welfare* geography, which he summarizes as 'who gets what where'.

---

†One of the most fruitful sources in examining modern industrial societies is obviously the framework of Karl Marx. Much of Marx's diagnosis of the trends in capitalist industrial society can be used as a basis for unravelling some of the complexities and outcomes of economic change. But this need not necessarily imply an uncritical acceptance either of the whole Marxist diagnosis or of the Marxist solution. Marxists would, of course, strongly disagree with this viewpoint, but as Smith has pointed out:

> Marxian economics is experiencing a revival, while in geography, familiarity with Marx is growing almost to the extent of the fashion effect that aided the quantitative revolution. But, as before, there is a tendency to apply new paradigms uncritically. Marx may have been able to dissect the operation of a capitalist economy with particular clarity, and see the essential unity of economy, polity and society that we so often miss today. But Marx does not hold the key to every modern problem in complex, pluralistic societies. A particularly disturbing aspect of the contemporary academic scene is the tendency to accept or reject things largely as a matter of faith – whether it be Marxian analysis, Samuelson's *Economics*, or the need for geography in a university curriculum.
> *Smith (1977), p.368.*

by jowl, as even cursory observation in most cities in both the industrialized and less-developed world shows. Zones of affluence exist next to zones of poverty.

CHOICES AND CONSTRAINTS

Such geographical unevenness – differences between places in human terms – is not entirely haphazard or random. There is a good deal of regularity about it. Why? Why does such 'regular unevenness' exist? What are the major processes underlying these spatial patterns observable at different scales? There is no simple answer, of course, to such a complex issue. But in trying to grope our way through the thickets of complexity it is useful to regard the spatial distribution of human activities as being the outcome of two connected elements:

1 the *choices* made by individuals, groups, organizations to behave in particular ways;

2 the *constraints* within which such choices are made.

Since the emergence of what has come to be called 'behavioural' geography, a great deal of emphasis has been placed upon *individual* decision-making and upon the motives, attitudes, preferences and choices underlying individual decisions. Writing in 1966 in the vanguard of the new behavioural geography, Gould argued that:

> the human landscape . . . is nothing more, but equally nothing less, than the spatial expression of the decisions of men.
> *Gould (1966), p.2.*

Ten years later, the introduction to a social geography text stated that,

> social geography focuses on individual spatial behaviour, for the geographical patterns produced by millions of people *can be understood only by examining the individual's decision making*.
> *Jakle, Brunn, Roseman (1976), p.xi (present authors' emphasis).*

The problem is that individuals are not completely 'free agents'; freedom of choice is not available to all. Indeed, in some circumstances, there may be no real choice at all; there may be only one option available. The Swedish geographer Torsten Hägerstrand is a leading advocate of an approach which concentrates upon the *constraints* within which choices are made rather than upon the individual choices. In his words,

> a society is not made up of a group of people which decides in common what to do a week ahead of time. It consists primarily of highly institutionalized power and activity systems. . . . In total, seen from the point of view of the individual, this is an enormous maze about which he personally can do very little.
> *Hägerstrand (1970), p.18.*

Individuals are rarely, if ever, totally free of constraints, obligations or rules which govern their behaviour. At the most general level, we are constrained to behave in certain ways by the kind of society in which we live. But it is not just individual people who are constrained in their behaviour. Business firms, educational institutions, labour unions, national governments also operate within a complex world of constraints. Thus, behaviour at the individual level needs to be seen within its broader context: the prevailing social, economic and political structure and the inherited culture. In order to understand how and why human activities are arranged spatially we need to understand the ways in which society operates.

However, there is a danger that, in adopting a *structuralist* viewpoint, in looking only at constraints, we may overlook the fact that individuals *do* make choices, albeit within a constrained environment. Some, of course, have a greater variety of choice than others. The wealthy and the powerful have more 'degrees of freedom' than the poor and the weak. The multinational business enterprise has a wider variety of options than the small local firm. On the other hand, to concentrate only on the choices of individuals as revealed in their actual behaviour blinds us to the fact that

> what people *cannot* do is just as important as what they are able to do, and often more revealing.
> *Thrift (1977), p.25.*

Our approach, therefore, is based upon the concept of *choices within constraints*.

NEEDS, WANTS AND THE BASES OF SOCIAL ORGANIZATION

A useful starting point is to recognize that human activities arise fundamentally from attempts to satisfy basic *needs* and *wants*. All human beings – indeed all living creatures – possess certain fundamental needs which must be satisfied in order to ensure survival. The social psychologist Abraham Maslow has suggested that human needs and wants may be arranged in a hierarchical sequence with 'lower' needs being satisfied before those of 'higher' needs (Figure 1.4). The most basic needs, of course, are those necessary for survival; they are related to human physiology. The primary concern then is for such needs as food, clothing, shelter and for the perpetuation of the species. Figure 1.4 suggests that other, increasingly less tangible, needs assume greater importance as the lower-order needs are fulfilled. As the individual develops, therefore, his or her set of needs and wants becomes increasingly complex. It would seem obvious, too, that the more basic needs of survival and safety would dominate in societies which are technologically and economically less developed. But it would be incorrect – as well as arrogant – to assume that inhabitants of such societies do not also possess the so-called higher-order needs. Conversely, as we shall see, there are many people in the affluent industrial societies who have to struggle even to survive in terms of the standards set by the particular society. This is, perhaps, the most important point. Above a certain very basic level, needs and wants are *relative*, not absolute. Hunger may be removed by a bowl of rice or maize, by a beefsteak or by a dish of caviar. Similarly, shelter may be a mud hut, a four-bedroom detached house or a penthouse suite. Each, in its own way, provides food or shelter yet not all would be universally acceptable. Thus, what is regarded as basic in one society may be an undreamt of luxury in another. What is standard diet to some may be culturally unacceptable to others. When we consider the driving force of needs and wants, therefore, we need to take into account individual and group perceptions of what is desirable. Such perceptions are themselves greatly influenced by the cultural values and customs, as well as the general level of affluence, of different societies. They are

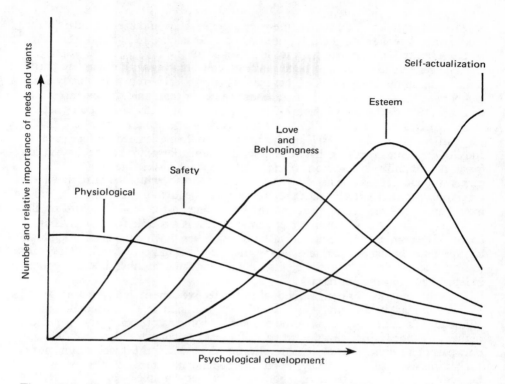

Figure 1.4 Maslow's model of the sequential development of needs and wants

Source: adapted from a hierarchy of needs in 'A Theory of Human Motivation' in *Motivation and Personality*, 2nd edition, by Abraham H. Maslow. Copyright © 1970 by Abraham H. Maslow. By permission of Harper & Row, Publishers, Inc.

also greatly influenced by people's *awareness* of differences, an awareness greatly enhanced by modern developments in the communications media (see Chapter Two).

However, regardless of the subtleties of meaning involved in defining needs and wants, two things are fundamental:

1 Very few, if any, of the basic needs and wants can be satisfied by individuals acting entirely alone.

2 Beyond a very simple level, such joint efforts need to be organized, co-ordinated, controlled and regulated.

Living alone on a desert island sounds very attractive to those of us who spend our time in large congested cities. We may well be able to survive in such isolation; to build a crude shelter, gather food, make simple clothing. But even if there were an abundance of natural resources on the island there would be a severe limit on how far we could satisfy our basic needs. Also, since most of our 'higher-order' needs (in Maslow's scheme) require interaction with other people, our life on the island would be extremely restricted. Of course, there are people who would prefer to live the life of a hermit, but they are the exception. Most of us choose to live and work with others (even though we may wish to 'get away from it all' from time to time).

The general advantages to be found from collaborating with others are partly summed up in the kinds of social messages which we learn from a very early age – 'many hands make light work', 'two heads are better than one', for example. But what precisely are these advantages? The most important one is based upon what the economist calls the *division of labour*. An individual operating alone would find it very difficult to provide himself and his family with the basic needs of food, shelter and clothing. But supposing that three individuals collaborate to provide these needs for all three families by each one *specializing* on a single task. One may be adept at carpentry, another may be handy with needle and thread, while the third may have green fingers. Alternatively, each specific task may be further subdivided: in building a house, one may concentrate on the walls, one on the roof, the third on the windows. This is a trivial example of course, but it is a simple form of division of labour. The point is that almost any task can be broken down into parts, individuals can specialize in just one part and, as a result, a number of people working together can produce more, in aggregate, than could the same number if each worked independently on the entire task.

Sharing of tasks, for both individual and collective benefit, is a very deep-seated form of human behaviour. It is certainly not confined to the economic sphere although it is in helping to solve the economic problems of society that it is most highly developed. Specialization in part of a task, or concentrating on producing only part of a person's basic needs, implies *interdependence*; the division of labour is the antithesis of self-sufficiency. Such interdependence thus involves *transactions* between individuals. The transactions may be very simple – for example, the exchange of one article for another – or highly complex as in modern industrial societies in which exchange is not directly in the form of products but indirectly through the medium of money or credit cards. Such economic transactions are, of course, only a small part of the myriad of transactions or *social bargains* which make up a society.

Social interdependence has a further, and particularly important, dimension. Most transactions and bargains, most forms of human behaviour, involve both benefits and costs. To the individual, the benefit of engaging in one particular action rather than another is the utility (value, pleasure, etc.) it provides. The cost is the 'opportunity cost' of not engaging in the alternative action. But benefits and costs invariably stretch way beyond the individuals directly involved: there may be *external effects* which 'spill over' to others either intentionally or unintentionally. We shall be much concerned with this question of *externalities* at various points in the following chapters; for the moment we merely provide some simple examples to illustrate the meaning of the term.

Consider, for example, the person who takes his transistor radio into the public park to listen to his favourite music. The action clearly provides the owner with pleasure; it may also provide pleasure – a *positive externality* – to other people within earshot who like the music being broadcast. But also it may generate a nuisance – a *negative externality* – to those who either want peace and quiet or who prefer a different kind of music. On the one hand, the playing of the radio is a 'good', on the other it is a 'bad'. Similarly, a factory producing, say, car tyres generates both positive and negative externalities, 'goods' and 'bads'. Apart from the tyres themselves (goods in the conventional economic sense), the factory provides employment both directly and indirectly in other businesses, it pays taxes which contribute towards the provision and maintenance of local facilities. But the factory may also produce 'bads'. It may dump its waste in the local river, it may pollute the atmosphere with its chimney, it may pollute the local environment with its noise, smells and unsightliness. All of these are external costs; they are inflicted on the local neighbourhood but, in most cases, they are not paid for by the producer.

A particularly significant feature of externalities or spillovers is that many of them are very specifically *geographical* in their expression: their impact, whether positive or negative, declines with increasing distance from their source. Since almost everything that an individual does, or refrains from doing, has some impact on others, then the greater the geographical concentration of population the greater will be the incidence of externalities.

The general issue of social interdependence takes us on to the second point about human behaviour:

> People do things or abstain from doing things, that affect others, beneficially or adversely. *Without appropriate organization, the results may be pretty unsatisfactory*.
> *Schelling (1974), p.27* (present authors' emphasis).

Beyond a very simple level, human activities need to be *organized* and *co-ordinated*. The finer the division of labour, the greater the degree of interdependence and the greater the need for co-ordination. Even at a simple level it does not follow that people will collaborate voluntarily. They may have to be cajoled, coerced, paid or bribed to do so. Hence all societies have evolved various types of control and co-ordination procedures to enable society to function – rules, regulations, customs, laws, codes of behaviour. These are designed to ensure social order and the fulfilment of society's needs.* In particular, they have to solve the 'economic problem' of society: the process of providing for the material needs of society against a background of scarcity. As Robert Heilbroner has pointed out, there are two elements to this process:

1 A society must organize a system for producing the goods and services needed for its own perpetuation – *the production problem*.

2 It must arrange a distribution of the fruits of this production amongst its members so that they will be encouraged to carry on their productive activities – *the distribution problem* (or who gets what).

The organizational problem is to devise social institutions which will mobilize human effort for a continued recycling of production and distribution. The type of

---

*The extent to which societies are based upon *consensus* or upon *conflict* is a matter of considerable argument. In the briefest terms, 'the *consensus* model gives considerable weight to the persistence of shared ideas. . . . The *conflict* approach, on the other hand, holds that the most important aspect of social order is the domination of some groups by others, that society is best understood as an arena of actual and potential conflict, and that when things *look* peaceful, it is only because someone is sitting on the lid. Conflict theorists do not ignore consensus and belief, but they emphasise that popular attitudes are often sustained and manipulated by groups in power' (Broom and Selznick 1975, p.8).

solution adopted has an important influence on the spatial dimension of society. Different types of *social* organization tend to produce different types of *spatial* organization. In examining different societies historically, Heilbroner suggests that only three basic ways of co-ordinating and organizing the production and distribution of society's needs have been devised, though they may be combined in various proportions in particular societies.

The oldest solution to the problem of providing society's material needs is based upon *tradition*. In Heilbroner's words,

> It has been a mode of social organization in which both production and distribution were based on procedures devised in the distant past, rigidified by a long process of historic trial and error, and maintained by heavy sanctions of law, custom, and belief.
> *Heilbroner (1972), p.21.*

In traditional societies, the *production* problem is solved by family continuity – sons do the jobs that their fathers did; birth determines a person's role in society. In this way, the skills needed to perform particular tasks are passed on from one generation to another. The *distribution* of the fruits of production in traditional society is based, to a large extent, on *reciprocal transactions* – the mutual exchange of goods and services. The precise method may be subject to complex rules of family, kinship or religion but reciprocity is the key element. An important characteristic of traditional societies is that they tend to be *static*. Change, if any, tends to come from outside the society.

An alternative way of co-ordinating efforts to produce society's needs is by centralized authority; what Heilbroner terms the *command system*. Such systems have a very long history, often being imposed upon traditional societies from outside. In a command system decisions to co-ordinate society's activities are taken by a central authority, an 'economic commander-in-chief'. Decisions are made in accordance with some more or less conscious objectives set out by those in authority. Those in positions of command may be either elected or self-appointed. Their programmes for solving the economic problem may be based on social jusice or self-interest or some particular combination of both. Regardless of the moral or philosophical basis of the command system, it provides another way of organizing human activity to produce a society's material needs. The *production* problem is solved by direct allocation of people and resources to particular tasks and the *distribution* problem by some conscious assignment of the fruits of labour on criteria determined by the central authority. Thus command systems are based upon the principle of *redistribution*.

The third basic solution to the economic problem is based upon *the market*. In the market or capitalist system there is, in theory, no overt control of either production or distribution. Economic life is governed by what has been called the 'invisible hand' of the market. Decisions are dispersed, not centralized. The key to the system is the *price* set by the market which is based upon supply and demand. What is produced and in what quantity depends theoretically upon what consumers are prepared to buy. This, in turn, depends upon the price asked and upon the financial means at the consumer's disposal. The end result, at least in theory, is a balance or equilibrium between supply and demand. This is what co-ordinates production in a market economy. *Distribution* – who gets what – is based upon *ability* *to pay* the market price. The underlying rationale of the market system, therefore, is the doctrine of 'intelligent selfishness' whereby every individual, by behaving in a way which brings him or her the greatest benefit, will supposedly enhance the total well-being of society at large.* To the advocate of the pure market system its intrinsic merit is that it (apparently) solves the production and distribution problem simultaneously.

In fact, most societies today contain a mixture of the three elements of tradition, command and market exchange. For example, most Western societies are basically market (capitalist) societies. But all of them contain elements of command systems; some to a very high degree (see Chapter Two). For example, all Western governments are increasingly involved in attempting to 'manage' their national economies. Although transactions may be based primarily on the market exchange mechanism, there are also strong elements of redistribution according to criteria established by government. Conversely, many of the command systems have begun to incorporate market elements within them. In this context it is useful to draw a distinction between *public* goods and *private* goods. Kuhn distinguishes between them in the following way:

> A compliment, a cup of coffee, a hat, or a bicycle produces satisfaction for one person. A radio, an automobile, a kiss, or a house can produce satisfaction for two or a limited group. Without attempting to state precisely the maximum number of people who can achieve satisfaction from any one good, we may say that goods of this sort are privately consumed, and will be called *private goods*. No matter what the nature of the system of social organization, many goods in any society are necessarily and by nature private, and are typically consumed by individuals or families. Some are also highly personal and give satisfaction to only one or a few people, like the faded boyhood snapshot of your grandfather hanging by his knees from the apple tree behind the old house on Sixteenth Street. *An important aspect of private goods is that, within the limits of his income, a person can consume or not consume any one good according to his personal preference*.
>
> In marked contrast is a good such as national defense. Although individuals can get satisfaction from having their nation defended, *this kind of good can be consumed only collectively, or publicly. It cannot be divided so that each person can have as much or as little as he likes*. By the same token, the values and costs of these *public* (or collective) *goods* cannot be allocated to the same individuals. Although there is no sharp dividing line between private and public goods, such things as fire and police protection, a system of justice, a

---

*That this may well not be the case is illustrated by Hirsch:

> Considered in isolation, the individual's demand for education as a job entrée, for an auto, for a country cottage, can be taken as genuinely individual wants, stemming from the individual's own preferences in the situation that confronts him. Acting alone, each individual seeks to make the best of his or her position. But satisfaction of these individual preferences itself alters the situation that faces others seeking to satisfy similar wants. A round of transactions to act out personal wants of this kind therefore leaves each individual with a worse bargain than was reckoned with when the transaction was taken, because the sum of such acts does not correspondingly improve the position of all individuals taken together.
> *Hirsch (1977), p.4*.

network of roads, a stable economy, a sound currency, and cleaning a polluted river are also public goods. A limited-access highway or a system or local trash paid for by tolls or fees of users is intermediate, showing some traits of public and some of private goods.
Kuhn (1966), p.559 (present authors' emphasis).

Thus, one basic difference between private and public goods is the extent to which an individual can buy as much, or as little, of the goods as he or she wishes (or is able). A second distinction relates to the principle of excludability. A public good is one from which no individual can be excluded. It follows from this that a public good should be equally available to all citizens. A 'pure' public good, therefore, is one which meets these two criteria of non-excludability and equal availability (Cox and Reynolds 1974). In fact very few, if any, public goods are totally pure. Everybody does *not* have equal access to such public goods as police and fire protection, education, a healthy environment or a public park. One of the most basic reasons why public goods are generally 'impure' is *geographical*: the frictional effect of distance. For example, the public park is theoretically available to all but it is 'more available' to those who live nearby. The fire service, similarly, is not deliberately discriminatory but houses nearer to the fire station are likely to get quicker fire-fighting service than those farther away. The general point is the same as that made earlier about externalities. The impact of a facility (whether positive or negative) generally declines with increasing distance from its source. Geography is a fundamental influence.*

Precisely what is included in the list of public goods and provided collectively varies a good deal between different societies depending upon their particular political complexion. For example, most Western industrial societies expect that not only national defence, police and fire protection but also such facilities as highways and air terminals should be provided publicly. Some regard health and education facilities as part of the public domain whilst others see these as, at least partly, private matters to be purchased in the same way as a refrigerator or an automobile – the richer the customer the more (or the better) he can have. But whatever the composition of the list of public goods, their availibility is a most important element in determining people's well-being, as we shall see in Chapter Five.

The characteristics of social organization we have been discussing have been largely economic, in that they are to do with the ways in which society provides for the material needs of its inhabitants. But the characteristics are more than simply economic. They also very much reflect – some would even say they determine – the broader social and political nature of society as a whole. They imply a particular set of *social values* and *social attitudes* which go beyond economic considerations. For example, although it would be a gross oversimplification to suggest that all the differences between, say, Republicans and Democrats in the United States, or between Conservatives, Labour and Liberals in Britain, are economic, the fact remains that much of the political debate today revolves around what are, in effect,

---

*Cox (1973), Cox and Reynolds (1974), Harvey (1972, 1973) and Smith (1977) discuss the geographical aspect of public goods and externalities in some detail. The topic forms an important part of our discussion in Chapter Five.

economic values. In addition, a major feature of all societies in which there is a substantial division of labour is that they tend to be organized *hierarchically* (Figure 1.5). People are *stratified* into status groups or classes based upon their 'place' in society. Most societies, even the most primitive, have some form of social stratification, whether this is based on religion, tribal status or some other cultural dimension. In general, 'place' in society is related to degree of power or influence over scarce resources (defined in the broadest sense). In urban-industrial societies the two most widely known social stratification schemes are those of Karl Marx and Max Weber.* Marx characterized capitalist industrial society as consisting of two major classes – the bourgeoisie, who owned the means of production, and the proletariat, who did not and who had to sell their labour in order to live. The sociologist Max Weber regarded such an *economic* basis of stratification as only one of three dimensions which, though important, is too restrictive to describe adequately the complexity of industrial society. A second dimension, he suggested, is *social* whereby people are stratified according to their styles of life, that is, by the way in which they dispose of their income rather than by the way they earn it. Style, rather than substance, is the essence of Weber's social status dimension, based as it is on the symbology of a culture, of attitudes, beliefs and value-systems. Weber's third dimension is *political* and is related to the way in which power is allocated in society and to a person's actual or perceived position in the power hierarchy. Thus, Weber provided a more flexible view of the social 'measuring rod' – seeing individuals as having not only an economically determined class situation but also a more open, culturally infused social position in which prestige, status, power, political affiliation as well as attitudes and beliefs serve to extend and blur the economic relationship. Weber saw *class situation* and what he called *market situation* as the twin pivots of socio-economic

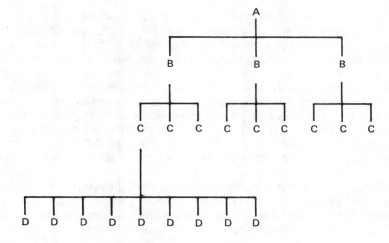

Figure 1.5   A simple hierarchy

---

*The question of social stratification is an immensely complex one whose detailed ramifications are beyond the scope of this book. The interested reader is advised to consult the sociological literature for enlightenment. Good starting points are provided by Broom and Selznick (1975) and Anderson (1971).

status. Whatever the precise form of the social stratification system in any particular society, however, an individual's position in that system is a major determinant of the kind of life he or she is able to lead.

Let us pause briefly to summarize the main points we have been making. In trying to understand the spatial organization of human activities we need to consider first how society itself is organized. At the most basic level, social organization arises from the combination of three basic elements:

1 Human behaviour is constrained, initially, by certain basic needs – especially these physiological needs related to survival.

2 Human behaviour is constrained further by the need to join with other individuals: to satisfy certain physiological needs more effectively, to satisfy 'higher-order' needs such as friendship and companionship, to produce society's economic needs more efficiently through collaboration, specialization and the division of labour. Thus, human behaviour is constrained by the nature of social relationships and the processes of social interaction.

3 Human behaviour is constrained by the overall organization of society and the structure of authority, control and social stratification which exists in the particular society. Key considerations here include the extent to which authority is centralized or dispersed, democratic or totalitarian, hierarchical or otherwise.

Such constraints apply to all types of human behaviour. The important point for us is that *they operate in both time and space*.

TIME-SPACE CONSTRAINTS

How these social constraints are expressed in time-space terms and how time-space affects their operation are fundamental questions which geographers are just beginning to ask.* Both space and time are *resources*. Society has to find ways of utilizing space and time in order to carry out its basic tasks. But for all practical purposes, space and time are *scarce* resources which, like most resources, can be put to alternative uses. All human activities take time; all human activities use space. Space and time can also be regarded as *frictions* which may have to be overcome in order to perform a particular task. The geographical literature, especially that of the 1960s, is full of references to the frictional effect of distance in explanations of the spatial organization of human activities. Space and time, then, are difficult concepts to handle even when considered separately. When we try to see how the two mesh together the difficulties are very great indeed.

The pioneer work in attempting to understand how this complex relationship between space and time affects human activities and social organization is that of the Swedish geographer Torsten Hägerstrand. In effect, he provides time-space equivalents of the three sets of social constraints summarized above. He begins by

---

*There is a growing literature concerned with 'time geography', stimulated by the work of Hägerstrand and his colleagues at the University of Lund, Sweden. See, in particular, Hägerstrand (1970), Thrift (1977), Carlstein, Parkes and Thrift (1978). Parkes and Thrift (1980) have produced the first comprehensive text entitled *Times, Spaces and Places*.

observing that human behaviour is limited by *capability constraints* 'which limit the activities of the individual because of his biological construction and/or the tools he can command'. Some capability constraints are essentially *temporal* in their effect, for example, the need to rest for a period of time and to eat at regular intervals. Both the regularity and duration of such physiological constraints determine when, and for how long, other activities can be engaged in. If we need eight hours' sleep in every twenty-four hours then we immediately reduce the amount of time we can devote to other activities. But capabilitity constraints are *spatial* as well as temporal. In particular from the individual viewpoint,

> People need to have some kind of home base, if only temporary, at which they can rest at regular intervals, keep personal belongings, and be reached for receiving messages. Assume that each person needs a regular minimum number of hours a day for sleep and for attending to business at his home base. When he moves away from it, there exists a definite boundary line beyond which he cannot go if he has to return before a deadline. Thus, in his daily life everybody has to exist spatially on an island.
> *Hägerstrand (1970), pp.12–13.*

Figure 1.6 illustrates this point. The vertical dimension shows the daily time-scale. H represents the location of an individual's home base. The length of time spent at H is represented by the vertical line immediately above H. If we assume that the person leaves home at 0800 and has to return by 2200 hours then the diamond shaped *prism* shows the maximum *spatial* extent that could be covered in the time available. For most inhabitants of modern societies this is a *daily* prism but for others it could be monthly, seasonal, annual or any other meaningful period, depending on how much time is spent continuously away from the home base.

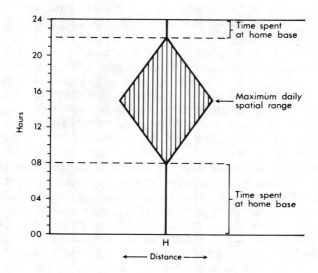

Figure 1.6 Capability constraints: a daily time-space prism

The time-space prism, then, is the *maximum* time-space range over which a person is able to operate. Its spatial extent depends on three basic factors (Figure 1.7). First, of course, it depends upon how much time is spent at the home base as a proportion of the prism's duration: Thus the housewife in Western society spends far more time at the home base than the husband who goes out to work. Figure 1.7a shows approximately how their daily time-space prisms might differ. As we shall see later, this has important social and economic consequences. The second source of variation in the spatial extent of the daily prism is the means of movement available: the individual's ability to overcome the friction of distance. In Figure 1.7b the difference in the potential size of the time-space prism between a person who has to walk everywhere and the person who has access to a car is clear. Again this is an issue we shall be taking up in more detail later.

The third element causing variation in the spatial size of the prism is the length of time that has to be spent in activities away from the home base, quite apart from time spent travelling. Figure 1.7c shows how the combination of having to spend a number of hours at one location away from home – for example, at work – with the means of movement available produces another kind of time-space prism. Of course, it is possible to transfer from the permanent home base to one or a series of temporary ones where this is necessary. Shifting cultivators, transhumance shepherds, migrant labourers and jet-set executives share this technique for increasing their effective territorial coverage given human physiological limitations. Once set in place again, however, the local constraints become the effective ones from the temporary base.

Thus, we would expect the average extent of time-space prisms to vary *between* societies according to technological and cultural differences and to vary *within* a specific society according to such considerations as age, occupation, income level and sex. Of course, only relatively infrequently will an individual operate at the absolute potential limit of his or her time-space prism. For the most part, life is carried on on a far smaller 'island' than that permitted by movement capability.

Within the time-space prism, the precise form of an individual's movement paths is greatly influenced by a second set of constraints. Recall that most of our activities are performed in conjunction with other people, either singly or in organizations such as business firms, schools, shops, public institutions. Each of these has a specific location in geographical space; most also have a location in time in that they operate only for certain time-periods during the day or week. Figure 1.8, for example, shows a very simple situation in which a person has to travel from home to a place of work some distance away. The distance is, essentially, time- or cost-distance rather than miles or kilometres. The workplace is assumed to operate only between the hours of 0800 and 1700.

The problem, then, is that the activities in which people or organizations need to join together to fulfil some common purpose must be co-ordinated in both space and time. Hägerstrand terms this set of constraints *coupling constraints*. They are, in effect, the time-space expression of the *social* nature of most human activities. In Hägerstrand's terminology, we form 'bundles' of activities with others in order to fulfil our needs and wants and to perform our roles in society. It follows that such bundles are possible only if they occur within the daily time-space prisms of all participants. Of course, the mere existence of overlapping or coincident time-space prisms does not guarantee interaction. The bases of social interaction lie in the social processes themselves. But without such overlap, social interaction is, by definition, physically impossible.

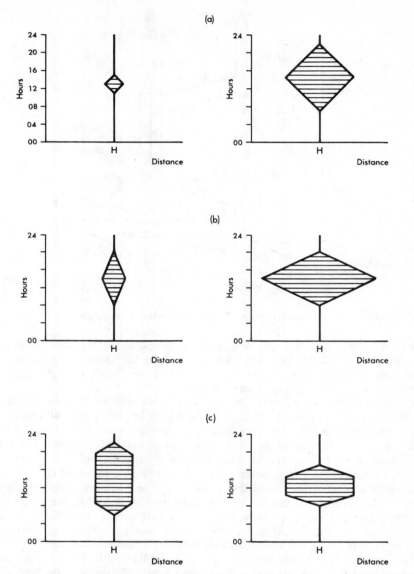

Figure 1.7   Some possible variations in the size and shape of a daily time-space prism:

    (a) Amount of time spent at home base
    (b) Means of movement available
    (c) Amount of time spent away from home base

It is for such reasons that geographers in particular have stressed the importance of *geographical proximity* in encouraging interaction and the role of distance in discouraging it. Although this 'distance-decay' concept may both overstate and

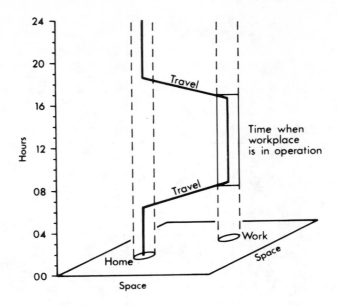

Figure 1.8 Coupling constraints: home-work relationship in time-space

oversimplify, there is little doubt that people will tend to interact more frequently with others closest to them geographically and that the likelihood of interaction will decline as distance increases. Again, of course, the nature of the available means of communication is fundamentally important.

Spatially, then, we can envisage coupling constraints as creating bundles of activities at particular locations. Figure 1.9 shows one hypothetical example. People leave their home bases to form a work bundle at a factory or office and then return to their home bases at the end of the working day. Note that such a bundle is not only co-ordinated in space but also in time. The work bundle only exists within a predefined time period. All societies, in fact, have to devise means of co-ordinating their multifarious activities in both space and time. The more complex a society and the more specialized its members, the more organized and synchronized it must be. For many activities co-ordination by some form of compulsory timetable has become the norm. Increasingly, the casual social or business meeting is being replaced by the formal appointment; diaries and appointment schedules, clocks and calendars regu-late the time-sequence of our lives. Indeed, Lewis Mumford, the eminent urban scholar, claimed the clock rather than the steam engine to be the 'key machine' of the industrial age.* The co-ordination of human activities in time and space through the operation of coupling constraints is a major cause of some of the highly regular temporal and spatial patterns characteristic of modern society (Figure 1.10).

---

*Another key time-space co-ordinator is the traffic light which controls and synchronizes flows of vehicles.

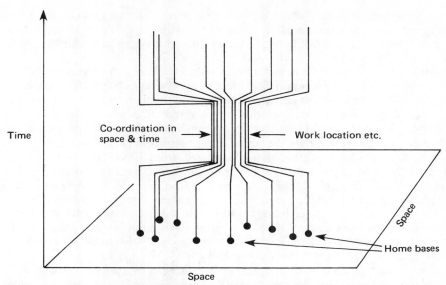

Figure 1.9   Coupling constraints: 'bundles' of activities co-ordinated in time-space

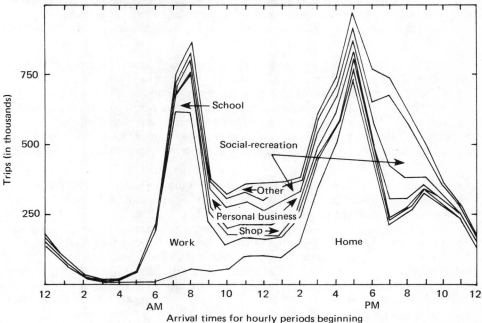

Figure 1.10   Regular daily rhythm of human activity in an urban area: hourly distribution of journeys in Chicago

Source: J. Schofer, *Systems Analysis in Transportation Planning*, Center for Urban Studies and Dept. of Systems Engineering, University of Chicago.

Although we have focused our discussion on the individual, we should not assume that capability and coupling constraints apply only at that level. They can be applied, too, to all organizations which have to interact with other organizations in space and time.

Precisely *where* and *when* joint activities occur, and *who* can participate in such bundles of activities, is constrained further by what Hägerstrand terms *authority constraints*. As we pointed out earlier, social organization is rarely the expression of spontaneous and voluntary co-operation between individuals or groups, except at the simplest level. Human activities are organized and co-ordinated in the interests of efficiency; in many societies the form of this organization is hierarchical.

From an individual's point of view and, indeed, from the viewpoint of organizations such as business firms precisely *where* and *when* activities occur is related to who controls the particular piece of time-space. Take the case of working hours, for example. For most people, this variable is outside their control. Society at large or individual employers generally define working hours. The precise *location* of activity nodes themselves – workplaces, shops, resources – arises out of decisions made in a previous time-period by 'higher-level' decision-makers, such as industrialists, property developers, government planners and so on.

Even if both capability and coupling constraints can be overcome, therefore, a particular act of social behaviour may be precluded or altered because the particular part of time-space in which the act is to take place is occupied so that entry is impossible. Such *domains* vary enormously in both their spatial extent and temporal duration; they may be very large or very small, ephemeral or quasi-permanent. They may also be protected in various ways:

> Some smaller domains are protected only through immediate power or custom, e.g. a favorite chair, a sand cave on the beach, or a place in a queue. Others, of varying size have a very strong legal status: the home, land property, the premises of a firm or institute, the township, county, state, or nation. Many of these have a long, almost permanent duration, such as nations, British universities, and Japanese companies. Others are only temporary such as a seat in the theater or a telephone booth at the roadside. *Hägerstrand (1970), p.16.*

Control over a time-space domain, then, however it may be exercised, adds a further and often very powerful modifying influence on patterns and processes of social behaviour. In particular, it is a source of potential conflict.

Geographical space, of course, is not infinite. Some parts of geographical space are regarded as more 'valuable' than others. They may be especially well located in relation to some highly desirable natural resource or to other activities with which close links are necessary. In addition, some human activities in themselves take up a lot of space whilst others are less space-demanding. Thus the need or desire to control various spaces creates problems of 'packing' – of fitting competing activities into finite spaces. The old adage 'possession is nine parts of the law' reflects the fact that existing occupation may prevent subsequent occupation or use by others. This emphasizes the importance of time in an evolutionary sense: the way spaces are occupied in one time-period greatly influences their use in subsequent time-periods where such occupation is carried forward. Thus, what Hägerstrand (1973) calls the ' "pecking order" between structures seeking spatial accommodation' is a central problem in all societies, though more so in those in which space is in short supply relative to competing demands. In societies in which land may be privately owned (as in Western urban-industrial societies, for example) competition is regulated through the land market. Land which generates the greatest degree of competition, for example, highly accessible locations such as centres of cities, or particularly desirable stretches of coastline, acquires the highest value expressed in rent or purchase price. Figure 1.11 is a well-known example of how the value of space may vary very

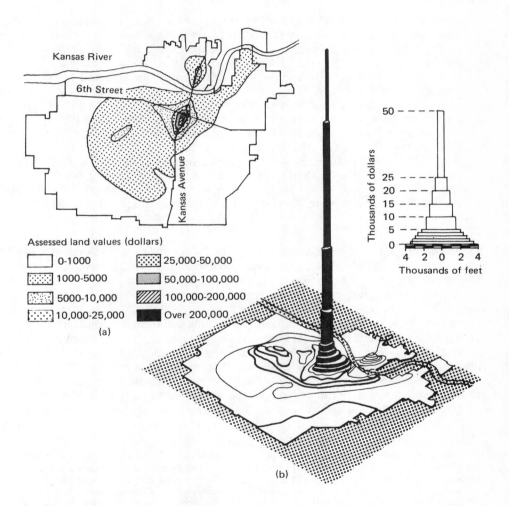

Figure 1.11 Authority constraints and the urban land market: spatial variations in land values in Topeka, Kansas

Source: D.S. Knos (1962) *The Distribution of Land Values in Topeka, Kansas,* University of Kansas Center for Research in Business, figures 1 and 2.

dramatically over extremely short distances. In such circumstances, the authority constraint is expressed through the ability to pay for the use of a particular portion of geographical space.

Authority constraints are control mechanisms. In general spatial terms they are expressed in the idea of *territory* which determines the use to which different portions of space may be put. Territories are evident at a variety of different scales, from the individual through the social group to the large business corporation and the nation state. In Soja's words,

> the surface of the earth is enmeshed in a labyrinth of boundaries created and maintained by man. Embedded within the pastel colors of a satellite photograph of the earth are layers of intricate and overlapping mosaics of spatial organization unseen by the distant eye but nevertheless profoundly influencing human activity and behavior. About one hundred and forty sovereign states partition the surface into distinctive territories, each further compartmentalized into smaller political divisions. A myriad of local administrative units carve up space in a variety of patterns to fulfill a wide range of functions. At a still more local level over most of the world there is a complex web of property lines and patterns of land ownership. If you are fortunate enough to be atop the Empire State building in New York City on a clear, smogless day, the urban panorama before you would encompass three states, 500 autonomous governments and about 1,000 additional governmental units with various legal and functional prerogatives.
> *Soja (1971), p.1.*

The means of control themselves may be explicit – for example, the existence of national borders with restricted access, the erection of signs and protective fences around a private residence or a firm or the territorial markers of urban gangs. On the other hand, control over pieces of space may be more subtle, being reflected, for example, in changes in custom or language.*

In the light of the existence of capability, coupling and authority constraints one way of looking at society is to see it as being made up of people, groups, organizations and institutions locked into a whole series of interconnecting *activity systems*. Their function is to ensure the production and distribution of society's needs and wants. Such activity systems have to be co-ordinated in both time and space and it is this which produces much of the observable spatial regularity in the distribution of human activities on the earth's surface. In addition, the operation of authority

---

*In addition to place-based territory, the anthropologist Edward Hall (1966) has suggested that individuals also operate a series of 'distances' which operate to separate them from their fellows, a kind of personal territory or spatial envelope which they, in effect, carry around with them. Using a particular sample of Western humanity – middle-class, healthy adults, mainly natives of the northeastern seaboard of the United States – Hall identified four distance zones: intimate, personal, social and public. In behaving territorially, he suggests, man and the other animals distinguish carefully between such distances and choose the one appropriate to the particular social transaction, the relationship between the individuals involved and what they are doing. Hall goes on to demonstrate that different cultures tend to develop characteristic attitudes towards spatial distances. But their function is universal: they act as 'space regulators' in human behaviour.

constraints serves to divide up geographical space into a complex overlapping and interweaving of territories.

Such activity systems may be very simple in organization and essentially static over time, as in traditional societies, or they may be highly complex organizationally and dynamic as in today's urban-industrial societies. But the basic principles on which they are organized are essentially the same; it is how these principles operate in specific circumstances which makes for differences – culturally, socially, economically, politically – between places and societies.

THE FOCUS: WESTERN URBAN-INDUSTRIAL SOCIETY

The concepts discussed in this introductory chapter could be applied in a variety of different circumstances. In this book, we apply them to a particular kind of society: the kind of urban-industrial society prevailing in the Western world at the present day. We are concerned with the ways in which people live out their daily lives in this complex and rapidly changing society. We are concerned with their *choices within constraints*.

Western urban-industrial societies are essentially *capitalist* societies, based upon the *market* mechanism, but with varying degrees of governmental involvement. All are, to a greater or lesser degree, *mixed economies*. But whatever the specific public-private mixture, all modern industrial societies are based upon the principle of *specialization* or the *division of labour*. This is something we have discussed already in general terms. The point about today's urban-industrial societies is that the *extent* of such specialization has become extremely fine and complex. An inevitable outcome is that such societies are strongly *hierarchical* and finely *stratified*. The nature of the work processes involved produces strong social differentiation, separating people into many fine grades of skills, functional roles, status categories and, most importantly, income brackets. No attempt is made to provide a historical account of the evolution of industrial society – our focus is upon the present, rather than the past. But it is useful at this point to sketch in some background very briefly.

In the industrial society which developed in Western Europe and later spread to North America in the eighteenth and early nineteenth centuries, organization of *production* shifted from the medieval craft guilds to capitalist entrepreneurs. At the same time, co-ordination of the *market* was left to what Adam Smith called the 'invisible hand' operating through the mechanism of supply and demand. Stephen Hymer has described the nature of these developments particularly well:

> The hallmarks of the new system were *the market* and *the factory*, representing the two different methods of co-ordinating the division of labor. In the factory entrepreneurs consciously plan and organize co-operation, and the relationships are hierarchical and authoritarian; in the market co-ordination is achieved through a decentralized, unconscious competitive process.
>
> To understand the significance of this distinction, the new system should be compared to the structure it replaced. In the pre-capitalist system of production, the division of labor was hierarchically structured at the *macro* level, i.e. for society as a whole, but unconsciously structured at the *micro* level, i.e. the actual process of production. Society as a whole was partitioned into various castes, classes, and guilds, on a rigid and authoritarian

basis so that political and social stability could be maintained and adequate numbers assured for each industry and occupation. Within each sphere of production, however, individuals by and large were independent and their activities only loosely co-ordinated, if at all. In essence, a guild was composed of a large number of similar individuals, each performing the same task in roughly the same way with little co-operation or division of labor. This type of organization could produce high standards of quality and workmanship but was limited quantitatively to low levels of output per head.

The capitalist system of production turned this structure on its head. The macro system became unconsciously structured, while the micro system became hierarchically structured. The market emerged as a self-regulating co-ordinator of business units as restrictions on capital markets and labor mobility were removed. (Of course, the State remained above the market as a conscious co-ordinator to maintain the system and ensure the growth of capital.) At the micro level, that is the level of production, labor was gathered under the authority of the entrepreneur capitalist.
Hymer (1972), pp.116–117.

Economic life in industrial society thus became increasingly associated with the gathering together of machinery, equipment and labour into factories. Investment of this kind presupposed the availability of *capital*. Whatever the initial sources of such capital – whether from the merchant or landowning segments of society – a continuing supply of capital for investment in machinery depended upon the *profits* derived from production. Profit, therefore, became a central feature of the capitalist market system. Thus we can envisage a circular and cumulative process providing much of the driving force underlying the evolution of modern industrial society. Division of labour leads to increased productivity, since a worker specializing in one part of a process can produce more than a worker who has to perform the whole range of processes. Increased productivity leads to increased profits. Some of these profits are re-invested to promote an even greater division of labour which, in turn, generates further profits and so on.

This is, of course, a massive oversimplification of a highly complex precess which, though inherently cumulative, may be diverted, inhibited or otherwise modified in many different ways. For example, profits may not be re-invested in the productive sphere but directed elsewhere (the massive flow of investment into speculative property-building in the late 1960s and early 1970s is one modern example). They may be distributed to company shareholders or simply squandered in riotous living. Profits may be appropriated by governments through taxation or redirected into increased wages and salaries to employees. Even so, the essence of the capitalist industrial process is its *circular* and *cumulative* nature.

Although today's Western industrial societies have evolved on the basis of these processes, there are particular contemporary characteristics which merit close attention. To some writers, particularly the sociologist Daniel Bell, we are witnessing *The Coming of Post-Industrial Society*, and the term 'postindustrial society' has become widely used in both popular, and some academic, circles. Like all such terms, however, it is often more misleading than illuminating, and we avoid its usage here while recognizing that many of the characteristics which Bell regards as diagnostic of postindustrial society can be identified in modern Western society.*

THE STRUCTURE OF THE BOOK

We begin in Chapter Two by taking a broad-ranging look at some of the major characteristics of present-day Western industrial society. No attempt is made to cover all its multifaceted characteristics and, almost certainly, the reader will be able to identify aspects we have omitted, either through design or through our own ignorance. The objective of Chapter Two is to outline the large scale 'organizational bases', hence the main body of what is a lengthy chapter is organized around four major topics – technological change (with particular reference to developments in the 'space-adjusting' technologies), the increasing dominance of giant multiloca-tional business organizations, the massive growth of the government sector and the changing urban face of modern Western society.

These major dimensions constitute the 'gameboard' on which the daily lives of individuals, households and social groups are played out. Like any gameboard, it is made up of sets of choices and sets of constraints. In a game it is perhaps the throw of the dice that presents the player with a ladder or a snake but our view is that, for the life game at least, the dice are loaded. Some individuals at some particular locations seem to get more than their 'fair' share of snakes, while others, perhaps, do rather better than expected in the matter of ladders. Some might suggest that this situation is the result of particular malign forces, a conspiracy of capitalism, that see to it that some prosper while others fail. We prefer to believe that no such consciously conspiratorial force exists but that the constellation of choices and constraints which has evolved is the outcome of an accumulation of decisions made over a long period of time which contain within them the seeds of uneven development.

Having examined some of the macro-scale characteristics of today's changing world, therefore, we move on in subsequent chapters to consider some aspects of the way people live their lives in this society. We are deliberately selective, identifying what seem to us to be the 'key nodes' around which peoples' lives are organized: work (Chapter Three) and residence (Chapter Four). For most people, their 'place' in society is inextricably related to their place in the labour market. This determines both social status and level of monetary income. Thus, how the labour market works and how it is changing at the present time are fundamentally important. The residential base is closely linked to the work base in a variety of ways, not least because income received from employment is the major basis for entering the housing market. But housing is, itself, a rather special commodity which is allocated through the operation of the housing market. Some people have a good deal of freedom in choosing where to live; others have virtually no choice at all.

---

*As we shall see in subsequent chapters there has been a pronounced shift of emphasis towards non-manufacturing activities; there is an increasing emphasis on knowledge as a central resource and upon planned technological change. We are increasingly conscious of social relationships and social problems related to the sheer scale, complexity and interdependence of living rather than simply those related to the process of material production itself. But whether those signify the emergence of a new type of society, as Bell and others of similar persuasion suggest, is open to doubt. Thus even though the term 'postindustrial' has begun to infiltrate the geographical literature we prefer to go along with Gershuny (1977, 1978), Heilbroner (1976) and others and view it with some scepticism.

A person's position in the housing market provides the geographical location from which he or she relates to the outside world. Since the sources for satisfying needs and wants are unevenly distributed geographically, the question of access to such sources (the 'goods' of life) and avoidance of less desirable qualities (the 'bads' of life) is greatly determined by the geographical location of the home base. It is in examining geographical variations in well-being in Chapter Five that the triad of time-space constraints discussed in this introductory chapter is particularly useful. In Chapter Five we look also at questions of community and at the kinds of locational conflict generated so frequently in our highly interdependent society. Finally, in a Postscript we draw together the main themes of the book and speculate, very briefly, on where we might go from here. Some of the material in the following chapters may strike some readers as being 'non-geographical'. Regardless of the fact that many would disagree on just what such a label means, our justification for such an approach is that set out in this introductory chapter. In order to understand how spatial patterns come about, in order to understand how and why peoples' lives vary from place to place, we need to explore the processes involved. Inevitably, we would argue, this takes us into some very diverse academic territory.

Chapter Two

Some major characteristics of modern Western society

GROWTH, CHANGE AND UNCERTAINTY

In the two and a half decades following World War II the world economy in general, and the industrially advanced W.estern societies in particular, achieved *unparalleled rates of economic growth*. Indeed, such growth was so widely experienced that for many of the privileged nations it came to be accepted as the *normal* state of affairs. Between 1948 and 1973, for example, world industrial production grew by an average of 5.9 percent a year – a rate never before achieved within the span of statistical records. This compared with an average annual rate of 2.9 percent in the preceding period from 1913 to 1948. Growth even accelerated during the 1960s to reach between 6 and 7 percent a year, reaching a peak between 1971 and 1973 at around 8 percent. Despite a number of minor fluctuations, the period from 1948 to 1973 was free of major economic recession (Kaldor 1976). For the Western societies we can, from the vantage point of the 1980s, see the postwar years as ones in which the *general level of affluence* increased very markedly. Although, as we shall see later, major inequalities continued to exist and even intensify, it is indisputable that most people in the rich nations are materially far better off than their parents or grand-parents. They live longer lives, they are generally more healthy, the standard of educational provision and of housing are incomparably higher for most people. In the postwar period in particular, incomes have steadily increased as Figure 2.1 shows.

This increase in the general level of affluence in Western societies has been accompanied by an acceleration of some long-established changes in the *pattern and nature of consumer demands*. It has long been argued that the relative importance which people attach to particular demands changes as their incomes rise. Beyond a certain level the amount spent on basic necessities grows less rapidly than the amount spent on more durable consumer goods. As incomes rise even higher, so the argument goes, the pattern of consumption changes further and more is spent on less tangible goods and services. Most statistics on changes in household consumption

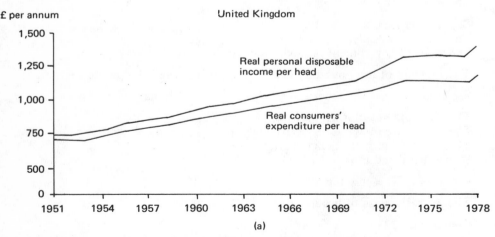

Figure 2.1   Increases in personal incomes, UK and US

(a) United Kingdom 1951–1978 (at 1975 prices)

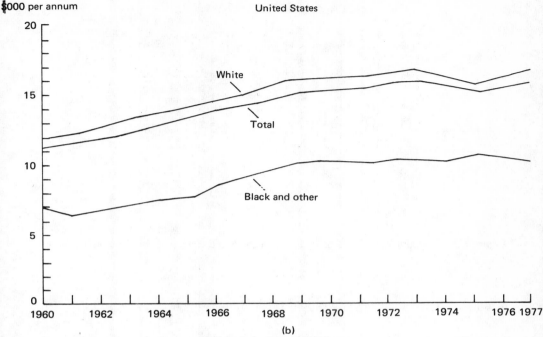

Figure 2.1   Increases in personal incomes, UK and US

(b) United States 1960–1977 (at 1977 prices)

Source: (a) Central Statistical Office, *Social Trends* 10 (1980), figure A.1. Crown Copyright.
(b) United States *Statistical Abstract* (1978), figure 14.2.

bear this out. In general, as Figure 2.2 shows, a smaller proportion of total expenditure has tended to go on food and clothing with a greater share being taken up by housing (as most people became owner-occupiers), by transport (as automobile ownership increased) and by leisure and recreational activities (as working hours shortened and became more flexible).*

However, as Fred Hirsch has pointed out, changes in consumer demands associated with increased general affluence are extremely complex. He draws a distinction between *material goods*, which can be produced in increasing quantities and consumed without loss of quality, and *positional goods*, which are either scarce in some absolute or socially imposed sense or are prone to 'congestion' from increased use. In this case, the enjoyment of a good is affected by how many other people have access to it. (An obvious example is a beautiful stretch of beach.) In pointing to what he terms the 'paradox of affluence' in modern Western society Hirsch argues that it is

---

*Such long-term shifts in the structure of consumer demands are frequently used to explain the changes in the *structure of employment* experienced by industrial societies, particularly the 'sectoral shift' from primary to secondary to tertiary and ultimately to quaternary activities. This topic is examined in some detail in Chapter Three.

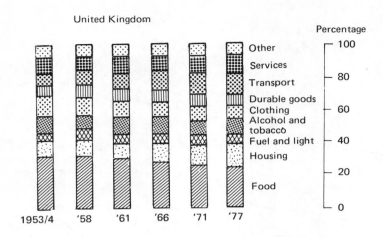

Figure 2.2   Changing patterns of expenditure on goods and services in the United Kingdom, 1953–1977

Source: Central Statistical Office, *Social Trends* 10 (1980), figure A.6. Crown Copyright.

relative, rather than *absolute*, position which is increasingly important in modern consumer societies for

> if everyone stands on tiptoe, no one sees better.
> *Hirsch (1977), p.5.*

More generally, throughout the 1960s in particular, there was a widespread feeling that the fundamental problem of meeting society's material needs was virtually solved. The futurologists tended to see the problems of the future as those of affluence and plenty rather than of poverty and paucity. Such complacent views of an assured future of continued economic growth and material prosperity received some rude shocks in the early 1970s. In 1972 a private research organization, the Club of Rome, published its document the *Limits to Growth* which predicted the imminent exhaustion of key resources. Although the document was very heavily criticized, it at least made many people pause to consider, perhaps for the first time, that economic growth might not continue indefinitely, that many resources are not infinite. More tangible was the oil crisis precipitated by the Arab-Israeli war of autumn 1973 which both dramatically increased the price, and threatened the availability, of the most basic resource whose cheapness and abundance had fuelled the golden era of economic growth.

In fact the oil crisis, though traumatic, was not the initiator of what has come to be the most talked about and written about phenomenon of recent years: *price inflation*. It is the experience of rapidly accelerating prices which has done most of all to change attitudes and perceptions and to fuel the idea that economic growth might not continue without intolerable levels of inflation, unemployment and the socially disruptive consequences associated with them. Thus, although world-wide in its impact, inflation has particularly served to alter the attitudes of the Western industrial nations toward the growth and expansion which had been characteristic of the postwar years. Its appearance in concert with economic stagnation has revived much talk of the 'crisis of capitalism' so common in the early 1930s but put into abeyance first by the war and second by the period of inflation-free growth that followed it.

Kaldor argues that the modern inflationary period in fact began around 1968. Until then the rate of inflation (measured by consumer prices) remained moderate with no clear sign of a trend toward acceleration. For example, during the fourteen years 1953–1967, price inflation in eleven leading industrial countries ran at just over 2 percent a year. From 1968 onwards, however, change set in. Labour costs per unit of industrial output rose sharply in all the key industrial countries though actual rates varied between them. The pressure on the international monetary system led to the abandonment of fixed exchange rates in 1971 and commodity prices moved sharply upwards during 1972–1973. A sudden twist to the evolving spiral was given by the fourfold rise in oil prices after the Arab–Israeli war in 1973, setting off a round of unprecedented inflation of consumer prices. In 1973–1975 inflation *averaged* 26 percent in *all* OECD countries. Figure 2.3 and Table 2.1 show how sharp and pervasive was this inflationary trend throughout the world economy in general, and among the Western nations in particular.

Whether or not the shocks of the 1970s really do mark a fundamental change in the world economy, whether the recession is merely a kink in the upward growth

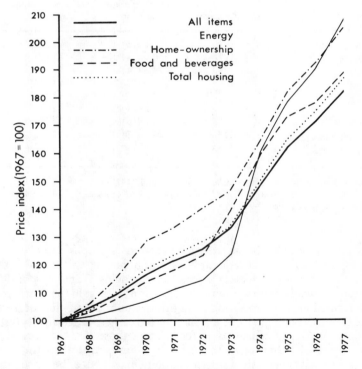

Figure 2.3 US consumer price inflation, selected items, 1967–1977

Source: U.S. Economic Report of the President (1979), tables B49–B51.

Table 2.1   *Inflation in Western industrial economies, 1961–1976 (Percentage change in consumer prices over preceding year)*

1961–1970

Country	Average	Highest average and year	Lowest average and year
Belgium	3.0	4.2 (64, 66)	1.0 (61)
Canada	2.7	4.5 (69)	0.8 (61)
France	4.1	6.1 (69)	2.4 (61)
West Germany	2.6	3.6 (66)	1.6 (68)
Italy	4.0	7.5 (63)	1.3 (68)
Japan	5.9	8.0 (63)	4.1 (64, 67)
Netherlands	4.1	7.5 (69)	1.2 (61)
United Kingdom	4.1	6.4 (70)	2.0 (63)
United States	2.8	5.9 (70)	1.0 (61)

1971–1976

Country	Average	Highest average and year	Lowest average and year
Belgium	8.6	12.8 (75)	4.3 (71)
Canada	7.4	10.9 (74)	2.8 (71)
France	9.0	13.6 (74)	5.4 (71)
West Germany	5.9	7.0 (73, 74)	4.6 (76)
Italy	7.4	19.1 (74)	4.8 (71)
Japan	11.4	24.5 (74)	4.8 (72)
Netherlands	8.7	10.2 (75)	7.5 (71)
United Kingdom	13.8	24.2 (75)	7.1 (72)
United States	6.6	11.0 (74)	3.3 (72)

Source: United Nations Economic and Social Council (1978)
Transnational Corporations in World Development: A Re-Examination, New York:
United Nations, table III-7

curve or the point at which it began to turn downwards, is impossible to determine at this point in time. Only the subsequent hindsight of history will tell. What is clear, however, is that at present society seems to be moving from self-confidence to uncertainty and from economic growth to stagnation (at least in the short term). It is within this transition from apparent certainty to doubt about the future that the subject matter of this book has to be set. But it is too early to see the likely outcome of current events. What we can do is to focus upon those key features of modern Western society which have had the most profound impact on the capability, coupling and authority constraints which Chapter One set out as being so fundamental to the relationships between man, society and space. Four closely related characteristics of such a society seem to be especially significant:

1 It is a society in which technology and technological change are widely regarded as being of central importance.

2 It is a society in which the media of transportation and communication have been revolutionized, thus permitting an unprecedented scale and complexity of social and economic organization.

3 It is a society in which all the major organizations and institutions have become progressively larger in scale and increasingly bureaucratic.

4 It is a society which is fundamentally an urban society but in which the urban form itself is undergoing considerable modification.

Let us now examine each of these in turn, bearing in mind that one clear thread links each of them – *specialization* – that most fundamental feature of Western industrial society.

TECHNOLOGY AND TECHNOLOGICAL CHANGE IN MODERN WESTERN SOCIETY

Technological change has been generally regarded as the major driving force underlying economic and industrial growth and the resulting increase in material living standards. Toffler, for example, describes technology as the 'great growling engine of change'. But technology and technological change affect more than just the growth of the economy; they impinge upon almost every facet of life in modern industrial society, greatly modifying the operation of capability, coupling and authority constraints. For example, technological change has fundamentally altered the jobs that people do and where they do them. It has affected the food we eat, the goods we buy and influenced prevailing life-styles. Our ability to move from place to place and to send and receive information has been drastically altered by the nature of technological change. Indeed, the massive *scale* of social, political and economic organization so characteristic of modern industrial society depends to a very great extent on its technological base and upon the choices made as to how such technology is used.

It is hardly surprising, then, that modern technology, its role as the engine of change and the way it is used, has provoked deep divisions of opinion. To many, modern technology is the basis of a good life for all – higher living standards, better diet, more comfortable living, the ability to traverse hitherto impossible distances and to partake in a world society through the media of communication. It has indeed facilitated, for many, the 'leap from necessity into freedom'. To the extent that technology is seen to make all these possible, then the pursuit of even newer and more sophisticated technologies may appear to be a desirable end in itself. However, to others modern technology is a Pandora's box to be opened only with great care and not a little distrust. Without denying many of the benefits of modern technology, they point to its high economic and social cost, its exploitative use of natural resources which may be irreplaceable, its propensity to pollute air, water and earth, its potential for misuse and mischief on a global scale, its possible alienating and dehumanizing effect on people. For followers of this line, technological change has to be implemented very carefully with a close concern for its social and ecological costs as well as its economic benefits.

Thus, any discussion of technology raises deep and complex issues regarding the relationship between technology and society – between means and ends, between costs and benefits, between 'goods' and 'bads', between who benefits and who does not. For one thing is certain: technology cannot be treated as a phenomenon independent of its social context. Both society and technology are each reflections of the other. Society makes the choices, not technology, but the nature of technology at any given time strongly influences subsequent choices; the two are mutually reinforcing. In our society, most technological change is motivated by *economic* criteria: profit, cost, economic efficiency and the like. In addition, technological change has become increasingly pursued in a *systematic* and *highly organized* manner. It has become, in Freeman's words, increasingly professionalized in the form of the *research and development (R and D) industry*. This industry has, in fact, become a major sector in its own right in all advanced industrial economies. The industries most characteristic of modern society, the rapid-growth industries – chemicals, electronics, aerospace, scientific instruments, nuclear engineering, for example – are highly research-intensive, science-based industries founded on the application of the theoretical principles of chemistry, physics and mathematics. These are the industries characterized by high levels of automation and sophisticated process control and associated with new types of materials.

In a book of this kind it is neither possible nor necessary to describe the history of technological change in detail. But to achieve our major objectives in understanding the impact of technology on society – on jobs, on incomes, on life-styles – it is important to identify some of the *major* recent technological developments and to see where they fit into the historical process. Despite the apparent acceleration in the rate of technological change during the last few decades, the process overall is gradual and cumulative. However, this gradual trend is punctuated from time to time by major developments which represent what might be called 'technological phase-shifts' – key innovations which either alter the direction of technology or vastly accelerate its progress:

> periodically throughout history, some technological innovations have been developed which have a very significant social and economic impact. They create a major new industry, displace or make obsolescent existing products, provide an important new medium of communication, or even alter the way we live. Such technological innovations as the steam engine, line-casting machine, telephone and telegraph, electric light and internal combustion engine fall into this category, as do more recent innovations as radio and television, the airplane, synthetic resins, the vacuum tube, the automobile, and synthetic fibers. Some recent technological innovations which appear to meet this criterion include electronic computers, semi-conductors and integrated circuits, synthetic leather, numerical control and atomic power generation.
> *National Commission on Technology, Automation and Economic Progress (1966), vol.II, p.36.*

To these we need to add more recent developments, for example, laser technology, communications satellite systems and the silicon chip (the basis of miniaturization in electronics).

The details are, for us, less important than the major trends which underlie the innovations themselves. At least three such trends can be identified when we examine the technological developments associated with the continuing process of industrialization:

1 developments which relate to *processes* and *methods* of industrial production, particularly those which affect their operation and control;

2 changes in the nature of *materials* used in industrial production;

3 changes in *transportation and communications* technology which permit the more rapid and/or cheaper movement of materials, products, information and people.

Let us now look briefly at each of these in turn.

New processes: mechanization and automation

A fundamental development underlying the early stages of industrialization was the gradual replacement of human physical effort by inanimate sources of energy. As industrialization proceeded throughout the nineteenth and early twentieth centuries a major strand of technological development was the progressive application and improvement of steam-driven production methods and their subsequent replacement by other forms of energy, especially electricity, which were both more flexible and more mobile.

The substitution of mechanical for physical effort in the production process made possible a massive increase in the *scale* of industrial production. This development of the huge factory with its very large labour force was facilitated by the revolution in transportation, a topic we look at in some detail below. Over time, therefore, production of almost all kinds became increasingly *mechanized*. The ultimate symbol of mechanization, of course, is the *assembly line*, a technique which combines the principle of specialization, or division of labour, with a means of moving materials and intermediate products and components from one worker to the next. The epitome of the assembly line was Ford's automobile plant in Michigan though, in fact, it had been used in the Cincinnati slaughterhouses as early as the mid-nineteenth century.

Mechanization, then, with its resulting mass production of goods, was the diagnostic feature of industrial technology in what some would call the first phase of the Industrial Revolution. Mechanization replaced human physical effort with mechanical devices, although the direct operation of these devices – of the machinery and equipment – remained in the hands of the factory worker. In contrast, a feature of latter-day industrial society is that the control of machine operations is becoming divorced increasingly from direct human involvement. In other words, the production process has become more and more *automated*.*

Automatic control is not, in itself, a particularly recent phenomenon. The thermostat, for example, which automatically controls heat output from a furnace, was invented in the first half of the seventeenth century. Automatic pattern-weaving of textiles using punched cards as a control mechanism was introduced by Jacquard

---

*Automation differs from mechanization in degree rather than in kind. Both are part of a single strand of technological development: the replacement of human labour by increasingly sophisticated machines. In the case of automation it is human *mental*, rather than physical, processes which are being replaced for a great many industrial operations.

in the late eighteenth century, and there were many other similar devices. But it is mainly in the last thirty years that automation has become particularly widespread as a result of developments in two other technological spheres. First, automatic operation and control depends upon highly sensitive instruments to monitor the production process as it proceeds. Second, the information collected or 'sensed' by such instruments has to be analysed very rapidly and the results fed quickly back to the machine to keep it on course. Thus, the basis of modern automation, as of so many other aspects of modern technology, lies in the sphere of *electronics* in general and of the *electronic computer* in particular. Thus, although the principle of automation is not new, its nature and impact have been changed beyond all recognition by the remarkable advances in electronics since the end of World War II.

The most recent developments, which have generated enormous discussion and controversy, involve the increasing *miniaturization* of electronic components. In particular, the development of the *micro-processor* promises to revolutionize not only a large number of industrial and other processes but also many aspects of daily life through the transformation of much existing technology. It is now possible to etch tens of thousands of transistorized circuits on to a wafer-thin 'chip' of silicon less than 1 cm² in size. Some idea of the effect of such technology is given by the fact that computations which, only a few years ago, would have needed an entire roomful of computers can now be carried out using a single slice of silicon smaller than a postage stamp. When produced in very large quantities these micro-processors become incredibly cheap.

Not only does this make possible vast numbers of new products and gadgets – from electronic watches and pocket calculators to pocket-sized television sets – and the transformation of existing products, but it also greatly increases the potential for automation throughout the industrial scene. It does this particularly because it introduces *flexibility* into automation. Until very recently it was feasible to automate only those processes which were repeated again and again over very long production runs, just as the mechanized assembly line could only be used to produce standardized products in vast quantities. However, the emerging development of microprocessors changes this relationship. Automation can be applied to a particular operation and then the control mechanism can be reprogrammed to perform another task. The potential implications of the micro-processor revolution are at the forefront of current economic, social and political debate, but since so much discussion of its impact revolves around its effects on work practices and employment we shall defer fuller discussion of it until Chapter Three.

New materials: from the natural to the synthetic

For most of its history, industrialization has been based upon the extraction and processing of naturally occurring materials, either those in the earth's crust – coal, iron ore, bauxite, copper, zinc, lead and so on – or those occurring in other natural forms such as cotton and wool fibres, grains and other food crops, timber and the like. Indeed the specific geographical distribution of some of the less mobile of these materials was responsible for much of the characteristic pattern of industrial settlement in the nineteenth century and, hence, today. This was particularly true of coal. As the primary energy source of early industrialization, and because of the high cost of transporting it, the coalfields gave rise to the massive urban-industrial agglomerations of the nineteenth and early twentieth centuries.

Given the nature, and often eccentric geographical distribution, of such materials, a good deal of technical ingenuity has been devoted to finding ways both of transporting and using natural materials more efficiently. For the most part such efficiency has been measured in the economic terms of the producers who have sought to assemble materials more cheaply and to produce more output per unit of input. But fears of eventual or imminent exhaustion of natural materials have added a new social dimension to their use and technology and conservation of resources has become an absolute target in its own right.

Until relatively recently, most of the materials exploited to meet society's needs were ones that had been in use for hundreds, in some cases thousands, of years. It is only during the last few decades that totally *new* materials – synthesized by man – have been developed. The first of the truly new materials was *plastic* but, like most new materials in their early stages, this was regarded initially as no more than a *substitute* for naturally occurring materials. It soon became evident, however, that the new synthetic materials possessed properties which made them very different from the traditional materials. Perhaps the most important difference between the two is the fact that the synthetic materials can be made into a number of quite different forms and, hence, tailored to specific uses. The same basic material – for example, nylon or polypropylene – can be produced as a fibre, a sheet, a film or moulded to form a component or product of a particular shape (Freeman 1974). As Freeman proceeds to point out, the synthetic materials have developed so rapidly that they already compare with the major natural materials in volume of production; indeed, they greatly outstripped them in rate of growth in the 1960 to 1970 period. Thus, plastics output increased by 16.8 percent and synthetic fibres by 21.1 percent in that decade compared with growth rates of 4.6 percent for steel and 0.8 percent for cotton. More than any other factor, it is the technical and production flexibility of the synthetic materials which explains their spectacular growth. We noted in our brief discussion of changing methods of production that a single industry – electronics – forms the basis of modern developments. When we look at the new materials technology we find a similar situation. In this case it is the chemicals industry which is significant in producing synthetic materials from hydrocarbon feedstocks.

A larger and larger proportion of the surroundings and trappings of modern industrial society reflects this new materials technology. Indeed it is often extremely difficult to distinguish the 'real' material from the simulated, so sophisticated have the synthetic materials become. The benefits of such developments can be very considerable in adding to the material comforts of life and, even more fundamentally, through their impact on agriculture and on medicine. But the costs may also be very considerable – not the least being the potential dangers inherent in some of the manufacturing processes and the problems of unwanted by-products, waste and the more general detritus of modern technology. From time to time the news headlines are dominated by reports of major accidents at industrial plants, some of which may have disastrous effects over large areas. Explosions and leaks at giant chemical plants are the most obvious examples. Less spectacular, but probably more significant because of its cumulative effects, is the increasing pollution of the natural and man-made environment by industrial processes. Natural materials degrade naturally; many synthetic materials such as the plastics are strongly resistant. Hence a growing problem of modern industrial society is what to do with its garbage as not only its total volume increases but also as its composition changes.

A rather different problem is posed by the dependence of many of the new materials upon the petrochemicals industry and, thus, upon fossil energy resources. It is significant that the massive growth of the synthetic materials occurred at a time when little or no thought was being given to possible shortages in the basic feedstock. Events since 1973, including the Iranian revolution of 1979, have produced the need for a re-evaluation of those activities which are heavily dependent upon petroleum supplies. This is particularly the case where problems in the field of energy *per se* are simultaneously compounded by shortages of those raw material feedstocks from which such a large proportion of our everyday products derive.

Quite apart from such considerations, the emergence of the new materials technologies has wrought major changes in industrial structures. As the shift to new materials has proceeded, old industries have been either totally or partially replaced by new ones. Very often this shift has been accompanied by both a total decline in employment, as the new industry is more capital-intensive and less labour-intensive than the old, and by particularly heavy job losses in those regions and communities highly dependent upon the obsolescent industry. One obvious example is the textile industry which has been altered so drastically in both scale and composition by the development of synthetic fibres during the last thirty years. Again the impact of such changes on the structure of employment opportunity lies at the forefront of contemporary debate and we shall examine these issues in some detail in Chapter Three.

A shrinking world: the modern revolutions in transportation and communication

Society cannot function without the constant transit of goods, people and messages.
Tornquist (1973), p.88.

Modern industrial society is a highly specialized society. It is a society which has become dominated by very large organizations and by a preoccupation with technological change. A society such as this cannot function without its highly elaborate system of *movements* and *flows* – of materials, semi-finished goods, components, finished products, workers and consumers, on the one hand, and of information and messages to monitor, co-ordinate, control and administer the specialists on the other. Technological change itself depends upon the *adoption* of new ideas and techniques which, in turn, presupposes access to, and awareness of, information about these ideas and techniques. It can be argued that the speed of technological change in society is very closely related to the prevailing media of communication and to the speed and extent of information flow.

It is hardly surprising, therefore, that modern society devotes so much of its energies and resources – human as well as financial and material – to overcoming what geographers usually term the *friction of distance*. Movement between places is costly, whether the cost is measured in dollars, pounds, time or general inconvenience. Geographical space may be perceived in one sense as a barrier or obstacle to be overcome as rapidly or as cheaply as possible. To business organizations (and to national governments) geographical space may also be regarded as something to be *controlled* or *captured* – as in the case of market areas, spheres of influence or political territories. From both viewpoints the characteristics and efficiency of the media of transportation and communication take on central importance. More generally, in modern industrial society there is a widespread obsession with mobility and with improving ease of access. Indeed, much technological change in industrial society has been characterized by deliberate efforts to 'adjust' geographical space, reducing the friction of distance through innovations in transportation and communication to overcome the capability constraints imposed by limitations on mobility. The result is clear for all to see. *Western industrial society is a media-rich society* whose general access to transportation and communications media is unparalleled in human history. What Abler calls the *space-adjusting* technologies are at its very heart. Thus, it is in this sphere that the effects of technological change on time-space constraints are most clearly seen. Although reduced capability constraint is the most obvious manifestation of the effect of space-adjusting technologies, both coupling and authority constraints are also modified by developments in transportation and communications technology which greatly enhance the possibilities of co-ordination and of control.

As a reflection of our obsession with mobility, the idea that we live in a *shrinking world* has become a highly popular notion much encouraged by commercial interests, particularly among the media themselves. It is certainly true that, in terms of transportation, there has been a remarkable shrinkage of geographical space. Beginning in the nineteenth century, the spread of railroad and highway systems transformed movement on a *continental* scale. More recently air transportation has shrunk distances at a *global* scale. In less than fifty years the speed at which individuals and freight can be moved has increased tenfold. Recent introduction of supersonic air passenger transportation, as the advertisements so insistently point out, has made it possible to 'leave Paris at 1.00 p.m. and be in Brazil tonight' (Figure 2.4). The

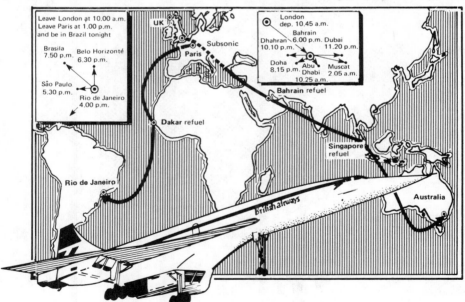

Figure 2.4   Effect of Concorde on intercontinental travel times

Source: Guardian 21 January, 1976, p.12.

Atlantic Ocean has been reduced to little more than a river; allowing for the time-zone differences it is very nearly possible to be in New York almost before leaving London! At the individual level, of course, the most potent transportation innovation has been the automobile. More than anything else, the automobile offers convenience and freedom from the restrictive locational influence of railroad stations and airports. Such freedom has had enormous repercussions on the scale and nature of urban living. It has also, as shown in Chapter Five, generated some very considerable social problems.

Thus the *potential* range of both individuals and organizations in modern industrial society has become truly enormous compared with the recent past. Their daily time-space prisms are more extensive than ever before. But it is all too easy to be seduced by the technology and its advocates into believing that the shrinking process has affected everywhere and everybody in the same way. The maps of the United States (Figure 2.5) and Canada (Figure 2.6) are typical of the widely held opinion that we live in a shrinking world. There is obviously some validity in this view. Yet such representations grossly oversimplify the real nature of the geographical shrinkage produced by technological changes in transportation. Such shrinkage is not regular; it is highly *ir*regular from place to place. The major reasons for this have been identified by Donald Janelle. He points out that a characteristic general feature of transportation improvements is that they tend to occur in and between

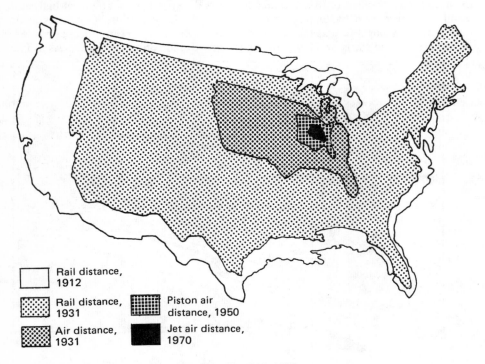

Rail distance, 1912

Rail distance, 1931

Air distance, 1931

Piston air distance, 1950

Jet air distance, 1970

Figure 2.5 The 'shrinking' United States, 1912–1970

Source: M. Clawson (1972) *America's land and its Uses*, Johns Hopkins University Press, p.13.

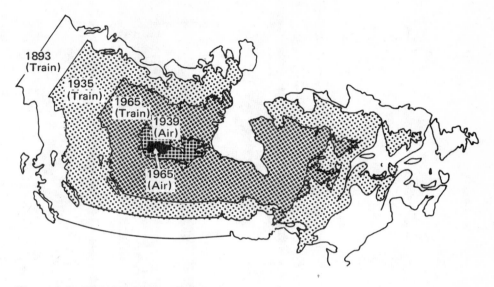

Figure 2.6   The shrinking map of Canada

Source: Economic Council of Canada, Annual Review. By permission of the Minister of Supply & Services, Canada.

places which already have achieved some degree of prominence or which have high potential for economic growth. These are the places that tend to 'converge' in time-space, that is, to get closer together in a relative sense.

The effect of such geographically selective development of transportation innovations is to 'pull' some places closer together while leaving others 'out on a limb'. Figure 2.7 illustrates this differential geographical shrinkage within Great Britain. The map focuses upon London (naturally!) and depicts fastest travel times from London to different parts of the country given the prevailing transportation system in the late 1960s. Quite clearly some cities have been pulled closer to London – indeed, this was the avowed claim of British Rail at the time of its massive, though highly selective, investment programme in electrification. Equally clearly, many places are disproportionately distant in time terms. Thus, Burnley is twice as far from London in time-distance as is Manchester, despite the fact that Burnley is a mere twenty-five miles north of Manchester. Pwllheli, a small town in North Wales, is almost as 'far' from London as is New York or Montreal even though it is less than one-tenth of the actual distance in mileage terms.

The result of technological developments in transportation, then, is a highly distorted time-space map rather than the regular ones so often presented. *Time-space convergence*, which undoubtedly occurs, is matched in many instances by relative *time-space divergence*. But not only is there a very great unevenness between places in the impact of technological developments in transportation, there is also very great variation at the individual and social group level. Only a small proportion of the total population of modern industrial society is able to partake in the delights (or disasters) of movement over vast distances. Although the size of the 'jet set' may well have increased it still constitutes a minority. As Adams has pointed out,

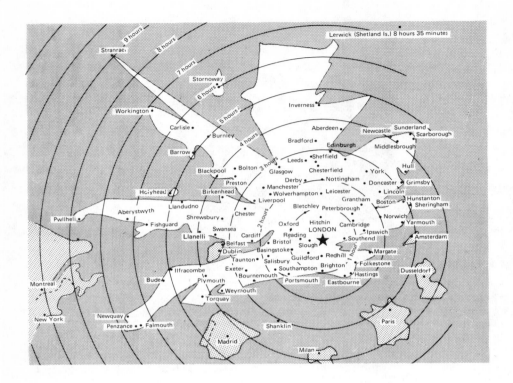

Figure 2.7   Britain's uneven shrinkage

Source: Richard Natkiel for *New Society*, London.

not even the most wildly optimistic Concorde salesman envisages the day
when all 800 million Chinese and all 500 million Indians, let alone all
Britons or Frenchmen, will be regular users of Concorde.
Adams (1972), p.383.

Although car-ownership has reached extremely high levels there are many people
who do not have access to a car. It is all too easy to overlook the existence of the
'transport poor' amidst the general euphoria about supposedly universal mobility.
This is a topic we return to again in Chapter Five.

Similar comments can be made about developments in interpersonal communication. The telephone permits people to speak directly to each other regardless of the
distance separating them. For those with access to it – and its adoption spread very
rapidly, especially in North America – social communication has been revolutionized. Telephoning friends or relatives began to supplement, or even replace,
visiting or writing. 'Keeping in touch' no longer necessitates physical proximity. As
Hägerstrand points out,

telecommunication allows people to form bundles . . . [of activities] . . .
without (or nearly without) loss of time in transportation.
Hägerstrand (1970), p.15.

As with all technological innovations in transportation and communication, the speed and sophistication of the telephone has increased enormously since Bell's initial experiments of 1876. The replacement of manual operation by automatic, and later electronic, exchange systems has generally reduced the time involved in making a telephone connection between distant places. Figure 2.8 shows the rate of 'telephonic-time-space convergence' between New York and San Francisco, in the period 1920 to 1970. Abler estimates that the two cities were converging at an average rate of sixteen seconds per year. In 1920, for example, it took approximately fourteen minutes to make a telephone connection between the two cities, by 1930 this had been reduced to a little over two minutes and by 1970 to a mere thirty seconds. Abler therefore concludes that 'in telephonic-time-space, all of Anglo-America is at the same place'. This is not the case in cost terms, however, even though there has been an average cost convergence of twenty-nine cents per year (Figure 2.9). Such developments at the national scale have also begun to spread internationally. Direct dialling is now possible between most parts of the industrialized world so that time-space convergence on a global scale is already in evidence (though it is important to know about time-zones). The combination of telephone and television technology has also produced the videophone whereby callers can both hear and see each other, while combination of telephone and computer technology now permits rapid transfer of information between computerized data banks and is beginning to have an impact in the business sphere.

Once again the allocation of telephone time-space convergence is uneven. Not every household has a telephone even though its use is especially high in the United States. There are, similarly, considerable differences both between and within countries in the ratio of telephones to population. It is, in fact, the big commercial and government organizations which appear to have gained most from transporta-

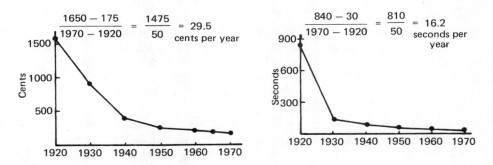

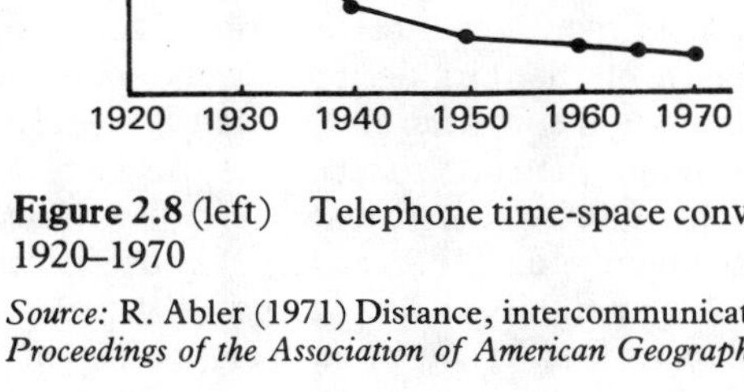

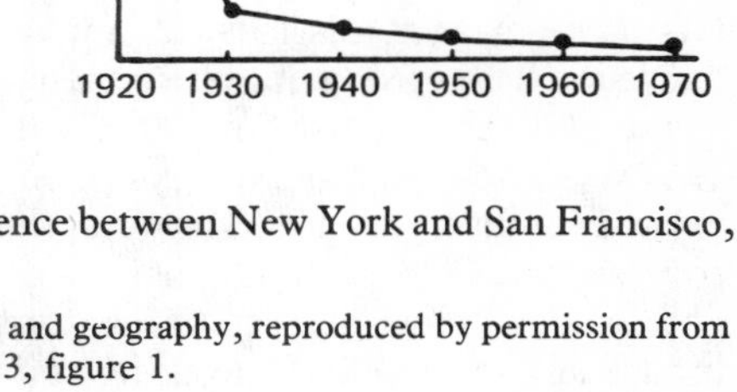

Figure 2.8 (left)   Telephone time-space convergence between New York and San Francisco, 1920–1970

Source: R. Abler (1971) Distance, intercommunications and geography, reproduced by permission from *Proceedings of the Association of American Geographers*, 3, figure 1.

Figure 2.9 (right)   Telephone cost-space convergence between New York and San Francisco, 1920–1970

Source: R. Abler (1971) Distance, intercommunications and geography, reproduced by permission from *Proceedings of the Association of American Geographers*, 3, figure 4.

tion and communications improvements. These have enabled them to operate over greater and greater distances. Indeed, the business historian Alfred Chandler traces the beginnings of modern large business enterprises to the development of the railroads in the United States in the nineteenth century. Not only did the rapidly expanding railroad network extend both supply and market areas, but it also made necessary and feasible a type of organization in which control became separate from day-to-day operations. In this sense it paved the way for the massive organizations discussed later in this chapter. It is also worth noting that the transportation industries – motor vehicle and aircraft manufacture, airline and railroad companies – are themselves dominated by a few giant corporations. Transportation, like so many other aspects of modern industrial society, is big business.

Changes in interpersonal communications have, therefore, had a particularly powerful impact upon interorganizational communications. It is no exaggeration to say that the giant business organization, operating on a national or multinational scale, simply could not exist without modern telephone and telecommunications facilities along with air transportation. Instantaneous, or very rapid, communication between corporate headquarters and branch plants or sales offices spread across the globe is a prerequisite of the survival of the large corporation. Such organizations are not produced or caused by technological developments in transportation and communication but they could not have developed without them. More generally, the fundamental point about these innovations – whether singly or collectively – is that they have brought about an enormous transformation of society and of social organization in space. They have achieved this by speeding up the flow of information, by increasing its range and scope and by facilitating control of operations over vastly increased distances.

In terms of the daily lives of most ordinary people in modern industrial society, however, probably the most pervasive development has been that of the *mass media*. Such innovations led McLuhan to claim that

> after three thousand years of explosion, by means of fragmentary and mechanical technologies, the Western world is imploding. During the mechanical ages we had extended our bodies in space. Today, after more than a century of electric technology, we have extended our central nervous system itself in a global embrace.
> *McLuhan (1964), p.11.*

Of all the mass media it is, of course, television which is most notable. Access to television has spread with phenomenal speed throughout modern industrial society. Figure 2.10 shows just how rapidly this innovation spread in the United States. In 1953 television coverage was confined to the major metropolitan centres; there were extensive unserved areas beyond the reach of television transmitters. By 1965 coverage was complete: in almost all areas between 80 and 100 percent of households possessed a television set. This pattern of ownership is now common in most industrialized nations. The effect and influence of television upon social behaviour continues to generate heated debate, debate which is beyond the scope of our present discussion. What is worth emphasizing, however, is the importance of television as a transmitter of information. As Johnson observed,

> the average male viewer, between his second and sixty-fifth year, will watch television for over 3,000 entire days – roughly nine full years of his life.

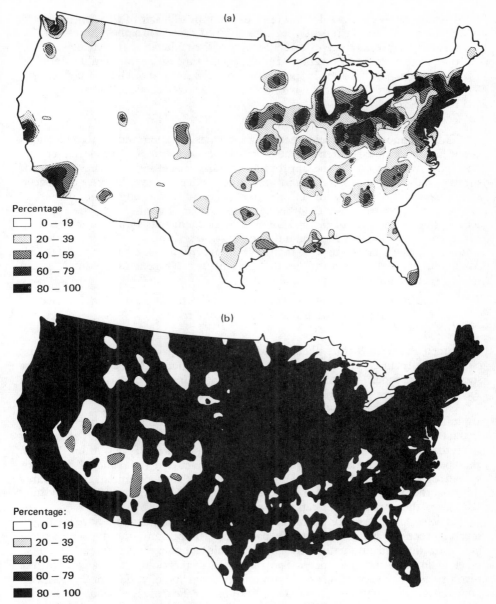

Figure 2.10   The spread of television ownership in the United States

(a) Percentage of households having a television receiver, 1953
(b) Percentage of households having a television receiver, 1965

Source: B.J.L. Berry (1972) Hierarchical diffusion: the basis of developmental filtering and spread in a system of growth centres, in N.M. Hansen (ed) *Growth Centers in Regional Economic Development,* New York: Free Press, figures 3 and 7.

During the average weekday winter evening nearly half of the American people are to be found silently seated with fixed gaze upon a phosphorescent screen. Americans receive decidedly more of their education from television than from elementary and high schools. By the time the average child enters kindergarten he has already spent more hours learning about his world from television than the hours he would spend in a college classroom earning a B.A. degree.
Johnson (1970), p.11.

Thus technological developments in the transportation and communications media have enormously extended the *geographical scale* of modern industrial society. For those with access to the appropriate media, space and time have, indeed, shrunk. We are all bombarded by information to a degree never before experienced and, as a result, coping with 'information overload' has become one of the key problems of modern living. Another problem is that of coping with the apparent acceleration in the *pace of change*. Many writers claim that we live in a period in which change is not only *endemic* but also *accelerating*. The theme that the modern world is changing at a faster rate than ever before has become widely popularized. Alvin Toffler, in particular, argues that present-day change is so rapid in Western society that we are being swept along by

the roaring current of change, a current so powerful today that it overturns institutions, shifts our values and shrivels our roots.
Toffler (1971), p.11.

He coined the term 'future shock' to describe the impact of such overwhelming change on humanity, and sees it as parallel to, but a more extreme form of, culture shock. Future shock, he claims, is 'cultural shock in one's own society' arising from accelerated change – the collision of the present with the future.

Not everybody agrees with this view or accepts Toffler's hyperbole. Much of the argument revolves around precisely what is meant by change, what exactly is changing so rapidly and how such change is measured. It does, however, seem fairly clear that it is not simply the more frequent appearance of 'new things' which characterizes present-day society as much as the fact that the *rate of diffusion*, or spread, of innovations through the population at large has accelerated. It is probably this, together with the impact of mass communications, which, more than anything else, gives the impression of rapid change.

In discussing the major characteristics of modern technology we have identified several processes which seem to be particularly important: the development of mechanization and automation, the new materials technology, the increasing importance of information and knowledge, the speed of technological change, and the revolutions in transportation and communications technology. Each of these aspects of modern technology has profound implications for the daily lives – and livelihoods – of the citizens of modern industrial society. They have greatly modified the operation of both capability and coupling constraints on human social behaviour and have altered the span of control of authority. At this point, we develop the thread of argument suggested by the last of these and turn to a more detailed consideration of the increasing organizational scale of Western industrial society. This is a development which, though by no means caused by technological change alone, has, as we have suggested, been much enhanced by it.

One major result of technological change during the continuing process of industrialization has been a *progressively increasing scale of production*. Factories have grown larger as technological developments have permitted increased output at lower unit cost. The enterprises controlling or owning the factories have grown still larger, extending their *control* over more and more production units in more and more geographical locations. They have extended both the diversity of their products and the geographical extent of their markets. Some writers go so far as to claim that the giant business corporation – which we propose to examine in some detail – is the inevitable result of modern technology. Galbraith is probably the leading proponent of this view. He argues that large organizations are made necessary by what he terms the 'imperative of technology':

> more even than machinery, massive and complex business organizations are the tangible manifestation of advanced technology.
> *Galbraith (1967), p.28.*

Galbraith suggests a number of factors which, he believes, underly such a relationship: for example, the high capital costs inherent in much modern technology, their specialized nature which requires co-ordination and organization, the time-scale involved which necessitates long-term planning and commitment of resources. While many would agree with Galbraith's view, there are many others who reject it and argue that modern technology need not inevitably require very large size. Indeed, some claim that the massive hierarchical bureaucracies characteristic of large organizations may well inhibit, rather than encourage, new ideas. The controversy over the relationship between technology and size of organization is only marginally relevant to our purposes. However, it leads us logically into a consideration of the extent to which Western industrial society has come to be dominated by very large organizations.

THE PERVASIVENESS OF THE GIANT ORGANIZATION IN MODERN WESTERN SOCIETY

Whether one accepts or rejects the relationship between technology and size, it is an indisputable fact that one of the most distinctive features of modern Western industrial society – one which sets it apart from its predecessors – is the all-pervasive embrace of the very large organization. Now, of course, big organizations in themselves are not new. The village dweller in eighteenth-century Britain or the settler establishing himself in the New World lived within the orbit of the 'Big Three': church, state, army. But most aspects of daily life were, until quite recently, untouched by the activities of large organizations:

> The social scene everywhere looked much like the Kansas prairie: the largest thing on the horizon was the individual. Most social tasks were accomplished in and through family-sized units.
> *Drucker (1969), p.213.*

Individuals were either self-employed or worked in small organizations which were invariably owned and operated by one person and whose continuity was based on family ownership. Relationships in such organizations were immediate and face to face; the owner more often than not knew each of his employees personally. Most of life's needs were also fulfilled locally, either through the small family-run store or through self-production. Entertainment was, for the most part, self-made entertainment. There were few large business organizations, no large labour unions or professional associations of any size and few large government departments. Life for the individual was predominantly family-based, communal and intimate.

Today, in the last quarter of the twentieth century, the picture is very different. There are still vast numbers of small organizations but their *relative* importance has tended to decline in the face of the trend – universal in all developed industrial societies – towards the very large organization. Such organizations form the dominant working environment for most people. They are, in many cases, light years removed from the small organization of yesterday. They are organizations in which the average employee would not recognize the owner if he fell over him in the street. (Indeed, in most very large organizations there is no such person. Since the development of the joint stock or limited liability type of company in the late nineteenth century, ownership can be transferred through the sale of shareholdings. In some cases, therefore, ownership is dispersed among literally thousands of individuals; in other cases the majority of the shares are held by other very large organizations such as insurance and pension companies, banks and other financial institutions.) They are organizations in which each person is a very tiny cog in a wheel so large that its size is often difficult to comprehend. This characteristic applies just as much to 'public' organizations – government departments and agencies, for example – as it does to 'private' organizations like business firms. *All tend to be impersonal, hierarchically organized bureaucracies*.

Such very large organizations with their massive bureaucracies have come to affect almost every aspect of life; they are the environment of modern man.* Indeed, it is difficult to think of many aspects of our daily lives that are not impinged upon, either directly or indirectly, by the large organization. With few exceptions it influences where we work and what we do there, what we eat and how we spend our leisure time. Large organizations make many of the decisions which affect the purity of the air we breathe or the rivers and lakes we swim in. They are the sources of most of the changes we see around us in the cities and towns. Large organizations spend vast sums of *their* money persuading us to spend *our* money on their products, or, as governments, in regulating much of our behaviour.

Thus we cannot hope to comprehend modern industrial society and the spatial organization of activities within it without some understanding of the role of large organizations as the major decision-making units.

---

*Lest you think that these are exaggerated statements, take time out to consider just how many 'contact points' in your average day are with large organizations. Your early morning radio programme probably comes to you on a set manufactured by a firm like ITT (employment: 376,000), Hitachi (employment: 146,447) or Philips (employment: 397,000). The radio station itself is probably owned by, or affiliated to, one of the handful of national networks: NBC, CBS, ABC in the United States, BBC or ITV in Britain, CBC in Canada. Light, heat and water are supplied by the massive public utility companies, whether 'privately' owned like Consolidated Edison (employment: 24,645) or 'publicly' owned like the British Gas Corporation (employment: 102,500). Breakfast, as we know from our television commercials, would be impossible without the wonderful products of General Foods (employment: 48,000), Nabisco (employment: 47,000) or Kellogg (employment: 17,000). Think, too, of the contents of your mail box. Apart from letters from your nearest and dearest, how much is in the form of bills from big companies like American

Telephone and Telegraph (employment: 939,064) or the Post Office (employment: 434,065) from credit card companies or from government departments? How much consists of advertising material and 'special-offers-not-to-be-missed' or of forms to complete whether to assess your tax liability or to permit you to vote?

If you drive a car it is more than likely to be the product of only a very small handful of automobile manufacturers, all of which are amongst the very largest manufacturing companies in the world. The origin of the gasoline in your tank is even more restricted – from what have been called the 'Seven Sisters', the world's major oil companies. In fact, seven of the ten largest business corporations in the world (measured in terms of their total sales) are oil companies and two of the other three are automobile manufacturers (General Motors and Ford). If you are employed you are more likely to work for an organization (private or public) employing several hundred or even several thousand workers than for one employing less than one hundred. If you are a college student you are more likely to attend a large college or university than a small one and, even if the college itself is small, it is probably financed and administered by a large state or local government department.

The pervasiveness of big organizations is also beginning to make many places in widely different geographical locations look much the same. If you were abducted and then released in some shopping centre or mall far from home you would probably have very great difficulty in deciding just where you were not, paradoxically, because of its unfamiliarity but because of its very familiarity. Most of the stores would be the ones that appear almost everywhere – the large retailing chains with their identical store façades and advertising slogans. A shopping mall with the usual cluster of Sears-Roebuck, Safeway, Kresge, and Woolco could be almost anywhere in North America just as the shopping centre with its group of Marks and Spencer, Woolworth's, and Tesco could be anywhere in Britain. Such organizational uniformity imposed upon geographical diversity is reinforced by the fact that shopping centres as a whole are increaingly planned as an entity, instead of evolving gradually. Since the shopping centre developers themselves also tend to be very large organizations with nationwide interests, the shopping centres as a whole, and not just the individual stores, take on a uniformity of appearance.

BIG BUSINESS

Big organizations in manufacturing industry

In the United States, less than 1 percent of all manufacturing firms controls approximately 88 percent of all industrial assets and generates more than 90 percent of total net profits. A mere one hundred firms (0.03 percent of the total) receive a larger share of net profits than the other 370,000 firms in the manufacturing sector put together (Reid 1976). These are the firms which each have assets of more than $1 billion. As Richard Barber points out,

> What this means is that the presidents of a hundred companies – a group sufficiently small to be seated comfortably in the reading room of the Union League Club in Philadelphia – represent almost as much wealth and control as large a share of the nation's economic activity as the next largest 300,000 manufacturers – a group that would completely fill four Yankee Stadiums. *Barber (1970), p.20.*

But what do such figures mean in terms of what really matters to most people – the number of jobs involved? Just how big in employment terms are the giant business corporations? In 1972, for example, eighty-eight firms in the United States and thirty firms in Britain each employed more than 40,000 workers. But many were very much larger than this as Table 2.2 shows. It also shows that, as we might expect, the largest US firms are much larger than the biggest UK firms. We can get a clearer perspective on the size of these largest corporations by comparing their employment with the population of various cities. Thus, as Table 2.2 reveals, General Motors employs as many workers as the entire population of San Antonio, Texas; Ford is as 'big' as Atlanta, Georgia; GEC compares with Southampton and ICI with Portsmouth.

Table 2.2 *Employment of the largest manufacturing firms in the United States and United Kingdom compared with populations of selected cities*

(a) United States

Corporation	Employment (000s) a 1972	City	Population (000s) b 1973
General Motors	760	San Antonio, Texas	756
Ford	443	Atlanta, Georgia	451
ITT	428	Buffalo, New York	425
General Electric	369	Newark, New Jersey	368
IBM	262	Sacramento, California	267
Chrysler	245	Richmond, Virginia	238
Westinghouse	176	Providence, Rhode Island	170
Goodyear	145	Bridgeport, Connecticut	148
Exxon	141	Las Vegas, Nevada	144
RCA	122	Peoria, Illinois	128

(b) United Kingdom

Corporation	Employment (000s) a 1972	City	Population (000s) c 1971
GEC	211	Southampton	217
ICI	199	Portsmouth	197
British Leyland	191	Walsall	185
Unilever	156	Brighton	166
Courtaulds	150	Bolton	153
British-American Tobacco	110	Newport	112
Guest, Keen & Nettlefold	109	Oxford	109
Imperial Group	108	Oldham	106
Associated British Foods	108	York	104
Dunlop	85	Darlington	86

Sources: (a) S.J. Prais (1976) *The Evolution of Giant Firms in Britain*. National Institute of Economic and Social Research, Economic and Social Studies, 30. Cambridge: Cambridge University Press, table F1; (b) United States *Statistical Abstract* (1975), table 25; (c) Census of England and Wales (1971) *Preliminary Report*, table 4. Crown Copyright.

These are impressive comparisons. But we can take them even further. If we examine the annual sales (in $ million) of the largest business corporations, then we find that they are of the same magnitude as the Gross National Products of entire nation-states. Only thirteen non-Communist countries in 1973 had GNPs larger than the sales of General Motors. Figure 2.11 compares the sales of fifteen of the leading world manufacturing corporations with the Gross National Products of a

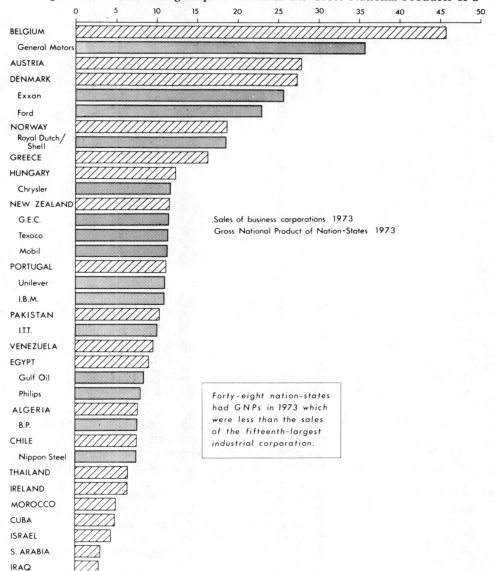

Sales of business corporations 1973
Gross National Product of Nation-States 1973

Forty-eight nation-states had GNPs in 1973 which were less than the sales of the fifteenth-largest industrial corporation.

Figure 2.11 Large business enterprises compared on a scale with nation states

sample of nation-states. The graph needs little further comment other than to note that no fewer than forty-eight nation-states had GNPs in 1973 that were less than the sales of the fifteenth-ranking business corporation.

Within Western industrial societies, then, the trend during the twentieth century has been for the relative importance of the largest enterprises to increase at the expense of smaller enterprises. One recent estimate suggests that in 1909 it took more than 2000 firms to produce one-half of the total manufacturing output in the United Kingdom. By 1970, a mere 140 firms were able to produce this same proportion (Prais 1976). Figure 2.12 shows how the importance of the 100 largest firms, in both the United States and Britain, has increased over this same period. Measured in these terms it appears that manufacturing industry in the United Kingdom is now more dominated by the 100 largest firms than is the United States, the traditional home of big business.

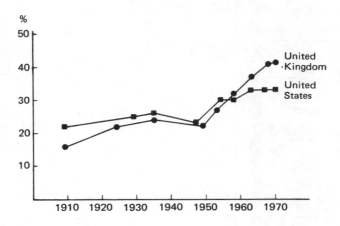

Figure 2.12   Shares of the 100 largest enterprises in manufacturing net output, United Kingdom and United States

Source: S.J. Prais (1976) *The Evolution of Giant Firms in Britain*, National Institute of Economic and Social Research, Cambridge: Cambridge University Press, chart 6.1.

Quite apart from the overall dominance of large firms in manufacturing as a whole, some individual industries are much more dominated than others. As Figure 2.13 shows, virtually the entire output of such industries as aluminium, automobiles, synthetic fibre and electric bulb production in the United States is supplied by only four firms in each industry. Each of these industries is what the economist would call an *oligopoly*. Of course, there is a lot of variation across the whole spectrum of manufacturing. Some industries are still shared between large numbers of firms, big, medium and small; others are composed of predominantly very small firms. However, the *general* trend in all the Western industrial economies is for an increasing share of most industries to be concentrated in a relatively small number of large enterprises.

But this does not mean that the large corporations themselves are involved only in a single industry. On the contrary, one of the most significant characteristics of the

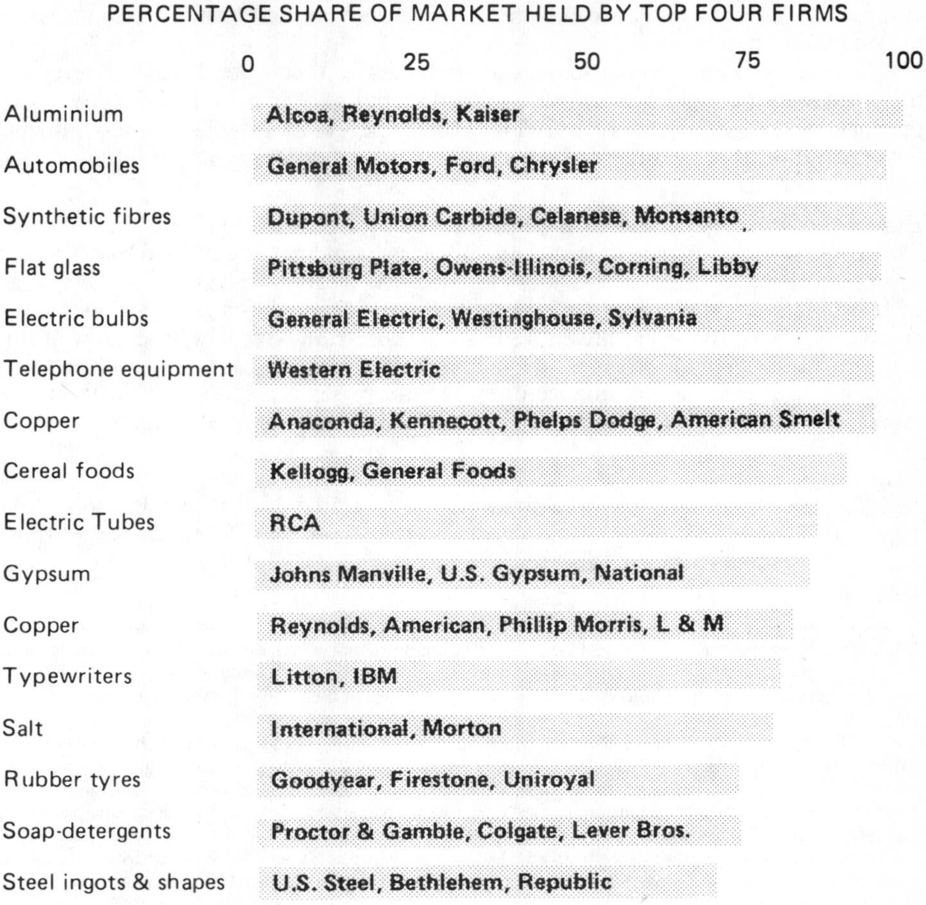

PERCENTAGE SHARE OF MARKET HELD BY TOP FOUR FIRMS

	0	25	50	75	100
Aluminium	Alcoa, Reynolds, Kaiser				
Automobiles	General Motors, Ford, Chrysler				
Synthetic fibres	Dupont, Union Carbide, Celanese, Monsanto				
Flat glass	Pittsburg Plate, Owens-Illinois, Corning, Libby				
Electric bulbs	General Electric, Westinghouse, Sylvania				
Telephone equipment	Western Electric				
Copper	Anaconda, Kennecott, Phelps Dodge, American Smelt				
Cereal foods	Kellogg, General Foods				
Electric Tubes	RCA				
Gypsum	Johns Manville, U.S. Gypsum, National				
Copper	Reynolds, American, Phillip Morris, L & M				
Typewriters	Litton, IBM				
Salt	International, Morton				
Rubber tyres	Goodyear, Firestone, Uniroyal				
Soap-detergents	Proctor & Gamble, Colgate, Lever Bros.				
Steel ingots & shapes	U.S. Steel, Bethlehem, Republic				

Figure 2.13   Industries in the United States dominated by a few large firms

Source: R.J. Barber (1970) *The American Corporation,* London: MacGibbon and Key, chart 1.

very large business corporation in the second half of the twentieth century has been the phenomenal spread of its involvement across an enormous variety of activities. This is one of the major differences between the giant firms of the late nineteenth and early twentieth century and the giant firms of today. In those earlier days, if a firm had a name like US Steel, US Rubber or General Motors you could be pretty sure that its efforts would be devoted entirely to producing steel, rubber or automobiles respectively, or, at least, to processes very closely connected to them. Not any more. A good deal of their energies is now devoted to such activities as real estate, domestic appliances, fertilizers, plastics and many others a long way removed from their original activities. For such reasons, a lot of large firms have changed their names to rid themselves of too close an association with a particular product. US Rubber is one of these; it is now called Uniroyal. American Tobacco is another, it changed its name to American Brands.

Most of the dominant business corporations, then, are highly diversified multiproduct or conglomerate firms. Indeed there has been a marked decline in the proportion of the largest firms which could be called 'single-business' firms. Diversification is the name of the game for the big corporation.*

Big organizations in the non-manufacturing sector

The increasing dominance of large enterprises is by no means confined to manufacturing industry. Wherever we look in modern Western industrial society – at wholesaling and retailing, at finance, at property development and real estate, at communications, indeed at the entire business spectrum – we see the shadow of the giant business corporation. Here we take just two examples, retailing and finance, although an increasing dominance of large enterprises is also evident in the mass media and in the development and construction industries (see Chapter Four).

Retailing

In 1973, total retail sales in the United States amounted to $459,040 million while 12,547,000 people were employed in providing retail services. Retailing is traditionally a small enterprise sector and this is still broadly the case. Even so, the leading

---

*One of the most active of these conglomerates, ITT, is a particularly interesting case not least because of the notoriety it attracted by its political involvements both within the United States and overseas (for example, in Chile). The development of ITT gives us some idea of the nature of a very large conglomerate corporation.

ITT began its life as a specialized telecommunications company and was one of the earliest of the large multinational corporations. By 1965, it was already widely diversified and active in more than fifty industrial sectors. But many of these were quite closely related to each other. For example, the corporation manufactured telecommunication equipment and related components, electronic products, control devices and so on, a good many of the products having defence and aerospace applications. But in the 1960s, ITT undertook an energetic diversification policy into areas very far removed from its existing products. By a vigorously aggressive policy of acquiring other firms ITT penetrated an enormous variety of sectors, especially in consumer goods and service industries. Between 1964 and 1969 it acquired forty-six corporations or parts of corporations in a bewildering variety of fields including, in particular,

> the nation's largest bakery, Continental, the largest hotel chain, Sheraton, the second-largest car rental service, Avis, the leading housing builder and developer, Levitt, one of the largest property and casualty insurance companies, Hartford, a leading vending machine company, Canteen, as well as two important consumer finance companies, Aetna and Thorp Finance. The acquisition of Hartford Insurance Company, with assets of $1,892 billion, is the largest recorded during this decade. *Thus the average citizen can buy his home from ITT, live in one of its 'planned communities', have the house insured by another of ITT's divisions, take a trip in one of ITT's rental cars, stay at one of ITT's hotels, or motels, purchase his bread and other bakery products from another of its divisions, buy his cigarettes and coffee from one of its vending machines, obtain a loan from one of its finance companies, and had it not been for antitrust objections, watch TV on an ITT-owned network.* Outside the consumer area ITT's major acquisitions have been of a major producer of automatic fire protection systems and equipment, Grinnell Corp., and of suppliers of raw materials which, however, have little in common; Rayonier, a leading forest products firm and the world's largest supplier of chemical cellulose from wood pulp; and Pennsylvania Glass Sand, a leading producer of silica used in glass manufacture.
> *Testimony of J.M. Blair to Subcommittee on Antitrust and Monopoly, US Senate (1969), p.4880* (present authors' ephasis).

fifty retailing companies accounted for 22 percent of the total sales and for 21 percent of retail employment. Again, therefore, we cannot fail to be impressed by the significance of what is, numerically, a minute fraction of the total number of firms. Using the same criterion as in our discussion of manufacturing – firms employing more than 40,000 workers – we find that sixteen of the leading fifty retailing companies in the United States in 1973 came into that category. Seven of these employed more than 100,000, whilst one – Sears-Roebuck – employed over 400,000 workers.*

The pattern is not dissimilar in other modern industrial societies. In Britain three retail companies – Marks and Spencer, Great Universal Stores and Woolworth's – are in the top fifty business corporations, while other very large corporations such as Sears Holdings and George Weston Holdings have major retail interests. Between 1961 and 1978 the large multiple retailers increased their share of total retail trade from 29 percent to 47 percent. In Canada eleven dominant corporations account for 45 percent of total retail sales though four of these are subsidiaries of United States companies and one, Simpsons-Sears, is a joint operation (Clement 1975).

The large regional shopping centres,† which, as Figure 2.14 shows, have become ubiquitous in the United States, provide a very clear illustration of the increasing dominance of very large corporations. A handful of large development

---

*Sears-Roebuck, in fact, can be regarded as the General Motors or the ITT of the retail sector. Barber describes its characteristics in a graphic manner:

> Sears is the biggest merchandiser in the world. It literally operates around the world selling, not just goods for the home, but almost everything that the consumer could possibly want in the way of products and services. Through acquisitions and internal growth, it has gained a position and developed a raison d'être that has pioneered the way for many other businesses. Sears is oriented to a function, namely meeting the needs of the household. To satisfy that demand the company has diversified wildly, not only selling through nearly a thousand retail stores (located in the U.S., Canada, South America, and Europe) but making many of those goods in wholly or partly owned subsidiaries.
>
> Sears manufactures and sells a full line of appliances, electronic goods (ranging from TV sets and radios to tape recorders and organs), lawn mowers and garden tractors, venetian blinds, wallpaper, paints and chemicals, outdoor cooking equipment, plumbing fixtures, sporting goods, and family apparel. It also services most of what it sells through wholly-owned service affiliates and will instal anything from a swimming pool to a heating-air conditioning unit. It offers comprehensive insurance, operates a savings and loan association, and provides the credit for its billions in instalment sales. Sears also franchises and operates restaurants in some twenty-eight states and supplies vending services for industrial plants and office buildings. In the breadth of its operations, in its aggressive search for new markets here and abroad, and in the degree of its self-sufficiency, Sears probably has no equal.
>
> Barber (1970), p.31.

---

†One architect of these centres regards them as 'the piazzas of America'. Breckenfeld claims that:

> in big metropolitan areas and smaller cities alike, such indoor piazzas are quickly reshaping much of American life. Giant regional shopping centers have arisen by the hundred across the nation and are still going up by the score. To an amazing degree they are seizing the role once held by the central business districts, not only in retailing but as the social, cultural and recreational focal point of the entire community. . . . The air-conditioned malls entice shop-

pers with year-round spring-time climate and the festive mood of a country fair. In the courtyards, developers plant tropical gardens dotted with kiosks, sculpture, benches, pools and – almost invariably – fountains. . . . As befits the place where all the action is, the typical regional shopping centre has grown to be immense. It is no longer just a department store and a few dozen shops and beaneries, but three or four department stores plus 100 or 150 smaller shops. Not only offices, but also apartments, a medical clinic, banks, stockbrokers, motels, and even churches cluster around the sea of asphalt that provides the quintessential free parking lot. Lauderwood Plaza, in the Cleveland suburbs, even includes a cemetery . . . regional centers have turned into mini-cities. Most important of all, they are attuned as downtown never was – to the age of the private auto.
Breckenfeld (1972), pp.80, 82.

---

companies is responsible for virtually all planned regional centres in North America and for most large city-centre developments in the United Kingdom. The largest retailing chains – the big department stores – often have an enormous stake in these centres. In the United States, for example, not only do they impose a substantial degree of control over the type of shop and merchandise which is permitted in the centres where they are the 'anchor tenants', but also they are heavily involved financially in developing new centres. Sears, for example, in 1972 owned nine regional centres and held a joint financial interest in seventeen others.

Finance

Geographers have long shown an interest in both manufacturing and retail activities. By contrast, they have virtually ignored the financial sector. Yet there is good reason to believe that this sector is the lynch-pin of Western industrial society. Capital tends to be channelled increasingly through a complex of financial institutions – commercial banks, finance corporations, insurance companies, pension funds and so on. We should not now be surprised to learn that these financial institutions have also been increasing in size and influence.

A House of Representatives Subcommittee (the Patman Committee) found that, in 1964, the 100 largest commercial banks in the United States (0.7 percent of the total) held almost 50 percent of all commercial bank deposits. A mere fourteen banks (0.1 percent) – the largest being Bank of America, First National City and Chase-Manhattan – held no less than 24 percent of all deposits. In Britain the banking sector is similarly concentrated, in this case by the Big Four of Barclays, National Westminster, Midland and Lloyds, which together had deposits of £42,000 million in 1975. The Canadian banking sector is one of the most concentrated of all: five banks (Royal Bank, Canadian Imperial Bank of Commerce, Bank of Montreal, Bank of Nova Scotia and the Toronto-Dominion) account for 90 percent of all Canadian banking assets. But the commercial banks are only a part of the financial structure of modern industrial society. Of increasing importance are the 'intermediary' financial institutions – the pension funds, insurance companies, mutual funds and unit trusts – which have grown especially rapidly during the last twenty years. The funds held by these institutions have reached staggeringly high levels. In 1969, the pension funds alone in the United States had $40 billion worth of assets. A similar sum was held in 1972 by the major financial institutions (excluding banks) in Britain.

The most important implication for our purposes is that these funds are increasingly being invested in industrial and commercial companies. In 1957, the financial institutions held roughly 18 percent of all ordinary shares in UK-quoted companies. By 1973 this proportion had risen to more than 40 percent (Prais 1976). This reverses

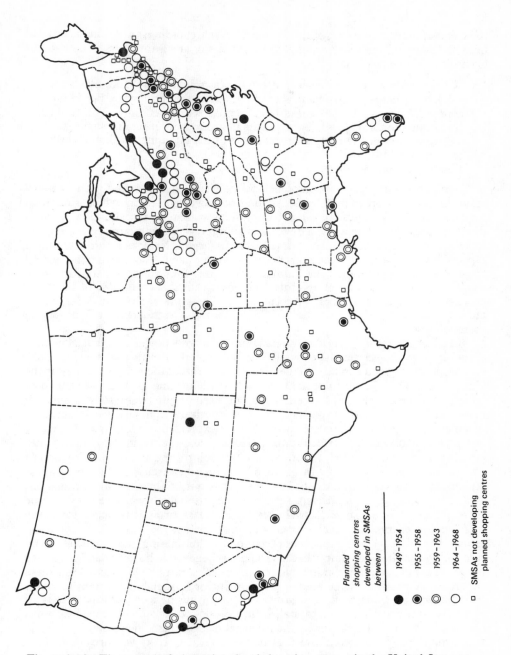

Figure 2.14 The spread of planned regional shopping centres in the United States

Source: Y.S. Cohen (1972) Diffusion of an innovation in an urban system: the spread of planned regional shopping centers in the United States 1949–1968, *Universtiy of Chicago, Dept. of Geography Research Paper* 140, figure 3.

the trend apparent for much of this century for shareholdings in business corporations to become fragmented among vast numbers of small investors. The Patman
Committee's view was that

> We see evidence of a reversed pattern of control whereby large blocks of
> stock in the largest non-financial corporations in the country are becoming
> controlled by some of the largest financial groups in the country. This trend
> is shifting economic power back to a small group, repeating in a somewhat
> different manner the pattern of the trusts of the late nineteenth and early
> twentieth centuries.
> *Patman Committee (1968).*

Such increasingly close relationships between financial and non-financial
institutions is reinforced by the maze of interlocking directorships which bind them
together. Interlocks between large corporations – that is, the situation where a
director of one company is also a director of another – are commonplace and may be
less insidious than is sometimes claimed. But *financial* interlocks would seem to be
especially important and at the heart of the business system. Again using the leading
500 industrial corporations, the Patman Committee found that a mere forty-nine
leading banks held a total of 768 interlocking directorships with 286 of them, an
average of three directorships per corporation. The same banks held 5 percent or
more of the stock of 147 of the 500 (5 percent is a significant and influential
shareholding).

In effect, therefore, a relatively small number of very powerful financial institutions act as *gatekeepers* in the flow of financial capital in industrial society. They
determine where such capital shall be invested in terms of the kind of activity or the
kind of company. To an important extent they determine in what way much of
society's resources are used – whether they are used productively, for example, by
investing in new industrial capacity, or non-productively, as in property or currency
speculation. A recent US Senate subcommittee expressed concern that the highly
interlocked nature of the sixteen leading financial institutions in the United States
gave them enormous power 'to influence if not control the shape and direction of
American corporate growth'. In terms of our present discussion of big business
organizations there is little doubt that the behaviour of financial institutions has
greatly encouraged the increasing scale of enterprise which we have shown to be
characteristic of modern industrial society. Business firms get bigger for many
reasons: for example, to achieve greater cost savings by large-scale operation
(economies of scale), to reduce uncertainty by dominating their market or by
controlling suppliers, or simply because bigger is believed to be better and biggest to
be best (a belief currently coming under some closer scrutiny). But factors like these
are greatly reinforced by the tendency for the major financial institutions to invest
their funds preferentially in large firms. The major business corporations rarely, if
ever, have difficulty in raising capital. If they cannot do so from their own earnings
they are looked on with favour by the financial institutions. The reason is basically
very simple: big corporations are regarded as safer, less risky ventures than small
firms. Bigness, it seems, equals security, although there are exceptions, as the
problems of Chrysler, British Leyland and Massey Ferguson, for example, have
recently demonstrated.

The global spread of business organizations

The days when the majority of business firms served only a relatively small local market from a single factory are long gone – even for many small firms – as the evolving transportation and communications media have caused distances to shrink. Today, most large business enterprises are *multiplant* firms; they operate production, administration, research and distribution activities in a wide variety of geographical locations. For example, the leading 100 industrial corporations in the United States in 1965 operated an average of forty-nine plants each within the United States itself. Sixteen corporations, in fact, operated more than 100 plants each. Even more significant than the fact that big firms operate a large number of plants in different regions within the same country is that they increasingly operate *across* national boundaries. Many large business enterprises are now *multinational* in their operations.

Table 2.3, based upon United Nations data, gives us some idea of this multinational involvement. Here a sample of twenty leading multinational industrial

Table 2.3 *Multinational activities of twenty leading business corporations, 1971*

Rank (in order of sales)	Corporation	Foreign content as percentage of employment	No. of countries where corporation has at least one affiliate
1	General Motors (USA)	27 (1965)	21
3	Ford (USA)	48 (1965)	30
6	IBM (USA)	36 (1965)	80
10	Unilever (Neths-UK)	70 (1969)	31
11	ITT (USA)	72 (1968)	40
15	Philips (Neths)	73 (1969)	29
24	Siemens (W. Germany)	23 (1970)	52
25	ICI (UK)	27 (1970)	46
29	Nestlé (Switz)	96 (1968)	15
43	Union Carbide (USA)	43 (1968)	34
44	International Harvester (USA)	32 (1965)	20
46	Eastman-Kodak (USA)	40 (1971)	25
60	Firestone Tire & Rubber (USA)	24 (1964)	33
78	Singer (USA)	66 (1968)	30
91	Xerox (USA)	38 (1970)	23
97	Ciba-Geigy (Switz)	71 (1968)	37
112	Courtaulds (UK)	16 (1970)	31
147	GKN (UK)	21 (1970)	27
156	Colgate-Palmolive (USA)	70 (1964)	55
174	Pepsi-Co (USA)	52 (1964)	25

Source: United Nations Department of Economic & Social Affairs (1974) *Multinational Corporations in World Development.* New York: Praeger, table 3

corporations is ranked in terms of their total sales in 1971. The extent of their 'multinationality' is shown in two ways: first, by the percentage of their total workforce which was employed overseas and, second, by the number of countries in which a corporation had at least one affiliated company (that is a subsidiary or a branch plant). With one exception, every corporation listed had at least one-fifth of its employment based *outside* its country of incorporation. In some cases well over half, or even three-quarters, of the firm's workforce was located overseas.

Until recently, the popular image of the multinational corporation was that it was American. The Europe of the 1960s had been much taken by Servan-Schreiber's book *The American Challenge*, and others of its kind, which portrayed not only European business but also its entire culture being destroyed by the invasion of American-based multinational corporations. But multinational business activity is not at all confined to United States companies even though US-based multinationals are still the most numerous. On the contrary, some of the largest – and earliest – of the very large multinationals are European or British, for example, Unilever, Philips and ICI, to name but three. In recent years, in fact, European and Japanese corporations have been increasing their overseas investments at a very rapid rate and a considerable proportion of this has been taking place in the United States itself as the activities of British Petroleum, ICI and Volkswagen testify. Thus the 'American challenge' is to some extent a misnomer; it is, rather, a challenge of the increasing geographical and economic scale of business enterprise in general rather than a dastardly plot devised by Uncle Sam. It is a challenge faced by all societies, including that of the United States itself.

Neither is multinational activity confined to industrial companies. All the major banks in the Western industrial economies now operate on a multinational scale. For example, in 1965, the twenty largest banks in the United States operated in a total of 211 foreign locations; by 1970 the same banks had increased their foreign operations threefold, to 627. The banks now lay very great stress on their international character. Hanover, one of the largest US banks, for example, describes itself as engaged in 'geobanking', which it defines as 'money moving and working around the world' enabling it 'to marshall strengths from the worldwide resources of a $30 billion organization' (headquarters, Park Avenue, New York City). Similarly, the Holiday Inns, Safeway Stores, Colonel Sanders' chickens and the 'Big M' of McDonalds which are proliferating across the globe (McDonalds now has more than 500 outlets in twenty-two different countries) are merely the more obvious signs of the inter-nationalization of what were formerly national activities.

We mentioned earlier that, in terms of products, the name of the game is diversification. We can now see that *the game board itself is global* in its geographical extent. The large business organizations – whether industrial corporations or banks, retail stores or hotel chains – slice through geographical boundaries at all scales: local, regional and, increasingly, national. Such internationalization of production and of capital is but a logical extension of the process which began when firms first set up production facilities in more than one location within their home country.

The path to bigness: mergers and acquisitions

Business enterprises grow in a variety of ways, but by far the most important contributor towards very large size has been the coming together of two or more firms by merger or acquisition. Although we need not probe at all deeply into what is a highly complex process, we cannot understand modern industrial society in general, or its changing geography in particular, without some awareness of the part played by mergers in producing the very large business organizations of the present day. Mergers affect jobs and employment opportunities, alter the variety of products available to the consumer and create an impact far beyond the confines of the boardrooms in which they are incubated and hatched. It is largely because of the big business firms' predilection for swallowing up – or joining forces with – other firms that ordinary employees, whether salesmen or shopfloor workers, clerks or cleaners, have found themselves part of larger and larger organizations and further and further removed from those controlling their livelihood.

Mergers between business enterprises are by no means new. As Figure 2.15 shows, there was an intense wave of merger activity at the turn of the century, a period which saw the emergence of the first truly giant enterprises epitomized by US Steel, Du Pont, American Tobacco and others. There was a second wave of mergers in the 1920s when firms like General Foods were formed by the merger of several food companies. But merger as the primary growth path of large firms and especially as the means of diversifying into multiproduct concerns became particularly important after World War II and most of all in the 1960s. Almost the entire *relative* growth of the very largest corporations in the United States was produced by merger. The Federal Trade Commission found that if they had *not* been engaged in mergers the leading 200 companies would have enlarged their share of total manufacturing assets from 42.4 percent in 1947 to only 45.3 percent in 1968. In fact, by very active merger activity, they increased their share to 60.9 percent.

In 1968 and 1969 almost 5000 mining and manufacturing firms 'disappeared' because of mergers. Between 1960 and 1971, a total of $53,015 million of assets was involved in the 13,134 mergers occurring in the United States. More and more firms were spending their investment capital on buying existing firms rather than in creating new capacity, an exercise of very dubious social value. (In 1968 almost 55 percent of total corporate investment went into mergers.) The emphasis in the 1960s merger wave was on product diversification, hence this was the era, above all, of the *conglomerate* corporation, the kind of enterprise epitomized by ITT, Gulf and Western, Lonrho and others. The characteristic feature of the acquisitive conglomerate is its tendency to move into and out of product markets almost at will. In some cases companies or parts of companies have been bought and sold in such a way that one observer was moved to comment that conglomerates 'serviced industry the way Bonnie and Clyde serviced banks' (*Business Week*, 30 November 1969, p. 74). Such firms developed virtually entirely through the process of merger and acquisition:

> by piling merger in one industry on merger in another, they entered within a few years into the ranks of America's largest corporations. Some did not exist prior to the start of the decade, but even those that had been rather large companies owe most of their present size to mergers made during this period.
> *Testimony of J.M. Blair to Subcommittee on Antitrust and Monopoly, US Senate (1969), p.4877.*

In some cases the effect was spectacular, with certain firms surging up the 'league table' of the largest industrial companies. Gulf and Western, Tenneco and Teledyne are three conglomerate corporations which were too small to be included on *For-*

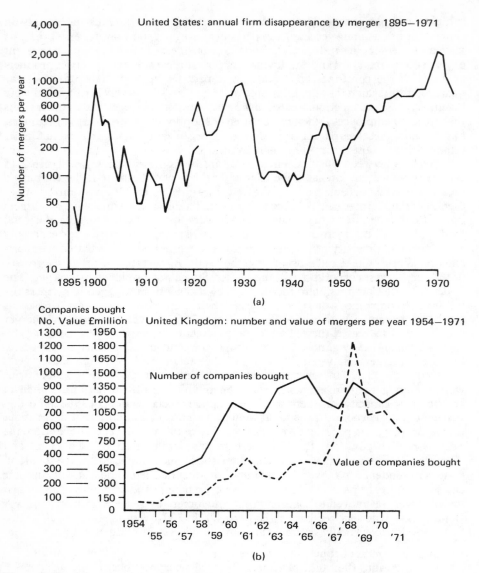

Figure 2.15   Merger activity in the United States and the United Kingdom

Source: U.S. Federal Trade Commission; Institute of Economic Affairs.

tune's list of the leading 500 industrial companies in 1960. By 1968 they were ranked 17, 16 and 74 respectively. Others already in the leading 500 vastly improved their positions by merger activity. ITT, discussed in some detail already, rose from 35th in 1960 to 9th in 1968. Ling-Temco-Vought soared from 335th to 22nd,

McDonnell-Douglas from 242nd to 62nd and North American Rockwell from 103rd to 58th. For the most part, however, it was those enterprises which were already very large which enhanced their positions through acquisition.

It is not surprising, therefore, that the very large corporations show a remarkable resilience in the face of change, an impressive ability to maintain their relative positions of strength. Despite the spectacular and rapid growth of some corporations there has been a great deal of stability in the relative positions of the largest enterprises. If we examine the 1973 list of the leading 200 industrial corporations in the United States and compare it with the 1929 list we see the same familiar names. In 1973, Exxon ranked number one in terms of assets, General Motors ranked second. In 1929 Exxon (then called Standard Oil of New Jersey) was number one and General Motors was number two. *Plus ça change . . .* ! Of the top twenty industrial corporations in 1973, fifteen were in the top twenty in 1961, four of the remaining five were in the top thirty. The other was ITT which ranked 47th in sales in 1961.

Geographical separation of corporate functions

As the business enterprise has become larger, it has had to modify its internal organizational structure. It has acquired, in Hymer's words, 'a more complex administrative structure to co-ordinate its activities and a larger brain to plan for its survival and growth'. The kind of organizational structure suitable for a small single-plant firm is totally inadequate for a giant multinational corporation making a diversity of products where the need to control and administer widely dispersed operations is of a totally different order.

Business organizations have therefore evolved highly sophisticated organizational designs to control their operations in what they see to be the most efficient and profitable manner. The detail of such arrangements is not relevant to us here but the *general* features are, because they greatly influence the differential impact which business corporations have on geographical space. Herbert Simon describes the structure of the modern business organization very neatly. It can be envisaged, he suggests

> as a three-layered cake. In the bottom layer we have the basic work processes – in the case of a manufacturing organisation, the processes that procure raw materials, manufacture the physical product, warehouse it, and ship it. In the middle layer, we have the programmed decision-making processes, the processes that govern the day-to-day operation of the manufacturing and distribution system. In the top layer, we have the non-programmed decision-making processes, the processes that are required to design and redesign the entire system, to provide it with its basic goals and objectives, and to monitor its performance. . . . *Large organisations are almost universally hierarchical in structure.* That is to say they are divided into units which are subdivided into smaller units which are, in turn, subdivided and so on. They are also generally hierarchical in imposing on this system of successive partitioning a pyramidal authority structure.
> *Simon (1960), p.40* (present authors' emphasis).

In fact, for a manufacturing enterprise, Simon's 'cake' would seem to be cone-shaped as in Figure 2.16a. The 'purpose' of each component part of the organization is to contribute to the efficiency of the organization as a whole. To understand the geographical impact of a manufacturing plant or administrative office, therefore, we need to know *where it fits into its parent organization*. Such modern organizational structures, with their high degree of internal specialization, exert a differential *geographical* impact in two ways:

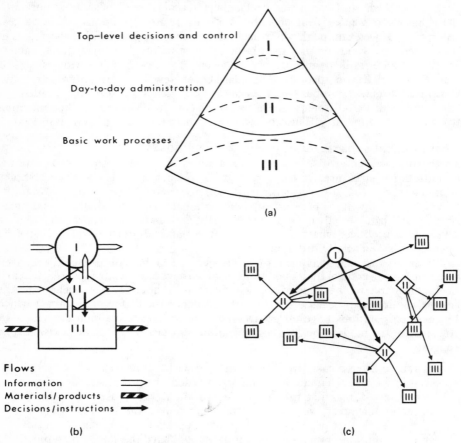

Figure 2.16 The organizational structure of a large business enterprise

1 Each 'level' has rather different locational requirements.
2 Each 'level' has rather different locational effects.

We shall look at the second of these in Chapter Three. As for the first, the fact that each level in the three-layered organizational 'cake' has rather different locational requirements means that each level tends to assume rather different geographical patterns. Figure 2.16b shows, in a very simple manner, how each level has a different relationship with the outside world (that is, with other organizations) and with the other levels *within* the organization. The top level decision-making and control functions, for example, seem to require what Armstrong calls 'environments of high interaction', where face-to-face contacts with similar functions in other organizations, both private and public, are most easily achieved. The more routine administrative functions also need an information-rich environment, although many of the activities of this level can be carried on without as much face-to-face contact, that is, by telephone, telex and written communication (Tornquist 1968). On the other hand, these functions require not only access to communications facilities but also (at least before the advent of the 'chip') to large numbers of 'white-collar' workers – clerks, typists, secretaries and so on.

The locational requirements of the upper two layers of the organizational cake are thus much the same regardless of its specific manufacturing function. Whether the enterprise is involved in the manufacture of iron and steel, ladies' apparel, television sets or chocolate-chip cookies makes little difference; they all have to be controlled, co-ordinated and administered. However, the locational requirements of the basic work processes themselves – Simon's bottom layer – clearly *do* vary. The production units of a steel company may have to be located to reduce the cost of raw materials; those of garment manufacturers or cookie manufacturers may need to be close to their respective consumer markets, while the TV manufacturers may be most concerned to locate where labour costs are as low as possible.

Thus both technological changes, particularly developments in transportation and communications, and organizational changes have combined to produce a multilayered organizational structure of multiplant enterprises with a distinct geographical expression. The three layers do not have to be located at the same place; each can be located, at least theoretically, where its locational requirements are best met. Figure 2.16c is a hypothetical arrangement showing the lines of control and administration passing from the head office (I) through administrative offices (II) to production units (III). The entire multiplant organization may, in fact, be spread over an enormous geographical range as in the case of a multinational enterprise. Here, the head office is likely to be located in a major city in the home country, the second-level administrative functions (regional or divisional offices) in key foreign cities and the production units in accordance with their particular locational requirements. Of course, some of the units may have been acquired by merger, so that their locations may be temporarily out of step with the needs of the organization as a whole, suggesting that some locational 're-adjustments' may be likely at a future date.

In the light of such organizational developments, it is not surprising to find that the trend towards increasing concentration of control in an organizational sense is strongly reflected spatially in the emergence of *geographical centres of control*. These are the cities where the control functions of major business corporations cluster, where the major business decisions are made which affect the lives of people both 'on the doorstep' and many thousands of miles away. Writing of 'élite' headquarters' locations (those of the leading 500 industrial corporations in the United States), Armstrong observed that

> the largest firms seem to have an affinity for each other and for a few selected large metropolitan areas. There is also an affinity for firms dealing in the same product to cluster together.
> *Armstrong (1972), p.37.*

Both these features underly the geographical pattern of headquarters' locations shown in Figures 2.17 to 2.23.

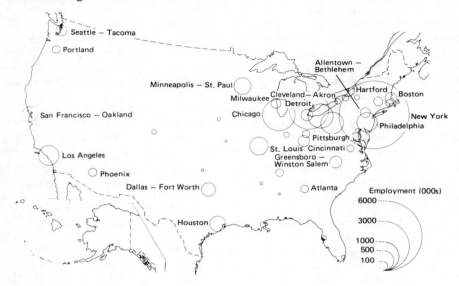

Figure 2.17   Headquarters' locations of the leading 500 industrial corporations in the United States, 1973

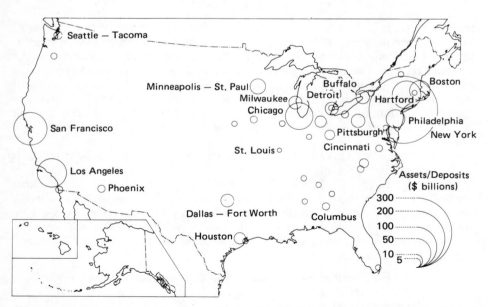

Figure 2.18   Headquarters' locations of the leading 150 financial corporations in the United States, 1973

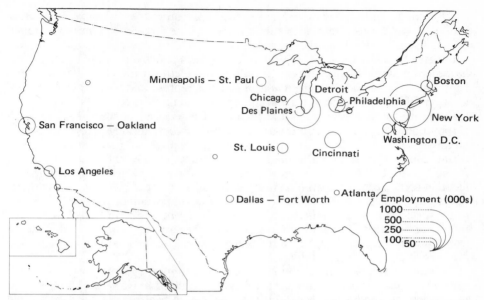

Figure 2.19   Headquarters' locations of the leading 50 retailing companies in the United States, 1973

Figure 2.20   Headquarters' locations of the leading 200 industrial corporations in Canada, 1974

Figure 2.17 identifies the major geographical control centres of *manufacturing industry* in the United States measured in terms of the total employment controlled by the leading 500 industrial corporations in 1973. Three metropolitan centres dominate: New York with almost 6 million workers employed by the leading firms headquartered there, Chicago with 1¼ million and Detroit with 1.8 million workers. In Figure 2.18 we focus on the *financial sector* as represented by the headquarters' locations of the 150 leading financial corporations in the United States. In this case, the measure of size adopted is the volume of assets and deposits held by each corporation. Here, the pattern is rather different in that, although New York again dominates, Chicago is less important as a financial control centre than as a manufacturing control centre and Detroit barely figures at all. On the other hand, San Francisco and Los Angeles are more prominent. Figure 2.18 also demonstrates the fact that certain centres may be very important in one respect and not at all in others. Hartford, Connecticut, for example, appears as an important control centre in only one respect: as a life insurance headquarters. In a sense it is the Detroit of the life insurance industry. Finally, Figure 2.19 shows the pattern of control of the leading fifty retailing companies in the United States. Here, as in the case of manufacturing, New York and Chicago dominate.

Quite clearly, certain metropolitan complexes appear again and again as headquarters' centres important not just in a single specialized activity (like Hartford) but in a variety of activities. Table 2.4 lists these leading control centres in the United States. The twelve metropolitan complexes listed possess the headquarters of more than two-thirds of the 800 leading business corporations in the United States (538). The table also shows more clearly the overall dominance of New York and Chicago. More than one-third of the leading corporations are headquartered there while, in the case of transportation and utility companies, their combined share is as high as 60 percent.

Most other industrial countries display a similar pattern whereby a few control centres are dominant. In Canada there is a very pronounced duality in the overwhelming dominance of Toronto and Montreal (Figure 2.20). These two metropolitan centres contained the headquarters of 127 of the leading 200 industrial corporations in Canada in 1974. There is an enormous gap between these two and the next most important headquarters' centres – Vancouver, and Calgary. In terms of the *number* of leading companies, Toronto is more important than Montreal, having the headquarters of seventy-seven of the leading 200 corporations compared with the fifty in Montreal. On the other hand, the Montreal-based corporations control a slightly larger share of the industrial assets of the leading 200 corporations (40.5 percent compared with 37.2 percent). However, as Figure 2.20 reveals, if the area around Toronto is included, stretching along the western edge of Lake Ontario through Oakville, Mississauga and Hamilton, then the centre of control of Canadian industry is clearly here rather than in Montreal.

If we take a broader view and include financial and merchandising companies, then the dominance of the two major metropolitan centres is even more apparent. Table 2.5 shows that Toronto and Montreal are the headquarters of twenty-six of the leading thirty financial companies and these account for 95 percent of the total financial assets. Of the five leading banks (which we noted earlier have some 90 percent of total bank deposits), three are headquartered in Toronto and the other two, including the largest (the Royal Bank) have their head offices in Montreal.

Table 2.4 *Leading geographical centres of control in the United States: headquarters of largest business corporations, 1973*

Number of corporations with headquarters in each centre

Metropolitan Complex	500 largest industrial corps.		150 largest financial corps.		50 largest retailing corps.		100 largest transportation & utility corps.		Total: 800 largest business corps.	
	No.	%	No.	%	No.	%	No.	%	No.	%
New York	150	30.0	34	22.7	14	28.0	20	20.0	218	27.2
Chicago	55	11.0	11	7.3	6	12.0	10	10.0	82	10.2
Los Angeles	22	4.4	12	8.0	3	6.0	7	7.0	44	5.5
Philadelphia	15	3.0	8	5.3	3	6.0	5	5.0	31	3.9
Cleveland-Akron	22	4.4	1	0.7	1	2.0	5	5.0	29	3.6
San Francisco-Oakland	14	2.8	7	4.7	2	4.0	4	4.0	27	3.4
Detroit	15	3.0	3	2.0	2	4.0	2	2.0	22	2.7
Minneapolis-St. Paul	13	2.6	6	4.0	2	4.0	–	–	21	2.6
Pittsburgh	15	3.0	3	2.0	–	–	1	1.0	19	2.4
St. Louis	10	2.0	1	0.7	1	2.0	3	3.0	15	1.9
Houston	8	1.6	3	2.0	–	–	4	4.0	15	1.9
Dallas-Forth Worth	7	1.4	5	3.3	1	2.0	2	2.0	15	1.9
Total	**346**	**69.2**	**94**	**62.7**	**35**	**70.0**	**63**	**63.0**	**538**	**67.2**

Source: calculated from data in *Fortune*, May 1974

Table 2.5 *Leading geographical centres of control in Canada: headquarters of the largest business corporations, 1974*

City	200 largest industrial corporations				30 largest financial corporations				20 largest merchandising corporations				Total: 250 largest business corporations			
	No.	%	Assets ($m)	%	No.	%	Assets ($m)	%	No.	%	Assets ($m)	%	No.	%	Assets ($m)	%
Toronto	77	38.5	33,266	37.2	14	46.7	60,536	48.0	11	55.0	3,180	63.1	102	40.8	96,982	43.8
Montreal	50	25.0	36,209	40.5	12	40.0	59,150	47.0	3	15.0	617	12.2	65	26.0	95,976	43.4
	127	63.5	69,475	77.7	26	86.7	119,686	95.0	14	70.0	3,797	75.3	167	66.8	192,958	87.2
Vancouver	16	8.0	4,722	5.3					1	5.0	205	4.1	17	6.8	4,927	2.3
Calgary	15	7.5	4,994	5.6									15	6.0	4,994	2.3
Hamilton	6	3.0	1,766	2.0									6	2.4	1,766	0.8
Mississauga	5	2.5	518	0.6									5	2.0	518	0.2
London	4	2.0	672	0.7	2	6.7	4,411	3.0					6	2.4	5,083	2.3
Kitchener	4	2.0	324	0.4									4	1.6	324	0.1
Winnipeg	2	1.0	648	0.7					2	10.0	849	16.8	4	1.6	1,497	0.7
Total	179	89.5	83,119	93.0	28	93.4	124,097	98.0	17	85.0	4,851	96.2	224	89.6	212,067	95.9

Source: calculated from data in J.E. Margetts & S.J. Meiklejohn (1976) *The Blue Book of Canadian Business*

Similarly, fourteen of the twenty leading Canadian merchandising companies are headquartered in the two major metropolitan centres. Overall, Toronto and Montreal account for 66.8 percent of the headquarters of the 250 largest Canadian corporations and for 87.2 percent of their total assets.

Geographical concentration of the leading corporations in Britain is even more pronounced than in either the United States or Canada. Figure 2.21 shows the headquarters' locations of the 500 leading industrial companies and Figure 2.22 those of major financial, life insurance and nationalized corporations. In both cases, London completely dominates as a headquarters' centre as it does in so many other aspects of British life. Some 327 of the leading 500 industrial companies have their head offices in the London Metropolitan Economic Labour Area – 65.4 percent of the total. The next centre, Birmingham, had only twenty-three head offices (4.6 percent), and Manchester eleven (2.2 percent). There seems to be a particularly strong relationship between company size and the propensity to be headquartered in London. Eighty-eight of the largest 100 companies in 1971 were controlled from the Southeast region and most of these were in London itself. More recent research covering the period to 1977 suggests increasing centralization of control in the Southeast region (Goddard and Smith 1978), much of it caused by acquisition and merger. Indeed, much of the geographical concentration of control as it existed in the early 1970s in all Western economies is the outcome of the vast amount of merger activity which we have already seen to be a major cause of corporate growth. When one firm acquires another there is a *de facto* shift of control from the latter organization to the former. If the two firms are located in different parts of the country, then there is a corresponding geographical shift of control as well. In most cases, the direction of this shift has been towards the already-powerful headquarters' complexes in the larger metropolitan areas and away from smaller cities.

Figure 2.23 illustrates headquarters' patterns in the broader European context. The dominance of a small number of centres is, again, clear. Spatial concentration of corporate control functions is especially high in France (similar to that in the United Kingdom), slightly lower in West Germany. This pattern holds for industrial headquarters, financial markets and banking assets. Retailing headquarters are somewhat more dispersed (Lee 1976), although the general trend towards increasing concentration is evident in this sector as well.

Although there are signs of geographical change in some corporate headquarters – for example, the increasing importance of Dallas, Houston, Atlanta and other rapidly growing 'Sunbelt' cities in the United States – the stability of the corporate control centres is strong (Borchert 1978). In fact much of the recent relocation of corporate headquarters has been part of the general process of suburbanization of economic activities within the same metropolitan areas (see Chapter Three).

The myth of the 'free' market

In the light of these clear trends towards economic dominance by very large business enterprises, it is difficult to believe that a free market economy in the pure sense exists any longer (if, indeed, it ever did). The major characteristics of such a system would include: (a) that it is made up of large numbers of relatively small firms of more or less equal size and strength; (b) that entry of new firms into the system is unhindered; and (c) that no individual firm can affect the price of any product – each accepts the price set by 'the market' through the interaction of supply and demand.

Figure 2.21   Headquarters' locations of the leading 500 industrial companies in Britain, 1971–1972

Source: P.W. Daniels *Office Location: An Urban and Regional Study*, London: Bell & Hyman, figure 26.

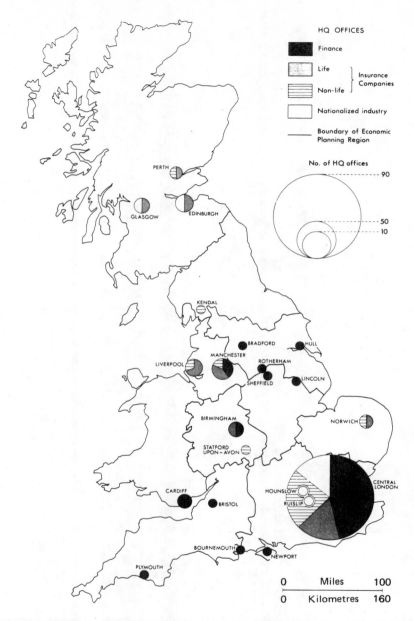

Figure 2.22   Headquarters' locations of the leading financial and nationalized corporations in Britain, 1971–1972

Source: P.W. Daniels *Office Location: An Urban and Regional Study*, London: Bell & Hyman, figure 27.

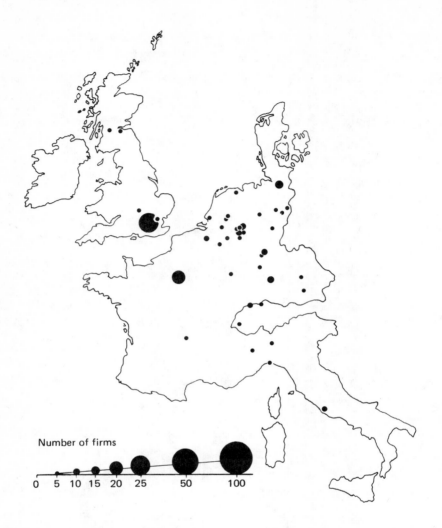

Figure 2.23 Headquarters' locations of the leading 100 industrial corporations in the EEC, 1974

Source: R. Lee (1976) Integration, spatial structure and the capitalist mode of production in the EEC, in R. Lee & P.E. Ogden (eds) *Economy and Society in the EEC*, Farnborough: Saxon House, figure 2.3.

Both Galbraith and Averitt argue that, in fact, the economic system in modern Western societies is a *dual* system. On the one hand there are the thousands of small and medium-sized firms – Averitt calls them 'periphery firms' – which are, in many respects, like the idealized firm of the theoretical *market system*. However, they are subordinate to, and often dependent upon, the giant firms which make up what Galbraith calls the *planning system* (Averitt calls these firms 'centre firms'). The key characteristic of planning or centre firms is that they can, and do, bypass the market mechanism. These firms do have the power to set prices and to inhibit the entry of new firms. In the case of firms in the consumer industries the behaviour of the very large enterprise is especially dependent upon its ability to persuade or manipulate consumer demand. It does this most clearly of all through mass advertising.

It is, of course, industries producing consumer goods which are most involved in, and dependent upon, mass advertising. Recent research in Britain has shown that a mere nine product groups, producing only 8 percent of total manufacturing output, account for fully 40 percent of all advertising expenditure by manufacturing industry. No television viewer would be surprised to learn of the identity of some of these big advertisers: soaps and detergents, toilet preparations, tobacco, pharmaceutical chemicals and preparations, miscellaneous foods, soft drinks companies. Not only were firms in these consumer industries very heavy spenders on advertising in absolute terms; such spending was also exceptionally high in relation to their other expenditures. Advertising expenditure exceeded capital expenditure on plant and machinery by 50 percent. In the toilet preparations industry, advertising expenditure was *four times* greater than capital expenditure (Prais 1976). Such highly advertised products are produced by industries which are heavily dominated by a few giant firms. Hence there is a relationship between size of corporation and level of advertising expenditure. Prais suggests, for example, that the 100 largest firms in Britain are in industries which are, on average, one-fifth more 'advertising-intensive' than manufacturing firms as a whole. The sums involved are staggering in both absolute and relative terms. In the case of advertising on United States television, for example, the annual expenditure on commercial advertising rose from $300 million in 1952 to $2.5 billion in 1968, a figure comparable with the Gross National Product of some entire countries.

A particularly intriguing feature of modern industrial society, therefore, is that although the free market philosophy still exerts a powerful influence on economic, social and political attitudes among large and influential sections of the population, the free market itself is, today, a myth rather than a reality:

> it was taken over long ago by big business, giant technology and the advertising industry as the determinant of what people shall be allowed to choose from and what they shall be taught to think they want.
> *Harford Thomas (1978).*

BIG GOVERNMENT

The trend towards increased organizational size is by no means confined to the private business sector. It is evident, too, in government, in non-profit institutions such as those in education and health, and in labour unions, for example. Not only this, but also there is a growing inter-relationship between many large organizations in different sectors of society, inter-relationships which are sometimes co-operative and sometimes conflicting in nature. We cannot look at all aspects of such a very complex issue so we shall concentrate primarily on the *government* sector in this section. For some reason, geographers have been very little interested in investigating the geography of government behaviour except in very limited ways, the most obvious being their long-standing interest in regional planning and development policies. Yet, in fact, most aspects of government behaviour have enormous geographical repercussions, particularly as the size and scope of the government organizations has increased so markèdly. Indeed, Borchert (1978) has pointed out that government control is even more heavily concentrated in very large organizations than is the private sector.

The increasing scale of the government sector

There is no country in the world today where the entire government establishment of 1910 could not comfortably be housed in the smallest of the new government buildings now going up, with room to spare for a grand-opera house and a skating rink.
Drucker (1969), p.214.

A similar observation can be made about other institutions in the 'not-for-profit' sector. The headquarters of the very large trade unions, often indistinguishable from the commercial office blocks that surround them, are a very far cry from their movement's humble origins. Certainly, Drucker's comment can be applied to the universities. But it is the growth of the government sector – national, state or provincial, and local – which merits primary attention. One clear example of the growth of big government is the way in which departments and agencies of government have proliferated over the years. In the United States, for example, there were only eight departments of the federal government in 1820, by 1900 there were seventeen, and by 1960 the number had reached seventy, and this figure did not include the many other less-permanent or special-purpose bodies which would swell the total considerably. There has been a particularly large increase in the number of government agencies: in 1900 there were only five (29 percent of the total number of government bodies), in 1960 there were forty-seven (67 percent). Not only have these institutions grown in number, each has also increased very greatly in size and scope. For example, the Department of Agriculture employed forty-five people in 1862, 560 in 1889, 25,000 in 1930, and almost 100,000 in 1960 (Warner, Unwalla and Trimm 1967).

In trying to place some perspective on the size of large private business corporations, we drew a parallel with the size of large cities or even nation-states (Table 2.2). Reversing this procedure somewhat, we can get some idea of the relative size of some government departments by comparing *them* with some of the largest business corporations. In the United States, the Department of Defence provides a graphic example. According to Borchert,

if its activities were assigned appropriate SIC (Standard Industrial Classification) codes, it appeared in 1971 as a conglomerate with assets of 133 billion dollars, approximately seven times the total assets of General Motors at that time. In fact, the DOD's wholly owned manufacturing facilities alone, if they were listed with private corporations, would have ranked fifth in number of employees and tenth in total revenue among the top 500 industrials.
Borchert (1978), pp.228–229.

In terms of aggregate expenditure, both federal expenditure on the one hand and state and local government expenditure on the other have come to account for a larger and larger share of the total Gross National Product of the United States as a whole. Figure 2.24 demonstrates this general upward trend between 1929 and 1976. In 1976 government expenditures of all kinds equalled almost one-third (32 percent) of United States GNP. In 1929 total government expenditure was only 10 percent of GNP, a share little different from that at the turn of the century.

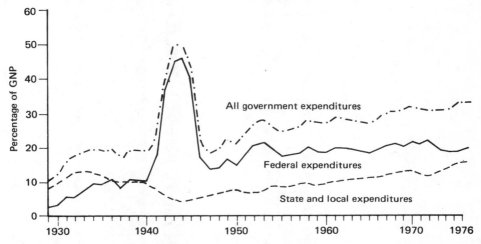

Figure 2.24 Growth of public expenditure in the United States as a percentage of Gross National Product

Source: United States *Statistical Abstract,* various issues.

Not surprisingly, such growth in the number of government institutions and in the level of government expenditure is reflected in the numbers of people employed by government. Figure 2.25 shows that for a very long period of time – in fact for 150 years – the *rate* of growth of federal civilian employment has been faster than that of civilian employment as a whole (the rate of growth is shown by the slope of the lines on the graph). Particularly rapid employment growth in the federal sector has occurred since 1930 (reflecting the expenditure pattern of Figure 2.24) with the upsurge in government involvement. Between 1930 and 1950, for example, total civilian employment increased by 31.4 percent. At the same time the number of civilians employed by the federal government grew by no less than 226 percent. By 1977, therefore, total government employment (federal + state + local) represented 16.2 percent of the total United States labour force compared with 13.5 percent in 1950. But if we break down the government sector into federal employment on the one hand and state and local government employment on the other, we find that it is the state and local sector which has gained particularly in importance. In 1950, 68 percent of government employment was in the state and local sector; by 1977, this share had increased to 81.5 percent.

A similar trend is evident in the growth of the public sector in all European economies, as Table 2.6 shows. In Britain, of course, direct government involvement in industrial production through the nationalized industries adds considerably

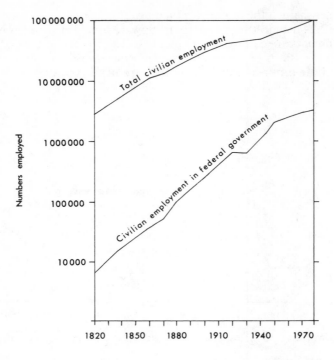

Figure 2.25   Growth of civilian employment in the US federal government, 1820–1977

Source: United States *Statistical Abstract*, various issues.

to the scale of the public sector. Thus, whereas the public sector in the United States is made up primarily of federal government and state/local governments, in Britain the structure is tripartite – central government, local government and the nationalized industries or public corporations.

In Figure 2.26 we show how public expenditure has come to account for an increasing proportion of the United Kingdom's Gross National Product. Prior to 1960, its share was below 40 percent, by 1970 it equalled exactly half the total GNP, and by 1975 the proportion was 56 percent (note that compared with Table 2.6 these figures include expenditure by public corporations). Reference back to Figure 2.24 shows that in 1974 the comparative United States percentage was 30 percent. But the difference between the US and the UK in terms of the public sector's share of total employment is far less marked. Table 2.7 shows the public sector's estimated share of total employment in the United Kingdom since the mid-nineteenth century. The major increase has occurred since the Second World War and it is interesting to note that in 1978 the public sector in Britain employed 29.7 percent of the country's total labour force compared with a figure of 16 percent in the United States. It is also significant that the greatest employment growth *within* the public sector of both countries has occurred in the 'local' rather than the 'central' sphere. In the United

Kingdom, for example, there were 1.87 million workers in local government in 1961; by 1978 this labour force had increased by 61 percent to roughly 3 million. Non-central government has been getting much larger.

Table 2.6   *Public expenditure in the EEC,* 1965–1974, as a percentage of Gross National Product*

	1965	1970	1974	Increase in expenditure 1965–1974 (%)
Belgium	32.3	36.5	39.6	+208.9
Denmark	30.1	40.1	44.3	+248.4
France	37.5	38.3	38.7	+127.5
Germany	36.4	37.4	41.8	+207.1
Ireland	32.7	38.0	47.7	+188.8
Italy	35.0	37.1	39.9	+133.7
Luxembourg	33.6	38.4	41.7	+208.7
Netherlands	37.6	46.3	50.6	+319.9
UK	36.3	39.7	45.0	+ 89.7
EEC	36.4	38.7	41.9	+155.6

* Figures exclude expenditure by public corporations for which no harmonized statistics are available at Community level.

Source: R. Lee (1976) Integration, spatial structure and the capitalist mode of production in the EEC, in R. Lee & P.E. Ogden (eds), *Economy and Society in the EEC*, Farnborough: Saxon House, table 2-1, p.15

Table 2.7   *Estimated growth of public sector employment in the United Kingdom, 1851–1978*

Year	Number employed in public sector	Percentage of total labour force
1851	250,000	2.4%
1900	1,000,000	5.8%
1914	*	7.0%
'inter-war'	2,000,000	10.0%
'1950s'	6,000,000	25.0%
1974	7,000,000	27.0%
1978	7,383,000	29.7%

* – figure not given in original source

Source: based on T.E. Chester (1976) The public sector – its dimensions and dynamics, *National Westminster Bank Review*, February 1976, p.38; *Annual Abstract of Statistics* (1980). Crown Copyright

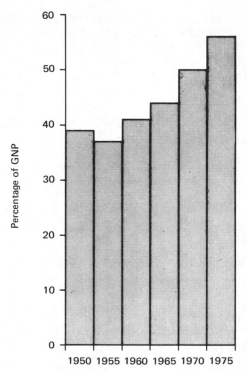

Figure 2.26   Growth of public expenditure in the United Kingdom, 1950–1975

Source: Annual Abstract of Statistics, various issues.

The major difference between the public sectors of the United States and Canada and such countries as Britain, Sweden and some others is, as we have mentioned, the existence in the latter countries of heavy *direct* involvement in industry and other activities. The nationalized industries in the United Kingdom accounted for 28.2 percent of all public sector employment in 1974 (of the remainder, central government employed 30.5 percent and local government 41.2 percent). These nationalized industries are made up of seventeen public corporations – and they exclude those business corporations in which the government has a very large shareholding but which are not public corporations. In total the public corporations had a combined turnover in 1974 of £12,662,879 and employed 1,818,695 workers. Some of the public corporations are gigantic by any criterion. Table 2.8 lists the leading six corporations in 1974. A quick comparison with Table 2.2 shows just how readily these fit into the league-table of giant business corporations. In fact four of the public corporations – British Steel Corporation, the Post Office, National Coal Board and British Railways Board – are larger, in employment terms, than the largest British private business corporation (General Electric Company). The Post Office employs more or less the same number of workers as the Ford Motor Company of the United States. The Electricity Board has swallowed up enough capital to build a new ICI every three years (Sampson 1974).

Table 2.8 *The six leading public corporations in the United Kingdom, 1974*

Public corporation	Turnover (£000)	Employees
Electricity Council & Boards	2,656,000	172,483
British Steel Corporation	2,255,800	223,000
Post Office	2,122,672	434,065
National Coal Board	1,589,600	321,000
British Gas Corporation	1,206,700	102,500
British Railways Board	914,900	255,902
Total	10,745,672	1,508,950

Source: The Times 1000, 1975–1976

These figures describing the size of the government or public sector and its increasing scale and scope reflect the trend throughout modern industrial societies, regardless of individual political or ideological variations between one nation and another. Thus, there can be no doubt regarding the *fact* of increasing government involvement in modern industrial society, an involvement transmitted primarily through very large government organizations and agencies. As we have seen, even in societies such as the United States the scale of government activity has grown markedly during the present century. There *is* disagreement, however, about whether such government involvement is excessive or whether it has not gone far enough; whether it is a 'bad thing' or a 'good thing'.* The particular attitude taken depends, of course, on one's political or ideological viewpoint. But quite apart from such value judgements, *why* has government become so much more prominent in modern Western society? To answer such a question we need to identify the various roles and functions performed by government. In doing this, we can also begin to understand the geographical impact of this enlarged activity. As in the case of the business corporation it is not size alone which is important but the differential geographical effect of the behaviour of large organizations.

Functions of government in modern Western society

Writing at the beginning of the Industrial Revolution, Adam Smith was able to define the role of government in quite narrow terms as being concerned with defence, administration of justice and the carrying out of certain public works. Even today some would argue that government involvement should go little or no further than these. But such a viewpoint is difficult to sustain in today's world. Regardless of political differences between countries, the most fundamental reason for the

---

* In the United Kingdom, the Conservative government, which came into office in 1979, did so on the basis of a programme which promised to reduce drastically the size of the public sector. This seems to have been difficult to achieve. More recently, the new Reagan administration in the United States has also vowed to prune the public sector.

increased scale of government involvement is simply the vastly increased scale and complexity of modern industrial society and the accompanying side-effects on particular segments of the population. The two have gone hand in hand even in countries such as the United States where there is probably greater opposition to government 'interference' than elsewhere. As Heilbroner has shown, the United States government was actively involved in economic affairs even before the Civil War, while the New Deal era and the post-World War II period have greatly reinforced this trend. Hence in all modern industrial societies,

> the functions of government have over the years been considerably broadened – from the 'law and order' state to the 'service state' and more recently from the 'welfare state' to the controller of the national economy. These changes have been reflected in the growth and complexity of public expenditure, the widening of public ownership and the increase in public employment.
> *Chester (1976), p.43.*

Expenditure on providing *public services* of various kinds accounts for a hefty proportion of growing government expenditure at all levels of government. Figure 2.27 depicts the composition of government expenditure for 1974 in the United States, Britain and Canada. It is unwise to try to compare directly the categories of expenditure between each of the three countries because of differences in the way some of the categories are defined. There is also the complicating factor that certain types of service provision are carried out at different levels of government – state, provincial, local. However, since much of this expenditure depends upon *transfer payments* from national government, the latter has an enormous influence on the provision of services. Indeed, the states

> have become more dependent on the federal government for the provision of a major share of their revenue growth. Many functions, notably welfare, transportation, and education, which historically have been a local or private responsibility, are becoming subjects of national concern and federal decision-making, especially via the grant-in-aid mechanism. *The states, in a sense, are becoming the retail distributors of funds that the federal Treasury disburses in a more wholesale fashion.*
> *Weidenbaum (1969), p.117* (present authors' emphasis).

Despite specific differences between the three political systems – the most notable being differences in defence expenditure – there are broad similarities between the three countries in the composition of their expenditure on public goods and services. If we define these social or welfare services as including:

1 income support programmes such as social security benefits, pensions and old age payments, public assistance, unemployment benefits;

2 health services;

3 education and training;

4 housing,

then we find that these account for a very high proportion of government spending in every case: roughly 49 percent in the United States, 45 percent in Canada and 49

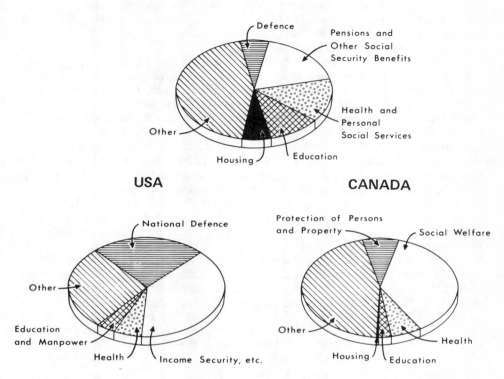

Figure 2.27 Composition of public expenditure by major categories: United States, United Kingdom, Canada, 1974

Source: U.S. Statistical Abstract, U.K. Annual Abstract of Statistics, Canadian Annual Statistical Abstract.

percent in the United Kingdom. In addition to these are the programmes relating to the provision of basic utilities such as water supply, sewerage and sanitation, transportation and so on. Some of this spending represents a real use of resources. For example, government purchases supplies for the bodies implementing its programmes, it pays wages and salaries to its personnel, it invests money in building projects and so on. But a large proportion of government spending takes the form of transfer payments to other levels of government, to private business, to individuals and families, which do not involve the receipt of goods and services in return. Such transfer payments typically account for between 40 and 50 percent of total government expenditure; the purchase of goods and services by government accounts for the remainder.

We examine the geographical impact of government provision of public services in later chapters. Here we simply make the point that *the increased involvement of government in modern society has a geography*. In the service and welfare sphere this takes the form of high levels of expenditure in some parts of the country and low levels of expenditure in others. Some areas are heavily dependent upon decisions taken in Washington DC, in London or in Ottawa regarding what is spent where; other areas are less dependent on such decisions. No area, of course, is in fact untouched either directly or indirectly by modern governmental activity, whether it is in the area of social and welfare services or in the economic sphere. It is to the latter that we now turn our attention.

Increasingly, governments have become *directly* involved in the economic management of modern industrial societies in ways which have profound effects on all our lives. Geographers have displayed very little interest in the geography of government economic activity with the primary exception of regional economic policies. These are, of course, one extremely important way in which the well-being of people in particular geographical areas is affected by government decisions. But they are only one – though perhaps the most obvious – of a much broader set of government measures. These range from the macro-scale activities of government to guide the national economy through to the increasingly complex and symbiotic relationship between government and private business corporations.

Government involvement in the economy dates back way beyond the present century. But it is really only since the 1930s in general, and since the Second World War in particular, that such involvement has become pervasive. The unco-ordinated nature of a market economy renders it highly susceptible to cyclical fluctuations – to boom and slump, depression (or recession) and growth – to events known as business cycles. The causes of business cycles are not fully understood; perhaps if they were we would be able to prevent their occurrence. But their effects are clear for all to see – rising unemployment, falling consumption and production, business bankruptcies and so on. The 1930s was a period of world-wide depression in which unemployment reached levels unknown for a century. At the trough of that depression something like one worker in every four was unemployed in the Western industrial nations. Within individual countries, unemployment levels could be very much higher than this, reaching 75 percent in some cases.

The massive depression of the 1930s convinced many people that governments had to intervene in the workings of the market system. J.M. Keynes was the leading proponent of the view that if the market economy were not to stagnate and if mass unemployment were to be avoided then governments had to act in a positive way. Spending and investment either had to be stimulated in the private sector or, in their absence, government must itself inject money and investment into the economy. Hence we can trace the origins of government involvement in economic management directly to the problems of the 1930s. Indeed, much of the social and welfare activity of government also began in that period. Thus Franklin Roosevelt's New Deal legislation and the measures taken by the British and other governments in the 1930s had both economic and social welfare dimensions. The major difference between the depression of the 1930s and that heralded by the oil crisis of 1973 is that in the latter period high levels of unemployment have been associated with persistently high levels of price inflation, a combination formerly believed to be virtually impossible.

In terms of macro-economic management, Chester summarizes the prevailing position as follows:

following the depression of the 1930s and the theories expounded by Keynes, there arose in most Western countries a demand for governments to intervene in the national economy. More specifically governments are now being charged with at least a four-fold responsibility:

(a) to promote full employment

(b) to safeguard stable prices and prevent inflation

(c) to watch that the external balance of payments does not go into the red; and

(d) to help in raising living standards by the growth of the economy.
Chester (1976), p.42.

In trying to achieve some or all of these objectives, governments have come to employ a complex battery of economic weapons, the balance varying from one nation to another according to their political complexion. The balance also varies over time within individual nations as circumstances or governments change. Among the most commonly used ways of regulating the national economy are: varying the level of government spending, altering levels of corporate and personal taxation, controlling the money supply, varying interest rates, regulating prices and incomes, controlling the inflow and outflow of money through foreign exchange controls, regulating trade through tariff and non-tariff measures. Most Western industrial societies also strive to influence the structure of industry through the regulatory mechanism. The Antitrust machinery in the United States and the Monopolies Commission in Britain, for example, have the power to permit or prevent the types of merger of firms discussed earlier in the light of what is regarded as the public interest.*

---

* Many observers are sceptical of the achievements of antitrust legislation. The political commentator Art Buchwald neatly caricatured such a view, writing at the height of the 1960s merger wave. Buchwald's 'scenario' looked forward to the year 1978 when, he predicted, there would be only two industrial corporations left in the whole of the United States – Samson Securities, which operated west of the Mississippi, and the Delilah Company which controlled economic activities to the east. The next logical step, of course, was for these two to merge but such a merger had to be sanctioned by the Department of Justice. The plot proceeds thus:

> At first the head of the Antitrust Division indicated that he might have reservations about allowing the only two companies left in the United States to merge. 'Our department,' he said, 'will take a close look at this proposed merger. It is our job to further competition in private business and industry, and if we allow Samson and Delilah to merge we may be doing the consumer a disservice.'
>
> The Chairman of Samson protested vigorously that merging with Delilah would not stifle competition, but would help it. 'The public will be the true beneficiary of this merger,' he said. 'The larger we are, the more services we can perform and the lower prices we can charge.'
>
> The president of Delilah backed him up. 'In the Communist system the people don't have a choice. They must buy from the state. In our capitalistic society the people can buy from either the Samson Company or the Delilah Company.'
>
> But if you merge,' someone pointed out, 'there will be only *one* company left in the United States.'
>
> 'Exactly,' said the president of Delilah, 'Thank God for the free enterprise system.'
>
> The Antitrust Division of the Department of Justice studied the merger for months. Finally, the Attorney-General made this ruling. 'While we find drawbacks to only one company being left in the United States, we feel the advantages to the public far outweigh the disadvantages. Therefore, we're making an exception in this case and allowing Samson and Delilah to merge.
>
> 'I would like to announce that the Samson and Delilah Company is now negotiating at the White House with the President to buy the United States. The Justice Department will naturally study this merger to see if it violates any of our strong antitrust laws.'
>
> *Art Buchwald*, Washington Post, *2 June 1966, p.A21, quoted in Mintz and Cohen (1971).*

In some cases, governments have actually encouraged and promoted mergers between large corporations and have set out deliberately to alter the structure of industry. In the latter half of the 1960s, for example, the British government set up the Industrial Re-organization Corporation which was designed to promote industrial efficiency, primarily by encouraging the re-organization of industry, and had access to £150 million of public money. In its four years of existence the IRC engineered a considerable number of mergers, both large and small, the two most noteworthy being the takeover of Associated Electrical Industries by GEC and their subsequent amalgamation with English Electric and the merging of Leyland and the British Motor Corporation.

Which of the many economic measures available to government are used to fulfil national economic objectives depends both upon what those objectives are and upon the prevailing climate of opinion. For example, there has been heated debate in recent years between those politicians and economists who follow a 'monetarist' line and urge strict control over the money supply and those who argue the need to increase public expenditure to create more investment and employment. Some are concerned primarily with increasing the size of the economic cake, others with the best way of dividing up the cake. These and other issues are matters for debate. But from our viewpoint they have markedly differential geographical effects. Such effects may be brought about in two ways. The most obvious is through those government policies which are directly and deliberately geographical in intent, such as regional, urban and other area-based policies. Less obvious, but almost certainly far more important in overall terms, are those government economic measures which are not deliberately geographical, for example, measures to raise or lower interest rates, to control trade, to make large-scale purchases, to allocate funds to particular industries or particular social groups. As we shall see at various points in this book, both of these types of government policy have enormous geographical repercussions.

The increased scale of the government, or public, sector thus parallels – in many instances exceeds – that of the private sector. Just as we were able to identify major corporate control centres so, too, we can identify major geographical concentrations of public organizations. For the most part, these coincide with the national capital; in the highly centralized systems of France and the United Kingdom most government functions are centred in Paris and London respectively, with smaller agglomerations of lower-order government functions in certain provincial cities. In a federal system such as the United States, Canada and West Germany the number of significant control points is rather larger. Even so, in the case of the United States, for example,

> with higher concentrations in a smaller number of organizations, public assets are controlled from a small number of points on the map. By 1971, the capitals of the large states and the seats of a few large counties had risen to the status of major public financial centers. Meanwhile, Washington had overtaken New York as a control point for the nation's assets. In Washington, 22 large federal organizations had assets of $641 billion; while the assets of 402 high order corporations based in New York totalled $615 billion. *Borchert (1978), p.229.*

THE BLURRING OF THE BOUNDARY BETWEEN THE PRIVATE AND THE PUBLIC SECTORS

It should now be clear that the trend towards an increasing scale of organization is characteristic both of private business corporations and of government at all levels. Not only are the two sets of bureaucracies becoming more alike in their organizational scale and form, but they are also increasingly crossing the boundary which traditionally separated them:

> In a fundamental sense, the dividing line between the public and the private sectors is shifting. The federal government is taking on functions that have often been performed elsewhere, at least in the past, and private organisations increasingly are being oriented to serving governmental, rather than private, customers or clients.
> *Weidenbaum (1969), p.vii.*

This blurring of the boundary between the private and public sectors can be appreciated more readily if we bear in mind the basic distinction between *private goods* and *public goods* introduced in Chapter One.

The goods and services available to, and consumed by, individuals, families and groups in modern industrial society may be either private or public in terms of their consumption characteristics. But what of their production? Following Alfred Kuhn, we can classify such production as follows:

(1)	(2)	(3)	(4)
Private production of private goods	Private production of public goods	Public production of private goods	Public production of public goods

The private production of private goods (1) is the responsibility of the kinds of business corporation discussed earlier. One of the bases of the growth of those large corporations, then, has been the increased demand for private goods as general affluence and spending power has increased. At the other end of the scale, the public production of public goods is the responsibility of government. One of the reasons for the massive growth of the public or government sector, then, is the increased production of public goods, in ways we shall examine in a moment. But, although we have long been accustomed to the sight of private organizations producing private goods and of public organizations producing public goods, we are less accustomed to the idea that private organizations may produce public goods (such as weapons for national defence) or that public organizations may produce private goods (as do some of the nationalized industries in Britain and elsewhere). Yet this is precisely what is happening today and on a massively increased scale. In other words, there has been a very large increase in categories (2) and (3) and it is this which contributes most towards the blurring of the public/private boundary.

The links between the private and public sectors have become closer in a variety of ways in recent years. One of the most obvious – and newsworthy – developments has been the growing number of cases in which government, in one guise or another, has intervened to prevent the collapse of private business corporations. Invariably, it is the very large corporation which is saved rather than the small firm, simply because of the magnitude of the likely economic, social and political repercussions of corporate collapse. For example, both British and United States governments have been involved in efforts to rescue the ailing Chrysler Corporation, the United States government prevented the collapse of the Lockheed corporation in 1970, whilst in the United Kingdom British Leyland was taken into public ownership to prevent its demise. Such rescue attempts have become characteristic of all Western industrial societies.

Government rescue efforts such as these are the kind of event which hit the headlines. But while they certainly increase the degree of government involvement in the private sector, they are probably less important overall than those relationships which exist to an increasing extent as part of day-to-day affairs. Government in modern industrial society invariably constitutes the largest single consumer of goods produced in the private sector. Much of this consumption is in industries which also sell to many other consumers, for example, automobiles, steel, machinery. A good deal of government consumption is also of the straightforward, 'arm's length' variety in which the goods are sold at the prevailing market price.

However, there are a number of very important industries where these two features are not present, where the government-producer relationship is of a quite different order. This is particularly the case in industries related to defence and aerospace but also in others such as telecommunications and power station equipment. In these, government is the dominant, if not the only, customer (who else buys space capsules, submarines or missiles?). Hence business corporations operating in these industries have inevitably become highly dependent upon government contracts, not just for their continued growth but often for their very survival. Conversely, the large government departments placing such contracts are dependent on such government-oriented corporations to perform tasks which they cannot perform themselves.

The most important sector in which such relationships exists is, obviously, that of defence and aerospace. A glance back to Figure 2.27 shows that in 1974 national defence accounted for almost one-third of total government expenditure in the United States. (In the late 1960s of course, at the height of the Vietnam War, its share was much higher – in 1968 it took up 43 percent of the federal budget.) Defence expenditures in the United Kingdom and Canada, though much lower than in the United States, are nevertheless a major item of government expenditure.

Defence happens to be the most publicized context of public-private involvement, but it is by no means the only field in which government buys the services of non-government institutions to perform certain tasks. A closely related area is that of research and development (much of which is defence- or aerospace-oriented anyway), where private corporations, universities and other non-profit institutions have acquired enormous sums of government money to perform research and development. Indeed, in the United States, some two-thirds of all money spent on research and development is by the government, though it carries out only about 15 percent of this work itself. The rest is, again, contracted out. Thus private industry, which performs roughly 70 percent of the research and development, finances only about 40 percent of this itself – the government pays the remaining 60 percent. Similarly some three-quarters of all research and development expenditure by the universities is funded by the federal government. In the United Kingdom, the government finances 50 percent of research and development and performs less than one-quarter itself. In research and development, then, as in defence contracting, new relationships have emerged between the private and the public sectors; in addition, entirely new types of organization have evolved of the kind represented by such institutions as the RAND Corporation, a non-profit agency which was set up specifically to do research for the United States Airforce. In other words, government today not only gets other organizations to do some of its work, it also gets them to do much of its thinking as well. As a result of these evolving relationships

> both parties – private and public – become 'locked-in' to a symbiotic relationship where they depend upon each other. . . . Because these high technology markets are so completely subject to the changing needs of the governmental customer, relationships between buyers and sellers differ from those typical in the commercial sector of the economy. By the selection of contractors, the government can control entry and exit, can greatly effect the growth of the firms involved, and can impose its way of doing business on the companies participating.
> *Weidenbaum (1969), pp.12, 37.*

Two closely related features of this relationship are important for our discussion of the geography of modern Western society. One is the tendency for major contracts to be awarded to a relatively small number of large corporations. The other is the resulting geographical impact of such awards (see Chapter Three). The fact that a limited number of corporations receives the bulk of the defence and aerospace contracts in the United States is illustrated by the following figures. During the 1960–1967 period a mere 100 corporations received two-thirds of all prime military contracts awarded by the Defence Department. In 1978, a mere ten corporations received more than one-third of the total value of Defence Department contracts. Table 2.9 identifies just five of these leading 'government-oriented' corporations in the 1960s. Their massive dependence on government defence contracts is abundantly clear. There was even greater concentration in the distribution of NASA contracts – here 100 corporations received 90 percent of the total. In some instances, the same corporations were involved in both NASA and Defence Department work: in 1966, sixteen of the leading twenty-five NASA contractors were also among the

Table 2.9 *Major defence contractors in the United States, 1961–1967*

Corporation	Approximate value of contracts 1961–1967	Relative importance to corporation
Lockheed	$11 billion	88% of total sales
General Dynamics	$ 9 billion	66% of gross receipts
McDonnell Douglas	$ 8 billion	75% of total sales
Boeing	$ 7 billion	50% of total revenue
Ling-Temco-Vought	$ 8 billion	70% of total sales

Source: compiled from data in R.J. Barber (1970) *The American Corporation*, London: MacGibbon and Kee, pp.191–192

leading twenty-five Defence contractors. Such contract work is dominated not so much by the truly giant corporations such as General Motors, Ford or RCA as by the 'medium-sized' corporations ('medium' is, of course, a relative term; in this context it refers to corporations with assets of between $100 million and $999 million!). The important characteristic of many of these firms is that more than one-quarter of their total sales were tied up in defence contracts. In a number of cases, the proportion was greater than 50 percent.

BIG ORGANIZATIONS IN MODERN WESTERN SOCIETY: A SUMMARY VIEW

We have spent a great deal of time in this chapter demonstrating that modern Western society has become characterized by the very large organization. Our discussion has focused upon the private business corporation and on big government organizations but, as we hinted earlier, the large organization is not at all confined to these two sectors. Big labour unions, big universities, big institutions of many kinds are diagnostic features of today's society.

Of these, the growth of large labour unions, and of confederations of unions such as the AFL-CIO in the United States and the TUC in Britain, is very much a response to the increasing scale of private and public organizations. The increasing concentration of union membership in a smaller number of large labour unions in the United Kingdom is shown in Figure 2.28, though there are still very many small unions in Britain. Membership of the giant individual unions has increased in much the same way as large business enterprises have grown – by acquisition and merger as well as by internal expansion. Similar general trends are evident in the United States, although the overall level of union membership is very much lower than in most European countries. In 1976, approximately 21 million United States workers belonged to labour unions of whom 16.5 million were affiliated to the AFL-CIO. Overall, 26 percent of the United States labour force was unionized, though there were enormous interstate variations in this level (see Figure 2.29). Union membership was highest in Michigan, New York, West Virginia and Pennsylvania, and lowest in the Carolinas, Mississippi, Florida and Georgia. There are, of course, very considerable differences in the organization and operation of labour unions in different countries, part of which is related to differences in labour legislation, though the ultimate objectives of labour unions are the same everywhere. In some cases, they exert considerable power, particularly where a monopoly labour situation prevails.

Such development of the very large organization in many spheres of life begs the age-old question of where power and authority lie in Western industrial society. There is no easy and straightforward answer to this question since much depends upon the ideological viewpoint of the questioner. At the institutional level, some would argue that power rests with the giant business corporation, some that government holds the key to power, whilst others would point to the labour unions as the centre of power in some societies such as Britain. An alternative view sees power as being dispersed amongst a plurality of institutions, each one being powerful in its own right and thus, in total, preventing the dominance of any single institution through the exercise of countervailing power. In this scheme of things, for example, government guards against the excesses of big business while the latter prevents total

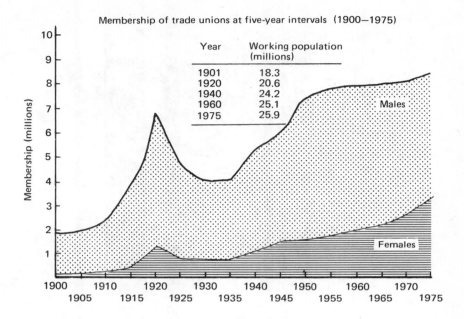

Membership of trade unions at five-year intervals (1900–1975)

Year	Working population (millions)
1901	18.3
1920	20.6
1940	24.2
1960	25.1
1975	25.9

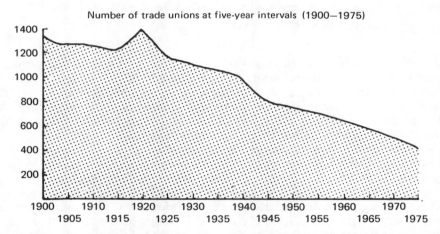

Number of trade unions at five-year intervals (1900–1975)

Figure 2.28 Membership of trade unions and number of trade unions in Britain, 1900–1975

Source: British Labour Statistics Historical Abstract and British Labour Statistics Yearbook Crown Copyright.

domination by the state. Others argue that the major institutions of society are becoming locked together in such a way as to produce a corporate state. Few would, however, disagree with the view that the large organizations collectively have become the units of effective social action and that an understanding of almost any

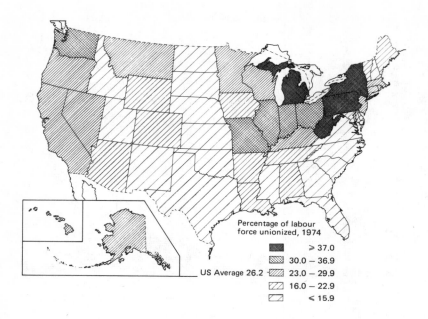

Figure 2.29   Interstate variations in labour union membership, United States, 1974

Source: U.S. *Statistical Abstract* (1978), table 699.

aspect of society's functioning cannot proceed very far without a thorough understanding of the organizational nexus which we have been describing.

What is perhaps most evident to the average person, however, is that the
all-embracing scope of the *large bureaucratic organization* projects a feeling of *remoteness* from the decisions which affect his life and that of his family. For most of us,
much of our day-to-day life, and that of our family and friends, is conducted by, in or
for large impersonal bureaucratic institutions. Some are 'privately' owned, some are
owned by the 'public', yet this distinction has become less and less clear as these
organizations have become increasingly alike because of their evolution towards a
common type of organizational structure. In such a structure, control and
decision-making are centralized in a *hierarchical bureaucracy*. Thus, as government
organizations have grown in size and complexity, as they have extended the span of
their operations, their form has become increasingly like that of the large business
corporation and vice versa. Both are characterized by large and complex bureaucracies; both make decisions at their remote 'head offices' which affect the lives of
millions of people in modern Western society. The emergence of supra-national
organizations such as the European Economic Community serves to increase this
feeling of remoteness and of an all-embracing bureaucracy.

A major consequence of these developments is that many people find themselves
less and less able to communicate with, let alone influence, such large organizations
because these appear to communicate most readily with others most like themselves.
It is perhaps not surprising, then, that there is an increasing body of opinion which is

disenchanted with the dominance of giant organizations in our lives and with the increased *centralization* of decision-making, an opinion which argues that they are not only unnecessary but often harmful. There is a growing feeling that 'small is beautiful', a rejection of the ethos of bigness, a feeling that smaller firms may be more desirable than giant firms. There is also a growing body of opinion which rejects the necessity of highly centralized government and urges a greater degree of regional or local autonomy. Where such a view is also identified with a strong cultural base it tends to generate *separatist* political movements, such as those in Scotland, Quebec, Brittany, for example. Despite these counter-movements, however, it is a fact that massive bureaucratic organizations dominate life in Western industrial society. As we shall see in subsequent chapters, the geographical repercussions are very substantial indeed.

THE ENLARGED SCALE OF URBAN LIVING

The urban face of Western society

The physical face of modern Western society is an *urban* face; the process of industrialization and the process of urbanization have proceeded hand in hand. As Lampard observes,

> the growth of the modern city and the march of the industrial revolution are joint products of a single cultural strand – specialisation.
> *Lampard (1955), p.91.*

The modern urban system, then, is the tangible, geographical expression of the process of specialization or the division of labour 'on the ground'. The Industrial Revolution saw the beginning of the demise of the craftsman and the rise of the specialist through the application of machinery to productive tasks. Specialization, the antithesis of self-sufficiency, as we suggested earlier, cannot exist without the interaction and communication of specialists for the exchange of materials, goods and information. All types of interaction must occur through time and space. Given the immobility of some factors of production under the kind of technological conditions prevailing during the nineteenth century, the agglomeration of people and production at specific points in space is readily understandable. The capability constraints operating on individuals and organizations were very considerable. Participation in the rapidly burgeoning 'bundles' of activities created by industrialization thus necessitated close physical proximity. Precisely where such urban-industrial agglomerations arose need not concern us here. In some cases, pre-existing settlements based on non-industrial functions, such as market towns or administrative centres, evolved into industrial centres. Not all did so of course; an important differentiating factor was their relative location on the evolving communications network. In other cases, entirely new urban-industrial centres were born, based upon a highly localized raw material like iron ore, for example, or on an energy source vital to the new industrial technology, such as coal.

More important for our present purposes, however, is the *general* relationship between industrial development and urban system development:

> Cities . . . are what make modern economic systems work. . . . It is the city
> that provides a direct link between all the macro-variables: capital forma-

tion, labour supplies, technological change, incomes, markets. Proximity – the essence of the urban system – permits the joining of these economic processes, and the high level of interaction among them provides the sustained thrust to launch modern economic growth.
Lithwick (1970), p.48.

The industrial system and the urban system are thus totally inter-related. The very term 'system' suggests this since it implies 'organized connectedness'. Both systems tend to be strongly *hierarchical* in structure, again a reflection of the division of labour. The industrial system depends upon the connected processes of production, circulation, exchange and consumption; the urban process creates the material, physical infrastructure in which these processes can take place. In Harvey's view, the urban system acts as a

surplus-creating, -extracting and -concentrating device. . . . Urbanism entails the geographic concentration of a socially-designated surplus product. This means a geographic circulation of surplus goods and services, a movement of people and, in a money economy, a circulation of investment, money and credit.
Harvey (1973), pp.238, 246.

Of course, the process of urbanization has long been underway in Western societies. Britain was already an urban nation by the mid-nineteenth century, Germany a few decades later, the United States and Canada by 1920. The point about the urban character of today's society is its vastly enlarged scale and complexity and the pervasiveness of its influence. Today, between 70 and 80 percent of the population of Western industrial societies live in areas officially designated as 'urban' and many more live within the influence of *daily urban systems* (the areas of regular interaction based on commuting in particular). Even those people who do not live in places which are *physically* urban are increasingly tied into the urban way of life either as participants (for example, the long-distance commuter or the farmer locked into the urban-based marketing system) or as observers through the urban-based media of communication.

The physical form of an urban system at any point in time reflects the *cumulative* result of two inter-related elements. First, it reflects the ways in which society as a whole is organized – in industrial society this involves, in particular, the organization of production and distribution – and the distribution of power. Urban forms are shaped by the major decision-making forces in society, whether these be the church in medieval times, the state in centrally planned societies, or the business corporation, property developer and government planner in most Western societies. The increased scale of such organizations and institutions has had a marked impact on urban form. In Bourne' view,

private developers are the prime initiators of structural change and they are the architects of urban spatial organisation in capitalist cities. . . . Public agencies are also corporate developers in their own right . . . [there is also] . . . the intermediate role of public sector institutions – the 'reluctant carpenters' of urban structure which shape private development decisions through their financial backing or building by-laws. Over time, the scale of operations and thus the imprint of decisions by large public and private

developers has increased. . . . The building and land development industries throughout North America have become increasingly oligopolistic,
more highly organised and more financially diversified. Similarly public
institutions have become larger and governments more centralised. That is,
fewer people are making ever larger investment decisions with greater
impact on the physical structure of the city.
Bourne (1976), p.539.

Since 'cities are primarily the result of investment decisions on what, when, and
where to build' they will reflect the prevailing balance between private and public
forces. In the late 1960s and early 1970s the most favoured development activity,
without any doubt, was office construction. The vast bulk of office building was
financed by the various finance capital institutions – the banks, pension funds,
insurance companies. Figure 2.30 shows in very simple terms how the land

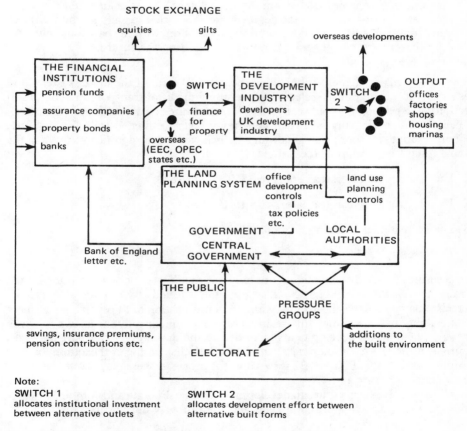

Figure 2.30   The land development system in the United Kingdom

Source: Shelter, *Report No. 1*, London.

development process operated in the United Kingdom context.*

The process is channelled through two 'switches'. The position of the first switch shows some of the possible outlets for investment: for example, speculation on the Stock Exchange, property development or overseas investment. In this case, the switch is set to property and channels funds through into the property development industry. The development industry, as the diagram shows, is constrained by government controls (both central and local) which control office development and land use. Switch two shows which particular kind of property development may be undertaken; the one chosen will be that which is perceived to yield the greatest financial return. Whichever one it is produces an addition to the built environment, an environment which can be seen to be

> a result of conflicts, taking place in the past and in the present, between those with different degrees of power in society – landowners, planners, developers, estate agents, local authorities, pressure groups of all kinds, insurance companies and so on. As the balance of power between these elements changes and as ideologies in society rise and fall, so the built environment is affected. It is a continuing situation, with the past constraining the present and together binding and limiting the future.
> *Pahl (1970), p.60.*

The second major element influencing the physical form of the urban system, and especially its geographical scale, is the prevailing media of transport and communication. The relationship between urban form and the transportation media is well documented in virtually all urban geography texts. Muller (1976), for example, identifies four transportation eras which he believes reflect significant stages in the geographical expansion of the United States city:

1 The walking and horsecar era (pre-1850 to late 1880s);

2 The electric streetcar era (late 1880s to 1920);

3 The recreational automobile era (1920–1945);

4 The freeway era (1945–   ).

As a result of such developments, not only has the Western city been transformed from the walkabout city of 150 years ago to the wheeled city of today, but also its precise spatial form has been closely linked to the location of the evolving transport routes. Figure 2.31 shows this relationship diagrammatically. It shows how the emerging suburban developments were tied to the developing transport network, initially as fingers of development, and later, with the coming of the automobile, as infilling of the gaps. Figure 2.32 shows how the processes were played out in the case of Manchester, England.

Frequently, such suburban development was a deliberate and combined operation between the transport companies and the property developers:

---

*Ambrose and Colenutt (1975) provide a detailed and illuminating study of the 'Property Machine' as it operated in the United Kingdom up to the early 1970s.

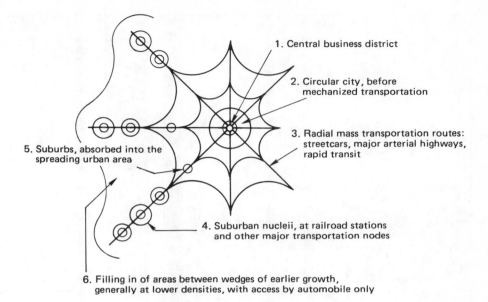

1. Central business district

2. Circular city, before mechanized transportation

3. Radial mass transportation routes: streetcars, major arterial highways, rapid transit

5. Suburbs, absorbed into the spreading urban area

4. Suburban nucleii, at railroad stations and other major transportation nodes

6. Filling in of areas between wedges of earlier growth, generally at lower densities, with access by automobile only

Figure 2.31   A hypothetical view of the relationship between urban form and methods of transportation

Source: H.M. Mayer (1969) The spatial expression of urban growth, *Association of American Geographers, Commission on College Geography, Resource Paper 7*, figure 9.

the middle class families' desire . . . for a cleaner, more livable environment created, particularly in the United States, the opportunity for land speculators to make sizable profits by combining trolley operations with real-estate developments. The device was simple. A trolley line, charging low fares, was built beyond the city to marginal land owned by the speculators. This land was then sub-divided into building lots. The result was a manifold increase in the value of these real-estate holdings, which more than made up for operating trolley lines that were at best barely profitable. This connection between real-estate profits and transit availability was thoroughly understood by U.S. land speculators from coast to coast. *Schaeffer and Sclar (1975), p.30.*

The importance of large institutions in the postwar suburbanization of urban population is discussed in more detail in Chapter Four. At this stage, it is important to stress the key role of mass automobile-ownership in enabling individuals and organizations to partake in a geographically more extensive existence. The transformation of the industrial city from its compact star-shaped spatial form in the nineteenth century to the sprawling amoeba-like metropolis of today could not have occurred without fundamental developments in transportation and communications technology which transformed capability and coupling constraints for many people and organizations. Again, we should stress that technology, though necessary, is not, in itself, sufficient for a particular change to occur; there has to be a willingness

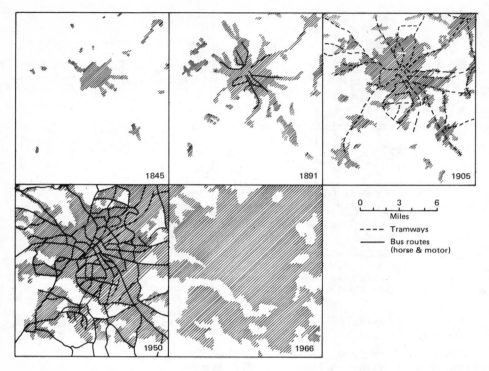

Figure 2.32   Urban expansion and developments in the transport system: the case of Manchester, England

Source: P. Hall et al. (1973) *The Containment of Urban England*, Volume 1, London: George Allen & Unwin, for Political and Economic Planning, now Policy Studies Institute, figure 2.4.

on the part of society to use the technology in a particular way. What we can say is that an innovation such as the automobile was necessary for the geographical constraints on urban expansion to be broken. Most of all, the automobile freed those possessing it from total dependence on mass transit routes and terminals. As automobile-ownership spread to larger and larger segments of the population of industrial society it facilitated the infilling of the industrial areas between the predominantly radial transportation arteries of the city and permitted suburban development beyond the terminal points of public transportation services.

The influence of the automobile obviously depended upon its possession by a large proportion of the population. As long as it was an expensive luxury possessed by the few its geographical impact was limited. But with the development of popular, mass-produced cars pioneered by Henry Ford's Model 'T', automobile ownership became widespread, as Figure 2.33 shows. By 1970 in the United States there was, on average, more than one automobile for every household in the land. Certainly, after the 1940s, the automobile came to epitomize modern industrial society. The unprecedented economic growth experienced by the advanced industrial nations between 1945 and the early 1970s was very much associated with the

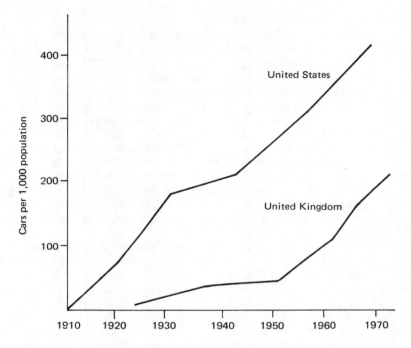

Figure 2.33 Increases in automobile ownership, United States and United Kingdom, 1910–1974

Source: K.H. Schaeffer & E. Sclar (1975) *Access for All: Transportation and Urban Growth*, Harmondsworth: Penguin, figure 2. Reproduced by permission of Penguin Books Ltd.

development of the automobile industry. The industry itself was so central to the economy as a whole that its fortunes came to be regarded as a critical barometer of national economic well-being. In most Western countries the exponential growth of automobile-ownership had, as its mirror image, the decline of public transportation – in some cases to the point of virtual extinction. Hence the possession of, or at least access to, an automobile became a necessity rather than a luxury in order for people to make a living, do the shopping, visit friends and relatives. Some of the problems of those with low mobility in modern Western society are dealt with in Chapter Five. Here we are concerned with the close relationship between the automobile and metropolitan development. Of course, it was not the only innovation involved. Developments in communications technology, especially the telephone, facilitated the further loosening of the bonds of physical proximity. As the general level of affluence increased, more and more people were able to substitute one kind of environment for another. For the most part this meant the suburbs of large cities.

Thus the major difference between the city of the nineteenth century and that of today is that, whereas the former reflected a process of *population concentration*, today's urban form is the outcome of the *expansion* of such centres and their *coalescence* with others to produce a vastly enlarged scale of urban living. We live increasingly in a *metropolitan world*, a world of giant cities.

The evolution of metropolitan society

It is rarely possible to date the precise beginnings of major changes in social organization mainly because most of them *evolve* gradually out of earlier forms. Certainly, as the figures discussed below suggest, the growth of metropolitan areas was well under way by the early part of the present century. But the forces which, in combination, generated pervasive, rather than localized, metropolitanization came together most clearly in the years immediately following World War I. Although they did not reach their peak for several decades, the 1920s were probably the years in which – at least in hindsight – these forces became clearly identifiable. In a number of respects, the 1920s seem to represent something of a turning point in the spatial organization of Western urban-industrial society. Not only does this date mark the beginning of major growth in automobile-ownership and in air traffic but also the upsurge in business concentration and the emergence of some of the giant business enterprises of the present day. By 1920 both the United States and Canada were, for the first time in their histories, more urban than rural in the sense that more than half of their populations lived in urban areas.

Figure 2.34 plots the change in the metropolitan population of the United States compared with the rate of growth of the population as a whole for the period 1900 to 1970. In every decade since 1900, without exception, the metropolitan population increased at a markedly faster rate than the total population. Quite clearly, a larger and larger proportion of the inhabitants of the United States came to reside in metropolitan areas. In absolute terms, the increase in the metropolitan population has been even more marked. Between 1900 and 1910 the metropolitan population of the United States grew by 10.4 million; in both the 1950–1960 and 1960–1970 decades, the metropolitan population increased by well over 30 million. These figures reflect a number of demographic changes, particularly those relating to *migration*. In the early decades of the twentieth century immigrants to the United States from Europe tended to settle in urban rather than rural areas. As the century progressed, millions of existing rural inhabitants left the countryside for the perceived attractions of the cities, especially the big cities which also drew a massive influx of population from the small towns, the non-metropolitan urban centres.

At the national scale, the pattern of metropolitan growth has shifted its geographical emphasis since 1900. Not surprisingly, in the early part of the century it was the Northeast of the United States – the industrial heartland – which experienced the bulk of the nation's metropolitan growth. But, as Figure 2.35 shows, there has been a clear shift in the pattern as the century has progressed. The South and, to a lesser extent, the West have come to account for a larger and larger share of national metropolitan growth. In the 1900–1910 decade, 45.1 percent of total population growth in existing and new Standard Metropolitan Statistical Areas (SMSAs) was in the Northeast region compared with 14 percent in the South and 11.7 percent in the West. By the 1930s, the Northeast's share of metropolitan growth had fallen to 22.6 percent while that of the South had increased to 36.1 percent and the West to 23.9 percent. These regional differences had become even more apparent by the 1960s.

Such regional variations in the rate of metropolitan growth are reflected in the wide differences in the growth rates of individual metropolitan areas. For the most part it is the newer, younger metropolitan areas which have experienced the most spectacular growth, particularly those in the more pleasantly endowed physical environments: the Miami-Fort Lauderdales, the San Diegos, the Dallases – what

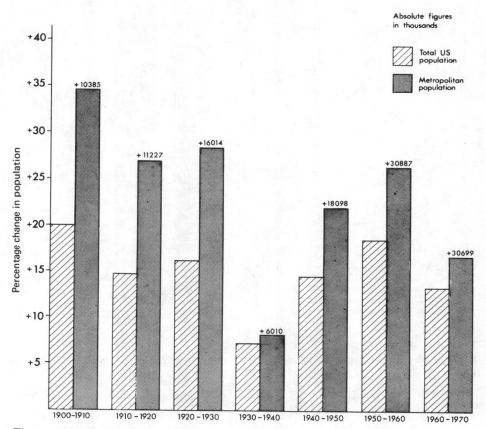

Figure 2.34 Metropolitan population growth in the United States, 1900–1970

Source: based on data in B.G. Zimmer (1975) The urban centrifugal drift, in A.H. Hawley & V.P. Rock (eds) *Metropolitan America in Contemporary Perspective*, Beverley Hills/London, Sage Publications, table 1.1.

have come to be termed the Sunbelt Cities. Conversely, it is the old metropolitan areas which have experienced the least growth. It is worth emphasizing, however, that the South still remains the least 'metropolitanized' region despite its very rapid recent growth. In 1970, only 56 percent of the South's population lived in metropolitan areas, compared with 83 percent in the Northeast, 67 percent in the North-Central region and 79 percent in the West.

When we look inside these aggregate statistics of metropolitan growth we find that virtually all of the growth of the metropolitan population has been occurring not in the central cities – the zone of greatest vertical development and massive skyscrapers – but in the surrounding suburban rings. Table 2.10 shows the population growth rates of the central cities and the suburbs as well as those of metropolitan areas as a whole and of non-metropolitan areas. It enables us to get a very general impression of the elements of metropolitan change. The table reveals that even in the

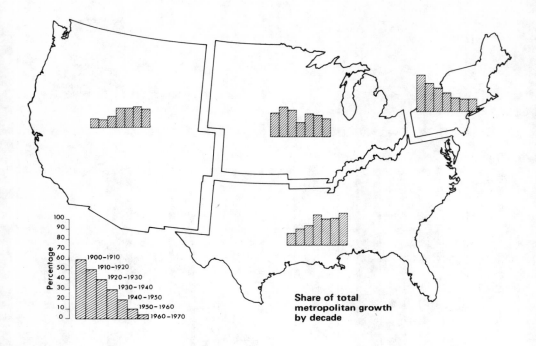

Figure 2.35   Regional pattern of metropolitan population growth in the United States, 1900–1970

Source: based on data in B.J.L. Berry & J.D. Kasarda (1977) *Contemporary Urban Ecology*, New York: Macmillan, table 8.2a.

Table 2.10   *Population change within metropolitan areas and in non-metropolitan areas, United States, 1900–1970*

	Percentage change			
	Metropolitan population	Central cities	Outside central cities	Non-metro-politan areas
1900–1910	34.6	33.6	38.2	16.4
1910–1920	26.9	25.2	32.0	9.6
1920–1930	28.3	22.3	44.0	7.9
1930–1940	8.1	5.1	15.1	6.5
1940–1950	22.0	13.9	35.9	6.1
1950–1960	26.3	10.7	48.6	7.1
1960–1970	16.6	6.5	26.7	−4.0

Source: B.G. Zimmer (1975) The urban centrifugal drift, in A.H. Hawley & V.P. Rock (eds), *Metropolitan America in Contemporary Perspective*, Beverly Hills/London, Sage Publications, table 1.1.

1900–1910 decade the rate of population growth within the metropolitan areas, but outside the central cities, was already greater than that in the central cities. But, at that time, the difference was small. Except for the 1930s, the gap has become progressively wider since then, so that by the 1960s the outer metropolitan areas were growing at an average rate more than four times greater than that of the central cities. Parallel with these changes was the relative and, in the 1960s, the absolute, decline of population in non-metropolitan areas. By 1960, therefore, not only was the United States a metropolitan society but also the majority of the metropolitan population lived outside the central cities.

In fact the difference in growth rates between central cities and suburbs was even greater than Table 2.10 suggests. This is because a good deal of the growth of central cities occurred through their annexation of adjacent suburban areas. This has the effect of inflating actual central-city growth rates and depressing actual suburban growth rates. Whereas with annexation the central cities grew by 10.8 percent and 6.5 percent between 1950–1960 and 1960–1970 respectively, without annexation the comparable figures were 1.5 percent and 0.1 percent. Since these are average figures it is clear that many central cities were in fact *losing population*. Again, it was the older metropolitan areas in the industrial heartland which were most affected, together with some smaller metropolitan areas elsewhere (Figure 2.36). Pittsburgh, in fact, was the only large metropolitan area – that is, those with a population of more than half a million – which experienced an *absolute* decline in population between 1960 and 1970.

The evolution of a metropolitan system is particularly clear in the United States. Obviously, there are certain aspects of American metropolitan development which reflect particular national circumstances. One of these is the absence of any major legislative restriction on the spatial extent of metropolitan areas. But the same general pattern is evident throughout Western industrial society. In their comparative study of urban change between 1966 and 1971 in Canada and Australia, Bourne and Logan (1976) identify large-scale population growth in the urban extensions of the metropolitan areas. They attribute such outer-area growth to congestion and increased costs in the metropolitan cores rather than to the deterioration of the cores evident in the United States.

The small geographical extent of Britain, together with its long history of intensive urbanization, make the identification of metropolitan trends rather more difficult. In addition, for the last three decades, Britain has operated planning legislation which has almost certainly modified the kind of metropolitan pattern which otherwise would have developed. New Towns have been created, the expansion of some of the larger cities restricted. Population has been deliberately 'decanted' from the decaying cities to towns elsewhere. Despite these 'local' circumstances, however, Britain's recent metropolitan development shows many of the characteristics evident in the United States and elsewhere.

A detailed analysis of developments in Britain's metropolitan system between 1951 and 1971 revealed that the dominant trend over the twenty-year period was 'accelerating decentralization' from the urban cores to the outer areas. In 1951, 52.7 percent of the nation's population lived in the urban cores; in 1971 this share had fallen to 47.4 percent with a corresponding increase in the proportion of the population living in the suburban rings. Table 2.11 shows how the relative performance of inner and outer metropolitan areas changed during the 1951–1971 period.

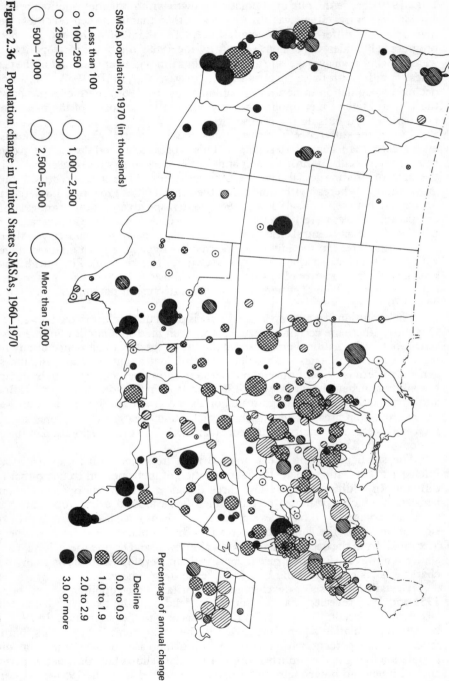

SMSA population, 1970 (in thousands)

- o   Less than 100
- o   100–250
- ○   250–500
- ◯   500–1,000
- ◯   1,000–2,500
- ◯   2,500–5,000
- ◯   More than 5,000

Percentage of annual change

- ○   Decline
- ◐   0.0 to 0.9
- ◑   1.0 to 1.9
- ●   2.0 to 2.9
- ●   3.0 or more

Figure 2.36   Population change in United States SMSAs, 1960–1970

Source: P.D. Phillips & S.D. Brunn (1978), Slow growth: a new epoch of American metropolitan evolution, *Geographical Review*, 68, figure 1. Reprinted with permission of the American Geography Society.

Two aspects of Table 2.11 are particularly relevant. First, the reversal in the fortunes of the urban cores is especially striking. Between 1951 and 1961 the cores as a whole were still increasing their population, though very slightly. In fact most of the urban cores of the large, old-established cities such as Manchester, Liverpool, Newcastle had been losing population for some time. Between 1961 and 1971 *all* urban cores were clearly in decline. The second striking feature of Table 2.11 is the increasing outward shift of population growth. Although the metropolitan rings continued to grow most rapidly of all (+13.3 percent and +17.2 percent) in both decades, the 1961–1971 period saw almost a 10 percent increase in the population of the outer rings. Hence 'the frontier of most active population change has moved progressively further from the urban cores'.

Table 2.11   *Rates of population change within British metropolitan areas, 1951–1961 and 1961–1971*

	Percentage change	
	1951–1961	1961–1971
Urban cores	+1.9	−2.8
Metropolitan rings	+13.3	+17.2
Outer metropolitan rings	+3.1	+9.8

Source: R. Drewett, J. Goddard & N. Spence (1976) British Cities: Urban population and employment trends 1951–1971, *Department of the Environment Research Report* 10, table 4. Crown Copyright

As in the case of the United States (Figure 2.35), there were considerable regional differences in the metropolitan growth rate in Britain. Figure 2.37 divides metropolitan growth performance compared with national population growth into four categories. The map shows clearly that the metropolitan areas experiencing below-average growth in both decades were mostly in the northern half of the country: Lancashire and Yorkshire, the Northeast and central Scotland. The exception to this clear geographical pattern was London. Metropolitan areas experiencing above-average growth in both decades were almost entirely those in central and southern England. The intermediate growth patterns are less clear, although Drewett, Goddard and Spence point to the changed fortunes of SMLAs in south Lancashire which, in the 1960s, were drawing population decentralizing from Manchester and Liverpool. For the most part, in fact, it was the largest SMLAs which experienced the greatest population decline, especially in the 1961–1971 period, a dramatic reversal of fortunes from previous decades of growth.

Urban 'field' and megalopolis

By the 1960s the progressive outward spread of metropolitan areas had come to

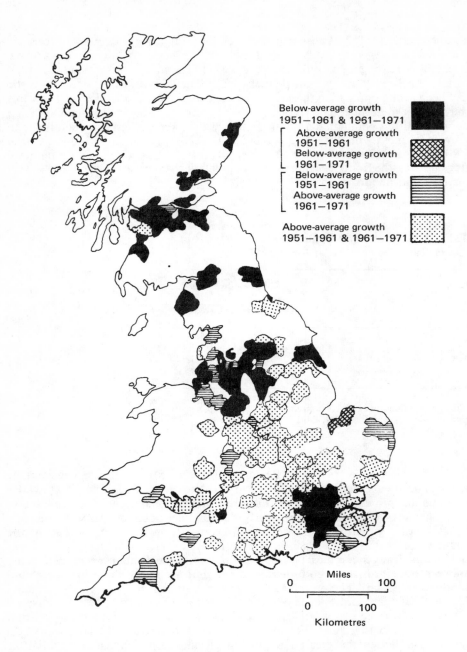

Figure 2.37 Population change in British Standard Metropolitan Labour Areas, 1951–1961 and 1961–1971

Source: R. Drewett, J. Goddard & N. Spence (1976) Urban Britain: beyond containment, in B.J.L. Berry (ed) *Urbanization and Counterurbanization*, Beverly Hills: Sage Publications, figure 5.

envelop almost the entire population of Western industrial societies. Figures 2.38 and 2.39 depict the daily zones of influence of metropolitan areas in Britain and the United States respectively. In the late 1960s more than 90 percent of the populations of both countries were resident within these daily urban systems. Writing in 1965, Friedmann and Miller coined the term *urban field* to describe what they saw as the fundamental unit emerging from the vastly enlarged scale of urban living.*

Figure 2.40 maps the '100-odd urban fields' identified by them. In some cases there is a clear coalescence of urban fields, a complex overlapping and clustering in which it becomes virtually impossible to distinguish where one urban field ends and another begins. Such large-scale coalescence of urban fields produces yet another, even larger, scale of urban organization: what Jean Gottmann terms *megalopolis*. There are various definitions of just what constitutes a megalopolis. Some argue for a threshold population size of 10 million, though Gottman himself holds to the much higher threshold of 25 million. On such a basis he recognizes six existing, and three embryonic, megalopolises. Five of the six are in capitalist-industrial societies (the sixth is in the Republic of China):

1 *The Northeastern Seaboard of the United States*. Stretches from Boston in the north, through New York, Philadelphia, Baltimore, to Washington and beyond

2 *Great Lakes Megalopolis*. Based on Chicago, Detroit, Cleveland

3 *Megalopolis England*. Stretches from the south coast northwards to Lancashire and Yorkshire. Includes most of the major cities, e.g., London, Birmingham, Manchester, Liverpool, Leeds

4 *Northwest European Megalopolis*. Includes Amsterdam, Rotterdam, Essen, Dortmund, Duisburg, Düsseldorf, Frankfurt, Mainz, Mannheim, Stuttgart

5 *Japanese Megalopolis*. Centred on Tokyo, Yokohama, Nagoya, Osaka-Kobe.

---

*The urban field may be viewed as an enlargement of the space for urban living that extends far beyond the boundaries of existing metropolitan areas – defined primarily in terms of commuting to a central city of 'metropolitan' size – into the open landscape of the periphery. . . . It is no longer possible to regard the city as purely an artefact, or a political entity, or a configuration of population densities. All of these are outmoded constructs that recall a time when one could trace a sharp dividing line between town and courtryside, rural and urban man. From a sociological and, indeed, an economic viewpoint, what is properly urban and properly rural can no longer be distinguished . . . The corresponding view of the city is no longer of a physical entity, but of a pattern of point locations and connecting flows of people, information, money, and commodities.

The idea of an urban field is similarly based on the criterion of interdependency. It represents a fusion of metropolitan spaces and non-metropolitan peripheral spaces centered upon core areas of at least 300,000 people and extending outwards from these core areas for a distance equivalent to two hours' driving over modern throughway systems (approximately 100 miles with present technology). This represents not only an approximate geographic limit for commuting to a job, but also the limit of intensive weekend and seasonal use (by ground transportation) of the present periphery for recreation. Between 85 and 90 percent of the total United States population falls within the boundaries of this system while less than 35 percent of the total land area of the country is included.
Friedmann and Miller (1965), pp.313, 314.

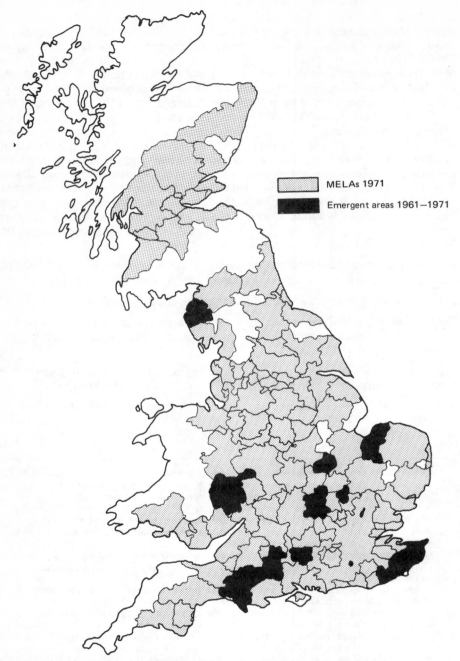

MELAs 1971

Emergent areas 1961–1971

Figure 2.38 Metropolitan economic labour areas in Britain

Source: R.J. Drewett, J.B. Goddard & N. Spence (1976) *British Cities: Urban Population and Employment Trends 1951–1971, Department of the Environment Research Report* 10, figure 4(b). Crown Copyright.

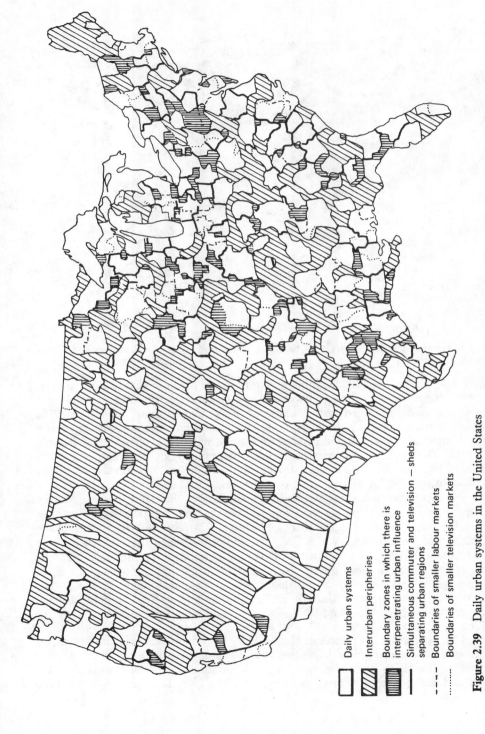

Key:

□ Daily urban systems

▨ Interurban peripheries

▥ Boundary zones in which there is interpenetrating urban influence

| Simultaneous commuter and television — sheds separating urban regions

– – – Boundaries of smaller labour markets

······· Boundaries of smaller television markets

Figure 2.39 Daily urban systems in the United States

Source: B.J.L. Berry (1970) The geography of the United States in the year 2000, *Transactions of the Institute of British Geographers*, 51, figure 3.

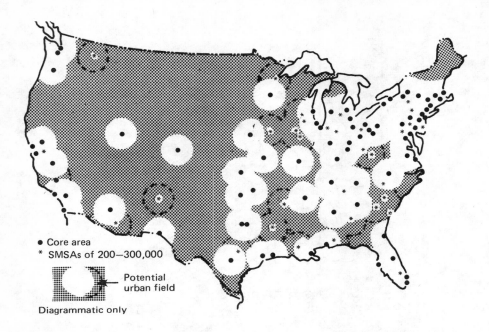

Figure 2.40   'Urban fields' in the United States in the mid-1960s

Source: J. Friedmann & J. Miller (1965) The urban field, *Journal of the American Institute of Town Planners*, 31, map 3.

Figure 2.41 shows the broad outline of the first two of these vast urban clusters. Gottmann's archetypal megalopolis was the 400-mile stretch between Boston and Washington along the northeastern seaboard of the United States which, in 1970, contained a population of some 37 million. This meant that almost 20 percent of the entire United States population resided on approximately 2 percent of the nation's land area. The Great Lakes megalopolis is spatially more extensive, but rather less homogeneous, and falls into three distinct groups of metropolitan areas: one centred on Chicago, one on Detriot and one on Cleveland-Pittsburgh.

By comparison, what has been called 'megalopolis England' is considerably smaller in spatial extent though, as a proportion of the country's population and land area, it is a good deal more significant (see Figure 2.42a). Roughly 70 per cent of the population of England and Wales lives in the 'coffin-shaped' belt which extends from the southeast coast northwards to a line running approximately between Preston and York. In fact, it could be argued that the English megalopolis is, in many ways, an extension of the northwest European megalopolis (Figure 2.42b) with its four major concentrations of urban population (Randstad Holland, Rhein-Ruhr-Aachen, Rhein-Main and Rhein-Neckar), and a total population of some 29 million.

Of the emerging megalopolises identified by Gottmann, one is in Brazil centred on the two large nuclei of Rio de Janeiro and São Paulo, another is in northern Italy, focused on the Milan-Turin-Genoa triangle. This extends westwards towards Marseilles and Avignon and southwards to Florence and Pisa. The third of Gottmann's nascent megalopolises is located in California with its central focus on Los Angeles and with extensions northwards to the San Francisco Bay area and southwards through San Diego and across the Mexican border. Other writers on these vast urban complexes recognize a larger number of emerging megalopolises. For example, Doxiadis (1969) suggested that an international megalopolis is developing astride the

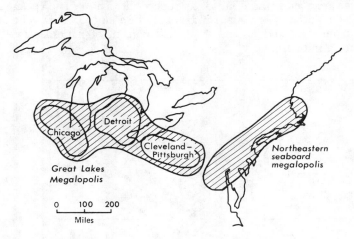

Figure 2.41   Northeastern seaboard and Great Lakes megalopolises

Source: C. Doxiadis (1969) The prospect of an international megalopolis, in M. Wade (ed) *The International Megalopolis*, Windsor: University of Windsor Press, figure 1.

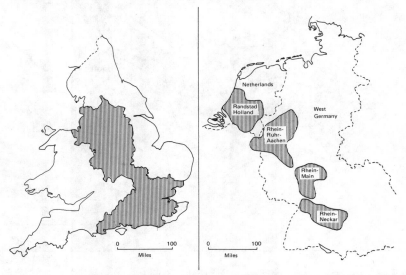

Figure 2.42   Megalopolis England and Northwest European megalopolis

Source: P. Hall et al. (1973) *The Containment of Urban England*, Vol. I, London: George Allen & Unwin, figures 1.4 and 1.5. By permission of PEP, now Policy Studies Institute.

Great Lakes in North America. Here he sees the Greak Lakes megalopolis branching northeastwards across the Detroit river through the Canadian city of Windsor and on through Hamilton, Toronto and Montreal. Figure 2.43 shows Doxiadis' view of this pattern together with a possible link via a 'Mohawk Bridge' to the northeastern seaboard megalopolis. Certainly there is an elongated cluster of rapidly growing metropolitan areas along the Windsor to Quebec City axis – what Yeates (1975) calls 'Main Street'. Within this Canadian axis is to be found 55.3 percent of the total Canadian population and no less than 71.7 percent of national employment in manufacturing industry.

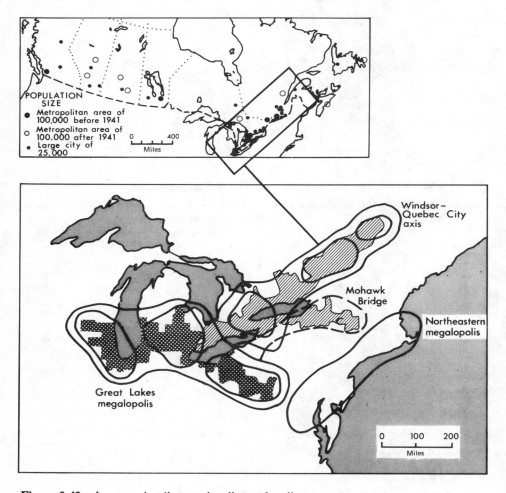

Figure 2.43   An emerging 'international' megalopolis

Source: C. Doxiadis (1969) The prospect of an international megalopolis, in M. Wade (ed) *The International Megalopolis*, Windsor: University of Windsor Press, figure 7; M.H. Yeates & B. Garner (1967) *The North American City*, 2nd edn, New York: Harper & Row, figure 2.9.

A NEW ERA? THE 'COUNTER-URBANIZATION' TREND

Every United States Census from 1900 to 1970 showed that the metropolitan population was increasing at a faster rate than the population as a whole. More and more people were residing in metropolitan areas. At the same time, the intermetropolitan periphery – those areas outside the daily urban systems of the metropolitan complexes – was losing population, largely through migration to the metropolis. Friedmann and Miller (1965) described the intermetropolitan periphery as a 'devil's mirror' which 'perversely reflects the very opposite of metropolitan virility'. As the century progressed, however, the metropolitan complexes themselves became increasingly differentiated in terms of population and employment growth. In particular, the central cities began to decline at an accelerating rate; the 'devil's mirror' was on the inside as well as the outside. To use a different metaphor, the metropolis took on a doughnut-like form. In the 1960s there was evidence of relative decline among the old-established metropolitan areas of the industrial heartland, but only one large SMSA, Pittsburgh, experienced absolute, as opposed to relative, population loss. Nevertheless, the growth of the metropolitan system as a whole seemed assured.

Yet by the 1970s things seemed to have changed. Not merely were some of the patterns of decline evident in the 1960s reinforced, but they became more extensive. More strikingly, some trends of the previous seventy years were apparently being reversed. According to Berry,

> a turning point has been reached in the American urban experience. Counter-urbanisation has replaced urbanisation as the dominant force shaping the nation's settlement patterns. . . . The trend has been one leading unremittingly toward the reversal of the processes of population concentration unleashed by technologies of the Industrial Revolution, a reversal finally achieved after 1970.
> *Berry (1976), pp.17, 24.*

Overall, the metropolitan population of the United States continued to increase between 1970 and 1974, from 137 million to 151 million. But the annual *rate* of growth was very much lower than in the previous decades. Between 1960 and 1970, for example, the metropolitan population increased at an annual rate of 1.6 percent. Between 1970 and 1974, this annual rate was halved, to 0.8 percent. Whereas only one of the largest twenty-five SMSAs actually lost population in absolute terms between 1960 and 1970, by 1974 ten of the largest group were experiencing absolute decline. Although most of the 'big losers' were in the Middle Atlantic and East-North-Central states not all were, as Figure 2.44 shows. For example, Los Angeles-Long Beach and Seattle-Everett both lost population. Overall, according to Morrison (1975), one-seventh of all SMSAs were losing population between 1970 and 1975 and one in three metropolitan dwellers lived in a declining area. The out-migration formerly confined to the central cities appeared to have aefected the suburbs closest to the city limits.

The more widespread decline in the population of metropolitan areas (and not just of the central cities) is a notable feature of the post-1970 period. But even more striking is the fact that *non-metropolitan* areas – which had been in persistent decline for several decades – not only reversed their previous decline but also grew at a faster

Figure 2.44   Standard Metropolitan Statistical Areas with declining population, 1970–1975

Source: P.A. Morrison (1975) The current demographic context of national growth and development, *Rand Corporation Publications*, P-5514, figure 1. Reprinted in L.S. Bourne & J.W. Simmons (eds) (1978) *Systems of Cities: Readings on Structure, Growth and Policy*, New York: Oxford University Press.

rate than the metropolitan areas. Table 2.12 shows that the areas outside the SMSAs grew by only 0.4 percent per year between 1960 and 1970 whilst 'entirely rural' counties experienced an annual population decline of −0.4 percent. Between 1970 and 1974, by contrast, these non-metropolitan areas grew by 1.3 to 1.4 percent per year. Metropolitan areas increased their population by only slightly more than half this rate (0.8 percent per year). The table also shows that the non-metropolitan increase was not simply a 'spillover effect' from SMSAs to immediately adjacent territory. Certainly counties with substantial commuting to SMSAs showed a clear population increase, but so, too, did those with very little metropolitan commuting and also the entirely rural areas. (At the state level, nine of the ten most urban states had population growth rates below the national average; eight of the ten most rural states had growth rates above the national average.)

Population change, whether positive or negative, is made up of two major components: natural increase (the relation between births and deaths) and net migration (the balance between in-migration and out-migration). Table 2.12 shows how these two components contributed to the changes in metropolitan and non-metropolitan areas. It is clear from the natural increase columns that there was a general slowdown in national population growth in the 1970s. Indeed, between 1955 and 1974, the United States birthrate was almost halved. Such slower population increase was reflected across all metropolitan and non-metropolitan categories. (It seems likely that the higher natural increase of the 1960s had obscured high levels of out-migration in many of the metropolitan areas.)

Thus, the key to the reversal of metropolitan growth trends is to be found in the migration figures. In the 1960s, the non-metropolitan counties were *losing* 300,000 people per year more than they were gaining. Between 1970 and 1974 these same

Table 2.12 *Components of population change for groups of metropolitan and non-metropolitan counties, 1960–1970 and 1970–1974*

Population category	1974 population (000's)	Annual population growth rate %		Annual natural increase rate %		Annual net migration rate %	
		1960–1970	1970–1974	1960–1970	1970–1974	1960–1970	1970–1974
United States	211,390	1.3	0.9	1.1	0.7	0.2	0.2
Inside SMSAs (Metropolitan)	154,934	1.6	0.8	1.2	0.7	0.5	0.1
Outside SMSAs (Non-metropolitan)	56,457	0.4	1.3	0.9	0.6	–0.6	0.7
In counties from which:							
⩾ 20% commute to SMSAs	4,372	0.9	2.0	0.8	0.5	0.1	1.5
10%–19% commute to SMSAs	9,912	0.7	1.4	0.8	0.5	–0.1	0.8
3%–9% commute to SMSAs	14,263	0.5	1.3	0.9	0.6	–0.4	0.7
<3% commute to SMSAs	27,909	0.2	1.1	0.9	0.6	–0.8	0.5
Entirely rural counties* **not adjacent to an SMSA**	4,618	–0.4	1.4	0.8	0.4	–1.2	1.0

Note: SMSAs as currently defined.

* 'Entirely rural' means the counties contain no town of 2500 or more inhabitants.

Source: P.A. Morrison (1975) The current demographic context of national growth and development, *Rand Corporation Publication P-5514*, table 1

areas were *gaining* roughly 350,000 extra migrants per year. The final two columns of Table 2.12 reveal that, whereas the net migration rate into SMSAs fell to a mere 0.1 percent, each of the non-metropolitan categories which had previously lost population by migration registered net increases.* These migration differences also largely explain the regional variations in metropolitan growth. As Figure 2.44 shows, almost all the declining SMSAs were in the East and Northeast. Migration of the white population out of the Northeast has been a persistent feature since the 1940s. Between 1940 and 1970 some 900,000 whites left the region, but this loss was more than offset by the influx of 1.6 million blacks from the South. Since 1970, however, there has been a complete reversal of black migration.

Overall, then, the metropolitan areas no longer seem to be experiencing net

*More recent figures show that 'between 1970 and 1978, more than 2.7 million more people moved out of metropolitan areas than moved into them. Whereas one-sixth of all metropolitan areas lost population, three-fourths of all non-metropolitan counties gained population' (Kasarda 1980, p.12).

in-migration from non-metropolitan areas. In a situation of slower national population growth this has resulted in a reversal of the fortunes of SMSAs and non-
metropolitan areas in the early 1970s. Now it is obviously unlikely that such a
reversal of long-established population trends occurred abruptly on 1 January 1970.
More than likely the changes began in the late 1960s. To some extent – especially in
the decline of the older, larger metropolitan areas – they are a continuation and
intensification of trends apparent throughout the 1960s. But it is at least possible that
the United States is experiencing a new era in its urban development. Whatever the
reasons underlying these developments in the United States' metropolitan system,
we need to ask whether they are unique to that country or whether they represent the
shape of things to come in other industrial societies. Certainly some of the trends
apparent in Britain, Canada and elsewhere towards the end of the 1960s could be
interpreted this way, even allowing for particular national circumstances. The
'accelerating decentralization' and the growth of smaller centres at the expense of the
ageing metropolitan centres are broadly consistent with American experience,*
though it is clear from recent work by Hall and Hay (1980) that patterns of change in
European urban systems are quite variable.

THE PERVASIVENESS OF URBAN VALUES

Whether or not recently observed trends do herald a substantial change in the
physical nature of urban forms, there can be little doubt that comprehensive
re-organization of urban living has occurred. Society has been transformed by the
processes of metropolitanization. As a result, the long-held distinction between
urban and rural, between town and country, can no longer be sustained. The
massive geographical expansion of long-established cities, the coalescence of
metropolitan complexes, the emergence of new metropolitan areas have all combined to produce an urban or, more accurately, a metropolitan society.

> The paradox here is that by the time ninety percent of the population are
> urban, the city has really ceased to have any meaning in itself. The converse
> of this phenomenon is the disappearance of rural life as a distinctive and
> peculiar sub-culture within the society. Over large parts of the United
> States this has already happened. The Iowa farmer has an occupational
> sub-culture but he does not have a rural sub-culture. He is merely an
> ex-urbanite who happens to be living on a farm, and he earns his living by
> thoroughly urban methods . . . he is far more remote, say, from the

---

*Certainly this seems to be Berry's opinion based upon recent urban experience in a variety of contexts.
He identifies

> a common response to the laissez faire industrial urbanisation that produced the big cities of the
> 19th century. . . . From these reactions have emerged three types of counter-urbanisation,
> each an expression of contemporary urbanisation policy: the individualistic decentralization
> that has culminated in the decreasing size, decreasing density, and increasing homogeneity of
> cities and the more ruralised life styles of the more liberal capitalist states; planned new towns
> as counterpoints to speculative private interest in the welfare states of Western Europe; and the
> Marxist search for a new settlement pattern for mankind, the city of socialist man in which
> traditional antagonisms between city and country are no more.
> Berry (1976), p.10.

European peasant than he is from the American factory engineer.
Boulding (1963), p.143.

Although the recently observed counter-urbanization trends may well herald a move away from *concentrated* urban living, it almost certainly does not presage a reversal or decline of urban *influence*. It is virtually impossible for any inhabitant of modern Western society to evade completely the urban embrace not least because of the revolution in the mass communications media.

Not only do the mass media play an enormously powerful role in modern Western society but also they are, first and foremost, *urban-based* and *urban-biased* media. The messages they transmit are overwhelmingly urban messages which reflect urban values, urban life-styles and urban viewpoints. Most of all it is the electronic media – radio and, especially, television – which are the all-pervasive transmitters of urban culture. The revolution in the electronic media led Marshall McLuhan to coin the term *global village* whilst other writers have suggested that the term *global city* may be more appropriate since it simulates the kind of experiences and interaction that a city provides even though the person experiencing it may live in a remote farmstead in the highlands of Scotland or in a cabin in Arctic Canada, many miles from the nearest human being. It is a 'city' because the media are essentially city-based: they emanate from cities, they are *of* the city, they represent and propagate urban values and urban life-styles. It is a 'city' rather than a village because it is based on interaction rather than intimacy. Thus whether he *actually* lives in a city or not, *modern industrial man is urban man*.

CONCLUSION

In this chapter we have emphasized the vastly increased scale of social and geographical organization which has come to characterize modern Western societies. Through the pursuit of economic growth, new technologies have been evolved which have both altered the physical processes of production and also greatly increased society's overall capacity to overcome the friction of distance. At the same time, developments in 'social technology' – of ways of organizing society's activities – have helped to create both the giant organization (private and public) and the massive urban forms of the present day. As part of this process, control over large segments of life has become very highly concentrated in a relatively small number of very large organizations. The remote bureaucracy has become endemic, though not to the same extent as in the command systems of the Communist bloc.

Such aspatial concentration, together with the specific internal characteristics of large organizations, has reinforced what all agree is an inherent characteristic of capitalist economies – the unevenness of their geographical development. We have shown how the headquarters of both private and public organizations tend to concentrate in certain locations to create geographical centres of control at the uppermost levels of the urban hierarchy. Once underway, the process of development has tended to be cumulative, reinforcing the dominance of specific centres and creating a complex centre-periphery structure.* In the case of the key decision-

---

*A detailed discussion of the cumulative process of economic development is provided in Lloyd and Dicken (1977), chapter 10.

making operations of large business corporations (the Level I activities), Figure 2.45 demonstrates how the cumulative process may operate.

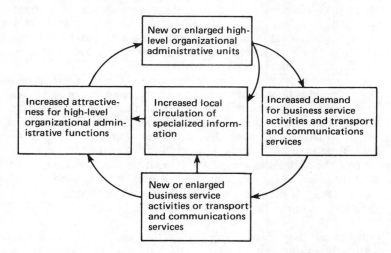

Figure 2.45   The accumulation of high-level control activities in a large metropolitan complex as a cumulative process

Source: A.R. Pred (1977) *City Systems in Advanced Economies,* London: Hutchinson, figure 3.1.

With the development of multinational business corporations the correspondence between centralization of control within the corporation and centralization of control within the international economy has become especially marked. Indeed, Roger Lee has likened the modern organization of production to a 'gigantic version of the putting-out system'. A spatial division of labour is evolving in which two sets of hierarchies – the urban and the organizational – are meshed together. Hence Hymer has argued that

> one would expect to find the highest offices of the multinational corporations concentrated in the world's major cities – New York, London, Paris, Bonn, Tokyo. These, along with Moscow and perhaps Peking, will be the major centres of high-level strategic planning. Lesser cities throughout the world will deal with the day-to-day operations of specific local problems. These in turn will be arranged in a hierarchical fashion: the larger and more important ones will contain regional corporate headquarters, while the smaller ones will be confined to lower level activities. Since business is usually the core of the city, *geographical specialization will come to reflect the hierarchy of corporate decision-making, and the occupational distribution of labour in a city or region will depend upon its function in the international economic system.*
> *Hymer (1972), p.124* (present authors' emphasis).

Although most would agree that a very strong cumulative element operates to preserve or enhance the relative positions of business corporations and of metropolitan areas changes, both positive and negative, major and minor, do occur. The fortunes of firms, of cities, of regions, of nations wax and wane. Some of the high fliers of one era become the stranded and disabled of another era as their attributes no longer meet the changing needs of the economy at large. Conversely, the ugly duckling may be transformed into the goose that lays the golden egg; perhaps the recent rapid growth in the southern United States, particularly the Sunbelt cities is an example of this. There is, of course, nothing new about such changes. What is perhaps different about the present day is that the developments of recent years have created extremely powerful interdependencies at a much enlarged geographical scale.

In addition, the degree of interdependence between individuals in modern society has increased very markedly. Taviss (1974) argues that modern society has become simultaneously both more individualist and more interdependent. She suggests that the 'phenomenon of individuals "rubbing against each other" has become unavoidable' and argues that there are three major reasons for this. The most obvious is the generally high population density of modern life. Despite the metropolitan decentralization trends outlined in this chapter, the predominantly urban environment of most people ensures that most actions spill over to other people. Externality effects, therefore, are especially pronounced in urban society. As Lowry observed, 'in the city everything effects everything else.'* A second, related, reason for increasing interdependence arises from the specialized nature of modern technology and its side-effects. Taviss suggests that a third cause of our increasing interdependence arises from the general increase in affluence which has helped to produce a shift in the composition of demand towards collective goods and services – public goods. Decisions about such goods have to be made collectively rather than individually.

This, then, is the dynamic context in which people live out their daily lives in modern Western society. The quality of these lives may depend as much, if not more, on decisions taken many thousands of miles away as on what is happening locally. Certainly this is true of one of the most basic aspects of most people's lives – the opportunity of earning a decent living. It is to the ways such opportunities vary, for different groups and in different places, and how they are changing, that we turn in the next chapter.

---

*Quoted in Harvey (1973), p.58.

Chapter Three

Making a living: geographical perspectives on the labour market

THE KEY ROLE OF WORK IN MODERN SOCIETY

For most adults [in modern industrial society] work occupies more of their time than any other activity. Their home and family life and system of living are built around, shaped by and integrated with their jobs. They plan every week, month, and year with close reference to the present and prospective future of their work. They time their meals, arrange for family outings, schedule their vacations, move from city to city, borrow and save, buy and sell, and educate their children all in terms of what their job responsibilities require and what their present and prospective earnings permit.
Heneman and Yoder (1965), p.9

In our highly specialized society, in which few people provide their own material needs and wants, most of us at some time in our lives have to work in order to live. (There are, of course, some highly dedicated people who live in order to work.) For all but the privileged few, work and the income derived from it provides the key to life-chances through the command it gives over resources and the social status it carries. At the same time, the demands of the workplace set and regulate the rhythms of day-to-day behaviour, giving pattern and form to the lives people lead. Much of our 'education for life' is, in fact, education for work or, more accurately, for employment. The majority of working people in modern Western society are employed in organizations of various kinds – increasingly very large ones as we saw in Chapter Two – rather than self-employed. Although major changes have occurred during the past century in working hours and conditions, the standard expectation for all males is that they will be gainfully and continuously employed for something like fifty years of their lives. Increasingly too, more and more females expect to be employed, albeit in many cases with a break in continuity associated with child-bearing and child-rearing.

In order to acquire the means of satisfying their multifarious needs and wants, therefore, people need jobs. At the same time, employers, whether they be private business firms or government organizations, need workers. The relationship is symbiotic; each depends upon the other. But the specific matching of job-seekers with job-providers is a far from simple matter. The mechanism through which such matching occurs is the *labour market*. Like any market its function is to bring buyers and sellers together. At the simplest level the labour market brings together employers as the buyers and potential workers as the sellers of what economists term in their impersonal way the 'factor of production', labour. The price paid by the buyer to the seller of labour is the wage or salary, together with any fringe benefits.

But outside the simple diagrams of the textbooks which relate the supply of, and demand for, labour in neat and unambiguous ways, the labour market in modern Western society is fiendishly complex. It consists of a vast, diffuse network of participants. Tens of thousands of companies seek to staff and maintain a bewildering variety of labour tasks; at the same time the potential labour force is numbered in millions, each individual offering a complex array of skills and personal attributes. Information between participants and the bidding process is transmitted through an equally complex constellation of agencies – job centres, employment exchanges, skill-finder bureaux – everything from government manpower offices to specialized firms of 'head-hunters'. With modern communications media, the range over which such information can travel is potentially global.

Not only is the structure of modern labour markets very complicated but also they are subject to continual, though not continuous, change. Indeed we are experiencing at present in Western societies very substantial changes in both the supply of, and demand for, labour. The operation of economic, political and social forces at the international and national scales – some of which we have discussed in Chapter Two – is having far-reaching, often dramatic, effects upon the world of work. The nature and quantity of job opportunities is changing rapidly but unevenly. At the same time, demographic and social changes are bringing increased pressure on those opportunities. Failures in the job-matching process between providers of jobs and providers of labour have generated major problems of unemployment in all Western societies. As always, the geographical outcome of these trends is extremely uneven. At the same time, the very fact that labour markets have a geographical dimension creates a further complication in their operation. The aim of this chapter, therefore, is to explore the changing world of work in modern Western societies from a geographical perspective. We begin by identifying the major elements in the operation of modern labour markets.

THE LABOUR MARKET: A GENERAL FRAMEWORK

Any model of modern labour markets must not only help us to identify the main elements involved but also set these elements into their dynamic context. Figure 3.1 is a widely recognized general model of the labour market which meets these two criteria.* In the diagram, the labour market is conceived as a set of *stocks* connected by a set of *flows*. The basic labour market *stocks* are:

1 *Employed workers* – a two-sided category: workers in work from the viewpoint of the job-seeker; filled jobs from the viewpoint of the employers

2 *Unemployed workers* – workers who are assumed to be actively seeking jobs but who are not currently employed

3 *Job vacancies* – jobs which are available but which are not currently filled

4 *Family members not in the labour force* – the 'economically inactive' from the viewpoint of the usual definition of the economy. Includes those too young or old to work as well as those not actively seeking work for reasons such as sickness, disability, family ties and so on.

Flows occur in the labour market as a result of changes in the level of some or all of these stocks. Suppose, for example, that a substantial increase occurs in the demand for a particular product. As Figure 3.1 shows, this will probably increase the amount of labour required so that the required workforce comes to exceed the existing stock of employed workers. There will be an *excess demand* for labour. As a result, new job vacancies are created; new 'hires' and 'recalls' will occur as unemployed workers are taken on. Thus, changes occur in each of the main labour market stocks: unemployment is lowered, job vacancies fall, the stock of employed workers

---

*The approach used here is based upon the innovative view of labour markets presented by Holt and David (see, for example, Holt 1970). Carmichael (1978), Cheshire (1979), Gleave and Cordey Hayes (1977) have explored the use of this framework in a geographical context.

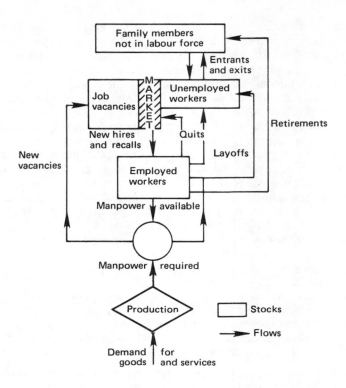

Figure 3.1   A general model of the labour market as a set of stocks and flows

Source: C. Holt (1970) Job search, Phillips' wage relation and union influence, in E.S. Phelps (ed)
Microeconomic Foundations of Employment and Inflation Theory, New York: W.W. Norton, figure 1.

rises. This is not the end of the story, however. Some vacancies created in the market
remain unfilled for rather longer than others and the average duration of unemployment shortens. Under these conditions some workers currently employed but
looking for a change might be persuaded that this is a good time to quit, given the
existence of the new opportunities and the increased likelihood of finding another
job. This follows through to raise the stock of the short-term unemployed while the
'quitters' seek the better jobs, to increase the stock of vacancies and to lower the
numbers of employees in employment. As both vacancies and unemployment rise in
tandem, there is perhaps a greater probability that unfilled jobs will find appropriate
workers among the voluntarily unemployed. New hires result and the stocks shift as
before. In the longer term, then, the number of employees steadily rises, unemployment falls and vacancies remain unfilled for longer. Where this situation per-
sists, however, newly active workers may join the labour force more readily and
migration to the area may increase – raising the supply of workers to the market and
matching the new levels of demand as the system returns to equilibrium.

Of course, the whole process may operate in quite the opposite direction. A
reduction in demand for the product, whether short term (*cyclical*) or long term
(*secular*), will reduce the demand for labour. In the latter case, for example, particu-

lar sectors or industries may be in long-term decline, shedding more workers in general than they take on to replace them and thus contributing more regularly to the build-up of pools of the unemployed and the closing-out of potential job vacancies. The stock of employed workers will exceed the requirements; in other words, there will be an *excess supply* of labour. Employed workers will be laid off either temporarily or permanently; the number of job vacancies will fall, the number of unemployed workers will rise. If the reduction in demand is very general – a recession at the level of the economy at large – the number of workers voluntarily seeking to change jobs is likely to be low. Vigorous attempts will be made by labour unions to protect jobs.

Whatever the direction of changes in the labour market system induced by increases or decreases in demand, there is the additional complication that *labour markets operate in geographical space*. Increased demand for labour may occur in one place but the stock of unemployed workers may be in another place. (In fact, as we shall see in the course of this chapter, this is most often the case in reality.) In a perfect world – or a spaceless one – adjustments would automatically occur through the transfer of available workers from the 'surplus' region to the 'deficit' region. In fact, of course, geographical space exerts a *frictional* effect on labour market adjustment. Where the surplus and deficit areas are virtually adjacent to each other, as, for example, with the inner and outer parts of the same metropolitan areas, labour market adjustment may take the form of commuting. Where, however, the labour markets are widely separated geographically, for example, different regions of the same country or even different countries altogether, then the geographical character of the connecting flows would be quite different. In this case, there would be a need to move home, or at least live temporarily away from it, and the frictional effect would be that of inter-regional (or international) migration rather than commuting.*
In addition, geographical distance often acts as a barrier to the flow of information about job opportunities in different labour markets. For some, geographical space poses insuperable difficulties in searching out vacant jobs, giving a frictional component to unemployment in addition to those of demand deficiency and structure.

We shall be looking in some detail at the operation of *local* labour markets later in this chapter. At this point, while we are taking a broad view of the labour market, it is worth pointing to the enormity of the flows which are continually occurring in the labour markets of modern economies. However crude they may be, the figures help us to appreciate that the labour market is far from static. Figure 3.2, for example, shows the various flow components in the United States labour market between 1960 and 1977. The figures reveal that between 4 and 5 percent of the entire United States labour force left or joined a job every month. They also reveal just how stable the flow components tended to be over the seventeen-year period, suggesting that a self-adjusting mechanism operates to damp down major swings. Figures for the United Kingdom demonstrate similarly large *gross* flows through the labour market:

> In a typical year, there are about 9½ million instances of people leaving their employer. Of these, about 2½ million are students leaving vacation employ-

---

*Cheshire (1979) has coined the terms *continuous* labour market mobility to describe adjustments which do not involve residential relocation and *discontinuous* labour market mobility where residential relocation is involved.

ment and people giving up second jobs. Of the remaining 7 million, about 1½ million move to another employer, 3½ million register as unemployed, 1½ million become sick or inactive and nearly 1 million die, retire or emigrate. These are replaced by 1½ million who find jobs after coming from other employers, ¾ million who leave education, 3½ million who find jobs after being unemployed, and a balance which is largely women entering the labour force and immigrants.
Thatcher (1979), p.33.

Labour markets, then, are complex and dynamic systems characterized, at the national scale, by large-scale flows between the component stocks. At the level of the individual seeking employment there is a host of further complexities. But before looking at these it is useful to outline the major recent trends in the supply of, and the demand for, labour – at changes in employment and unemployment. Such trends, which exhibit a number of disturbing features, are the context within which individual attempts to make a living have to be seen.

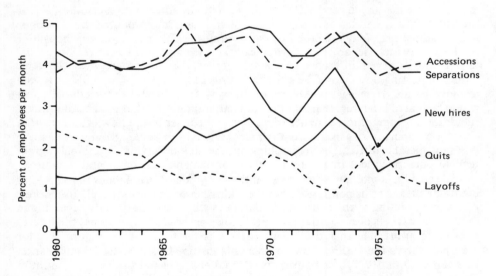

Figure 3.2   Flows in the United States labour market, 1960–1977
Source: United States *Statistical Abstract*, various issues.

LABOUR SUPPLY AND DEMAND: RECENT TRENDS IN EMPLOYMENT AND UNEMPLOYMENT

It is always difficult to make a clear and unambiguous distinction between supply and demand, whatever the object in question, because the two are so intimately related. One of the basic tenets of elementary economics is that supply tends to adjust to demand and demand to supply. Nevertheless, it is useful to make a distinction between the two in order to identify their major features. In examining recent changes in labour supply and demand it is important to distinguish between two broad types of change:

1 Short-term or *cyclical* trends, and

2 Long-term or *secular* trends.

Having said this, it is not always easy in practice to distinguish between them.

What appears at first sight as merely a temporary perturbation may turn out to be the beginnings of a long-term change and vice versa. This is a point we have made already with regard to current developments in the world economy. Most of the empirical examples used in this chapter are drawn from North American and British experiences. However, the *general* characteristics of recent change have been common to virtually all Western industrial societies to a greater or lesser degree. In the following discussion we look initially at recent aggregate changes in employment and unemployment. In the subsequent section we look at the geographical pattern of such changes.

Recent trends in labour supply

Demographic changes
The outside bounds of the labour resources available to a national, urban or regional labour market are determined by the size of the economically active population potentially accessible to its employers. Normally this is seen as the number of people between the effective school-leaving age and the retirement age. While these ages vary with convention from nation to nation they are generally set at around fifteen to sixty-four years of age. Leaving aside other complications for the moment, it is immediately clear that the scale of the economically active population is by no means a constant over time. It is subject to demographic shifts which affect the population as a whole. Wars, baby-booms, the effects on birth and death rates of prosperity and depression will all have their impact on the numbers of people passing through the active age ranges at a given period of time. Migration may also be a substantial variable both internationally and within nations, swelling the active populations of some nations or regions and drawing it down in others. For Britain and the USA, our primary interest here, international migration has been relatively insignificant in recent years although inter-regional migration remains important in determining the stocks of active workers in *local* labour markets.*

Figure 3.3 illustrates the general population trends in the United Kingdom and the United States over the last five decades. Since the death rate does not fluctuate greatly, the main influence on the size of the potentially active population in any one year is the size of the age cohort born some fifteen or sixteen years earlier. On this strictly demographic basis the potentially active population of the United Kingdom

---

*This statement refers to conditions prevailing at the present time when most Western countries impose very stringent and selective immigration regulations. It clearly does not apply to the situation in the 1950s and 1960s in countries such as Canada, Australia and some European countries, including the United Kingdom, France and West Germany. In the latter case, guest workers (*Gastarbeiten*) particularly from Turkey, have been an important element in the labour supply of certain industries, such as motor vehicle manufacture.

first rose and then fell over the period 1961–1971, giving a net increase over the decade of around half a million. During the 1970s, however, the number of young people coming onto the labour market began to increase again and this upward trend will increase the size of the potentially active labour force by approximately 2 million, from 32.5 to 34.5 millions in the early 1990s.*

These trends reflect the passage of the baby-boom after the war, which recorded its peak of live births in the mid-1960s. After this, births fell sharply and are only now beginning to show a slight increase. This more recent upturn is, however, a function of the growing number of women of child-bearing age in the population rather than of increased fertility (number of children per female), which is sharply reduced. Given that the peak of live births was in the mid-1960s, then the United Kingdom is experiencing at present the peak input of young people into the labour market at fifteen–sixteen years of age. In the immediate future this will fall quite sharply to rise again in the mid-1990s.

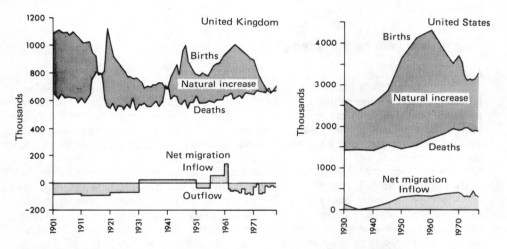

Figure 3.3   Population changes in the United Kingdom and the United States

Source: (left) Central Statistical Office, *Social Trends* 10 (1980), chart 1.5, Crown Copyright; (right) United States *Statistical Abstract* (1978), table 8.

In the case of the United States, demographic trends are similar to those in the United Kingdom but about four or five years ahead. Its active population is also destined to continue growing for much of the 1980s, though a sharp recent drop in live births will see a dip in labour force entry of young people in the mid-1990s. While the active population of the United States will continue to grow, the next decade will see growth at a rather slower rate since the peak of the US baby-boom had its maximimum impact on the labour market in the mid-1970s. Table 3.1 gives some idea of this, showing how different age cohorts account for varying proportions of the total population at different dates. In terms of our present discussion the

---

*These figures, together with much of the discussion in this section, are based upon Gleave (1980).

interesting groups are those of fourteen–seventeen years and eighteen–twenty-one years. In 1950 these made up 5.5 percent and 5.9 percent respectively of the United States population. In 1977 their shares had increased to 7.7 percent and 7.8 percent respectively.

Table 3.1   *Age cohorts in the United States population, 1950–1977*

Year	Under 5 years	5–13 years	14–17 years	18–21 years	22–34 years	35–54 years	55–64 years	65 years and over
	Percentage of total population at each date							
1950	10.8	14.7	5.5	5.9	20.5	25.7	8.8	8.1
1960	11.3	18.2	6.2	5.3	16.3	24.8	8.6	9.2
1970	8.4	17.9	7.8	7.2	17.2	22.7	9.1	9.8
1975	7.4	15.7	7.9	7.7	19.7	21.8	9.3	10.5
1977	7.0	14.9	7.7	7.8	20.7	21.7	9.4	10.8

Source: United States *Statistical Abstract* (1978) table 5

Such national demographic trends will, of course, manifest themselves differently at various geographical scales. For example, metropolitan decentralization will pro-duce a 'stirring' of the population characteristics of urban areas, with the younger, active age groups more concentrated in the suburbs and the older, retirement groups in the urban cores. The processes are too complex for us to enter here, but the subnational spatial implications of broad national demographic trends should be borne carefully in mind.

Changes in participation rates
The demographic changes we have been describing have obviously had an important influence on the changing level of labour supply. In particular, certain periods have seen large numbers of young people entering the labour market. But these are essentially *cyclical* trends; they are short-term in their effect even though they may help to create especially difficult social problems at particular times and in particular places. In the longer term or *secular* sense, the most significant impact on labour supply in recent years has been the result not of broad demographic shifts but rather of changing rates of participation in the labour force among different groups of the population. In this the new role of women in the labour force has been critical, since it has altered both the scale and composition of labour supply. In all Western industrial societies the increasing emancipation of women has been associated with their growing involvement in the labour force. Such involvement has been facilitated by some of the changes in the demand for labour, particularly for labour of different types, which we examine in a subsequent section of this chapter. Particularly important for female participation in the labour market has been the much faster growth rate of jobs in the service sector, jobs which have been taken up predomin-antly by women. Figure 3.4 shows how female participation varied by industry in the United Kingdom in 1971. Within individual industry sectors female participation

Male and female shares of employment in different industries, 1971

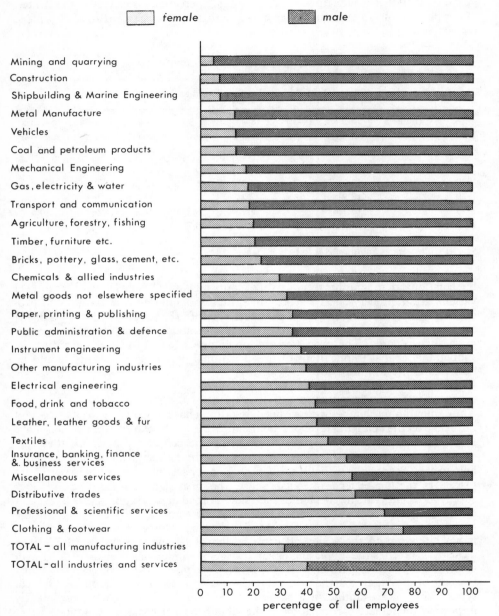

Figure 3.4   Male and female shares of employment in different industries, United Kingdom, 1971.

Source: Department of Employment *Gazette*, January 1975, p.13. Crown Copyright.

grew particularly in the clerical and administrative jobs in manufacturing industry and in professional and scientific services, health and social services.

Figures 3.5 and 3.6 demonstrate the extent to which females have become increasingly involved in the labour forces of the United States and Great Britain in recent years. In 1960, 37 percent of the US female population over sixteen was in the labour force; by 1977 the percentage share had increased to 48. Over the present century as a whole female participation rates in the United States have doubled. Figure 3.5 shows how the recent increase has affected the various age groups differentially. Although the twenty–twenty-four-year age group had the highest labour force involvement in 1977, it was the twenty-five–thirty-four-year age group which showed the biggest increase in participation rate between 1960 and 1977 (from 36 percent to 60 percent). The increased participation rate of both the twenty-five–thirty-four-year and the thirty-five–forty-four-year age group reflects the major feature of change. It is the increase in *married* women in the labour force which accounts for most of the growth in the female labour force.

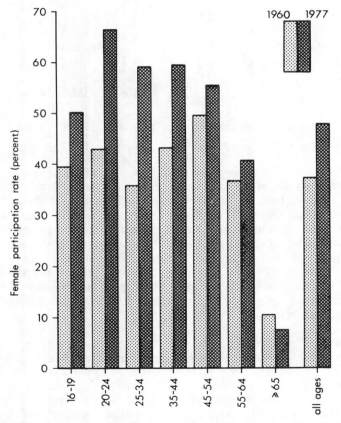

Figure 3.5 Female participation rates in the United States labour force, 1960 and 1977

Source: United States *Statistical Abstract* (1978), table 644.

Figure 3.6 shows this especially clearly for Great Britain. Between 1971 and 1978 the proportion of married women in the labour force increased steadily compared with non-married women and men (in the latter case, male participation rates have remained extremely stable over a long period of time). By 1978, in fact, 50 percent of married women in Britain had jobs (many, of course, were part-time) compared with 10 percent in the 1930s. In the United States approximately 40 percent of married women now have jobs compared with only 5 percent in 1900.

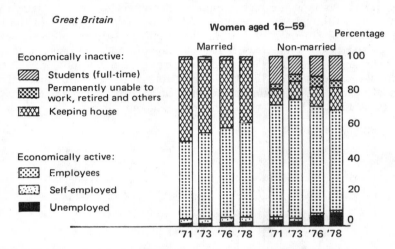

Figure 3.6   Changing female participation rates in Great Britain, 1971–1978

Source: Central Statistical Office, *Social Trends* 10 (1980), chart 5.3. Crown Copyright.

Thus there has been a major social revolution which has affected not only the economy but also society as a whole. One of the characteristic features of modern Western society (though it is by no means unique in this respect) is the emergence of the multiworker family where both mother and father have full-time occupations and the children, according to age, find a variety of short-time, part-time and full-time money-earning occupations. A society dedicated to consumerism and the advertising media has perhaps 'hooked' a more substantial number of its members on the need to earn money for the 'good life' and, in the process, second household incomes have moved from a luxury or necessity (depending on social position) to a norm in most families. In 1970 more than half of all US families had two or more gainfully employed workers.

Recent trends in labour demand
Very substantial changes have been occurring in recent years both in the *level* of labour demand (the numbers of jobs on offer) and in the *nature* of labour demand (the kinds of jobs on offer) in most Western societies. In general, it would seem, there has been more variation in the growth rate of the labour force as a whole between individual countries than in the changes in the type of labour demanded. The United States, for example, saw its employed labour force grow by almost 25 million workers between 1960 and 1977, an increase of nearly 40 percent. Apart from a

minor fall in 1975, the growth trend was positive throughout that period. On the other hand, the United Kingdom's employed labour force grew by a mere 500,000 over a similar period (1961–1976), a growth rate of only 2 percent. In further contrast to the United States, the employed labour force in the United Kingdom peaked in 1966 and has declined since then.

But although experiencing very different employment demand trends in the aggregate, both the United States and the United Kingdom – and most other Western nations – have experienced very similar trends in both the sectoral and occupational composition of their labour forces. Such trends are extremely important in any consideration of how individuals attempt to find jobs and make a living. In the following sections we deal with each one in turn.

Sectoral shifts: the changing balance of functions in the economy

> Fewer people grow things or make things: more people service, entertain, consult, supervise.
> *Hirsch (1977), p.43.*

Hirsch's statement highlights one of the most significant characteristics of modern industrial society: that major shifts have been, and still are, taking place in the relative balance of society's economic functions. Many of these changes are the result – either direct or indirect – of the kinds of technological changes and the organizational and public sector developments we have discussed in Chapter Two. To make our discussion easier, we need to consider for a moment the broad structural – or more properly sectoral – elements of the modern economy. Figure 3.7 provides an outline sketch of the sectors and of the more important flows which make up each sector. The centre of the diagram shows that the economic activities of modern societies are generally divided into four main sectors, while the right-hand side indicates the characteristic links and flows of each sector. The terminology – primary, secondary, tertiary, quaternary – indicates the degree to which each sector is removed from direct involvement with the earth's physical resources. Thus the primary sector is concerned with the direct extraction and manipulation of earth resources. Its output consists of commodities and raw materials which are taken up by the *secondary* (or manufacturing) sector and transformed into manufactured products. These are designed for use either by other producers (producer goods) or for purchase by the population at large (consumer goods).

Few manufacturers sell directly to the domestic consumer; this is one of the functions of the *tertiary* sector in the form of wholesaling and retailing. But the tertiary sector also provides a whole range of other services. At one time, the whole of the so-called non-production sector was included under the tertiary heading, but the sheer heterogeneity of such a classification rendered it somewhat valueless. After all, there is an enormous difference (in function at least) between, say, a junior sales clerk in a retail store and a consultant surgeon, or between a gas station attendant and a nuclear physicist. Yet each was often included in the tertiary category. Such anomalies led the geographer Jean Gottmann (1961) to propose the creation of a new and distinct *quaternary* family of economic activities involving those services that involve transactions, analysis, research or decision-making, as well as education and government. The quaternary sector is now commonly regarded as consisting of those activities which control, administer and co-ordinate a nation's economic activities

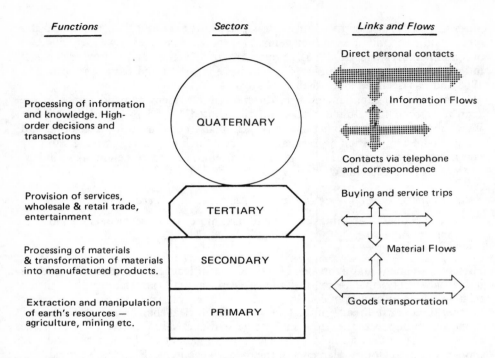

Figure 3.7   Characteristics of the major economic sectors in modern industrial societies

Source: based on G. Tornquist (1973) Contact requirements and travel facilities: contact models of Sweden and regional development alternatives in the future, in A.R. Pred & G. Tornquist *Systems of Cities and Information Flows: Two Essays. Lund Studies in Geography, Series B 38,* figure 1.

and which also provide 'higher-order' services such as finance, research, education and others commensurate with the complexity of modern industrial society. Parts of the public sector, the growth and importance of which we described in Chapter Two, form one of its key elements.

The right-hand section of Figure 3.7 illustrates one of the fundamental differences between the quaternary sector and the others. The primary and secondary sectors are characterized chiefly by flows of materials and of material products through the transportation system. Similarly, the tertiary sector generates material flows through buying and service trips. The quaternary sector, on the other hand, transmits, receives, processes and uses *information* rather than materials. Hence the various parts of the quaternary sector are connected with each other, and with the other major sectors, by flows of information, rather than of materials, either through direct personal contacts or by indirect communication via telephone and correspondence. Figure 3.7, therefore, illustrates the increasingly complex sectoral structure of modern industrial society as well as the growing interdependence of the various sectors which has arisen from its extreme specialization and division of labour.

Over a long period of time the relationship between these four sectors has been changing and the pattern of such change has been extremely regular. Figure 3.8 provides a highly generalized picture of those sectoral shifts which industrial

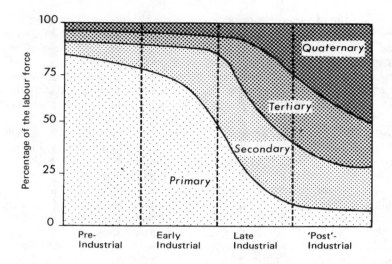

Figure 3.8 Sectoral shifts in the labour force of industrial societies

societies have experienced. It is often argued that economic development in *all* countries will tend to be associated with such a pattern of sectoral change. We do not need to enter that controversy here; for our purposes it is sufficient to regard the sequence shown in Figure 3.8 as a description of how the economic structure of modern industrial societies has changed over time without implying that today's underdeveloped and developing countries will necessarily experience the same pattern of development.

Although we are concerned chiefly with recent changes, it is important to set these against the more general historical sequence. Prior to nineteenth-century industrialization, the primary sector (especially agriculture) employed most of a country's labour force. For example, more than half the total United States labour force in 1870 was employed in agriculture, mining and forestry. As industrialization proceeded, however, and industrial societies matured, the proportion of the labour force employed in the primary sector, especially in agriculture, declined spectacularly. By the late 1970s, only 3.2 percent of the labour force in the United Kingdom and 4.8 percent in the United States continued to find jobs in the primary sector. The same general trend has been evident in all modern industrial societies though with differences of level and timing between one country and another.

Initially, of course, jobs lost in agriculture were replaced by new jobs in the growing manufacturing industries of the cities and towns. As the Western nations became more and more industrialized, the proportion of the labour force employed in the secondary sector increased. For a lengthy period – between the mid-nineteenth and mid-twentieth centuries – manufacturing industry in such industrial societies as the United States, Britain, Canada, Holland and Germany employed between one-quarter and one-third of each country's growing labour force. Taken together, therefore, the primary and secondary sectors consistently employed more than half of the labour force in industrial societies.

This pattern persisted throughout industrial societies until relatively recently.

The first indication of a real change occurred in the United States. Some time in the 1940s, the proportion of the United States labour force employed in the 'service industries' (our tertiary and quaternary sectors) began to exceed the proportion in the primary and secondary sectors – the 'goods-producing' activities. The United States became, in Fuchs' terms, the world's first 'service economy', the first country in which more than 50 percent of the labour force was *not* employed directly in the production of tangible, material goods. By the mid-1970s some two-thirds of the entire United States labour force was employed in the service sector.

Between 1970 and 1976 the general services category, including business and personal services, added 4½ million workers to its payroll and increased its employment share from 25.8 percent to 28.3 percent. Finance, insurance and real estate gained substantially and so also did the wholesale and retail trade category. Together the three main expanding groups in the service sector took up almost 8½ million extra workers during the seven-year period and saw their combined share of the workforce rise by some 4.5 percentage points. The trend has spread to most other industrial nations. Britain's employment in the tertiary and quaternary sectors exceeded half the total labour force by the 1960s and by 1975 these sectors employed 57 percent of the total. The two most prominent growth sectors in terms of their demand for labour over the period 1970–1978 were finance, business, professional and scientific services and the heterogeneous miscellaneous services category. The first of these raised its employment by almost a million or over 25 percent, while the second saw a gain of 269,000, equivalent to a 21.5 percent rise on the 1970 base figure. The much-debated growth of employment in the area of public administration amounted to 155,000 or 10 percent of its earlier stock.

Thus, a very large proportion of this 'service sector' growth is in quaternary activities. As Abler has observed, the advanced nations of the world

> are fast becoming quaternary societies in which most people earn their livings by taking in each other's information.
> *Abler (1975), p.49.*

The size of the quaternary, or information-handling, sector of the economy is directly related to the functional and technological complexity of a society and the organizational and geographical scale of its operations: it varies directly with the degree of *specialization*. The more specialized a society, the greater is the need for such specialized activities to be co-ordinated and controlled or organized. The flow of information is fundamental to this process. The evolution of those large business organizations described in Chapter Two as characterizing the modern business scene epitomizes this relationship, as does the growth of government activities.

Modern industrial society therefore is heavily committed to the collection, production and transmision of information. Such a commitment is reflected in the growth to a position of great importance of what has been termed the *office industry*. This represents a tangible expression of the shift of emphasis in employment terms from the physical processes of production to the processes of organization and control. As Barnet and Muller observe,

> the aluminum-and-glass warehouse on Park Avenue with its rows of steel desks and electric typewriters is the assembly line of the service economy.
> *Barnet and Muller (1975), p.327.*

Initially, the increasing importance of the tertiary and quaternary sectors reflected their faster relative growth rate compared with manufacturing industry, both gaining relatively from the continued decline in agricultural employment. But in the last fifteen to twenty years a quite new phenomenon has become evident: *the proportion employed in manufacturing in most industrial societies has begun to fall*, in some cases quite drastically. Figure 3.9 shows how the manufacturing labour force has been changing in a sample of eight industrial countries between 1950 and 1975. There is, obviously, some variation in the experience of individual countries. Two countries – Japan and Italy – run completely against the general trend in that they have been experiencing rapid manufacturing employment growth (though from far lower 1950 levels than the others). West Germany's manufacturing sector also increased its share of national manufacturing employment at least up to 1970, though it has joined the league of relative employment decline since then. France's manufacturing sector has remained fairly constant at between 27 and 28 percent of the total labour force. The other four nations in Figure 3.9 – the United States, the United Kingdom, the Netherlands and Sweden – all experienced very considerable declines in the proportion of their labour forces employed in manufacturing.

The decline was especially rapid during the 1970s. In the United States, the manufacturing labour force was some three-quarters of a million smaller in 1976 than in 1970. In Britain the decline of the labour force in manufacturing has been very pronounced indeed. For example, between 1948 and 1966, 1.5 million new jobs were created in British manufacturing industry. Between 1970 and 1978, more than 1 million manufacturing jobs disappeared in net terms, a fall of 12.5 percent (the percentage decline in manufacturing employment in the United States was less than one-quarter of this). Table 3.2 shows that every individual sector was in decline in employment terms. Among those changes not distorted by small number bases, the most noteworthy losses were in metal manufacture (-22.6 percent), mechanical engineering (-15.6 percent), textiles (-27.0 percent), leather (-18.4 percent), clothing and footwear (-15.8 percent), bricks, pottery, glass (-15.7 percent) and paper and printing (-13.4 percent). However, the most depressing aspect of the changes is the performance of former growth sectors – vehicles (-8.2 percent) and electrical engineering (-9.7 percent). Thus, traditionally, successful industries like vehicles and engineering have recently joined the long-term group of depressed industries like textiles, clothing, metals and the food industries.

The experience of the United Kingdom may well be rather extreme and the result of particular national circumstances. On the other hand, what has been termed *de-industrialization* could well be the future experience of other 'advanced' Western economies.* Certainly, as Figure 3.9 demonstrates, there is a clear *general* trend

---

De-industrialization has become a widely used term in the British context. While some economists see the loss of employment in manufacturing as no more than a rather extreme form of sectoral shift in an economy which, after all, was built on a foundation of manufacturing and of exports of industrial products, others view it with a deeper concern. The essence of the de-industrialization debate is discussed at length in Blackaby (1979) and the reader can explore the issue more deeply there. Briefly, two schools of thought have emerged on the possible causes of Britain's industrial demise. On the one hand there are those who see it as public sector growth squeezing out national enterprise (the Bacon-Eltis group), on the other those who see it as a function of low export performance and an endemic propensity to import (the Cambridge group).

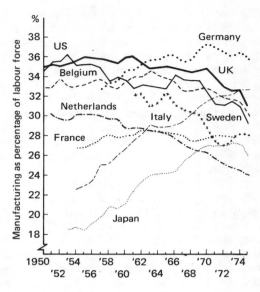

Figure 3.9 Changes in the proportion of the labour force employed in manufacturing industry, selected industrial countries, 1950–1975

Source: C.J.F. Brown & T.D. Sheriff (1979) De-Industrialization: a background paper, in F. Blackaby (ed) *De-Industrialization*, London: Heinemann Educational Books Ltd., chart 10.2.

towards a relative decline in the manufacturing labour force. For the most part such decline has been matched by an increase in labour demand in the tertiary and, more particularly, the quaternary sectors of all Western economies.

Occupational changes

The sectoral shifts in labour demand discussed in the preceding section refer to changes in the type of economic activity in which people work. The sectors, in fact, are defined in terms of what they produce, their characteristic output. But quite apart from a consideration of where people work (in the sense of which economic sector), there is also the question of what kinds of tasks people perform when they are at work. In other words, we should also ask about the kinds of changes that have been occurring in the demand for different *occupations*. In addition to the sectoral shifts there have also been occupational changes of very great significance.

The most obvious changes relate to the broad categories of blue-collar (manual) workers and white-collar workers.* In all Western industrial societies, a larger and larger proportion of the labour force is to be found in white-collar occupations and a declining proportion in blue-collar occupations. Figure 3.10 demonstrates this trend for the United States. Blue-collar workers as a percentage of the total labour force

---

*Some critics have objected to the traditional blue-collar, white-collar dichotomy on the grounds that many service and clerical jobs are actually blue-collar in that they demand a significant amount of manual labour (see Levison 1974).

Table 3.2   *United Kingdom: manufacturing employment change, 1970–1978*

	Employment (000s)		Percentage change
	1970	1978	1971–1978
Food, drink and tobacco	792	717	−9.5
Coal and petroleum products	48	37	−23.0
Chemicals and allied industries	442	431	−2.5
Metal manufacture	593	459	−22.6
Mechanical engineering	1106	934	−15.6
Instrument engineering	163	149	−8.6
Electrical engineering	828	748	−9.7
Shipbuilding and marine engineering	191	183	−4.2
Vehicles	842	773	−8.2
Metal goods n.e.s.	595	540	−9.2
Textiles	678	495	−27.0
Leather, leather goods and fur	49	40	−18.4
Clothing and footwear	455	383	−15.8
Bricks, pottery, glass	318	268	−15.7
Timber, furniture, etc.	271	264	−2.6
Paper, printing	626	542	−13.4
Other manufacturing	345	335	−2.9

Source: Annual Abstract of Statistics (1980) table 6.1. Crown Copyright

reached a peak between the 1920s and 1950s when they formed the largest single occupational group in the country. In 1920, for example, blue-collar workers accounted for 40 percent of the total labour force, compared with farm workers 27 percent and white-collar workers 25 percent. By 1977 the relative position of blue-collar and white-collar workers was reversed: almost one worker in every two was in a white-collar occupation by that date, while the blue-collar percentage had declined to 33 percent. These changing proportions reflect major differences in the relative growth rate of the two occupational groups (see the inset in Figure 3.10). Between 1960 and 1977, white-collar employment in the United States increased by almost 60 percent, blue-collar employment by 25 percent.

But the changes have not been evenly spread within the white- and blue-collar occupation groups, as Table 3.3 demonstrates. Within the white-collar occupations it was the professional and technical category which showed the greatest growth. In the blue-collar group, operatives declined in relative importance as did labourers. The farm workers group continued its sharp decline, halving its share between 1960 and 1970 and falling still further to account for only 3 percent of the active population in 1977. The service group of workers, who by the blue-collar/white-collar tag might be described as perhaps 'uniformed' – janitors, elevator attendants, policemen, firemen, hospital workers, etc. – maintained a comparatively stable 12–13 percent of the employed workforce over the period.

The demand for labour is, of course, a derived demand arising from shifting needs and wants and from the means for satisfying them in society. Hence the detail

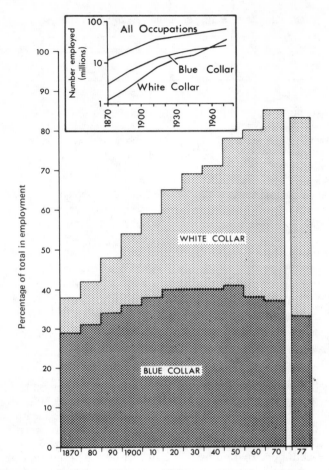

Figure 3.10   The changing relative importance of blue-collar and white-collar workers in the United States, 1870–1977

Source: United States *Statistical Abstract*, various issues.

of the job shifts can tell us something about the nature of changing demand. For example, within the fast-expanding professional, technical and kindred workers class (+83 percent 1960–1977), the fastest growing element was that consisting of programmers, systems analysts and other computer specialists. There were also sharp increases in employment in higher education, in the 'knowledge-based' society. University teachers as a group increased by 150 percent in the decade 1960–1970 and high school teachers by 80 percent. In part, of course, this also reflects the extra demands on the educational system made by the passage of the postwar baby-boom through the high schools and onto the campuses. Clerical workers became the largest single occupational group in the USA during the 1960s, replacing the blue-collar operatives group which dominated the labour force before 1960. Sixteen million

Table 3.3   *United States: distribution of employment by major occupational groups, 1960, 1970 and 1977*

	1960 Millions	1960 %	1970 Millions	1970 %	1977 Millions	1977 %
White-collar workers	28.5	42.7	38.0	48.3	45.2	50.0
Professional, technical	7.5	11.2	11.1	14.1	13.7	15.1
Managers and administrators	7.1	10.6	8.3	10.6	9.7	10.7
Salesworkers	4.2	6.3	4.9	6.2	5.7	6.3
Clerical	9.8	14.7	13.7	17.4	16.1	17.8
Blue-collar workers	24.1	36.1	27.8	35.4	30.2	33.4
Craftworkers	8.6	12.9	10.2	13.0	11.9	13.1
Operatives except transport	} 12.0	} 18.2	} 13.9	} 17.7	10.4	11.5
Transport equipment operatives					3.5	3.9
Labourers except farm	3.5	5.2	3.7	4.7	4.5	4.9
Farm workers	5.1	7.6	3.1	3.9	2.8	3.0
Service workers	8.9	13.3	9.7	12.3	12.4	13.8

Source: United States *Statistical Abstract* (1978) table 679

Americans now hold clerical jobs, catching up rapidly on those 25 million craft-workers and operatives who find employment in what some call the 'real' economy – physically making things. Elsewhere 12 million Americans find jobs providing personal services for their fellow citizens. The majority of these are in the food industries, in cleaning and in health-service occupations.

Such major occupational shifts, experienced to much the same general degree in all Western societies, reflect in part those broad sectoral changes we described earlier, with the progressive shift of labour demand from the primary and secondary sectors to the tertiary and quaternary sectors. In particular, much of the increase in white-collar employment results from a massive increase in public sector employment generally – especially education, health, government and the other public institutions – plus the growth of finance, insurance and other high-level business and professional services. But this is not the whole explanation. Cutting across those occupational changes associated directly with sectoral changes is the fact that occupational change has been occurring *within* sectors and industries. This, too, is primarily a shift of emphasis from blue-collar to white-collar employment, an increasing 'professionalization' of all sectors, though at varying rates:

Just as over time there is a flow of labour from the primary and secondary industries into the more advanced, there is a progressive net movement

from the unskilled manual occupations into the educated ranks of the professions, even within older industries.
Foote and Hatt (1953), p.367.

This shift in the relative importance of production and non-production workers has been especially large within the manufacturing sector itself and contributes further to the increase in white-collar employment in the economy as a whole. Table 3.4 shows that in the United States between 1947 and 1976 the number of non-production workers in manufacturing more than doubled while the number of production workers grew by only 4.6 percent. (By non-production workers we mean administrative, sales, research, personnel and other technical staff; production workers are those who are employed in manual jobs on the 'shopfloor'.) Similarly in the United Kingdom, as Figure 3.11 shows, non-production workers have steadily become a larger and larger proportion of total manufacturing employment. In 1924, a little over 10 percent of the manufacturing workforce was in non-production activities; by 1975 the proportion had increased to almost 30 percent.

Table 3.4 *Production and non-production workers in United States manufacturing industry, 1947 and 1976*

	1947		1976		Increase 1947–1976	
	Number (millions)	%	Number (millions)	%	Number (millions)	%
All manufacturing	15.6	100.0	19.0	100.0	+3.4	+22.6
Production workers	13.0	83.3	13.6	71.6	+0.6	+4.6
Non-production workers	2.6	16.7	5.4	28.4	+2.8	+108.0

Source: U.S. Department of Labor (1974) *Manpower Report of the President*; United States *Statistical Abstract* (1977) table 657

The implications of these major occupational shifts in modern industrial society are very considerable indeed. As Fuchs observed,

changes in the industrial distribution of employment have implications for where and how men live, the education they need, and even the health hazards they face. . . . [They affect] . . . the kind of work people do, the kinds of organizations they work for, the location of the work, and many other critical aspects of their lives.
Fuchs (1968), pp.183, 184.

White-collar occupations, in particular, possess a number of attributes which set them apart from the rest. First, they have proved, so far at least, to be far less susceptible to cyclical instability. Estall makes the point that, whereas production occupations in United States manufacturing fell markedly in the recessions of 1954 and 1971, non-production occupations were hardly affected at all. Second, the

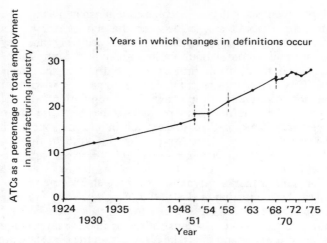

Figure 3.11 Growth of non-production employment in UK manufacturing industry, 1924–1975

Source: G. Gudgin, R.E. Crum & S. Bailey (1979) White collar employment in U.K. manufacturing industry, in P. W. Daniels (ed) *Spatial Patterns of Office Growth and Location*, London: Wiley, figure 5.1.

general level of salaries in white-collar occupations tends to be relatively high, even though the category does contain some low-paying jobs. Closely related to this is the fact that working conditions tend to be more congenial and career structures more in evidence than in blue-collar employment. Finally, the white-collar occupations generally demand higher levels of educational qualifications.

This latter point is especially important. The increasing professionalization of occupations, the shift from unskilled to skilled work, the movement from manual to non-manual employment, the growing importance of the quaternary sector are all associated with, and based upon, wider access to higher standards of education. Educational institutions, therefore, are becoming ever more important in the assignment of prestige and occupational position in industrial society, and social mobility and economic advancement are very much a function of such access. More and more tasks in modern industrial society demand higher levels of education. The sectoral and occupational changes occurring in modern Western societies are thus leading to

> the escalation of education credentials . . . the job formerly open to high school graduates now demands a college degree.
> *Hirsch (1977), p.31.*

Mismatches between labour supply and demand: trends in unemployment

Rising unemployment

One of the clearest, and most perturbing, features of the labour markets of Western nations in the last decade is their increasing inability to provide enough jobs. High levels of unemployment seem to have become endemic in many nations. Of course, a perfect balance in the labour market between the demand for particular types of labour and the supply of precisely matching types is probably unachievable in a real world. As we have pointed out, labour markets are dynamic, not static. Demand for labour changes over time – sometimes very rapidly – so that even under ideal circumstances there is likely to be some delay in matching it with labour supply. Even in boom conditions some proportion of the population is likely to be unemployed. Indeed, boom conditions may promote some *short-term* unemployment as workers are persuaded to quit their present job in an atmosphere where they are more confident of finding another. Any rise of this kind in the levels of labour turnover will inevitably find rather more people 'between jobs', registering as unemployed while they search for new work opportunities.

Not only are labour markets dynamic, they are also segmented in a number of ways, particularly by occupation or skill and by geography. As a result, certain basic *frictions* occur in matching flows of workers to new vacancies. Where, in addition, demand is falling for certain occupations and rising in others, problems of *mismatch* occur even where these rises and falls take place within the same labour market area. The skills acquired in those jobs now less in demand are not necessarily translatable to the new generation of job opportunities.

Nevertheless, there is a growing awareness that, apart from short-term problems of adjustment, the underlying trend of long-term unemployment is rising in many Western nations. The capacity to absorb both new and displaced workers seems to be declining. Table 3.5 shows that over the ten-year period 1967–1976 unemployment rates doubled in the four industrial countries. More significant, however, is the fact that, with the exception of West Germany, unemployment rates were already moving sharply upwards *before* the 1973 oil crisis.

Table 3.5   *Unemployment in selected Western nations, 1967–1976*

	Percent unemployed		
	1967	1971	1976
United States	3.8	5.9	7.7
United Kingdom	2.3	3.5	5.8
Canada	4.1	6.4	7.1
West Germany	2.1	0.8	4.6

Source: International Labor Office (1977) *Yearbook of Labor Statistics*

Two features of the current employment situation are particularly significant. One is the tendency for the *duration* of unemployment to be getting longer: for the long-term unemployed to constitute a larger proportion of the unemployed total. Figure 3.12 demonstrates this trend for Great Britain. In 1951, approximately

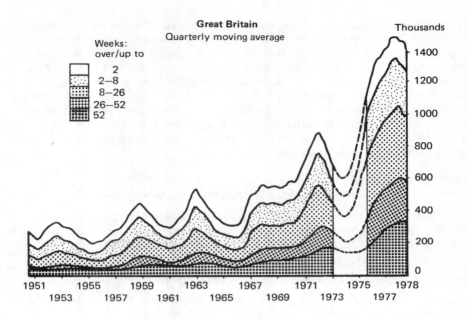

Figure 3.12   The increasing duration of unemployment: Great Britain, 1951–1978
Source: Central Statistical Office, *Social Trends* 10 (1980), chart 5.14. Crown Copyright.

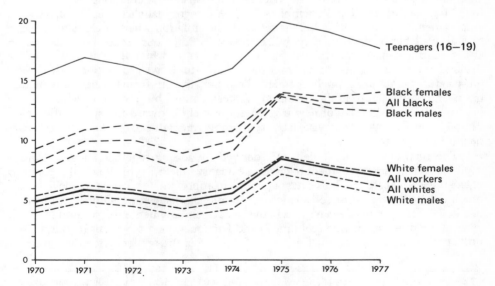

Figure 3.13   Unemployment rates by population group, United States, 1970–1977
Source: United States *Statistical Abstract* (1978), table 667.

12 percent of the unemployed population had been out of work for more than one year. In 1978, 23 percent were in this category. The second feature is that unemployment tends to be much higher among some sections of the population than amongst others. Young people, members of ethnic minorities and women, in particular, tend to experience higher rates of unemployment. Figure 3.13 gives some indication of such variation in the United States during the 1970s. The pattern of 'unemployment stratification' is extremely regular. Youth unemployment is consistently very much higher than that of adults, black unemployment much higher than white. Within both the black and white groups, female unemployment is consistently higher than male unemployment.

Types of unemployment
Conventionally, unemployment is divided into three basic types:

1 *Frictional unemployment.* Theoretically, when the supply of labour equals the demand for labour there should be no unemployment. But there are inevitably delays or lags in workers finding jobs, hence frictional unemployment.

2 *Structural unemployment* is produced by long-term shifts in the economy, in particular the decline of certain industries or occupations.

3 *Cyclical unemployment* is produced by deficiencies in demand produced by downswings in the economy – slumps and recessions.

Although each of these categories has particular characteristics it is not always possible to distinguish between them in practice. Table 3.6 is one attempt to disaggregate the unemployment performance of some industrial nations into its component parts. In the table, the frictional and structural components are combined together as 'frictional unemployment'. A category labelled 'capital-shortage employment' is also identified. This refers to the situation where there is too little capital available to equip and mobilize the available labour force. For example, either existing capacity may be established in sectors for which there is insufficient demand or new capital investment may be in capital-intensive production with a low job-product per unit of capital expended. Traditionally, this form of unemployment has been relatively rare in the advanced Western nations but more recently, either because of a real shortage of new investment or a shift toward the substitution of capital for increasingly high wage labour, unemployment due to capital shortage has begun to reappear.

The final column of Table 3.6 is derived by adding together frictional and capital-shortage unemployment to create a category 'unemployment at full capacity of existing capital stock'. This category seems to approximate what has come to be a much-debated notion – the so-called *natural rate of unemployment.** Quite apart from detailed differences between nations in the basic unemployment rate (column 1), the cyclical unemployment rate (column 2) and frictional unemployment (column 3), probably the most significant feature of Table 3.6 is the tendency for the natural

---

*The debate over the natural rate of unemployment is part of the current monetarist controversies taking place in most Western economies and stimulated in particular by the work of Milton Friedman. For a discussion of the relationship between unemployment and inflation see Friedman (1975).

unemployment rate to be rising in *all* cases. More specifically, the evidence of Table 3.6 seems to suggest that the gloomy underlying truth is of a growing inability of the advanced industrial nations to 'soak up' available labour supply even at full economic capacity.

Table 3.6 *Components of unemployment change*

	Unemployment rate	Cyclical unemployment	Frictional unemployment	Capital-shortage unemployment	Unemployment at full capacity of existing capital stock
United States					
1974	5.5	0.6	4.9	0.0	4.9
1975	8.4	3.3	4.9	0.2	5.1
1976	7.6	2.1	4.9	0.6	5.5
France					
1974	2.8	0.3	2.4	0.1	2.5
1975	4.1	1.3	2.4	0.4	2.8
1976	4.5	1.1	2.5	0.9	3.4
United Kingdom					
1974	2.2	0.1	2.0	0.1	2.1
1975	3.4	0.7	2.2	0.5	2.7
1976	5.0	1.7	2.4	0.9	3.3
Germany					
1974	2.2	0.4	1.5	0.3	1.8
1975	4.2	1.2	2.2	0.8	3.0
1976	4.1	0.6	2.5	1.0	3.5
Italy					
1974	5.9	0.1	5.0	0.8	5.8
1975	6.7	0.3	5.0	1.4	6.4
1976	7.2	0.4	5.0	1.8	6.8
Netherlands					
1974	3.0	0.5	1.6	0.9	2.5
1975	4.3	1.4	1.8	1.1	2.9
1976	4.7	1.2	2.0	1.5	3.5

Source: OECD (1978) *A Medium Term Strategy for Employment and Manpower Policy*, Paris: OECD, table 4

Summary

A number of clear general trends are apparent in the changing supply of, and demand for, labour in modern Western societies. The *supply* of labour, of individuals in the relevant age groups, has grown in recent years. At the same time, its composition has been changing. The two main forces producing such changes have been cyclical upturns in birth rates in the postwar period, which have eventually brought large numbers of young people onto the labour market, and a secular increase in the participation of females, especially married females, in the labour force. Of course, these are not the only factors involved. Other developments which tend to reduce the labour supply are the longer period of time spent in formal education (for example, the raising of the school-leaving age and the increased numbers in post-school education) and the trend towards earlier retirement. Migration – both inward and outward – may be another influence, although in recent years its importance has been expressed at the subnational rather than the national scale. Significant as these and other influences may be, however, it is the combination of high birth rates at particular times since 1945 and the more general trend of increased female participation which have been the major influences on changing labour supply.

The level and composition of labour *demand* in Western economies have also been changing radically in recent years. Sectoral and occupational shifts, in particular, have created a whole series of changes. Tertiary and quaternary jobs have increased while the manufacturing demand for labour has declined. This general trend towards a smaller manufacturing labour force is particularly intense in the United Kingdom, reflecting, some would argue, a tendency towards de-industrialization of the economy. A good many of these non-manufacturing jobs have gone to women as their involvement in the labour force has grown. Occupationally, the trend is away from production activities to non-production activities, from blue-collar to white-collar occupations. The economic and social repercussions of these changes are very considerable, particularly when they help to produce mismatches between the supply of labour and the demand for labour. One clear feature of recent years is the rising rate of unemployment. Although to some extent this is caused by the recession of the 1970s (partly precipitated by the oil crisis of 1973), there seems to be an underlying trend towards both higher unemployment rates and also unemployment of longer duration. In addition, unemployment tends to affect some parts of the population more than others.

THE GEOGRAPHY OF RECENT EMPLOYMENT CHANGE

In examining recent trends in employment and unemployment we have been concerned with aggregate trends at the national scale. But jobs are created and jobs are destroyed or displaced in specific geographic locations within national economies: the broad aggregate trends have a particular geographical expression. In this section, therefore, we first of all examine the geography of recent changes in employment at different spatial scales and, secondly, explore some of the more important processes which are producing such changes.

Spatial patterns of recent employment change

When we try to look at spatial changes in employment we are very much dependent upon the geographical scale at which data are available. As we suggested in Chapter One, our view and interpretation of any spatial distribution is greatly influenced by the 'level of resolution' adopted.* However, allowing for such complications, and for the fact that there are detailed geographical differences in employment change between different nations, it seems possible to identify three *general* spatial trends:

1 Broad geographical or 'inter-regional' changes;

2 Intermetropolitan and urban-rural changes;

3 Intrametropoltan changes, specifically the differential employment performance of central-city and suburban areas.

Of course, these three trends are not independent of each other. For example, some of the broad inter-regional employment shifts are, in part, a reflection of differential changes at the intermetropolitan and urban-rural level. Similarly, the nature of intrametropolitan changes depends, in part, upon their regional location. Despite these problems of overlap, however, these three general trends appear to express much of the currently changing geography of employment in modern Western societies. The empirical examples used to illustrate them are drawn from United States and United Kingdom experience.

Inter-regional changes in employment

Broad geographical shifts in economic activity and, hence, in levels and types of employment are particularly clearly seen within the United States. Traditionally, the United States has displayed a classic core-periphery pattern of employment; the industrial base of the nation was the manufacturing belt of the Northeast. In 1958 Edward Ullman described the dominance of the belt bounded by Boston in the North, Chicago in the West and Baltimore in the East in graphic terms. He showed that 68 percent of United States manufacturing activity and 43 percent of its population were located in the manufacturing belt on a mere 7.7 percent of the nation's land area.

The belt also provided the focus for transport flows, the organizational pivot of the nation's enterprise with its concentration of headquarters' activities and, perhaps more important, the source of new ideas and technological innovation. It was, in short, the classic core region dominating the national economy and casting its net of hegemony across its 'colonial fiefs' in the states of the periphery. The belt exported its products to them, supplied them with capital, imported their raw materials, drew away their young families as migrants.

Some twenty-two years after Ullman described the dominance of the manufacturing belt, the broad geography of employment in the United States looks very different. As Figure 3.14 shows, the relative growth trends of the traditional core and periphery have been reversed, at least in terms of manufacturing employment.

---

*In the particular case of employment change in the United Kingdom, for example, Fothergill and Gudgin (1979) point out that although we have generally adopted a 'regional' level of resolution – specifically the eleven official regions – there is far more variation in employment change *within* such regions than between them.

Figure 3.14   Changing manufacturing employment between the manufacturing belt and 'the periphery' in the United States, 1954–1977

Source: R.D. Norton & J. Rees (1979) The product cycle and the spatial decentralization of American manufacturing, *Regional Studies*, 13, figure 1.

Norton and Rees (1979) set the year 1966 as the 'historical breakpoint', but the years 1969–1977 present the most revealing shifts. Between 1969 and 1977, for example, the traditional manufacturing belt lost 1.3 million jobs while the periphery gained 700,000.

The current popular view of broad geographical change within the United States gives it a climatic label – the Sunbelt is seen to be gaining at the expense of the Snowbelt.* But although the cities of the South and Southwest have certainly experienced spectacular economic growth in recent years, the pattern of employment change seems to be rather broader than the Sunbelt–Snowbelt dichotomy suggests. Certainly Norton and Rees see the post-1966 developments as core-periphery rather than as North-South changes. They base their view on the pattern shown in Figure 3.15, pointing out that the twenty-nine states which had manufacturing employment growth greater than that of California (+10.1 percent) were outside the traditional core region. Figure 3.15 also reflects the broad sectoral changes which have occurred in recent years. Whereas seventeen states experienced a decline in manufacturing employment between 1966 and 1977, every state increased its service employment. But with only a few exceptions, the states experiencing most service employment growth were outside the traditional core.

---

*See Perry and Watkins (1977), *The Rise of the Sun Belt Cities*, for a series of essays on this phenomenon.

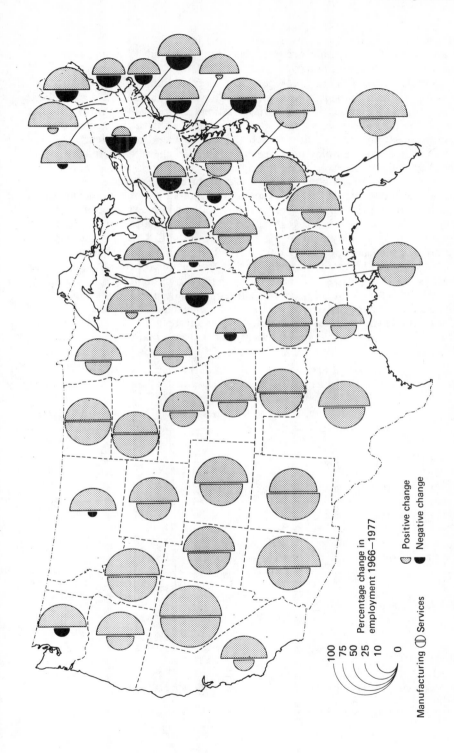

Figure 3.15 Employment change in manufacturing and in services in the United States, 1966–1977

Source: based on R.D. Norton & J. Rees (1979) The product cycle and the spatial decentralization of American manufacturing, *Regional Studies*, 13, table 1.

These sectoral trends are also paralleled by occupational changes. Table 3.7 shows the broad regional shifts which occurred between 1960 and 1975 in white-collar occupations and production employment.

Broad regional changes in employment are also evident in the United Kingdom. Although it is difficult to identify Sunbelts and Snowbelts – a nationwide 'Rainbelt' is probably more accurate, though with variations in intensity – rather similar core-periphery shifts are apparent in recent experience.* As in the United States, it is manufacturing employment change which shows this trend most clearly. Figure 3.16 shows considerable employment growth in the peripheral areas in addition to substantial growth in the South (excluding London). But there was either slow growth, or even absolute decline, in many parts of the core. Figure 3.17 gives some idea of how the broad spatial pattern of manufacturing employment changed quite dramatically between 1959 and 1966 on the one hand and between 1966 and 1971 on the other. In 1959, according to Keeble, the core regions contained 54 percent of total manufacturing employment in the United Kingdom. This was the result of massive growth focused upon the London and Birmingham conurbations. In the 1960s, however, there was a 'dramatic reversal' in the fortunes of core and periphery.

The 1959 to 1966 period was one of national growth in manufacturing employment. Spatially, only ten of the sixty-two subregions shown in Figure 3.17 experienced an absolute decline in manufacturing employment (mainly the old-established large industrial conurbations of London, Manchester, West Yorkshire and Clydeside). Although most peripheral areas gained some manufacturing employ-

Table 3.7   *Regional changes in white-collar and production occupations, United States*

	North-east	Central	South	West	Nation
White-collar occupations					
1960 (percent)	28.1	28.3	26.4	17.2	100.0
1970 (percent)	26.8	26.9	28.0	18.3	100.0
Percent annual average change	2.8	2.8	4.0	4.0	3.3
Production employment					
1963 (percent)	31.8	32.3	24.5	11.4	100.0
1972 (percent)	26.4	32.0	29.6	12.0	100.0
Percent annual average change	–0.5	0.6	1.9	1.0	0.7

Source: R.B. Armstrong (1979) National trends in office construction, employment and headquarter location in U.S. metropolitan areas, in P.W. Daniels (ed) *Spatial Patterns of Office Growth and Location*, Chichester: Wiley, table 3.6

*In discussing manufacturing employment change, Keeble (1976) defines the core in terms of proximity to the London-Birmingham axis.

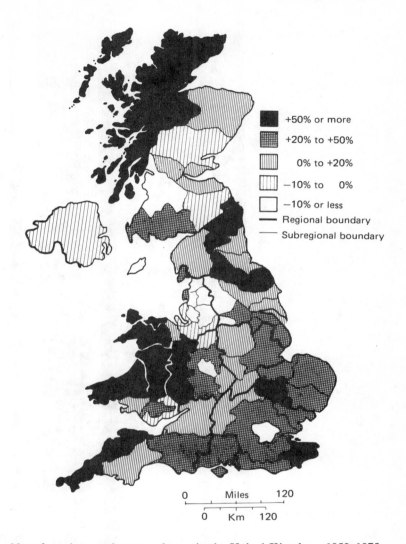

Legend:
- +50% or more
- +20% to +50%
- 0% to +20%
- −10% to 0%
- −10% or less
- ——— Regional boundary
- —— Subregional boundary

0   Miles   120
0   Km   120

Figure 3.16 Manufacturing employment change in the United Kingdom, 1959–1975

Source: S. Fothergill & G. Gudgin (1979) Regional employment change: a subregional explanation, *Progress in Planning*, 12, figure 2.1.

ment during the early 1960s the map was still dominated by the core – particularly the outer metropolitan area of Southeast England and the West Midlands. The pattern altered substantially after 1966 – which was also the year in which national employment in manufacturing began to decline. Spatially, decline was experienced in virtually all the major industrial centres, particularly the five largest conurbations. In contrast, the periphery gained manufacturing jobs, as did areas adjacent to the declining major cities. Service employment change differed substantially from that of manufacturing. Figure 3.18 shows that the fastest growth rates of service em-

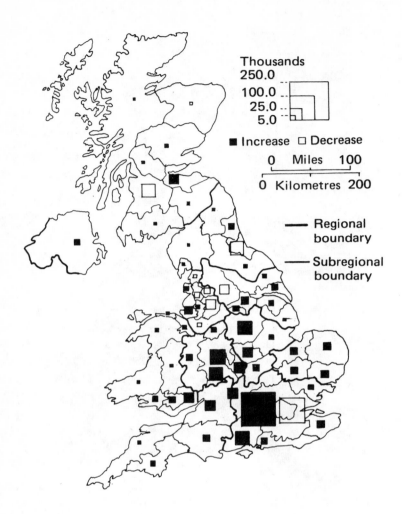

Figure 3.17a   Regional change in manufacturing employment in the United Kingdom, 1959–1966

Source: D. Keeble (1976) *Industrial Location and Planning in the United Kingdom*, London: Methuen, figures 2.3a and 2.3b.

ployment were in the Southeast, East Anglia and parts of the Midlands. Service employment did not grow substantially in the periphery.

Some idea of the changing geographical distribution of occupations over time in Britain can be gained from Table 3.8. The table is in the form of a regional 'balance sheet' and shows very clearly how professional and managerial occupations in particular became more highly concentrated into the Southeast region. Five of the

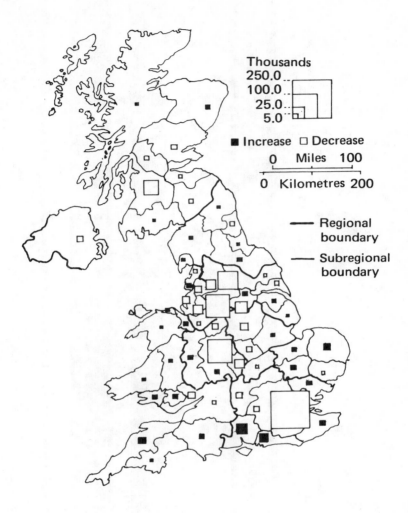

Figure 3.17b   Regional change in manufacturing employment in the United Kingdom, 1966–1971

Source: D. Keeble (1976) *Industrial Location and Planning in the United Kingdom*, London: Methuen, figures 2.3a and 2.3b.

ten regions had a net gain of professional and managerial occupations but the net gain by the Southeast region was more than double that of the combined gain by the other four. These regions made substantial gains in the lower-level administration category and in manual occupations. Two regions, Yorkshire and Humberside and the Northern region, lost substantial numbers of professional and managerial jobs, gained some administrative jobs but lost manual jobs. The Northern region is

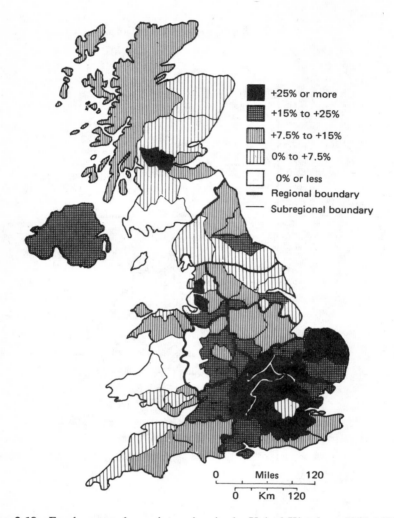

Figure 3.18   Employment change in services in the United Kingdom, 1959–1971

Source: S. Fothergill & G. Gudgin (1979) Regional employment change: a subregional explanation, *Progress in Planning*, 12, figure 2.2.

interesting in that it gained more than 5000 administrative jobs but lost almost 25,000 manual jobs. Finally, three regions – Wales, the Northwest and Scotland – lost substantial numbers in all occupations.

In terms of non-production occupations in manufacturing – which we have seen to be a rapidly growing occupational group – Table 3.9 shows just how uneven geographically such occupations are in Great Britain. Column 3 shows the difference in non-production employment between actual employment (column 1) and that which might be expected on the basis of the national ratio of non-production workers

Table 3.8 *Regional 'balance sheet' of shifts in professional/managerial and administrative occupations, Great Britain, 1961–1966**

Region	Professional & managerial†	Administrative	Manual
Southeast	+14,336	+2,133	−2,149
Southwest	+574	+3,452	+21,769
West Midlands	+4,178	+7,894	+39,588
East Midlands	+1,517	+4,825	+21,299
East Anglia	+93	+608	+19,453
Yorkshire & Humberside	−5,546	+1,000	−1,950
North	−2,664	+5,047	−24,835
Wales	−4,929	−2,272	−11,519
Northwest	−1,738	−7,348	−19,865
Scotland	−5,823	−15,357	−40,918

* Refers to economically active males only.

† Includes males working in all non-manufacturing sectors, plus doctors and schoolteachers.

Source: J. Westaway (1974) Contact potential and the occupational structure of the British urban system, 1961–1966: An empirical study, *Regional Studies*, 8, table 4

Table 3.9 *Regional employment disparities of non-production employment, Great Britain, 1971*

	Employment in thousands		
Region	Actual employment (1)	Expected employment (2)	Actual minus expected employment (3)
North	137.6	171.5	−33.9
Yorkshire & Humberside	246.8	295.0	−48.2
East Midlands	184.5	223.4	−38.9
East Anglia	68.1	70.8	−2.7
Southeast	981.6	698.6	+283.0
Southwest	149.9	144.0	+5.9
Northwest	387.4	435.1	−47.7
West Midlands	354.9	403.8	−48.9
Wales	97.5	127.3	−29.8
Scotland	215.5	254.2	−38.7

Source: G. Gudgin, R. Crum & S. Bailey (1979) White collar employment in U.K. manufacturing industry, in P.W. Daniels (ed) *Spatial Patterns of Office Growth and Location*, Chichester: Wiley, table 5.7

to operatives (column 2). The spatial differences shown in column 3 are very striking. Every region outside the Southeast and Southwest had a 'deficit' of non-production workers in manufacturing in 1971. But it is the sheer size of the 'excess' in the Southeast which is so remarkable: the region had 282,000 'extra' non-production jobs. In fact, most of these were in managerial and clerical occupations.

Intermetropolitan and urban-rural changes in employment

The broad regional shifts in employment outlined in the previous section are an amalgam of changes occurring at smaller geographical scales, in particular at the intermetropolitan scale. Thus employment growth in the United States has been especially rapid in the metropolitan areas of the South and the Southwest – for example, in Atlanta, Phoenix, Dallas, Houston. Together with the counterpoised decline of large northern industrial metropolises, these intermetropolitan changes are part of the general geographical shifts which have been occurring in the United States economy. But there is an additional dimension of change involved which relates to the metropolitan system itself and to the urban-rural dimension.

The intermetropolitan and urban-rural pattern of employment is changing in ways which, in some cases, cut across the broad regional shifts. We have already pointed to the redistribution of population which is occurring in the United States in Chapter Two. In employment terms there is a growing involvement of non-metropolitan and rural areas in manufacturing activity in both the core and the periphery. Some of this development is, in effect, an 'overspill' of activity from the adjacent metropolitan areas and is really part of the process of intrametropolitan decentralization discussed in the next section. But not all is of this kind. For example, Heaton and Fuguitt (1978) calculate that between 1950 and 1970 the percentage of the labour force employed in manufacturing increased from 14.2 percent to 19.8 percent in urban areas which were *not* adjacent to SMSAs and from 9.1 percent to 14.8 percent in rural areas not adjacent to SMSAs. They also show that such increases in non-metropolitan areas were not confined to the Sunbelt but were also evident in 'Frostbelt' areas, though to a lesser degree.

The relative shift to smaller metropolitan areas and to non-metropolitan areas continued in the 1970s:

> While the 225 largest Standard Metropolitan Statistical Areas suffered a net loss of 513,000 jobs in manufacturing between 1970 and 1978, non-metropolitan counties experienced an increase of 619,000 manufacturing jobs. . . . An additional 3,452,000 service sector jobs emerged in the non-metropolitan counties between 1970 and 1978. . . . By 1980, nearly two-thirds of all non-metropolitan workers were employed in the expanding service-performing sector and the trend shows no signs of abating. *Kasarda (1980), pp.13–14.*

In the United Kingdom, differential changes in employment within the metropolitan system are also evident. The decline of large centres and the growth of smaller ones, together with the relative shift from urban to rural areas, are clearly shown in Fothergill's and Gudgin's study. They classify the sixty-two United Kingdom subregions into eight categories; Table 3.10 shows how employment changed substantially differently between these categories in the 1959–1975 period. Manufacturing employment, in particular, shows a very clear progression across the eight categories. Manufacturing employment performance between 1959 and 1975 varied directly with the degree of rurality. London and the major conurbations experienced massive employment decline in manufacturing of more than 1 million. In contrast, the industrial non-city category gained a quarter of a million jobs. The biggest percentage increase, though from a small base, was in semi-rural and rural areas.

Table 3.10 *Employment change by type of subregion in the United Kingdom, 1959–1975*

	Manufacturing employment			Total employment		
	% U.K. employment	Change 1959–1975		% U.K. employment	Change 1959–1975	
Type of subregion	1959	(000s)	%	1959	(000s)	%
London	18.4	−585.9	−37.8	21.2	−517.1	−11.4
Conurbations	32.5	−433.7	−15.9	26.0	−258.2	−4.7
Major free-standing cities	21.8	+61.6	+3.4	20.8	+437.7	+9.9
Smaller free-standing cities	4.3	+64.0	+17.9	5.8	+209.7	+17.0
Industrial non-city	18.7	+254.8	+16.3	17.4	+816.7	+22.0
Urban non-industrial	1.3	+41.7	+38.8	2.4	+96.3	+18.8
Semi-rural	2.1	+78.2	+44.9	3.3	+131.7	+19.0
Rural	1.1	+73.1	+77.2	3.1	+94.5	+14.3

	Service employment			Total employment		
	%U.K. employment	Change 1959–1975		% U.K. employment	Change 1959–1975	
Type of subregion	1959	(000s)	%	1959	(000s)	%
London	27.0	+58.9	+2.3	21.2	−517.1	−11.4
Conurbations	22.4	+112.1	+5.2	26.0	−258.2	−4.7
Major free-standing cities	18.8	+289.6	+16.1	20·8	+437.7	+9.9
Smaller free-standing cities	6.5	+88.9	+14.3	5.8	+209.7	+17.0
Industrial non-city	14.6	+401.1	+28.7	17.4	+816.7	+22.0
Urban non-industrial	3.3	+41.1	+13.1	2.4	+96.3	+18.8
Semi-rural	3.7	+48.4	+13.8	3.3	+131.7	+19.0
Rural	3.9	+4.6	+1.2	3.1	+94.5	+14.3

Source: based on S. Fothergill & G. Gudgin (1979) Regional employment change: A subregional explanation, *Progress in Planning*, 12, tables 3.2, 3.3, 3.7

Such urban-rural employment shift is a good deal less evident in service industries. All types of area increased their number of service jobs, perhaps not surprising in view of national trends. In fact, Fothergill and Gudgin suggest that the big cities gained especially in the rapid-growth service categories which we have seen to be insurance, banking and finance, health and education.

Intrametropolitan employment change: inner-city decline and suburban growth

The third general trend in the geography of employment is that of decline in the central areas of large cities and of growth in the suburbs. Again, this is a trend which partly underlies both the broad regional shifts and intermetropolitan and rural shifts. In the latter case, especially, the decline of employment in some of the large, long-established metropolitan areas is the critical element. In all but a few it is the heavy weight of inner-city job loss which tips the balance of the area as a whole towards decline. So-called decentralization of industry from inner to outer metropolitan areas is, of course, no new phenomenon.* It has been evident, particularly in the case of manufacturing industry, for a good many decades. In recent years, however, the scale of the shifts has become especially great.

Table 3.11 summarizes the broad pattern of change in manufacturing employment in United States metropolitan areas between 1947 and 1967. Manufacturing

Table 3.11 *Changing manufacturing employment in 245 SMSAs in the United States, 1947–1967*

	Employment		Absolute	Percentage
	1947	1967	change	change
Central cities	7,356,733	7,063,426	−293,307	−3.9
Suburban rings	4,141,704	8,044,030	+3,902,326	+94.2
SMSAs	11,498,437	15,107,458	+3,609,021	+31.4

Source: B.J.L. Berry and J.D. Kasarda (1977) *Contemporary Urban Ecology*, New York: Macmillan, table 12.1. © 1977 Macmillan Publishing Co., Inc.

employment in the SMSAs as a whole increased by almost one-third, but significantly the suburban rings virtually doubled their manufacturing employment. By 1967 there were more manufacturing jobs in the suburban rings than in the central cities. Only twenty years earlier there had been almost two manufacturing jobs in the central cities for every one in the suburbs.

Of course, 1967 is roughly the time at which the broad regional trends in manufacturing employment in the manufacturing belt turned downwards. Superimposing the regional shifts on the urban trend sees the cities of the Northeast experiencing not simply low growth in their cores but also absolute declines. Kasarda (1980), for example, shows that the central cities of the thirty-three SMSAs over 1 million population in 1970 (over half in the manufacturing belt) lost more than 880,000 manufacturing jobs between 1947 and 1972. While manufacturing em-

---

*Decentralization need not imply the physical outward movement of businesses from centre to periphery. In fact, in most cases it reflects differential growth involving closures and slow growth in one place compared with new openings and faster growth in another.

ployment in the suburbs grew in the same cities by over 2.5 million, it is tempting to speculate that such growth in more recent years has been less strongly evident in the suburbs of large cities in the Northeast. As yet, however, we can do no more than speculate while awaiting the results of the 1980 Census of Population in the United States.

As at other spatial scales, changes in sectoral employment have been accompanied by spatial shifts in occupational distribution. Table 3.12 shows the changing occupational profile of central-city and suburban-ring employees in United States SMSAs between 1960 and 1970. Most of the major occupational categories declined very substantially in the central cities. Losses were especially heavy in the blue-collar categories (craftsmen, operatives, labourers). Only professional/technical and clerical workers showed an increased presence in the central cities. In comparison, all occupational groups, both blue and white collar, increased their employment in the

Table 3.12 *Occupational groups in central city and suburbs: 101 United States SMSAs, 1960–1970*

Occupational category	Mean number of central-city employees		
	1960	1970*	Change 1960–1970
Professional and technical	16,015	20,138	4,123
Managers and proprietors	12,458	11,354	−1,104
Clerical workers	26,915	30,002	3,087
Sales workers	11,113	9,813	−1,300
Craftsmen	18,041	16,043	−1,998
Operatives	25,078	19,838	−5,240
Labourers	5,676	4,668	−1,008
Service workers	15,669	15,713	44

Occupational category	Mean number of suburban-ring employees		
	1960	1970*	Change 1960–1970
Professional and technical	9,392	16,203	6,811
Managers and proprietors	5,787	8,288	2,501
Clerical workers	10,066	18,411	8,345
Sales workers	5,209	7,921	2,712
Craftsmen	11,684	14,575	2,891
Operatives	14,263	17,501	3,238
Labourers	3,649	4,363	714
Service workers	8,393	12,630	4,237

*Central-city and suburban employment figures adjusted for annexation between 1960 and 1970.

Source: B.J.L. Berry and J.D. Kasarda (1977) *Contemporary Urban Ecology*, New York: Macmillan, table 12.3. © 1977 Macmillan Publishing Co., Inc.

suburbs. White-collar growth was especially strong. At the same time, those blue-collar categories which declined in the central city grew substantially in the suburbs.

In the United Kingdom, inner-city employment decline has become a major topic of concern since the second half of the 1970s. Hitherto, most of the problems concerning the geographical distribution of employment had been viewed at the regional scale. During the 1970s, however, it became clear that enormous employment losses were being experienced not only in the central cities of assisted areas but also in the supposedly high-growth areas of London and Birmingham. Figure 3.19

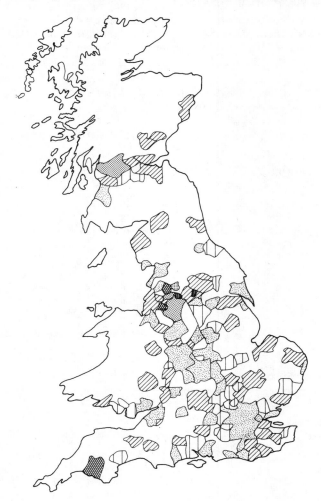

Figure 3.19 Centralization and decentralization trends in employment in SMLAs, 1951–1969 (left) and 1961–1971 (right)

Source: R. Drewett, J. Goddard & N. Spence (1976) British cities: urban population and employment trends 1951–71, *Department of Environment Research Report*, 10, figure 13. Crown Copyright.

shows how the pattern within Standard Metropolitan Labour Areas changed between 1951 and 1971. During the 1950s, decentralization of employment was confined to the larger cities of the core. During the 1960s, not only had decentralization become extremely widespread but also some cities had experienced a complete reversal. Having experienced a centralizing trend in the 1950s, they had become decentralizing cities in the 1960s.

Table 3.13 shows the inner-outer changes in more detail for six major conurbations. All except one of the six (Tyneside) lost employment in their inner areas.

Employment

Centralization | Decentralization

During decline | Absolute | Relative | Relative | Absolute | During decline

London, Manchester and Clydeside each lost more than one job out of every five – almost one in four for London. All except London experienced employment growth in their outer areas but only in the cases of the West Midlands and Tyneside was this sufficient to offset inner-city decline. London, in fact, lost almost three-quarters of a million jobs between 1952 and 1976. As in United States cities it is blue-collar jobs which have declined particularly in the inner cities, both in manufacturing and in services (Townsend 1977).

Table 3.13　*Employment changes in the inner and outer areas of six large British conurbations, 1952–1976*

	Inner		Outer		Total	
	No. (000)	%	No. (000)	%	No. (000)	%
London	−644	−24.0	−97	−6.6	−741	−17.8
Manchester	−114	−23.2	+47	+15.3	−67	−8.3
Merseyside	−79	−16.6	+29	+18.5	−50	−7.9
Clydeside	−117	−20.7	+45	+16.0	−72	−8.5
Tyneside	+5	+1.5	+20	+19.4	+25	+5.7
West Midlands	−102	−12.0	+173	+63.6	+71	+6.3

Source: based on M.W. Danson, W.F. Lever & J.F. Malcolm (1980) The inner city employment problem in Great Britain 1952–1976: A shift-share approach, *Urban Studies*, 17, table 6

Spatial variations in unemployment

Finally in this survey of the changing geography of job opportunities we look briefly at spatial variations in unemployment. The picture is not a simple reflection of the pattern of employment trends examined so far. Unfortunately, the shortage of unemployment data at appropriate spatial scales makes it difficult to obtain a clear impression at all but the more general levels.

Figure 3.20 shows in very approximate terms how interstate unemployment varied around the United States average in two time-periods, 1958 to 1962 and 1974 to 1977. In the earlier period, the national unemployment rate was 5.1 percent, in the more recent period it was 7.1 percent. At the state level, the highest unemployment rates were not precisely the same in the two time-periods. In 1958–1962, the highest rates were in Maine and West Virginia, followed by Michigan, Washington, Montana, Pennsylvania, Kentucky, Tennessee and Arkansas. In the 1974 to 1977 period of much higher general unemployment, the highest state rates were in Arizona, Michigan, New Jersey and Massachusetts (all with unemployment rates of 9 percent or more). The West Coast states had rates of well over 8 percent as did Florida, New York, Maine, Delaware. On the other hand, West Virginia's unemployment rate, though still high, was less extreme than in 1958–1962. It seems likely that out-migration may have reduced the West Virginia figure whilst in-migration may well have contributed to the higher unemployment rates in the West and Southwest.

Regional variation in unemployment in Britain over the 1966 to 1979 period is

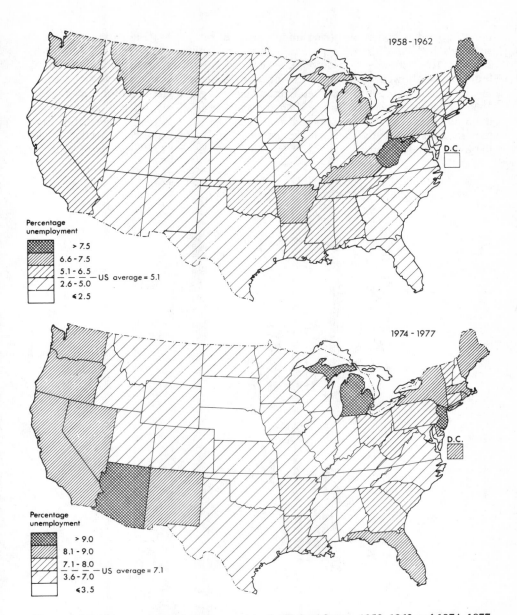

Figure 3.20 Average unemployment rates in the United States, 1958–1962 and 1974–1977

Source: United States *Statistical Abstract*, various issues.

shown in Figure 3.21. Each region's unemployment rate is expressed as an index of the national rate. Again, it should be remembered that the national rate was higher in each succeeding year shown: in fact, the national unemployment rate in 1979 was 4.3 times higher than that of 1966. Three regions – the Southeast, East Anglia and the

East Midlands – consistently had unemployment rates below the national average, although the East Midlands experienced some worsening of its position. At the other extreme, five regions – all peripheral – were consistently worse off. The position of four of these showed some improvement over the period. The Northwest, however, saw its unemployment rate worsen from being on a par with the national average in 1966 to being 23 percent higher than the average in 1979. But the region whose unemployment position deteriorated most was the West Midlands, even though it remained just below the national average in 1979. In 1966, the West Midlands had the lowest unemployment rate in Britain, 0.8 percent. By 1979, its unemployment

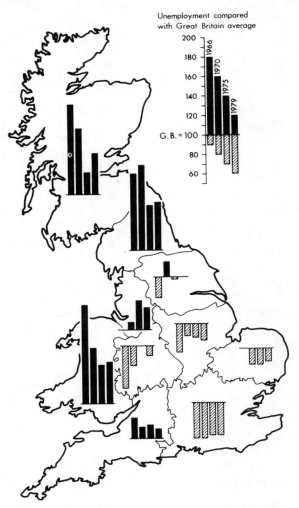

Figure 3.21   Regional variation in unemployment within Britain, 1966–1979

Source: Department of Employment *Gazette*, various issues.

rate had increased almost sevenfold. It is interesting to compare the West Midlands experience with that of Michigan in the United States. Both have been hard hit by the impact of the oil crisis on the motor vehicle industry.

As in the case of employment, such regional scales of analysis tend to obscure substantial intraregional variations in unemployment. For example, unemployment rates in some of the large industrial conurbations in the United Kingdom are very much higher than both the region in which they are located and the nation. For example, in 1979 the unemployment rate in Northwest England was roughly 7.4 percent; in Liverpool more than 12 percent of the working population was unemployed. In the same year, Scottish unemployment stood at 8.6 percent, that of Glasgow was well over 9 percent. At even finer spatial scales, unemployment may be especially high, particularly in those inner-city areas which we have seen to be losing employment. Again the case of Liverpool is illuminating. Thrift (1979) points out that the risk of being unemployed is about four times as great in the inner city as in Liverpool as a whole.

Processes of change

There is no single – or simple – explanation of these aggregate and geographical changes in employment and unemployment. During the recessionary conditions of today it is tempting to attribute the recurring reports of job losses, plant closures, corporate rationalizations, in some cases bankruptcies, to the energy crises of 1973 and 1979. Obviously the shock to the world economy of the unparalleled rise in oil prices has had a major impact upon the level of economic activity and, hence, upon jobs. But as we pointed out at the beginning of Chapter Two, the Western world was already experiencing economic difficulties before 1973. The basic causes, then, lie deep within the processes of industrial change at international and national, as well as local and regional, scales. A whole complex of processes is involved and it is extremely difficult to disentangle one from another. Having said this, however, some basic forces can be identified which quite evidently affect the scale, type and location of job opportunities. These are the ones we discussed in Chapter Two. Having outlined some of their major attributes in that chapter, we can now try to show how their particular operation helps to alter patterns of employment and unemployment. Each of the elements in fact merits a book in its own right; we can do no more than suggest in outline the way they are operating.

Some effects of changing demands and changing technologies on the geographical pattern of job opportunities
The demand for labour is what economists call a *derived* demand. It arises at second hand as a product of the labour input required to satisfy society's needs for goods and services. Clearly, a number of things can alter the nature of that input. For example, if society should decide to purchase fewer goods made in the more labour-intensive industries, demand would fall. Similarly, if the costs of labour rose, or its productivity fell, by comparison with other factors of production, producers might opt to use less labour and perhaps more capital equipment. The basic need for labour might also be significantly altered by changes in the technology of production, some innovations might call for more labour, others for less. The picture is made more complicated by the fact that national, and especially regional or local, economies, are

not closed, self-contained systems. Through the mechanisms of international and inter-regional trade, products flow from one place to another. Demands for many products, therefore, are met from outside sources with important implications for local producers and, thus, for employment.

A standard explanation of the broad sectoral shifts in employment discussed earlier relates the progressive shift of emphasis from primary to secondary to tertiary to quaternary activities, to changes in consumer demands associated with increased affluence. The conventional argument runs as follows. As overall incomes have risen, the aggregate pattern of consumer demand has changed in ways which have had a differential impact on the economic sectors. The result of higher incomes is that, beyond a certain level, the amount spent on basic necessities such as food grows less rapidly than the amount spent on durable goods and, as incomes rise even higher, less rapidly than the amount spent on leisure and other activities, which in turn become more important as the average person's leisure time increases with the decrease in working hours. An affluent society demands more and better services and amenities such as schools, higher education establishments, hospitals, libraries and so on, while, as society becomes more complex, more people are needed to organize and co-ordinate the work of specialists, to bring together the necessary factors of production, to transport materials and goods, to facilitate communication. For all of these reasons, therefore, the tertiary and quaternary sectors become increasingly important and it is the expansion of these areas of the economy which, for some, epitomizes the post-industrial society.

But this does not necessarily imply that modern Western economies are becoming service-producing rather than goods-producing economies as the proponents of the post-industrial model of society seem to suggest. Gershuny argues that

> with the exception of medicine and education, the consumption of services in Britain has actually decreased considerably as a proportion of total consumption over the last twenty years. Though a new category of needs, corresponding to post-industrial demands for more recreational and other personal products does emerge, these are met not by services but by goods. Precisely, we see a process of substitution; services which were previously provided from outside the household are increasingly replaced by production within the household using goods, essentially capital goods, acquired from manufacturing industry.*
> Gershuny (1978), pp.138–139.

Gershuny suggests, therefore, that the growth of service employment comes largely from two sources: first, the growth of employment in education and health care and, second, the growth of activities related to material goods production. These include banking, insurance, finance and those co-ordinating and controlling activities (managers, technologists, etc.) which we have seen to be growing.

---

*In contrast to conventional views of a 'service' economy Gershuny argues that we are evolving a 'self-service' economy: 'Instead of capital investment taking place in industry, and industry providing services for individuals and households, increasingly capital investment takes place in households, leaving industry engaged in what is essentially intermediate production, making the capital goods – the cookers, freezers, televisions, motor cars – used in home production of the final product. This is the trend towards the do-it-yourself economy – almost the antithesis of Bell's service economy' (Gershuny 1978, p.81).

Within manufacturing industry itself there has been very substantial differential growth and decline of individual manufacturing sectors. Massive job losses have been experienced in textiles, clothing, iron and steel and shipbuilding, for example. But the causes of such declines, and of growth in other sectors such as electronics, are to be found in a combination of demand changes, technological changes and global shifts in patterns of production. Obviously, there is still a high level of demand for textiles and for clothing, yet employment in these industries in Western economies has plunged dramatically. One reason is, undoubtedly, the emergence of new geographical centres of production which can produce these, and other goods, at lower cost than the Western producers. In other words, the emergence of an *international division of labour* – global specialization in particular goods – is affecting demand for such goods from domestic producers in Western economies.

For example, apart from productivity improvements, one reason for the small proportion of the labour force employed in agriculture in the United Kingdom is the high proportion of the nation's food that is imported from overseas. Similarly, one frequently suggested explanation for the recent downturn in manufacturing employment in most advanced industrial nations is the growth of competition from some Third World countries in certain labour-intensive manufacturing industries. For example, countries such as South Korea, Mexico, Turkey and Brazil are exporting textiles, clothing, footwear and, increasingly, vehicles, ships and steel. These are essentially labour-intensive industries for which these countries have the advantage, at present, of relatively low labour costs. Quite apart from the effect of an economic recession on the general level of demand for such products and also on technological change, competition from low-wage, low-cost producers is doing a good deal to reduce employment in these and other industries in advanced industrial societies.*

It is extremely difficult to disentangle the effects on employment of such competition from other factors. But it is certainly the case, as Figure 3.22 shows, that the newly industrializing countries (NICs) have been capturing an increasing share of imports into the OECD (developed) countries. Between 1963 and 1977, for example, the NIC's share of OECD imports of clothing increased from 19 percent to 38 percent, of electrical machinery from 1 percent to 12 percent, of footwear and related goods from 7 percent to 32 percent.

Of course it is not only imports from such newly industrializing countries which are creating employment problems. A much-remarked upon feature of the United Kingdom economy is its generally very high propensity to import manufactured goods, particularly consumer goods, from developed as well as developing countries. The changing demands of the UK population, therefore, are increasingly being served from outside rather than by domestic production. At the same time, the overseas demand for British goods has been, with exceptions, far from buoyant. This trading problem is at the heart of the de-industrialization issue. But it is also a problem which is experienced to a greater or lesser degree by most Western economies. Europe and the United States, for example, see their populations'

---

*Some would argue that industrialized nations must protect themselves against such job losses by erecting tariffs and quotas against imports. Others take the view that the advanced industrial nations should be encouraging newer, more sophisticated production and accepting the shift of low-skill, labour-intensive production to less-developed countries.

demand for motor vehicles being satisfied by Japanese imports. European textile fibre producers feel they are being threatened not only by NICs but also by the United States. In a highly complex, interconnected world economy the effects of changing demands are extremely difficult to disentangle.

It is perhaps rather easier to identify the impact of technological change on both the level and nature of employment. As we showed in Chapter Two, technological innovations have created substantial changes in materials, products and processes, as well as in the media of communication. Perhaps the most important general effect of technological change on employment comes from those innovations which reduce the quantity of labour used in the production process, innovations which increase *labour productivity*.

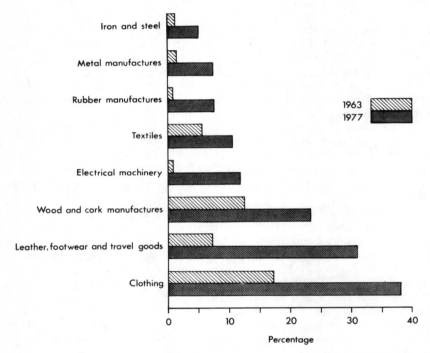

Figure 3.22   The increasing share of OECD imports accounted for by newly industrializing countries

Source: OECD (1979) *The Impact of the Newly Industrializing Countries,* Paris: OECD, chart C.

Mechanization and automation have substituted mechanical and electronic devices for human operation. As a result, overall output per worker has risen in all modern industrial societies, though to greatly varying degrees, as Figure 3.23 shows. In both the United States and the United Kingdom, productivity was almost 30 percent higher in 1974 than in 1967. Compared with the other countries shown, however, these were relatively low rates of increase. The most spectacular increase in productivity amongst industrialized nations was clearly experienced by Japan where

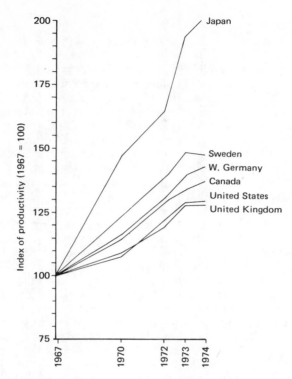

Figure 3.23 Indexes of output per man-hour in manufacturing industry in selected industrialized nations, 1967–1974

Source: United States *Statistical Abstract* (1975) table 1405; (1978) table 1568.

the 1974 output per man-hour was almost twice as high as in 1967. The point of Figure 3.23 is neither to draw detailed comparisons between these countries nor to suggest reasons for individual differences. Rather it is designed to reinforce the point that the increase in productivity has been a general phenomenon throughout modern industrial society. As productivity increases, fewer workers are needed to produce the same – or an even larger – volume of output. Thus, for example, over a seven-year period the US meat-packing industry lost 40,000 jobs while productivity in the industry increased by more than 50 percent. Between 1951 and 1963 employment in the United States steel industry declined by 28 percent though total steel production increased. Similarly, in the motor vehicle industry over the same period employment declined by 20 percent though 1 million more cars were produced.

Of course, technological change is not the sole influence on levels of employment and unemployment. Indeed its precise impact depends on its interaction with at least two other forces: the rate of growth of the labour force itself and the rate of growth of demand for goods and services. At an aggregate level of, say, the United States, it is possible to have rising productivity without a corresponding increase in unemployment provided that either more new jobs are being created elsewhere in the economy or that the rate of growth of the labour force is lower. For example, between 1947 and 1965 output per man-hour in the United States was increasing at a rate of 3.2 percent per year. In the early part of this period, 1947 to 1953, not only was economic growth at a high level (output increased at 5.2 prcent per year) but also the labour force was increasing at only 1 percent per year as a result of low birth rates in the 1930s. As a result the national level of unemployment remained relatively low. But between 1953 and 1960 economic growth slowed considerably (output increased by only 2.4 percent per year), while the rate of growth of the labour force speeded up. Increased unemployment was the result (National Commission 1966). Since 1973 the forces leading to high levels of unemployment have been very strong. Economic growth has fallen to very low levels while more and more people are entering the labour market, especially young people and married women as we have seen. If, as many believe, the days of rapid economic growth are now over, then the impact of technological change on employment and unemployment will be correspondingly greater.

Such a view is reinforced if we accept the fact that we are probably only on the threshold of even more massive technological change, especially in the sphere of automation based upon the micro-processor revolution. Predictions that many millions of jobs will be destroyed throughout North America, Europe and the rest of the industrialized world simply through the introduction of micro-processors have become commonplace. Many of these predictions convey a false air of precision, but there is no doubt at all that the impact on employment will be enormous and that both governments and industry will have to make major adjustments. In view of the growth of white-collar employment even while blue-collar employment has been declining, the possible effects of micro-processor technology could indeed be serious, particular for female workers. Many routine clerical tasks have already been affected by developments in computer and data-processing technology, photocopying equipment and so on. The advent of the word-processor seems likely to revolutionize a good deal of secretarial work. It is suggested by some that growing numbers of secretaries and typists will be made redundant since, it is argued, one word-processor can do the work of three or four typists.

It is, of course, still too early to predict with any real accuracy the future impact of automation both on numbers of jobs and on the kind of tasks involved. Some would argue that jobs displaced by the new technology will be offset by the creation of jobs in other spheres which result from the increased overall growth. In other words, as the pace of technology grows in society it raises the total scale of output and creates more jobs rather than removes them. Further, work by the National Economic Development Council and the Institute of Manpower Studies in Britain suggests that technological innovations proceed much more slowly and are more diffused through the economy than popular views would suggest. As a result they consider that automation is unlikely to provide, by itself, dramatic increases in structural unemployment. Whatever the precise numerical outcome, it is likely to be the routine tasks which are automated, the tasks normally performed by unskilled or semi-skilled manual workers. Demand for this kind of labour declines drastically, while that of the highly skilled workers able to design, maintain and supervise the automated processes increases. There are two counterpoised views of these changes. One view regards automation as a blessing because it relieves industrial workers of the boredom and drudgery of monotonous, repetitive operations. Hence the overall skill level of the labour force tends to increase. The opposite view argues that the logical outcome of this process is the displacement of the average worker who does not possess the education, training and skill necessary to occupy the new jobs in an automated factory.

The spatial outcome of these inter-related changes in demands and technology depends very much on the prevailing geographical distribution of the economic activities affected. A major characteristic of many regional economies has been a tendency to specialize in particular industrial sectors. Numerous examples spring to mind: steel manufacture in Pittsburgh and in Northeast England, cotton textiles in the towns of New England and of Lancashire, shipbuilding on Clydeside. As we have seen, there have been massive employment losses in both the United Kingdom and the United States in these, and other, traditional industrial sectors. Since such sectors tended to be very strongly localized geographically, these aggregate losses were also specifically spatial losses. In Doreen Massey's words,

> sectoral decline brought with it specifically *regional* decline.
> *Massey (1979), p.236.*

In general terms, much of the regional employment change in both the United States and the United Kingdom has been attributed to the influence of industrial structure. The declining regions of the northeastern United States and of Scotland, Wales, North and Northwest England have suffered employment losses mainly, it is argued, because they contained an unfavourable 'mix' of industry sectors. In particular, they contained a preponderance of sectors either for whose products demand had declined or which were subject to technological obsolescence, or both. In the United Kingdom case, the influence of industrial structure on regional employment change, though important up to the end of the 1950s, seems to have become less important in the last twenty years.*

Studies of recent employment changes at the regional level in the United States see industrial structure as being of some importance. For example, Beyers (1979) suggests

> that much of the slow growth of the Northeast can be attributed to an 'adverse' industrial structure – the concentration of many types of manufacturing activities experiencing slow growth in demand . . . [at the same time]. . . . The types of manufacturing industries that expanded rapidly at the national scale over the 1965–1975 period also tended to be located in the South and West, possibly suggesting that the technologies of these industries are 'new' and not represented strongly in components of the same industries in the Northeast.
> *Beyers (1979), pp.40, 43.*

Norton and Rees (1979) claim that the traditional pattern of industrial mix effects altered dramatically in the early 1970s, favouring the periphery rather than the core. However, the main thrust of their explanation of broad inter-regional shifts in employment in the United States is technological. Thus, they attribute the

---

*Both Keeble (1976, 1980) and Fothergill and Gudgin (1979) reach this conclusion. The topic of regional specialization in particular industrial sectors together with the problems of regional adjustment are discussed in some detail in Manners, Keeble, Rodgers & Warren (1980).

employment changes shown earlier in Figure 3.14 to a decline in the ability of the manufacturing belt to act as a 'seedbed' for new technological innovations. They point out that many standardized and routine manufacturing operations had been shifting away from the Northeast for a number of years. Until quite recently, however, the manufacturing belt had been able to offset such decentralization by spawning new technologies. Now, they argue, not only has this ability deteriorated but also the 'periphery' – specifically the South and West – is generating new technology as well as continuing to attract the manufacture of standardized products. In addition, the rapid growth of certain metropolitan areas of the periphery – for example Houston, Dallas-Fort Worth and Atlanta – is creating sufficiently large regional markets to generate internal growth. Agglomeration economies – the benefits available to firms and individuals from clustering together in geographical space – are beginning to characterize such metropolitan centres. As yet they have not accumulated the diseconomies of agglomeration associated with many of the old-established metropolitan areas of the Northeast. The result of such technologically based changes is that

> the periphery states now tend to specialise in the economy's "rapid growth" industries, and core states in slow growing ones.
> *Norton and Rees (1979), p.142.*

But as these authors rightly observe, the regional shifts in economic activity and their associated job changes are not simple processes attributable only to technological change. Technology, as we pointed out in Chapter Two, is not an independent entity. It is initiated, utilized and spread by organizations in particular. Changes in the spatial distribution of economic activity are the outcome of a myriad of decisions made by business enterprises – especially the very large corporations – and by governments. It is to their impact upon the geography of employment that we now turn, looking first at corporate behaviour.

The impact of corporate strategies of organization and re-organization on the changing geography of employment
In Chapter Two we identified the emergence of giant manufacturing corporations as a major feature of modern Western societies. From the viewpoint of the impact of such organizations on the changing geography of employment, the significant factor is not so much their sheer size as their geographical flexibility, in particular their ability to locate different functional parts of their operations in different geographical locations (refer back to Figure 2.16). As we pointed out, each functional 'level' in the corporate hierarchy has rather different locational requirements. Hence there has been a tendency for the high-level control functions to cluster in one type of geographical location and for other functions to be oriented towards different types of location. But because each functional level not only has different locational requirements but also different locational *effects*, each has a differential impact on both the number and types of jobs available from place to place. Thus, where each functional level is located, and how these locational choices are changing as economic circumstances change, are important influences on the geography of employment.

Recent locational trends in corporate organization arise from the pressures of the competitive environment at international and national scales. The basic goal of private business enterprises is to grow: to get bigger, more profitable, to have a larger share of the market, and so on. To achieve such aims, enterprises strive to produce and distribute their output in the most efficient, that is, least-costly-to-the-firm manner. As part of this process, they are driven to update their technology both to make production more efficient (for example, by mechanization and automation which increases the productivity of the labour force) and to create new products. These pressures are put in a rather different light in times of economic recession when the problem becomes one of survival rather than growth. As overall demand falls, the competition to hold on to existing markets becomes more intense. The precise response to such pressures obviously varies from one firm to another. Commonly, however, it involves efforts to reduce labour costs and to get rid of old and obsolescent capital equipment and buildings.

The changes in the geography of employment outlined earlier in this chapter can be seen as very largely the outcome of the response of business enterprises to changing internal and external pressures and to their attempts to adjust the spatial organization of their operations accordingly. In deciding how to organize their operations geographically, firms are faced with a spatial surface of opportunities and constraints. This is a multifaceted surface, made up of spatial variations in resources and materials, suppliers and customers, capital availability and labour availability. In terms of labour, for example, there are areas of high labour costs and low labour costs, areas of skilled labour and areas of unskilled labour, areas of strong unions and weak unions, areas of highly productive labour and areas of low productivity. In view of such spatial variations, we should not be surprised to find that firms which have a degree of locational flexibility take advantage of them to improve their labour position. Indeed, the firm's ability to achieve its goals may depend upon its ability to exploit spatial variations in labour supply.

Much of the manufacturing growth in the Sunbelt of the United States, much of the new employment created in the peripheral and rural regions of the United Kingdom, has been in the branch plants of large multiplant corporations engaged in standardized production activities (Level III of Figure 2.16). The reasons for the choice of specific locations obviously vary greatly. In the case of the rapid growth of manufacturing in the southern United States, for example, there is general agreement that a combination of low labour costs and low levels of unionization (see Figure 2.29) related to a previously 'non-industrial' population have been key factors.* In the United Kingdom, inter-regional wage differences are less marked than in the United States, while the level of unionization is both higher and more uniform geographically. But there are considerable variations in the availability of labour of different skills. One of the attractions of peripheral and rural locations (quite apart from the influence of government policies) has been the availability of a large supply of semi-skilled, often female, labour suitable for standardized manufacturing processes.

Within metropolitan areas, the growth of employment in the suburbs at the expense of the inner cities also partly reflects the branch-plant behaviour of large

---

*Of course, these have not been the only factors involved. Others often cited include lower costs of living in the South (including lower energy costs), lower business taxes, a more pro-business climate and the fact that transport and communications improvements have greatly reduced the region's relative isolation.

firms. Of course, some suburban employment growth in manufacturing is, literally, decentralization through the outward migration of firms previously operating in the centre. Some is also due to the fact that many newly-born firms are locating their initial operations in the suburbs (although the inner cities still spawn large numbers of new, often short-lived, firms). But it is also the case that those large national and international firms which do locate in the older-established metropolitan areas choose the suburbs rather than the inner cities for their branch plants. Such suburban choices are not necessarily based on labour factors. Changes in production, transportation and communications technology, together with the more widespread availability of public services, have all contributed to the internal resorting of manufacturing in metropolitan areas. For example, the need for extensive single-storey factories by modern manufacturing processes can rarely be satisfied in congested central areas. Increasing orientation towards the movement of materials and products by highway reduces the attractiveness of central cities. The availability of fully serviced industrial sites with both good transportation facilities and modern plant layout has exerted a strong pull on manufacturing industry. As a location for many – though not all – branches of manufacturing, the central area has become less attractive.

Although it has been the standardized, routine manufacturing functions which have displayed the greatest tendency towards geographical dispersal by large corporations, locational changes have been occurring in other operations of the large firm. We noted in Chapter Two that there have been recent changes in the location of corporate headquarters, even though the established geographical centres of control show a remarkable degree of locational stability. Table 3.14 lists thirty-three major corporations which transferred their head offices out of Manhattan between 1967 and 1971. Twenty-eight of them moved to suburban locations in the outer parts of the New York metropolitan complex. This process of the suburbanization of head-quarters has continued into the 1970s in both the United States and the United Kingdom. Table 3.14 also shows the relocation of several corporate headquarters to cities such as Houston, Texas.

Some locational shifts are evident also in other high-level corporate functions such as research and development. Malecki (1979) has shown that the R and D operations of large firms have become more widely dispersed in that they appear in a larger number of metropolitan as well as non-metropolitan areas. Although R and D by the largest firms is still strongly concentrated in the largest metropolitan areas, some considerable changes have occurred. For example, the New York urban region lost fourteen R and D laboratories between 1965 and 1977, the Los Angeles region gained thirty. In the United Kingdom, R and D functions seem to remain strongly concentrated in the southeastern corner of the country (Goddard 1980). The kinds of locations sought for the higher-order corporate functions relate very strongly to their attributes of interpersonal communication and also of social and recreational amenities. The former explains the continued concentration of headquarters in central-city locations, the latter helps to explain some of the suburban and longer-distance moves, particularly those to more pleasant 'amenity-rich' locations.

All of these changes in the locational arrangements of corporate functions have a differential impact on the geography of employment. The corporate processes generating spatial change are extremely complex. They involve not only locational changes of the kind traditionally examined by geographers, for example, the move-

Table 3.14 *Corporations which moved their headquarters out of Manhattan, 1967–1971*

Company	1970 sales ($ millions)	New location
American Can	1838	Greenwich, Conn.
AMF	636	White Plains, N.Y.
Avco	758	Greenwich, Conn.
Bangor Punta	342	Greenwich, Conn.
BASF (US Division)	56	Parsippany, N.J.
Cheseborough-Pond	261	Greenwich, Conn.
Columbia Gas System	828	Wilmington, Del.
Combustion Engineering	957	Stamford, Conn.
Continental Oil	2964	Stamford, Conn.
CPC (Corn Products)	1376	Englewood Cliffs, N.J.
Flintkote	355	White Plains, N.J.
Foster Wheeler	391	Livingston, N.J.
General Telephone and Elec.	3,439	Stamford, Conn.
Great Northern Paper	355	Stamford, Conn.
Hooker Chemical	N.A.	Stamford, Conn.
Howmet	250	Greenwich, Conn.
ICI America	67	Stamford, Conn.
Ingersoll-Rand	766	Woodcliff Lake, N.J.
M.W. Kellogg	N.A.	Houston, Texas
Kraftco	737	Chicago, Illinois
Lone Star Cement	265	Greenwich, Conn.
Lummus	192	Bloomfield, N.J.
Metro Goldwyn Meyer	171	Culver City, Calif.
Microdot	155	Greenwich, Conn.
Olin	1125	Stamford, Conn.
Panhandle Eastern Pipeline	419	Houston, Texas
PepsiCo.	N.A.	Purchase, N.Y.
Richardson-Merrell	381	Southern Connecticut
Shell Oil	4299	Houston, Texas
States Marine International	123	Stamford, Conn.
Stauffer Chemical	483	Westport, Conn.
Union Camp	462	Wayne, N.J.
U.S. Tobacco	86	Greenwich, Conn.

Source: *Time* Magazine, 26 April 1971, p.87. © Time Inc. 1971.

ment of plants from one location to another, the opening of new plants and the closure of existing ones, but also changes at existing sites in the number and type of workers employed. The process of corporate re-organization may also arise from involvement in merger and acquisition. As we noted in Chapter Two, this has been a most important element in the growth of giant corporations. Whatever the detail of the corporate processes the effects on employment may be felt in two ways. First, there may be changes in the *number* of jobs provided from place to place and, second, there may be changes in the *types* of jobs available.

Major geographical changes in the numbers of jobs are continually being produced by processes of corporate re-organization and restructuring. Regular reading of the daily newspapers will confirm this. The incidence of such job changes – particularly job losses – has been especially great during the recession of the 1970s and early 1980s. Hardly a day goes by without news of yet another large-scale job loss in one place or another. But such events, though intensified by economic recession, are not confined to recessionary periods. They are a continuing feature of industrial change in all modern societies in which large multiplant organizations operate under the pressures of competition. Two examples can be given to illustrate some geographical aspects of the process.

Litton Industries is one of the largest United States conglomerate corporations, one of those which grew especially rapidly in the 1960s, diversifying both functionally and geographically. One of its many business interests was typewriter production based upon its acquisition of the Royal Typewriter Company in the United States. In 1966 Royal acquired the Imperial Typewriter Company, a British firm (in fact it was the last remaining British-owned typewriter manufacturer) with production units in two British cities, Hull and Leicester. Apart from selling machines to the United Kingdom and other markets the Hull plant supplied components to the Royal factory at Hartford, Connecticut.

The Hartford plant was the last remaining large factory in the United States manufacturing non-electric typewriters. Early in 1972, Litton announced that it was closing down the Hartford plant in order to concentrate its typewriter production in Europe – much of this at Hull and Leicester. Some 1300 jobs in Hartford were lost by this move. However, Hartford's loss was Hull's gain (though only temporarily as it turned out). A small number of supervisory staff were transferred from Hartford to the UK, the Hull plant's labour force was increased from around 500 to more than 2000 and more were being recruited and trained. But the new arrangement was short lived; the UK operations failed to achieve profitability in the eyes of the Litton management and, a mere three years after the closure of the Hartford plant, the Hull and Leicester plants were also closed down with the loss of 3200 jobs. This represented half of all typewriter employment in the United Kingdom.

An even more extensive rationalization programme was carried out in the late 1960s and early 1970s by the giant British firm GEC. In 1967 and 1968 GEC, with much encouragement by the Labour government of the day, had been involved in a series of massive mergers involving other large electrical firms, especially Associated Electrical Industries (AEI) and English Electric. The new combine employed many thousands of workers in plants – some very large, some quite small – throughout the country. There were especially large concentrations in parts of inner London, in Manchester, Liverpool and the Midlands. Since the objective of the mergers was to improve GEC's competitive position in domestic and foreign markets, it was not surprising that a major rationalization programme ensued. Tens of thousands of jobs were lost in the period between 1966 and 1972. Some losses were especially large. The biggest single job loss was at the Woolwich, London, factory, previously owned by AEI, where its closure led to the disappearance of 5500 jobs spread over a period of time. On the other hand, some locations benefited from the rationalization. For example, some 2000 new jobs were created in Scotland and in other less prosperous parts of Britain.

A recent detailed study of the employment changes involved in industrial restructuring, of which the GEC changes were a major part, shows how the corporate changes had a particularly serious impact on four British cities.* Firms were restructuring their operations for two major reasons: to eliminate excess production capacity and to reduce their costs. To achieve these aims, some plants were closed entirely, others had their labour forces drastically reduced. There was also some locational re-arrangement whereby some production – and jobs – were transferred from one location to another. Two types of employment change occurred, therefore: absolute changes, the gain or loss of jobs at the level of the economy as a whole, and locational changes where the gain or loss was specific to a particular geographical area. Table 3.15 shows how these job changes resulting from corporate re-organization in twenty-five firms had an especially serious impact in four major British cities. Not only were most of the job losses absolute losses but also the four cities gained no new jobs as part of the restructuring process. In fact, almost two-thirds of the locational job shifts – a little over 2000 in all – were gained by the Development Areas.

Table 3.15 *Geographical changes in employment as a result of corporate re-organization in twenty-five firms in the British electrical, electronics industries, 1966–1972*

City	Total employment in the firms, 1966	Jobs lost		Jobs gained		Net change	Percentage change 1966–1972
		Absolute loss	Loca-tional loss	Absolute gain	Loca-tional gain		
Birmingham	11,950	−3,020	0	0	+40	−2,980	−25
Greater London	26,473	−10,228	−2,563**	0	+20**	−12,771	−48
Liverpool	11,350	−4,910	−250	0	0	−5,160	−45
Manchester	22,740	−8,955	−542†	0	+93†	−9,404	−41
Total	72,513	−27,113	−3,252‡	0	+50‡	−30,315	−42

** Excludes 30 jobs transferred within London but includes 103 jobs transferred to other cities.
† Excludes 240 jobs transferred within Manchester.
‡ Total column does not add up as it excludes all jobs transferred within and between cities.

Source: D. Massey & R.A. Meegan (1978) Industrial restructuring versus the cities, *Urban Studies*, 15, 273–288, table 4

*Full details can be found in Massey and Meegan (1978, 1979). The changes were stimulated by a government agency of the time, the Industrial Re-organization Corporation, whose aim was to increase the international competitiveness of British firms in certain sectors.

Both of the examples given above refer to situations in which large corporations were striving to increase their efficiency. In the British example, this was seen to be a national priority aided by government finance. The examples illustrate a key problem of conflict of geographical interest inherent in corporate strategies of reorganization. The fact that the enterprises as a whole may prosper or even that particular places gain new jobs is cold comfort to the losers. Aggregate changes may be favourable – for example, the country as a whole may benefit from a stronger nationally based firm operating in competitive world markets – but the effects may be highly deleterious locally. As Barnet and Muller have observed in writing about the impact of US-based multinationals on domestic employment:

> On computer tapes, jobs may be interchangeable. In the real world they are not. A total of 250,000 new jobs gained in corporate headquarters does not, in any political or human sense, offset 250,000 old jobs lost on the production line. When Lynn, Massachusetts becomes a ghost of its former self, its jobless citizens find little satisfaction in reading about the new headquarters building on Park Avenue and all the secretaries it will employ. The changing composition of the workforce and its changing geographical location brought about by the globalisation of U.S. industry are affecting lives of millions of Americans in serious and largely unfortunate ways.
> *Barnet and Muller (1975), p.302.*

However, it is not only changes in the number of jobs which is involved in corporate re-organization. The *types* of jobs involved must also be considered. For example, Massey and Meegan claim that a 'deskilling' process was involved in the job changes they studied. Most of the job losses recorded in Table 3.15 were relatively skilled jobs. Most of the jobs gained in the smaller towns of the Development Areas were less skilled. More generally it is important to recognize that each 'level' in the corporate hierarchy tends to have a different employment profile. Each, therefore, tends to offer different kinds of job opportunities. The clearest distinction in this respect is between the headquarters and higher-order functions on the one hand and the standardized production processes carried out in branch plants on the other.

A headquarters' unit generally employs almost entirely 'white-collar' workers whilst a branch assembly plant has a predominantly 'blue-collar' labour force. Many of the headquarters' jobs are at the higher-executive level, many are highly specialized and highly skilled, for example, in finance, the law, marketing and business systems analysis. A large proportion of the lower-level headquarters' jobs are also skilled – secretaries, stenographers, computer programmers and the like. However, the employment profile of the typical branch assembly plant is very different. There are probably few executive employees, and these may be quite junior in level, and relatively few white-collar workers. Most modern assembly operations either do not require a high level of skill or they involve a skill easily and quickly learned. Most employees, therefore, are semi-skilled or even unskilled. In many industries, much of the assembly work is performed by female workers.

Quite evidently, therefore, those regions which contain large concentrations of corporate headquarters and higher-order functions such as research and development will have different employment and occupational profiles from those regions which consist predominantly of branch plants whose headquarters are elsewhere.*

The major developments in corporate growth and concentration during recent decades have resulted in many regions having a very large proportion of their total employment in branch plants. For example, Pred (1975) has calculated that 74 percent of manufacturing employment in the Phoenix SMSA in 1972 was controlled from elsewhere. At a similar scale, 86 percent of Merseyside's manufacturing employment is externally controlled (Lloyd and Dicken 1981). Almost 60 percent of manufacturing jobs in Scotland are in externally headquartered branch plants. In the latter case, Firn summarizes some of the major causes for concern created by these trends:

> the major problem with any regional economy that is dominated by externally controlled enterprises is probably that of the effects of the changing balance between innovative, entrepreneurial-type decision-making and routine management-type supervision. When major decisions, such as on investment, sales, or purchasing are made elsewhere, the plant managers in the regional subsidiaries or branch plants are reduced to what Baumol calls 'competent calculating machines'. Thus much of the drive, enthusiasm, and invention that lies at the heart of economic growth is removed, reduced, or at best, suppressed. . . . It is also probable that a region dominated by branch plants is unlikely to have a large research and development (R and D) component. . . . Thus one would expect that the region would not be a leader in developing new products, processes, and technologies, which in turn suggests that innovation will not be a major force in the local economy, which further implies that there will not be a substantial development of new enterprises or indeed of growth within existing enterprises. . . . There is also the likelihood that a high degree of external control will express itself in terms of a very open regional economy, with a high degree of integration with other economic systems . . . global economic fluctuations are transmitted into the Scottish economy relatively quickly, and the large American component in Scottish manufacturing has been a prime point of entry for externally generated economic fluctuations. . . . The final problem of external control that will be briefly raised here is that concerning the type of personnel employed in many of the new external plants that have set up in Scotland during the last 20 years . . . there are two possible causes for concern. First, because of the large number of branch plants present, there have been very few senior management and professional jobs created per 1000 employees. Therefore, young Scottish professionals wishing to enter companies at middle management levels are increasingly forced to leave Scotland. This is turn will reduce the potential pool of entrepreneurs, for it is from within such management levels that the majority of the founders of new enterprises seem to emerge. Second, there seems to have been a mismatch in terms of the male-female ratio between the jobs that have been

---

*A good deal of attention is now being devoted to the general problem of 'external control', the effects of the geographical concentration of headquarters on those regions whose economic autonomy is thereby reduced. For an indication of the broader issues involved see Dicken (1976), Firn (1975), Westaway (1974).

lost to the region, and those that have replaced them in new enterprises. . . . The nature of new jobs provided by external plants has been principally oriented towards female, semi-skilled assembly operations . . . whereas the jobs lost have been mainly of male, highly paid, skilled craftsmen. Therefore, there seems to have been a net wage reduction per new job provided, as well as an element of de-skilling, although this assertion remains to be proved.
Firn (1975), pp.410, 411.

There is no doubt that the creation of branch plants by multiplant firms has created large numbers of jobs in certain locations. In the short-term, at least, they have alleviated many of the problems associated with the decline of traditional industries and of agriculture. Whether such developments are beneficial in the longer term to the regions involved is an open question. As we have seen, much of the branch-plant employment is of the low-skill, routine job variety. There is also the question of the likely permanence of such jobs. It is, of course, nonsensical to argue that branch plants, in general, are either more or less stable in the face of cyclical changes in the economy. However, since the giant business corporations have shown considerable spatial flexibility so far, it is unlikely that they will cease to do so in the future. As the geographical scale of such flexibility continues to increase, the assembly and routine operations recently located in the peripheral areas of the United States, the United Kingdom and other countries may well be relocated outside these countries altogether. At the international scale there are already a good many instances of this. Quite evidently, the changing geography of employment within Western industrial societies cannot be isolated from developments at the global scale.

Government activities, government policies and the changing geography of employment

As a very substantial employer in its own right, government clearly exerts a significant influence on employment both in aggregate and in different geographical locations. Government employment is obviously particularly high in national, state and provincial capitals. Some governments have also deliberately decentralized some of their functions, and hence some of their employment. Examples in the British context include the major social-service offices relocated to Newcastle-upon-Tyne, the vehicle-licensing centre relocated to Swansea and the regionalization of some Inland Revenue activities. Quite apart from government's role as employer, very many government actions and policies have a major influence on the changing geography of employment. Some of these actions are deliberately geographical in design, others, though non-spatial in intent, have very substantial employment implications in different places.

In recent years, all governments in modern industrial societies have begun to implement policies which *directly* aim to influence and modify the geographical distribution of the nation's economic activities and resources. For the most part, the geographical focus has been *regional* though more recently the city in general, and the inner city in particular, have become prominent in policy terms. Although, as with government policies of all kinds, there are differences between countries in the types of regional economic policies actually used, all share certain common characteristics:

most of the tools of regional policy are used to subsidise capital expansion in areas where labor is relatively unemployed or working at relatively low wages. The objective is not only to encourage capital to move to target areas but also to induce local capital in those areas to be invested locally rather than in more advanced regions where, under market conditions, the rates of return are higher.
Hansen (1974), p.24.

Geographically-oriented economic policies obviously demand the selection and designation of those geographical areas which are to receive government funds. The other side of the same coin is that areas not so chosen do *not* benefit and, indeed, may lose out. For the most part, areas have been designated on the basis of their high levels of unemployment, in some cases supplemented by such criteria as low income levels, large-scale out-migration of population or poor basic amenities. A general tendency has been for a larger and larger proportion of the population to be included in designated areas. For example, in the United States the designated areas in 1968 contained roughly 26 million people; by 1973 this had increased to more than 100 million (Estall 1976). In the United Kingdom the increase was even more pronounced. The handful of Special Areas of 1934 had, in effect, spread to such an extent that by 1972 the various types of designated area covered almost 50 percent of the total United Kingdom population. However, recent government measures in the United Kingdom have drastically reduced the geographical coverage of assisted-area policy (Figure 3.24). By 1982 the percentage of the population included will have fallen to roughly 25 percent.

In addition to explicitly regional policies, there is a trend towards policies targeted at the urban, and especially the inner-city, scale. Again, Britain provides a clear indication of this trend. For example, under the 1978 Inner Urban Areas Act certain areas were designated as Partnership Areas and Programme Areas in which central government and local authority initiatives to improve both employment and the physical environment were to be co-ordinated. As Figure 3.25 shows, the areas to be assisted cut across the areas qualifying for regional assistance. An additional element was introduced in 1980: a small number of 'enterprise zones' are to be established in which the hope is to stimulate new activities – and jobs – by offering both a high level of financial incentives and also a good deal of freedom from planning controls and other regulations.

The most common form of spatial economic measure used by all governments has been the provision of grants, loans or tax allowances for capital investment. The primary object clearly has been to stimulate the building or extension of factories in the designated areas on the assumption that such investment either would not have occurred at all or, if it did, it would have been located in more prosperous parts of the country. In some cases, for example, the United Kingdom, government has subsidized employment as well as capital by granting those firms located in the designated areas a sum of money for every worker employed. This, in effect, reduces the firm's wage bill as an incentive for it to provide jobs. A good deal of public money has also been channelled into public works, or what is generally called *infrastructure*. These include basic physical amenities ranging from highways to public utilities, industrial parks and advance factories, health and education facilities. In the United States, between 1966 and 1973, some three-quarters of total regional expenditure of $2 billion was used for public works (Estall 1976).

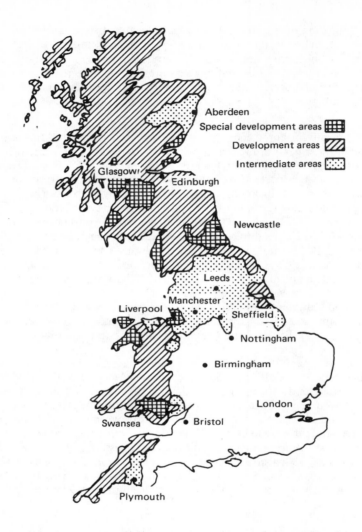

Figure 3.24a   Changes in the geographical distribution of Assisted Areas in Britain, 1978

Source: Department of Industry. Cr   Copyright.

For the most part, government regional economic policies have been of the 'carrot' variety, the carrot being the financial and other incentives offered to private industry to locate or expand their operations in designated areas. In some cases, however, there has been a 'stick' to go along with the carrot. Such sticks tend to be wielded in countries with unitary rather than federal government structures for fairly obvious reasons. In the United Kingdom since the Second World War industrial development has not only been encouraged in the designated areas, it has also been prevented (though not totally) in the more prosperous areas. Thus a major

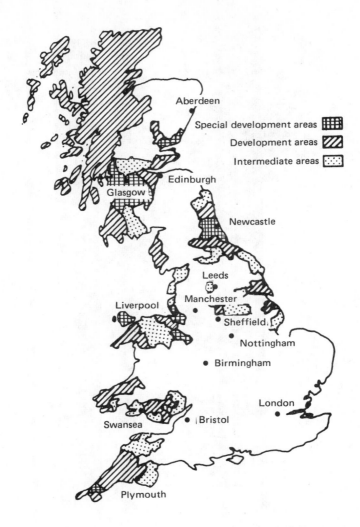

Special development areas
Development areas
Intermediate areas

Figure 3.24b   Changes in the geographical distribution of Assisted Areas in Britain, 1979

Source: Department of Industry. Crown Copyright.

plank in British regional policy has been the restriction of new development, particularly in the Southeast and the Midlands.

A further way in which government can explicitly alter the geography of the nation's employment is through the location or relocation of its own productive organizations. We noted earlier (Table 2.8) that the nationalized industries in Britain are comparable in scale to the very largest private business corporations. In such cases, government can greatly affect the jobs and incomes of entire communities either positively or negatively through its investment or disinvestment decisions.

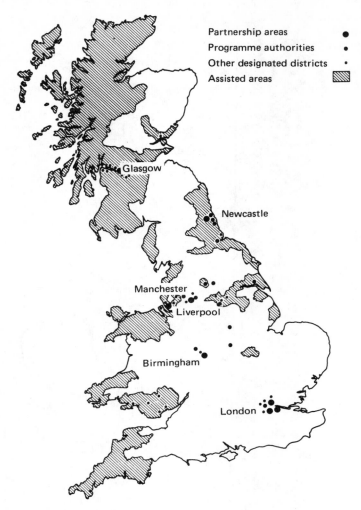

Figure 3.25   Designated urban areas in Britain, 1979

Source: based on G. Manners, D. Keeble, H.B. Rodgers & K. Warren (1980) *Regional Development in Britain*, 2nd edn, Chichester: Wiley, frontispiece.

Although there has been a strong 'social' element in some decisions – for example, to retain an uneconomic steel works in an area of high unemployment (or high political sensitivity) – recent government policy in Britain has insisted upon the commercial viability of public corporations. In other words, they are supposed to show a profit just as a private corporation must. The result, inevitably, is that the spatial rationalization process occurs in both the public and private industrial sectors. For example, the publicly owned British Steel Corporation is closing down its high-cost plants and concentrating its production on a small number of modern, low-cost plants. The outcome, inevitably, is major job losses in parts of the country, some of which are very heavily dependent upon employment in the steel industry. In 1980, for example, the British Steel Corporation closed its plants at Consett in northeastern England, Corby in Lincolnshire and Shotton in northwestern England with the loss of many thousands of jobs.

Although this is not the place to assess the effectiveness of regional economic policies, there can be little doubt that they have had a not inconsiderable impact on the geographical pattern of employment.* Encouraging investment in some areas and discouraging – or even restricting – it in others produces a geographical arrangement of jobs and incomes which probably would not have occurred otherwise. Designating some towns or cities as 'growth centres' alters the geographical flow of both public and private investment since it implies that those centres not so designated are 'no growth' or even 'decline' centres. Thus, decisions taken at national level regarding the geographical allocation of financial or other resources materially affects the livelihood of people and communities in places far removed from where the decisions are made. This point applies to almost all decisions made by government, even though, unlike regional policies, they are *not* deliberately geographical.

Suppose that a government decides to increase the rate of sales tax (or its equivalent) on automobiles. The objective may be simply to increase government revenue or perhaps to discourage automobile purchase in order to conserve energy. In itself this is a 'non-geographical' decision, but its *effects* will be very strongly geographical. The decision will have the greatest impact on those areas where the major automobile manufacturing plants are located – on southern Michigan in the United States and on the West Midlands in Britain, for example. Production targets may be revised downwards, workers may be dismissed or temporarily laid off. But the effects will be felt far beyond these assembly plants and their labour force. Automobile manufacture draws upon thousands of different components which are produced in a wide variety of geographical locations. Firms supplying the automobile manufacturers with transmission units or silencers, windscreens or tyres, will suffer a reduction in orders which, in turn, may lead them to reduce *their* labour force. The resulting loss of income by employees in all the affected plants will eventually feed through to local retail businesses as people cut back on domestic purchases. Thus, we can envisage a situation similar to that of rocks being thrown into a lake. The rocks (in the form of sales tax increases) have their primary impact at certain key points but their effects ripple outwards to involve other parts.

Much the same kind of differential geographical effect may result from other apparently non-geographical government behaviour. For example, the use of tariffs

*There is a continuing debate in the United Kingdom concerning the effect of government regional policy on employment. One school of thought, reflected in the work of Moore, Rhodes and Tyler (1977) and Keeble (1976, 1980), claims that regional policy may have increased employment in the Assisted Areas by roughly 280,000 between 1951 and 1970. Massey (1979) on the other hand, whilst agreeing that regional policies may well have contributed towards new jobs in the peripheral areas, suggests that other factors were also involved. In particular, she suggests that the changes in corporate organization, especially the increasing standardization of production, which we have discussed in this chapter, encouraged firms to seek out suitable labour concentrations. In other words, she sees the employment needs arising from production changes within large firms as coinciding with government efforts to attract industry to the assisted areas.

or quotas to regulate the inflow or outflow of products will have primary repercussions on those areas having a large stake in their production. The effects, again, may be either positive or negative. Regulations which restrict the import of textiles or clothing, of television sets or typewriters may well stimulate their domestic production and, thus, increase jobs and incomes in particular areas. Conversely, the reduction or removal of taiffs and quotas will have the reverse effect, especially if imported versions are much cheaper. Consumers in general may benefit, but jobs in the major producing areas may well be lost. For example, it was estimated in 1977 that some 1.6 million textile jobs in the EEC countries and some 2.3 million jobs in the United States were at risk because of increasingly high levels of low-price foreign imports of textiles. But these jobs are not evenly spread. In the United States it would be the communities of New England and the southern states which would be hardest hit; in Britain, the traditional textile areas of Lancashire and Yorkshire would be most seriously affected by such central government decisions.

Other ways in which non-spatial government actions may affect the geography of employment include policies on interest rates which, indirectly, may also affect the foreign exchange value of the nation's currency. High interest rates increase the cost of borrowing. For business firms it raises their costs in a variety of ways and tends to hit small businesses especially hard. Many may be forced to give up altogether and jobs are lost. High foreign exchange rates not only make imports cheaper in relation to domestically produced goods but also make the country's exports more expensive and less able to compete in foreign markets. Again, therefore, non-spatial policies may have an important effect on employment. On the one hand, some areas are hit by foreign imports; others depending on export trade are hit by the high price of their goods in foreign markets. The British economy in the early 1980s provides numerous examples of these effects, although it has to be said that it is very difficult to calculate precisely the impact of these various strands of government policies on employment change in particular places.

As a final example of government influences on the geography of employment, there is the effect of government purchases from the private sector. In Chapter Two we noted the example of the allocation of defence contracts to a relatively small number of prime contractors.* A major outcome of such uneven distribution of government contracts between corporations is that their *geographical* pattern is also uneven. Some areas derive great benefit, others do not. At the same time some areas are so heavily dependent on government contracts that any reduction in government spending on their particular activity will have serious, and perhaps catastrophic, effects. Figure 3.26 maps one aspect – the value of prime military contract awards by state for 1977. There is a clear dominance by a few states. In fact, a mere seven states received 50 percent of the total value of such contracts. Of the seven, California received almost one-fifth and is, as Brunn observed, 'quite literally a "contract" state'. Indeed, it was largely the cushioning effect of defence contracts which helped California through a period of massive decline in its aerospace and related industries in the late 1960s and early 1970s. In fact, California's share of the defence budget has been increasing even though the budget as a whole became a smaller proportion of

---

*Government expenditure of all kinds helps to create employment. Other aspects of such expenditure are examined in Chapter Five.

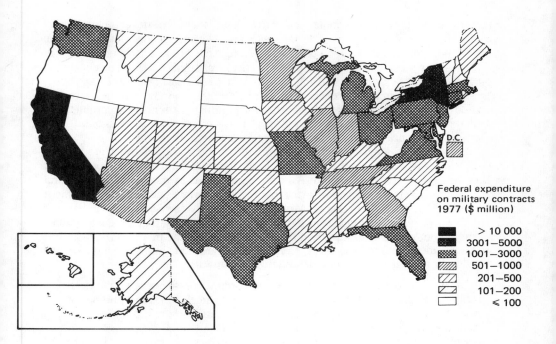

Figure 3.26 Allocation of federal defence contracts by state, 1977

Source: United States *Statistical Abstract* (1978), table 597.

GNP. The other major defence contract states in 1977 in order of contract value were New York, Texas, Massachusetts, Missouri, Virginia and Connecticut.

The West of the United States is especially strongly oriented towards industries in which federal expenditure is vital. Thus, the local economies of San Diego, Los Angeles and Seattle are inextricably tied to the federal purse-strings. Elsewhere, the aerospace complexes of the South around Houston and in Florida, the defence contractors in Connecticut (especially around Hartford) and the defence and aerospace activities of St. Louis all reflect the geographically uneven impact of federal government policies. Rees (1979) suggests that federal outlays have been an 'invisible hand' in stimulating employment growth in the peripheral states:

> Implicit in the economic history of the South . . . has been a recognition that if the northern states controlled the economic allocation of resources, one way to counter this was through the political process, particularly the seniority system in Congress. In this way a political allocation of resources could be achieved. Examples that immediately spring to mind are the military bases set up in the south west during the 1940s. These have been cited by many as the catalyst for inducing the movement of military personnel and procurement contracts into the region. More recently, the Space Triangle (between Houston, Huntsville, and Cape Canaveral) in the Johnson era steered NASA and DOD contracts southward.
> *Rees (1979), p.51.*

Although such a pattern may be less clear in Britain, there are, nevertheless, many parts of the country which have a big stake in government contract work. The telecommunications and the power-generator industries in the 1970s are cases in point. In good times, of course, the benefits to the local inhabitants can be enormous – increased job opportunities and high wages benefit both workers in these industries and the communities in which they spend their money. But government demands in defence and other high-technology industries tend to fluctuate very considerably. Indeed, there have been some massive booms and slumps in local economies which are heavily dependent on government contracts.

Local effects of dependence on government contracts are well illustrated by the case of Seattle. In 1970, roughly four in every ten workers in manufacturing industry in the Seattle-Everitt Metropolitan Area were employed in producing aircraft and aircraft parts. A very large proportion of this employment was geared to government and government-related contracts. Much of the activity focused upon the Boeing Corporation which has its headquarters in Seattle and is very much a government-oriented corporation with more than half of its total revenue in 1961–1967 derived from government defence contracts. Employment variations in Seattle have tended to be closely related to variations in Boeing's fortunes:

> Boeing's total employment and Seattle's economic performance have been intimately related in the past. . . . Three times since 1958, the influence of Boeing's employment pattern has reversed national growth or decline trends for the Seattle area. Twice, in 1959–1960 and 1963–1964, declines in Boeing's fortunes created minor recessions in Seattle during periods of general national prosperity, while Boeing's expansion in 1966–1967 reversed a nationwide recession for the Seattle area. Three times over the past fifteen years, Boeing's local employment dropped by over 20 percent. During 1966 alone, on the other hand, it grew from 64,000 to about 92,000. . . . Only a short time later, between mid-1968 to October 1971, Boeing's employment in Seattle fell again from its all-time high of about 101,500 to 37,200. Boeing's payroll declined from $958 million in 1969 to $515 million in 1971, while Seattle area unemployment increased from 21,200 (3.2 percent) in mid-1968 to 98,200 (15 percent) in mid-1971. It was estimated that the total direct, indirect and induced employment impact . . . 'would be at least 100,000 jobs lost, and an income decline of at least $1.4 billion'.
> *Krumme and Hayter (1975), pp.349, 350, 351.*

Although such massive fluctuations in employment were not totally caused by Boeing's role as a government contractor, there is little doubt that this was a major contributory factor, together with the corporation's attempts to diversity its activities. Thus, the employment increases in 1958–1959 were associated with the build-up of missile and aircraft programme and the award of the Minuteman contract. The ensuing decline was related to the reduction in B-52 sales and in first-round orders for 707-720 aircraft. Post-1969 employment losses were largely related to the decline of 747 orders, the cancellation of the SST programme and the generally low level of military aircraft and aerospace sales (Krumme and Hayter 1975).

Summary

Quite clearly the aggregate changes in employment and unemployment discussed earlier in this chapter have been associated with particular geographical outcomes. Some quite fundamental changes appear to have been taking place in the spatial allocation of job opportunities within both the United States and the United Kingdom during the past ten or fifteen years. Such changes are evident at a variety of geographical scales – inter-regional, intermetropolitan, urban-rural and intra-metropolitan. There is clear evidence of a changing regional balance of labour demand, particularly for manufacturing. At the intermetropolitan level the large, long-established industrial centres have been in relative – in some cases, absolute – decline. It is the smaller non-metropolitan centres in particular which have been gaining manufacturing jobs. Within metropolitan areas the long-standing trend of decline at the centre and growth of employment in the suburbs became even more pronounced during the 1970s. Massive job losses have been experienced by many inner-city areas. Geographical patterns of unemployment also show a good deal of variation over time. Some regions have maintained a favourable position in relation to the national average, others have even improved a little, albeit with larger actual numbers of workers unemployed. But a significant number have seen their unemployment position worsen in both relative and absolute terms. Again it is the older cities and their inner areas which are suffering particularly high rates of unemployment.

Such changes in the geography of employment opportunities are being produced by the combined effect of three major processes: changes in demands and in technology, developments in corporate strategies and the activities of governments. Although we have dealt with each separately, it is important to bear in mind the strong overlaps and interconnections between them. Shifts in demand, both nationally and internationally, together with changes in product and process technology, have had a particularly powerful effect on those geographical areas with a heavy dependence on certain industrial sectors. Changes have been occurring in the geography of technological change itself which have stimulated differential regional employment growth. These developments do not occur in some disembodied manner; they are outcomes of the growth and re-organization strategies of business corporations. The giant multiplant corporations are reshaping the geography of employment through their increasing tendency to separate their internal functions into different types of location. Each of the major functional levels of the firm tends to bring a rather different range of occupations and incomes to the areas in which they are located. The third major influence on the geography of employment is government. Most government policies, whether spatial or aspatial in design, have a geographical outcome. Although the various regional policies are the most obvious way in which government influences the geography of employment, other policies, for example, those relating to taxation, trade, interest and exchange rates, and government purchasing may be equally, if not more, important.

FINDING A JOB: CHOICES AND CONSTRAINTS IN THE LABOUR MARKET

Local and non-local labour markets

The trends in employment and unemployment discussed so far in this chapter represent the broad context of the supply of, and demand for, labour. It is against this general background that specific individuals seek employment and specific employers seek labour. The labour market is, as we pointed out earlier, the device for bringing the participants together and, as Figure 3.1 demonstrated, it is a complex and dynamic mechanism. In fact, of course, there is no such thing as a single, homogeneous labour market; there is, rather, a myriad of submarkets. In particular there are submarkets for different *types* of labour – for teachers, welders, cab drivers, secretaries, chemical engineers and so on. A further complication is that these submarkets tend to have rather different geographical dimensions.

How individuals relate to such labour submarkets, how they are able to find employment, depends on two important variables:

1 The propensity to respond to job opportunities away from home

2 The spatial range of information about job opportunities.

The process can be conceived within the framework of time-space constraints outlined in Chapter One. Hägerstrand's coupling and authority constraints define both the nature and location of places of employment and also the rules of entry to such employment. Given these constraints the key variable becomes the capability constraints operating upon the job-seeker. If the home base is fixed, then, as we have seen in Figures 1.6 and 1.7, there will be a spatial limit beyond which the person cannot travel and return on a daily basis. A combination of personal mobility and domestic responsibilities will determine the spatial range within which employment can be engaged in without relocating the home base. In general, individuals with access to a private car will have greatest spatial flexibility of employment within the local labour market. Those with conflicting allegiances, such as married women with domestic responsibilities, will have a more restricted spatial range than those without.

Whatever the variation between individuals in their capability constraints, if the home base is fixed, then the job-seeker is clearly locked into the *local* labour market. Quite obviously, localities vary very substantially in both the range and the quality of jobs they offer. For example, the great metropolitan complexes like Greater London or Greater New York offer almost the entire range of employment types within commuting range. By contrast, predominantly rural communities like those in Mid-Wales or, say, the Appalachians offer only the most limited job spectrum to their residents. Of course, as we saw in Chapter Two, commuting fields generally and those of the metropolitan areas in particular have expanded enormously in recent decades. Innovations in transport and communications media during the last half-century have seen the labour markets of the major urban centres explode. In doing so they have absorbed within themselves the jobs and workers of hundreds of previously discrete communities around them. Reference back to Figure 2.39 reminds us of the way in which commuting fields and their associated local labour markets have spread themselves out around the cities of the United States. In this process populations from 50,000 to several million have been assembled together within daily commuting range. For the United Kingdom, Figure 2.38 provides a similar picture defined by its Metropolitan Economic Labour Areas (MELAs). It is clear from this that in such a small country as Britain the expansion of commuter fields has drawn all but the most peripheral regions into an urban-dominated network of metropolitan labour markets.

However, although the potential variety of jobs is greatest in large metropolitan areas, only the higher-paid and most mobile sections of the workforce can effectively choose from the total variety available. Even within the broad sweep of opportunity presented within the urban commuter field, there are some workers whose job choices remain very closely constrained by the influences of time and distance. Working mothers present a classic example, constrained by the needs of their children to work close to home. Similarly, the low-paid may also represent a confined case under the particular circumstances where their access to jobs involves travel costs which eat quickly into net wage returns. More subtle influences associated with the functioning of information networks may also lead to the creation of relatively isolated labour submarkets within the general urban setting. For some ethnic communities, for example, the free flow of job information may be confined to the community itself, falling off sharply outside the immediate neighbourhood and effectively closing-off information about job opportunities outside. Genuinely *local* labour markets do, therefore, still exist even within the flexibility and variety available in urban labour catchment areas. *

Characteristically, employers seek labour according to their expectation of being able to recruit suitable applicants. This also has a geographical dimension. There is no point in wasting money and effort on advertising nationally for jobs which can be filled easily from the local area. Thus some jobs, particularly lower-grade manual and service jobs, routine clerical jobs and so on, tend to be advertised within, and filled from, the local labour market. However, with the progression to more specialized job skills, or where demand is less likely to be localized, or in the cases of those particular activities where workers tend constantly to be on the move – migrant farm workers, construction workers, sales representatives, for instance – the labour market tends to operate over a wider geographical area. This may cover several localities, whole cities or broad regions. For many of these occupations a move away from home either on a temporary basis or through migration tends to be built into the functioning of the labour market mechanism. At the very top of the market in, say, the professional and executive grades, markets tend to be national or even international in their scope, with many of their participants committed during the most progressive stages of their careers to a semi-nomadic existence, moving temporarily at first and later bringing family with them to a succession of venues. For these groups – civil servants, managers, professional engineers and scientists, doctors,

---

*The obvious way to break out of the constraints of the local labour market is to relocate the home base: to migrate. But residential migration is a far from simple process, particularly for households with several dependent members. We shall be looking in some detail at residential mobility in Chapter Four. At this stage it is only necessary to point out just how difficult residential movement can be, particularly for the low-paid. Moving house is not only a very costly process but also there are frequently social and institutional barriers to movement.

academics and so on – the market tends to revolve around job information supplied by the prestigious national newspapers or by professional journals.

In summary, then, although overall generalization is difficult, it is possible to visualize the general labour market as consisting of clusters of submarkets with different spatial ranges. Some are highly localized, straying little beyond the bounds of the local community. Others extend over whole regions or metropolitan areas, whilst, at the extremes, some are national or even global in their scope.

An institutional approach to the labour market

Until relatively recently, most labour market studies were set within a neoclassical economic mould of self-adjusting, competitive markets. However, the elegant abstractions of the theoretical models of labour markets seem increasingly remote from the real world in which people seek jobs and employers seek workers. One reaction to the neoclassical approach emphasizes the key role of *institutions* in the labour market. Since we have stressed the importance of large organizations and other institutions in modern Western society, the institutional approach fits neatly into our framework. Two aspects of the approach are especially relevant for our purposes. One is the tendency for large organizations to operate *internal* labour markets, the other is the notion that labour markets possess a *dual* structure which divides jobs into 'good' ones and 'bad' ones.

Internal labour markets of large organizations

One of the starting points of the institutional theorists' argument is that, while traditional economic models assume the labour market to be something *outside* the firm – a pool of labour in which employers freely compete – substantial labour markets also exist *within* firms. Indeed, it is suggested that this internal labour market is the one with which the majority of today's wage-earners are involved. (We have already seen in Chapter Two that some of the largest business organizations employ more than half a million workers.) A good deal of competition between employees is, therefore, wholly set *within the context of a single organization* as workers vie with each other for company jobs as foremen, managers, chief clerks, chargehands and so on. They compete with each other in this context not simply for better wages but for a combination of wages and other important non-monetary benefits, such as job security, status, fringe benefits and general job satisfaction.

In fact, in the big company sector the contact with the external labour market is confined to particular levels in the hierarchy of jobs within a firm. These are the limited *entry points* through which newcomers join from the outside world. Workers, often school-leavers or college graduates, compete with each other on the open market *only for initial entry*. Once appointed, they become subject to the evaluation procedures and informal rules laid down by the institution itself and competition to climb the company ladder on the inside tends to vary in accordance with these. While most entry points are restricted to the bottom rungs of the promotional ladder, there is also some entry from the external market at the very highest career levels. Between the two, contact with the external market is, of course, still possible for those who wish to leave the company but, given that internal labour markets dominate most large companies, it is often difficult to join another career ladder part way up. Another feature of the internal labour market is that it influences the nature of information flow in the labour market. Opportunities within the company are better known than those outside. Even where there are better wages and benefits to be had, workers may well be happy to stay where they are out of sheer ignorance of the alternatives. The imperfect nature of job information generally is, in fact, a fundamental component of the institutionalist's critique of neoclassical labour market theory.

The geographical significance of the internal labour markets of large organizations with their limited entry points arises from the ways in which such organizations arrange their operations spatially. As we have seen, large business corporations tend to separate their major functions into different types of geographical location. Since each level in the corporate hierarchy tends to have a different employment profile, the mix of jobs varies geographically according to which 'parts' of firms a region has. The internal labour market of the large organization intersects with its functional-geographical structure to create important repercussions for the availability of jobs.

Take first the corporate headquarters. These tend to be located in the core areas of national and regional economies. They are staffed almost exclusively by white-collar workers, from higher-company executives through professional specialists like lawyers and accountants to more general grades like programmers and typists. They also employ a number of manual workers in service occupations such as catering, cleaning and driving. The labour submarkets within which each of these occupational grades operate are strikingly different, even though they all work for the same company. The highest managerial grades, for example, tend to be filled by 'company people' closely tied into the firm's internal labour market. They will probably have been recruited through the discrete entry points mentioned earlier, although the most senior executives may have been acquired from other large corporations through 'head-hunting' activities. These, however, will be something of an exception. Most executives will have been recruited some time previously from, perhaps, the graduate entry scheme and acquired varying amounts of company service. For them the promotional ladder is the basis for incentives, and competition will tend to exist in relation to this with less regard for the world of opportunity outside. While the market through which they entered the company was almost certainly national in its scope, that in which they now compete for preferment is as spatially distributed as those individuals in the company with similar ambitions. Some may be within 'visual' range, others doing their stint in the more peripheral operations of the company.

The same sort of national-internal market also covers the more specialist and professional company servants, although the overall range of opportunity is probably narrower. Few such workers will have been recruited in any genuinely 'local' sense. Whether or not many of them find themselves close to their original roots will be a function more of the social mix of the area in which the headquarters is located (measured, for example, by its relative share of graduates per head of population) than by any local component in the firm's labour market. These, then, represent the 'best' jobs on offer in the corporate hierarchy, their highly mobile occupants are recruited from a national pool and move, both occupationally and spatially, largely at the behest of the company itself.

In the middle ranks of the headquarters' hierarchy come those with rather more generalized skills. For them, the probability is that the original labour submarket through which they entered was one bounded by the commuter field of the headquarters or other higher-level establishments. Once appointed, they too might be unwilling to pass through the external labour market *en route* to another company. They may be content to limit their horizons to their present employer in bargaining for pay and conditions. For this group, then, there is a local labour market bounded generally by the travel-to-work area. Within this, submarkets for typists, programmers and clerks have varying degrees of job turnover and intercompany mobility. Headquarters and other higher-level units thus exercise a powerful *regionalized* demand in such labour submarkets, providing entry points which may stimulate inter-regional migration on the part of those willing and able to move.

At the bottom of the headquarters' personnel ladder, conditions for the manual service workers are rather different. There is a lower degree of attachment to the company *per se*. Hiring may well be on a short-term basis, part-time and week by week, with the headquarters' unit this time figuring as just another office among many utilizing the services of cleaners, tea ladies, janitors, drivers and the like. The market for such workers, many of them married women, tends to be genuinely local and often confined to the immediate neighbourhood. Turnover rates are probably high and the overall operation of the market hardly influenced by those internal factors which characterize other worker groups. Thus, internal labour markets may not necessarily be co-extensive with companies. Only the better jobs tend to be involved in them while lower-grade employment reflects more closely the conditions of the traditional external market.

Let us now take the contrasting case of the branch assembly plant, more likely to be located in a peripheral region, to see how, within the same company, organizational structures common in the contemporary world influence the labour market. Whatever the degree of devolved management control the branch assembly plant offers a substantially different mix of white-collar and blue-collar jobs. For the small numbers in the managerial and professional grades, conditions are similar to those described for the headquarters' case. National markets feed discrete entry points and the employees are moved around corporate divisions and plants in accordance with the company's needs. The smaller numbers of typists, clerks, programmers and so on will be drawn from occupational submarkets operating within the travel-to-work area of the plant. Cleaners, janitors and catering staff also reveal similar patterns at the branch as at the headquarters, with weaker attachment to the internal labour markets of the company and a narrowly confined labour market catchment area.

It is the shopfloor manual workforce of the branch that provides the greatest contrast. The blue-collar group operates under institutional conditions emanating from *two* sources – the company itself and the trade unions. Whilst entry points from the company side are determined by tasks to be performed, it is the trade unions which, in many cases, act as secondary 'gatekeepers', controlling labour supply and the assignment of tasks to particular groups of workers. For the time-served tradesmen whose skills, on balance, remain in short supply, union control tends to remain strong and union rulebooks, rather than the strict laws of supply and demand, govern pay differentials and conditions of work. For other blue-collar groups, trade unions also tend to be involved with varying degrees of power in the wage-bargaining process although less control tends to be exerted than in the case of skilled craftsmen. Clearly, this is no place to open up the debate on the role of trade unions in the contemporary workplace, although we have already seen that many corporations have sought to minimize the power of trade unions by relocating their production plants in areas of weaker union influence. Nevertheless, the unions represent an institutional force whose power on the shopfloor is hardly less than the power of the corporate hierarchy on the lives of white-collar executives. In both cases there is a solid interface of power relationships and group pressure between the economic laws of the market place and the real behaviour of employers and employees.

In spatial terms the shopfloor workforce is supplied from within the local travel-to-work area. There is little inter-regional mobility, partly because of the reluctance of such workers to move from their home area, partly because of the costs of moving and partly because of the operation of housing markets (a topic developed more fully in the next chapter). Within the commuting field of the plant, labour submarkets for various worker groups tend to operate with differing degrees of spatial freedom. Some skilled, high-wage workers may willingly travel long distances to work, while part-time, female assembly hands and the lowest paid generally tend to operate within much tighter spatial constraints. As with the white-collar grades, there may be more or less willingness to accept the narrow horizons imposed by working continually with the same company. Here again, however, the bias inherent in the flow of job information will often mean that workers remain ignorant of wage differentials in the local market, making it possible to observe sharp variations in pay over short distances even for the same jobs.

The existence of internal labour markets within large organizations, together with the particular geographical arrangement of their functional units, adds considerable complexity to the structure of labour markets. It also helps to produce some of the geographical contrasts in occupations and skills discussed earlier in this chapter. Quite clearly, for large organizations, only certain types of workers are drawn from local labour markets. Higher-level employees are drawn from the national, or even international, scale in ways which contribute to the 'brain drain' from regions (and countries) which cannot offer high-level career opportunities themselves. At the other extreme, the lowest grades of workers in the corporate hierarchy – those in the poorest-paid manufacturing and service jobs – seem to operate almost indifferently of the corporate structure which so powerfully affects jobs above them. They remain closely constrained, regardless of location in core or periphery, or classification as production or service personnel. For these workers, local labour markets exist in a realistically narrow sense – little changed, it would seem, by transportation developments or corporate functional re-organization.

'Good' jobs and 'bad' jobs: the concept of the dual labour market

For the most part, jobs in the internal labour markets of large organizations are 'good' jobs, offering not only good financial rewards but also good working conditions, career prospects and, for some grades, substantial fringe benefits. In contrast to such 'good' jobs, there are many jobs in modern economies which might be termed 'bad' jobs, with

> low wages and fringe benefits, poor working conditions, high labour turnover, little chance of advancement, and often arbitrary and capricious supervision.
> Doeringer and Piore (1970), p.165.

Doeringer and Piore term the labour markets in which such 'bad' jobs occur *secondary* labour markets. *Primary* labour markets, the other component of their *dual labour market* concept, are broadly synonymous with the internal labour markets of large organizations.* The primary and secondary sectors not only have very different qualities and characteristics but also, it is suggested, very little mobility between them. Secondary workers, then, are viewed as being trapped in the bad jobs sector and denied access to the good jobs of the primary sector. Powerful pressures seem to exist which prevent 'mixing' at the boundaries of the two sectors.

In the primary sector, for example, employers and workers (largely through active trades unions) put a premium on job *stability*. This simultaneously reduces the costs of labour turnover to the one and guarantees job security to the other, binding both parties into conservative positions and encouraging restrictive and protective hiring practices. There is, as a result, a tendency to 'off-load' destabilizing influences like short-term cyclical fluctuations onto secondary sector firms and workers. This action reinforces the *instability* that forms the characteristic feature of the secondary low-wage economy. By contrast with conditions in the primary sector, employers here seem adjusted to high rates of turnover, absenteeism and unpunctuality, while workers rarely expect job security and accept arbitrary and capricious management. Dualists, therefore, see the two employment sectors as 'locked-in' to certain kinds of mutually exclusive behaviour that appear to characterize their operations and to condition the nature of the interaction between them.†

Hiring and firing practices in much of the secondary sector reflect conditions very much like those of the competitive market conditions of traditional labour market theory. Examples of these include casual labouring jobs in the construction industry, general domestic work and casual catering employment (e.g., dishwashing). There are also some secondary sector jobs attached to, but not fully integrated with, primary sector activities. We have already mentioned office cleaners, labourers and catering staff in the big company office. We could also add labouring jobs in the engineering industries or temporary packaging lines in assembly and light manufacturing. Perhaps the reader's shortest guide to this particular subset of the secondary employment spectrum is to consider those jobs regularly open to students on vacation who, with working mothers and 'moonlighters', form the most regular members of the large part-time contingent among secondary market clientele.

Part-timers in particular, but also many full-time employees, typically exhibit one of the most characteristic traits of the secondary sector worker – *a low degree of*

---

*The terms 'primary' and 'secondary' when applied to labour markets should not be confused with the primary and secondary sectors of the economy as a whole. In the latter case, the terms refer to the type of economic activity involved. Thus, the secondary sector of the economy is composed of manufacturing industries. In labour market terms, manufacturing *industries* contain both primary and secondary *labour markets*.

---

†Internal labour markets do, in fact, exist in the secondary sector but they are of particular types and are characteristically underdeveloped. In particular, internal markets here have many ports of entry and there are only short chains of horizontal or vertical mobility. Jobs in them, like the majority of those in the secondary sector, tend to be low paying and working conditions are often unpleasant. Doeringer and Piore suggest that typical examples of the secondary internal market are provided by blue-collar jobs in foundries, stitching and pressing jobs in clothing factories and menial jobs in hospitals.

attachment to the job or workplace. Such attitudes are, of course, reciprocated by secondary sector employers who often show a *low degree of commitment to their workers*. Both exist in symbiosis and it neither pays the worker to become too attached to his job in a generally unstable, high-turnover situation, nor the employer to invest his resources in the provision of training for his short-term workers. By such inter-relationships as these the secondary sector is built up, with the attitude of the one participant hardly interpretable except in relation to the other. Similar two-way responses typify other areas of employer-employee relations. Undisciplined work habits become met with arbitrary justice and supervision (or vice versa). Endemic pilfering is met by exploitatively low fringe benefits (or vice versa). Ageing, ill-maintained machinery is met with low standards of use and operator care (or vice versa). The list could go on, but repetition would serve only further to reinforce the essentially *negative* nature of secondary sector workplace relationships and of attitudes which work directly against self-improvement in any form.

Thus, while the primary sector of the labour market is characterized by employment stability, internal promotion and good pay negotiated by strong unions, the secondary sector is very different. It is, first and foremost, the sector in which the low-paid are concentrated. It offers little on-the-job training, unstable employment, poor promotion prospects and has low levels of unionization. Generally, it is a sector more subject to intensive competition and is at the lowest level of the hierarchy of business activities. Since it depends heavily on work subcontracted from the mainstream companies, it also tends to have a sharply cyclical employment performance, expanding and declining quickly in response to change. It is in this sector, then, that the dualists see most disadvantaged workers trapped, primarily by attitude and custom but also by economics and geography. On the demand side its jobs are generated by small business in the less enlightened forms, by particular low-level worker requirements among the public institutions and by the need to perform menial tasks among the larger corporate enterprises. As such the secondary labour market cannot be firmly associated with any one sector of the economy or subset of corporate enterprise. It cuts horizontally across the labour rungs of the employment ladder in the economy as a whole, representing 'bad' jobs wherever they may be found.

One particular subset of the secondary labour market which is receiving increasing attention at present is the *informal sector*.* Most of the workers in this sector tend to be missing from official accounts. It is broadly divisible into a legal and an illegal subset. Typical activities on the wrong side of legitimacy are prostitution, drug-peddling, handling stolen goods, book-making, etc. More legitimate but less 'well-paid' tasks are house-painting, car-washing, floor-scrubbing, lift-minding, paper-selling and a variety of low-grade short-term store jobs. The workforce often comprises children, teenagers, moonlighters, parollees, as well as the unemployed. There are very low entry requirements. High turnover rates and informal work

---

*See, for example, Pahl (1980). The informal sector is also known by a variety of other terms: 'hidden', 'underground', 'black', for example. It gives concern to governments because it is a cash economy outside the net of the income tax authorities. The scale of the black economy is often underestimated, particularly in countries with high levels of regulation and taxation. Only recently, for example, government explanations of the large shortfall in tax receipts in the United Kingdom have evoked interest in the black economy and its probable scale.

patterns are typical. The only training is on the job and it offers limited prospects for advancement. These are ghetto jobs *par excellence* with particularly unstable employer-employee relations. For the most part, this is the sector most accessible to those cut out of other labour markets in society by racism, poverty, poor education and the informal discrimination we have just been describing. In the short term wages may well be high, but over the long run they are very low. Pahl has suggested that informal labour markets, particularly for the residents of inner-city areas, provide the basis for their 'real' economy – an economy generally cut off from the mainstream of national life.

The kinds of jobs, both formal and informal, which are filled by participants in the secondary labour market are those for which society exerts a demand, and someone is likely to have to fill them. However, the essence of the dual labour market view is that where such jobs become 'reserved' for particular groups who are permanently disenfranchised from the 'good' jobs of the primary sector, this becomes a key source of class division in modern society. Where such jobs become closely associated with particular groups – blacks, immigrants, 'guest' workers – the operation of the labour market provides yet another of those hidden mechanisms for the reinforcement of discrimination.

Further exaggerated by the operation of the housing market, which we examine in the next chapter, there has been a tendency for the forces of discrimination to provide the secondary labour market with a geographical habitat around the centres of the older cities. Here the so-called *trapped* hypothesis applied to the high levels of unemployment in the inner areas of the older cities has, as its basis, the notion that while 'good', primary sector jobs exist they are often *too far away* spatially for their labour demand to have any impact on the unemployed poor of the central city. Since the elements of labour demand most strongly expressed in central-city locations are those in the white-collar internal markets, then inner-city and ghetto residents are often cut out of them by all those factors which impede entry from the secondary to the primary labour market. Further, the decentralization and suburbanization of manufacturing during the past fifty years or so has removed even those primary sector job opportunities for which the inner-area resident may be considered better matched – manual jobs in industry. Frequently, it is suggested, the new industrial parks of the suburban and exurban fringe are simply too far away for central-area manual workers even to perceive job opportunities let along physically take them up. As a result, the 'trapped' theory sees the inner-urban poor both disenfranchised by education and skill from those top-grade, white-collar jobs close to where they live and, at the same time, prevented by sheer distance from taking those jobs in the industrial mainstream to which their skills render them better suited. In the event, it is argued, ghetto residents tend to be claimed by the submarginal or informal labour market on the fringes of legality, thereby confirming the view from the affluent suburbs of their general idleness and dubious moral character.

In many ways the case is overdrawn and the nature of the causal chain too simplistic in its outline. Nevertheless, there is clearly some degree of truth in a view that sees the inner-urban poor ground between the millstones of labour market dualism and the evolving geography of urban manufacturing which leaves them far from the sources of industrial employment to which they might be better suited. The existence of the inner areas of the older cities as pockets of high endemic unemployment, for whatever reason, is not in dispute.

Summary
Labour markets, the means through which people seek jobs and employers seek workers, are extremely complex. Submarkets exist for different skills and occupations and these vary greatly in location and geographical scale. Some jobs are filled by residents in the immediate locality, others from regional, national or even international sources. Similarly at the individual level, there are substantial differences in the geographical scale over which jobs are sought and in the awareness of job opportunities. Although the geographical scale of local labour markets has increased enormously with developments in transport, strongly localized labour markets still exist for some groups in the population. This is particularly true of the low-paid who cannot afford high commuting costs and of married women with children who cannot afford lengthy commuting times. The internal labour markets characteristic of large organizations cut across the simple distance dimension of the labour market. Limited entry points into the firm, together with the particular way in which organizational functions are distributed spatially, produce a pattern of job opportunities which favours some areas rather than others. These internal labour markets make up most of the primary sector identified in the dualist concept of the labour market. Contrasted with the 'good' jobs of the primary sector are the relatively 'bad' jobs of the secondary sector and the 'invisible' jobs of the hidden economy. Jobs in the secondary sector of the labour market, though found throughout the economy, tend to be concentrated in certain geographical areas, especially the inner areas of large cities.

The ways in which the labour market works clearly illustrate the operation of choices and constraints both for people seeking employment and employers seeking labour. Job-seekers are constrained, initially, by their basic set of skills and personal attributes, but also they are constrained by their knowledge of appropriate job opportunities and by their ability to travel to such opportunities. Further constraints are imposed by the operation of the internal labour markets of large organizations, particularly their limited points of entry, and by the dual nature of the labour market. Employers also face sets of constraints imposed by the availability of labour of suitable types within reach of their production plant or office. However, the large business organization has a good deal of locational flexibility and may be able to overcome the constraints of local labour markets by opening a branch plant in a more favourable (for the firm) location. Job-seekers also can, and do, migrate, but in general workers have been less mobile than enterprises. The constraints on residential relocation are very considerable.

WHO GETS WHAT IN THE LABOUR MARKET: VARIATIONS IN EARNINGS AND INCOMES

It should be apparent from our discussion so far that it is unrealistic to consider the workings of the labour market in isolation from the workings of the housing market. People have to have a home base from which to search for jobs and to travel to work on a daily basis. The matching of people to jobs depends, to a great extent, on the degree of matching between particular labour markets and particular housing markets. Access to housing depends primarily on income. Thus a logical link between our discussion of labour markets in this chapter and housing markets in the next chapter is the income derived from employment. The extent to which such income varies is an important element in a person's ability to find a home. In turn, the location of that home helps to determine the variety of job opportunities available. How income is generated through the workings of the labour market, how wages and salaries are determined, are part of the complex bargaining processes which are beyond our scope. The point we are making is simply that people derive income from employment.

Figure 3.27 illustrates the main sources of individual and household income. Income from employment (wages and salaries) is by far the largest source of income for the majority of people in Western society. In the United Kingdom in the late 1970s, earnings accounted for 69 percent of total personal income; in the United States the figure was only slightly lower at 64 percent. However, there are substantial

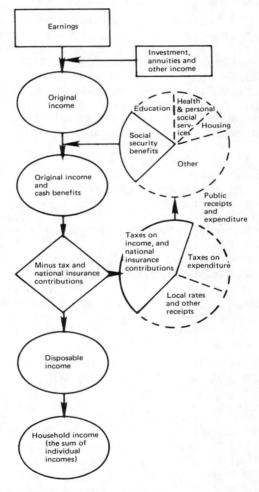

Figure 3.27   The main components of income

Source: Central Statistical Office, *Social Trends* 10 (1980), p.133. Crown Copyright.

variations in the *distribution* of earnings within the labour force. Such variations reflect a variety of influences – education, skill, responsibility, status, risk – are some of the explanations generally given for differentials in earnings. The extent of the differential between the lowest- and highest-paid occupations reflects the general values which society places on some occupations compared with others. In a society in which market forces operate, this can produce some intriguing anomalies – entertainers and sportsmen, for example, earning more than Prime Ministers.

One example of an 'earnings tree' is shown in Figure 3.28; it shows the relative distribution of earnings of male occupations in the United Kingdom. The height of the tree, and the relative positions of occupations along it, are measured in multiples of the pay of the lowest-paid worker, in this case the farm labourer. Two features stand out in Figure 3.28. First, most occupational groups are tightly packed near the base of the tree. Second, the height of the tree – in whose branches sit a very small number of occupations – is equivalent to fifty times the pay of the lowest-paid worker. Although the precise form of earnings trees will differ from one Western country to another, there is no doubt that, in general, the financial rewards from

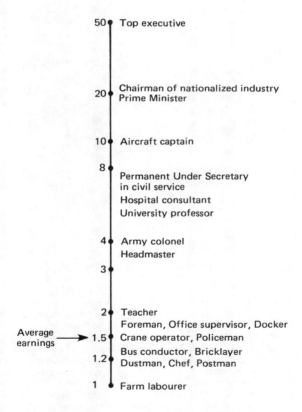

Figure 3.28   An earnings tree for male workers, United Kingdom

Source: A.B. Atkinson (1975) *The Economics of Inequality*, London: Oxford University Press, figure 2.4.

employment are highly skewed in their distribution. Over the years there has certainly been some convergence of earned incomes between occupations, perhaps more so in the United States than in the United Kingdom, but the occupational differences remain very great.*

The combination of differential incomes between occupations, together with the kinds of variations in the geographical distribution of occupations arising from the processes discussed in this chapter, helps to produce substantial geographical variations in income levels. Figures 3.29 and 3.30 demonstrate some of this variation. In the United States the highest per capita incomes at the state level (excluding Alaska) were in the District of Columbia, followed by Connecticut, New Jersey and California. Altogether nineteen states in continental USA had per capita incomes above the national average of $7019 in 1977. In general, incomes were highest in the Middle-Atlantic and Western regions and lowest in the South and South-Central regions, although there were individual exceptions.

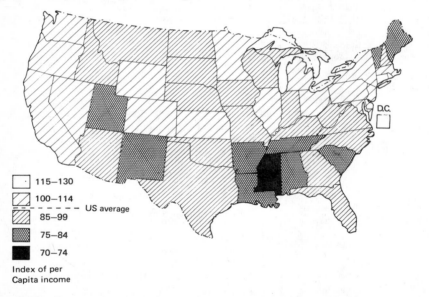

115—130
100—114
— — — — — US average
85—99
75—84
70—74

Index of per
Capita income

Figure 3.29   Geographical variations in personal income by state, United States, 1977

Source: United States *Statistical Abstract* (1978), table 725.

*It is important to distinguish between income derived from employment and income derived from wealth. Those with the highest earned incomes in society, while no doubt 'well-off', are rarely the most wealthy. Unearned incomes, that is, incomes derived primarily from wealth, are particularly highly concentrated in their distribution. Britain, for instance, still has one of the highest concentrations of wealth, despite its long tradition of liberalism and the increased power of the labour movement during the last fifty years. Estimates of this concentration vary with the quality of the data and, even more often, with the subjective views of the analyst. Even so, it is agreed that the degree of concentration is very high. Atkinson (1975), for example, claims that the richest 7 percent of the population own 84 percent of the private wealth and the richest 2 percent own roughly 55 percent. At the other end of the spectrum, the vast majority of the population owns no wealth at all, although the increase in home-ownership is changing this somewhat.

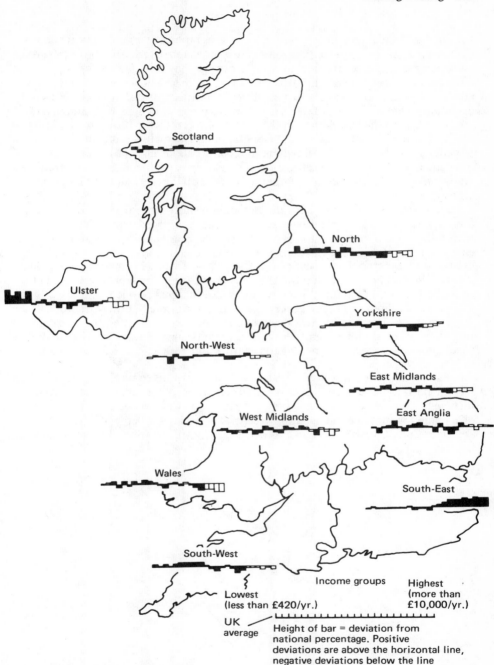

Figure 3.30   Geographical variations in income by region and major conurbation, 1971–1972

Source: based on B.E. Coates, R.J. Johnston & P.L. Knox (1977) *Geography and Inequality*, London: Oxford University Press, figure 5.1.

In the United Kingdom (Figure 3.30) geographical variations in income are shown rather differently. Here, incomes are divided into twenty-four groups and the percentage of regional income in each group is shown as a ratio of the United Kingdom average. The height of each column above or below the horizontal shows how far the incomes in each category differ from this national average. Where the deviation is significantly different statistically from the United Kingdom average, the columns are shaded. Although the pattern looks rather complicated it confirms the existence of higher incomes in the South and East and lower incomes elsewhere. In general the more peripheral regions and conurbations have larger proportions of their incomes in the lower categories. The extremes of income distribution geographically are represented by Southeast England on the one hand and Ulster on the other.

Of course, these variations do not only reflect occupational differences.* Incomes tend to be higher, on average, in big cities compared with small cities. Even within the same occupational group there may be pronounced geographical differences in rates of pay; one of the more obvious reasons for such differences is the existence of geographical variations in the cost of living. Living costs tend to be substantially higher in London and the Southeast than in the North, reflected in the common practice of paying a 'London allowance' in most public sector jobs. In the United States, living costs are generally much lower in the South. Variations in the wages and salaries of individual occupations will also be affected by geographical variations in the supply of, and demand for, that occupation. If a particular skill or occupation is scarce in one place and plentiful in another, this will be reflected in income differences.

For all of these, and other, reasons, data showing geographical variations in income need to be treated with caution. Nevertheless, there are major variations in income between occupations and between places. As we have seen, the major source of income for most people is employment. To see how income affects a person's ability to find a suitable place to live we turn to a consideration of how the housing market works.

---

*See Coates, Johnston, Knox (1977), p.145.

Chapter Four

Finding a home: geographical perspectives on the housing market

Although they are often treated separately, the labour market and the housing market are extremely closely inter-related. The relationships are both *functional* and *geographical*. From an individual's viewpoint, access to the housing market is determined very largely by income. As we demonstrated in the previous chapter, the dominant source of income for the majority of people in Western society is employment. Thus, the ability to become a home-owner or to pay the rent depends upon the individual's position in the labour market, particularly the income earned from employment. The close *geographical* relationship between the housing market and the labour market arises from the operation of time-space constraints which place outer limits on the possible geographical separation between home and workplace. Jobs need to be near to homes and homes to jobs. Hence, in examining how people find a home through the operation of the housing market, we need to keep these close relationships with the labour market firmly in mind. Our basic concern in this chapter is with how, and to what extent, housing needs are met and with the geographical form that the residential pattern takes. We begin by identifying some of the special characteristics of housing as a 'commodity'.

HOUSING AS A SPECIAL COMMODITY

> Houses are things other people live in. To the cabbie a house is a street number; to the tax office a revenue source; to the school so many desks; to the speculator an investment; but, to the occupant, it is home.
> *Bourne (1976), p.111.*

In any list of human needs, shelter is one of the most basic; it is one amongst a set of needs to do with a person's survival. But in modern Western society a house provides a great deal more than mere shelter. Because a house is fixed in its geographical location it provides the geographical pivot around which each person's regular activities occur; it is the focus of his time-space prism. Where a house is located in relation to all the activities which are necessary to fulfil a person's needs and wants is, therefore, a critical influence on that person's well-being. In our society, too, a house has two distinct types of value (Harvey 1972). First, it has a *use value* to its inhabitants: the value of having private space for individual and family use, the value of the house's location in relation to people and places. But a house has a second – *exchange* – value which is realized when the house is offered for sale in the housing market. In this sense, therefore, the house is a means of accumulating wealth. Harvey points out that use value and exchange value are closely related though they are not necessarily identical. He also summarizes the unique characteristics of housing as a commodity especially well and it is worth quoting his words at some length:

> *First, a house is not a commodity which can be moved around at will* (except mobile homes of course, but even most of these are rather immobile). It is therefore a very different commodity from things like wheat, iron ore, Cadillacs, stereo sets, and the like. *It is fixed in space because it has an absolute location. Second, a house is a commodity which changes hands infrequently* and most of the population will purchase a house only once or twice in a lifetime (although the rate of change is increasing). *Also, when a purchase is made*

there are very high transaction costs to be borne so that the marketing mechanism contains a barrier to free exchange. Third, shelter is something which no individual can do without and it is therefore impossible to substitute housing against apples in the way that apples can be substituted for oranges in our food supply. This means that *every individual will have to purchase housing no matter what its price. Fourth, the house has many uses and it therefore possesses a multitude of values* compared with apples which are only for eating, automobiles which are almost entirely for driving, and utensils which are only for cooking. *Finally, because housing is such a permanent feature in the built form of the city it is itself a form of stored wealth* which people use to preserve their own equity. The implications of this last point are legion. It means, for example, that the purchase of a house is not geared simply to use values, but to the future market exchange value of the property. For the individual who purchases a house, it becomes important to preserve the market value of the house because this represents much of his lifetime savings. It also means that a certain proportion of the housing stock will be 'used' by investors, landlords, real estate operators, and the like to generate income or to increase their net worth. This is a very different use from that described under 'use value' and it implies that money is to be made through market operations with respect to housing. . . .

A house is, therefore, a special commodity. It is fixed in geographical space, it changes hands infrequently, it is a commodity which we cannot do without, and it is a form of stored wealth which is subject to speculative activities in the market and the object of use by capital itself as a means for reaping income or for increasing capital value. In addition, the house has various forms of value to the user and above all it is the point from which the user relates to every other aspect of the urban scene.
Harvey (1972), p.16 (present authors' emphasis).

A house, therefore, represents a complex package of characteristics, including, for some people, an outward, visible indication of their social status. To live on the right side, rather than the wrong side, of the tracks is, for many, a primary aim in life. More generally it is an important determinant of our security, comfort, well-being, status and autonomy. As the background to childhood, and the primary socialization of the individual, many of life's more memorable experiences become associated with it. For many women in society the home is also simultaneously both residence and workplace. By its association with the nuclear family the home becomes a cultural focus within the social value-system. It is something to be 'fought for' and 'preserved' at all costs. Politicians speak loudly for it and governments legislate to enhance and preserve it. Despite all the changes that have occurred in Western society during the process of industrialization and urbanization, the home remains a primary focus of life.

RESIDENTIAL NEEDS: THE DEMAND FOR HOMES

It should be obvious from these introductory remarks that a definition of housing need or demand is a far from simple matter. The multifaceted nature of housing as a commodity means that any assessment of housing need based on simple tables of numbers of household units will be quite inadequate as an expression of real demand. Needs for privacy, security, autonomy and community are no less genuine than those for shelter and, since these embody elements of the general living environment as much as they do the physical structure of a home, they are all measured far less easily. However, in surveying the very large literature on housing and residential matters, two elements recur again and again as important explanatory factors in residential demand. One of these is the *family life-cycle*, the other is *social status* (including income, life-style and so on). Let us look at each of these in turn.

The family life-cycle and housing needs

The concept of the life-cycle can be applied at a variety of scales. Clearly, every individual moves through a number of 'stages' in the process of passing from birth to death. But from the viewpoint of residential need it is more useful to apply the life-cycle concept to the *household* or the *family unit* since this allows for variations in size and composition which are especially significant in producing changes in residential needs.

Precise definitions of each stage in the family life-cycle vary somewhat from one researcher to another. Table 4.1 presents a fairly widely accepted scheme and, although one could no doubt quibble about some of the detail, the general sequence is valid. For each identified stage in the cycle the table suggests the most likely emphasis of the household in that stage on a number of aspects of housing – both the kind of physical unit itself and its environmental setting.

The family life-cycle begins when an individual or a couple set up an independent household unit for the first time. The likelihood is that both members of the household will be occupied full-time outside the home, either in employment or perhaps as students. Space, in terms of the physical size of the dwelling, is unlikely to be an important consideration. In some cases a limited income may reinforce this and produce a demand for a low-rent apartment. In other cases, however, the combination of two incomes and few family expenses may produce a demand for higher-quality accommodation. In either case, the accessibility of the household to work-place(s) and to social facilities is especially important at this stage in the cycle.

The next major change in household needs is likely to come with the starting of a family. With this kind of change in family status the relative importance of household space and accessibility begin to be reversed; a process which continues through several subsequent stages. Access to the high life becomes far less important than space of the right kind. However, the loss of one income which follows child-bearing, even if only temporary, may not permit an immediate move to a house with its own garden. But as the stage shifts from 'child-bearing' to 'child-rearing' and 'child-launching' the need for more adequate household space becomes more acute. Initially it is the home itself which is most important: the number and size of rooms; the size, safety and access of yard or garden. It is at this stage that the unsuitability of high-rise apartments is most evident:

> It's no place to raise a family. A mother can't look out for her kids if they are fifteen floors down in the playground.
> *Quoted in Hall (1966), p.159.*

As children reach school age, however, access to neighbourhood facilities, especially schools and social facilities, becomes increasingly significant. In most urban-

Table 4.1 *The family life-cycle and changing housing needs*

Stage		Space	Median tenure	Housing age	Mobility	Locational preference
I	Prechild	Unimportant	Rented flat		1 move to own home	Centre city
II	Child-bearing	Increasingly important	Rented house	Old	High 2–3 moves	Middle and outer rings of centre city
III	Child-rearing	Important	Owned	Relatively new	1 move to owned home	Periphery of city or suburbs
IV	Child-launching	Very important	Owned	New	1 move to second home	Suburbs
V	Postchild	Unimportant	Owned	New when first bought	Unlikely to move	
VI	Later life	Unimportant			Widow leaves owned home to live with grown child	

Source: B.S. Morgan (1976) The basis of family status segregation: A case study in Exeter, *Transactions of the Institute of British Geographers, New Series,* 1, table 1

industrial societies these are the family life-cycle stages which have contributed most to the massive suburbanization developments discussed in Chapter Two. In contrast to these child-centred stages of the family life-cycle, the onset of the 'postchild' stage signifies a marked diminution in both space needs and in those environmental attributes which are specifically child-oriented. Many 'postchild' couples remain where they are but others move to smaller accommodation, though probably of a higher quality than that occupied at the start of their family life-cycle. Finally, in the 'later life' stage of the cycle, especially when only one person is left, a move to live with son or daughter or to a home for the elderly is common.

Quite obviously this is an idealized sequence. Not every household passes through every stage. For example, there has been, in recent years, a marked decline in the birth rate in both the United States and Britain. As a result, not only are families becoming smaller in size but also the number of voluntarily childless households has been increasing. Perhaps more important, not every household *can* adjust its housing in line with family life-cycle changes. This is a vitally important issue to which we return below in discussing the *constraints* on residential choice. The fact remains, however, that changes associated with the family life-cycle are a very significant element in changing residential demands. Rossi's pioneering study of residential mobility in Philadelphia during the 1950s showed that changes in family size associated with changes in the family life-cycle were the most important single cause of household's voluntarily seeking a new residence. A survey conducted in Britain by one of the major building societies produced similar results. As Table 4.2 shows, some one-third of a total of 5000 mortgage applicants were seeking a dwelling because of family life-cycle-induced factors. Allowing for the problem of interpreting responses, it seems likely that some of the 'mixed and other reasons' in the table were also associated with changes in the family life-cycle, particularly those related to *size* of accommodation.

The family life-cycle, therefore, is a very important element in the demand for housing since different stages of the cycle produce different housing requirements. A house in a particular neighbourhood appropriate for a family at one stage may be quite unsuitable for a family at a different stage. Thus, in terms of the *aggregate* demand for housing in any particular area, family or household composition is a key variable. For example, a pronounced rise in the birth rate – as in the baby-boom of a few years ago – will drastically alter housing demand in areas where birth rates were previously low and the area's housing stock adjusted to such rates. But, again, this is a question of the relationship between demand and supply to which we return later.

Social status and perceived housing needs

Needs related to the family life-cycle – especially those pertaining to the physical size of the dwelling and its access to essential facilities – are common to all segments of the population. But cutting across these are the kinds of *aspirations* households have regarding the 'quality' of their housing needs at different stages in the cycle. There is no doubt that a household's perception of its housing needs is very closely related to that household's perception of its *social status*. (Housing is, in Hirsch's terms, a 'positional good').

A cursory glance at any city will show that people of similar social status tend to live near to each other (of course where they live is, in any case, a partial determinant of that status). The earliest urban analysts saw such residential segregation as either a product or a reinforcer of class/status differentiation in society. Frederick Engels was probably the most powerful early commentator on the subject. Writing about Manchester in 1843, he commented that

Table 4.2 *Principal reasons for moving house*

		%
A. Life-cycle reasons		
Getting married		33.1
Increase in family size		1.9
Decrease in family size		0.8
To be nearer schools		0.5
To be nearer social facilities		0.1
	Subtotal	36.4
B. Career/income reasons		
Change in income		1.9
Change in job		12.0
Retirement		0.6
To be nearer work		5.3
More modern house		8.5
Obtain garage		0.6
Obtain better garden		0.7
Seek better neighbourhood		3.9
	Subtotal	33.5
C. Mixed and other reasons		
Accommodation too small		16.1
Accommodation too large		1.6
To be nearer shops		0.1
To be nearer relatives		1.2
Other		11.1
	Subtotal	30.1

Source: Nationwide Building Society (1970)

Owing to the curious layout of the town it is quite possible for someone to
live for years in Manchester and to travel daily to or from his place of work
without ever seeing a working class quarter or coming into contact with an
artisan. He who visits Manchester simply on business or for pleasure need
never see the slums because the working class districts and the middle-class
districts are quite distinct. This division is due partly to deliberate policy
and partly to instinctive and tacit agreement between the two social groups.
In those areas where the two social groups happen to come into contact with
each other the middle classes sanctimoniously ignore the existence of their
less fortunate neighbours.
Frederick Engels, The Condition of the Working Class in England,
in Henderson and Chaloner (1958), p.54.

More recent commentators would bear witness to the continued existence of social segregation of residence in modern society, though their descriptions and explanations might well differ from Engels. We shall turn later to the impact of class/status as a constraint on residential choice and to a more detailed analysis of the geography of residence. For the moment, however, let us concentrate our attention solely on class and status as a variable which impinges on housing need. Michelson (1970) has suggested that the inhabitants of modern Western society can usefully be categorized in the following way:

1 *Lower class*: low income, often no steady job or one subject to the whims of the employer; little education

2 *Working class*: regular blue-collar employment

3 *Lower middle class*: regular white-collar employment, usually for others; moderate salary at most

4 *Upper middle class*: high amount of education; comfortable salary or fees; sometimes self-employed but skills are transferable regardless

5 *Upper class*: great personal wealth either at present or within the family at some past date; at least moderate education; occupation, if any, is respectable.

Such categories are important in any estimation of housing needs. In the class/status game of ranking in society a key perceived need for many people is to see one's place in society reinforced in terms of home and neighbourhood, to live near one's 'own kind' and to ensure that offspring, at least in associating with others, and more important in marrying and reproducing the family, maintain and preferably improve the family status. As we shall see, however, freedom of choice is not equally distributed across these social classes.

Michelson points out that in the specific case of housing choice there are significant income overlaps between blue-collar and white-collar workers with the former also sometimes better-off in real terms. Even so, the white-collar groups tend on average to choose better homes. It may well be that it is education as a variable in choice which promotes this distinction. After all, it is education that moulds attitudes and values and is more concerned with the symbology of society. White-collar groups – generally the better educated – simply choose to spend more of their income on housing than on other competing goods. Within such groups there may also be subtleties of choice depending on individual value-systems. Some may value 'good neighbours' highly while others may seek a home in isolation surrounded by a high fence. For some status groups, safety, security and a sense of autonomy from what happens outside are highly prized. This is particularly so, it is sometimes suggested, among the lower classes. For upper and upper-middle classes it may be a community that they seek, with home itself as a secondary consideration. A good address, high-quality civic and recreation facilities, and top schools become the primary perceived needs and the search for a home begins with these. In short, aspiration levels differ among status groups and accordingly so does the nature of demand for home and neighbourhood. In Western society at large, of course, aspiration levels generally tend to be rising still, despite current economic crises.

In summary, then, the demand for housing in modern Western society is not simply expressed in terms of number of households. It is a complex demand within which the two most important influences seem to be the changing needs associated with progression through the family life-cycle and those related to the social expectations and aspirations of different groups in society.

RESIDENTIAL PROVISION: THE SUPPLY OF HOMES

Just as housing demand is a far from simple issue so, too, is the question of housing supply. At the beginning of this chapter we noted some of the special features of housing as a commodity. In terms of housing supply one of the most important of these characteristics is its relative permanence – and, therefore, its fixed geographical location. Hence a nation's – or a city's – housing stock is built up cumulatively over a lengthy period of time, the stock being made up of housing of different ages according to the area's specific history. The housing stock is differentiated in many ways other than age – we shall be examining some of these later – but an especially important consideration is the *form of tenure* on which housing is supplied. The major distinction to be made is between *owner-occupation* and *renting*. Over the last few decades the general tendency in most Western urban-industrial societies has been for the relative importance of owner-occupation to increase. In the United States, for example, roughly 47 percent of all housing units were owner-occupied in 1900. By 1950 the percentage had increased to 55 percent. However, the ensuing two decades saw a very rapid increase in owner-occupation so that by 1976 almost 65 percent of all United States housing units were owner-occupied. In the United Kingdom there is a much more even balance between owning and renting: in 1978 approximately 50 percent of all dwellings were owner-occupied and 50 percent were rented. To a very great extent, the larger rented sector in the United Kingdom reflects the scale of *public* housing since housing legislation in recent years has almost eliminated the privately rented housing sector.

Figure 4.1 summarizes the major elements which, together, combine to produce changes in the supply of housing. We can usefully organize our discussion of housing supply around this diagram.

New housing construction

An area's existing housing stock may be changed in three major ways. The first, and most obvious way, is by new construction ('simple growth' in Figure 4.1). As Figures 4.2 and 4.3 show, the volume of new housing construction tends to fluctuate very considerably from year to year. It is, in other words, strongly *cyclical*. Figure 4.2 depicts new housing construction in the United States between 1960 and 1977. During this period there were three major upsurges in house-building; the first peak was in 1963, the second – much higher – peak was in 1972, while there was another upsurge in housing construction in 1977. The deepest troughs in house-building during the 1960–1977 period were in 1966 and 1975. In the United Kingdom (Figure 4.3) a similar cyclical pattern is evident although the timing of the peaks and troughs was more or less the reverse of that in the United States. For example, whereas United States housing construction was very depressed in 1966, it was relatively buoyant at that time in the United Kingdom. Conversely, the United States peak of the early 1970s was matched by a trough in United Kingdom housing construction.

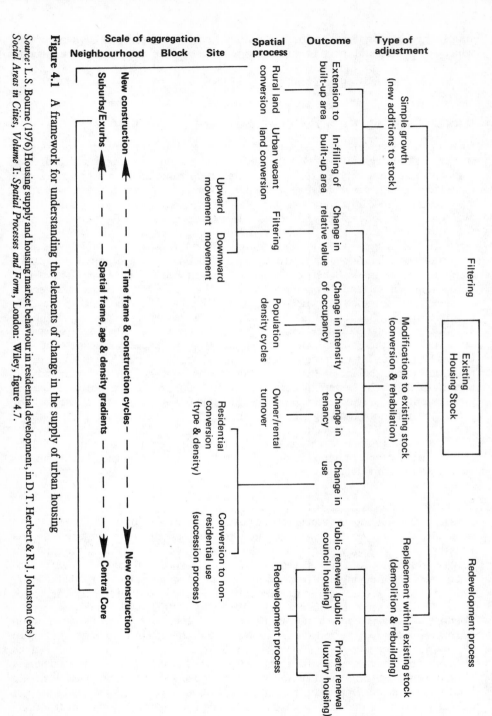

Figure 4.1 A framework for understanding the elements of change in the supply of urban housing

Source: L.S. Bourne (1976) Housing supply and housing market behaviour in residential development, in D.T. Herbert & R.J. Johnston (eds) Social Areas in Cities, Volume 1: Spatial Processes and Form, London: Wiley, figure 4.7.

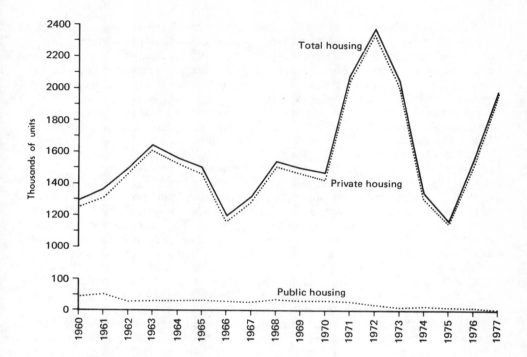

Figure 4.2 New housing units started in the United States, 1960–1977

Source: United States *Statistical Abstract* (1978), table 1366.

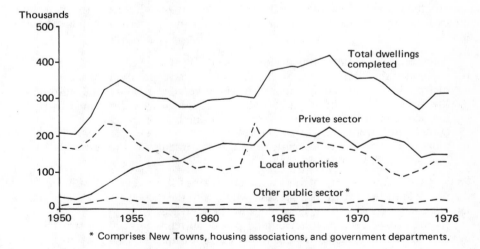

Figure 4.3 Permanent dwellings completed in the United Kingdom, 1950–1976

Source: Central Statistical Office, *Social Trends* 8 (1977), chart 9.3. Crown Copyright.

The main difference between the United States and United Kingdom housing markets, however, is not the different timing of the ups and downs of the construction cycle. Far more significant is the different relative importance of the private and public housing sectors. Figures 4.2 and 4.3 show this difference very clearly. In the United States, public housing is very small in volume so that the house-building cycle as a whole is almost entirely a reflection of private housing construction. Overall, public housing in the United States accounts for less than 2 percent of the total housing stock. The United Kingdom situation is very different. Since the 1920s, and especially since 1945, the public housing sector has grown very markedly. Thus Figure 4.3 shows that for most of the 1950s public housing construction far exceeded that in the private sector and there was a further public housing peak in the early 1960s. As a result almost one-third of total United Kingdom housing stock in 1976 – 31.8 percent – was public housing. A considerable proportion of public housing construction is, in fact, *replacement housing* (see the right-hand side of Figure 4.1), especially in the inner areas of the large cities. The massive urban renewal programmes of the 1950s and 1960s swept away thousands of substandard and dilapidated houses (including many which could easily have been renovated). Between 1956 and 1973, for example, some 1.4 million houses were demolished in England and Wales by local government authorities. Thus, almost 40 percent of the 3.7 million houses constructed in the public sector were straight replacements rather than actual additions to the nation's housing stock.

Despite the apparently high volume of new housing construction, its actual net contribution to a nation's aggregate housing stock is very small – probably only about 2–3 percent per year. But such an aggregate figure can be highly misleading. Housing is built in particular places. During periods of urban growth of the kind outlined in Chapter Two a city's housing stock may be increased very dramatically over a short period of time. Consequently, some cities have a much 'younger' housing stock than others. For example, of the 17 million new housing units constructed in the United States in the 1960s only one-eighth were in the metropolitan areas of the Northeast whilst one-quarter were in the metropolitan areas of the South.

> The result, of course, was a much newer inventory and a more rapidly changing mix of units in the South. A worker looking for living space in the metropolitan South could choose from an inventory in which one-third of the units had been built since 1960. . . . If that worker happened to be interested in apartment living, more than one-half of the units he could choose from were new. In the Northeast, however, only one-sixth of all units were new and only one-fifth of the apartment units were new.
> *Barabba (1975), pp.65, 68.*

Thus, between 1960 and 1970 there was an increase of 18 percent in the total number of housing units in the United States as a whole. But the increase in the South was 22 percent compared with only 12 percent in the Northeast.

At the urban scale, new housing construction tends to occur in two kinds of location (Figure 4.1): as an extension to the built-up area or as infilling of the built-up area. The first of these is, quantitatively, by far the most important. Most new housing construction – especially that of single-family dwellings in the private sector – occurs at the periphery of the built-up area. Hence, most urban areas have grown spatially by a process of accretion around a nucleus, the successive growth phases being recognizable as a series of housing age contours, rather like the annular growth rings on a tree. In most large cities, therefore, there is a clear 'age-of-housing gradient' with increasing distance from the city centre. Figure 4.4 illustrates such a pattern for the city of Minneapolis.

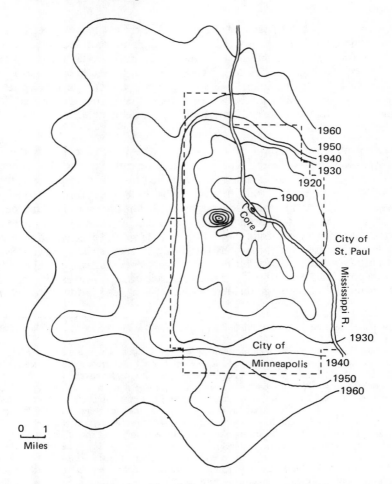

Figure 4.4   Housing age contours: the median age of housing in Minneapolis and vicinity

Source: J.S. Adams (1970) Residential Structure of Midwest cities, *Annals of the Association of American Geographers,* 60, figure 16.

The precise spatial form of new residential development on the periphery of a city – *suburbanization* – is the result of a number of inter-related forces, some of which have been referred to briefly in Chapter Two. Most important would seem to be the decisions by key institutions – both private and public – to develop the invariably cheaper peripheral land in a particular way. A recent study of the United States suburbanization experience by Checkoway (1980) throws some interesting light on this aspect of housing supply and is worthy of examination. Checkoway argues that the key element in postwar suburbanization in the United States was the emergence of the large-scale residential builder and the supportive policies of the federal housing agencies:

> The growth of many post-war suburbs was precipitated by decisions by large residential builders to select and develop suburban locations. There was nothing new about suburban development in America. What was new in this period was the developed capacity of large builders to take raw suburban land, divide it into parcels and streets, instal needed services, apply mass production methods to residential construction, and sell the finished product to unprecedented numbers of consumers.
> *Checkoway (1980), p.22.*

Such a process reflected the considerable changes which occurred in the residential construction industry after World War II, in particular, the emergence of the very large-scale builder. Whereas the large building firms were responsible for only 5 percent of all houses built in the United States in 1938, they constructed 64 percent of the very much larger number of houses by 1959. The big residential builders came to possess many of the characteristics of big business in general: they operated on a national rather than a local scale, they employed a large and specialized labour force, they had sophisticated and large-scale purchasing arrangements, they were heavily involved in advertising and marketing, they had access to finance to make large-scale operations possible.* In terms of our present discussion, however, the most important characteristic of the large residential builder was his predominantly suburban

---

*The epitome of the large-scale suburban builder in the United States was Levitt. Checkoway characterizes the firm as follows:

> Levitt adapted assembly line techniques to the mass production of housing. An army of trucks speeding along new-laid roads stopped and delivered neatly packaged bundles of materials at exact 100 foot intervals. Giant machines followed the trucks, digging rectangular foundations in which heating pipes were embedded. Each site then became an assembly line on which houses were built. Men, materials and machines moved past each site in teams, each performing one of 26 operations over and over again from site to site according to standards derived from systematic studies of time and motion. Every possible part and system was preassembled, prefabricated or precut to specification and size in the factory, and then brought to the site ready to assemble with machinery developed just for the purpose. Mechanization and labor-saving machinery, forbidden or prohibitive in traditional operations, were everywhere evident in Levittown. Levitt was less a builder, more a manufacturer of houses. Each Levittown house was controlled by Levitt from start to finish (pp.26–27).

Checkoway goes on to depict Levitt's practice of either producing most of his own materials supplies or buying in bulk at preferential prices. He points to Levitt's 'enviable capital position and a profitable partnership with government' which provided huge amounts of credit. He also describes the large involvement in consumer research – 'the Levitt house – and Levittown itself – was meticulously designed to match consumer preferences. Each house was small, detached, single family, Cape Cod in style, and centrally located on a small lot in a development in the suburbs. . . . For middle income consumers, Levittown offered a virtual dream house, and Levitt was the dream's entrepreneur' (p.28). In addition, Levitt, handled the whole purchasing process so that 'the entire financing and titling transaction was reduced to two half-hour steps. . . . Contract forms already stamped with fixed title enabled clerks to sign up to 350 buyers per day' (p.28).

orientation: the mass-production techniques being applied to new house building necessitated very large parcels of land at low cost.

The massive suburban development of the postwar period in the United States, which added so substantially to the new housing stock, could not have occurred without government support for the large building programmes. Checkoway argues that US federal housing policy in this period was predominantly suburban in its orientation. By encouraging home-ownership, new housing construction in the suburbs and by the preference for dealing with the large building firm, FHA policy seems to have contributed very materially to the particular form of new residential development. Other federal and state programmes reinforced the suburban trend. We have seen already how the spatial form of cities has been closely related to transport developments. One major result of the US federal highway programme was that it opened up large areas of land for residential development.

In Britain, the geographical scale of new housing construction on the periphery of cities has been less than in the United States. This is not only because of the relative scarcity of land but also because the public planning mechanism has operated to control the nature and direction of the development process. Even so, large-scale residential builders, such as Wimpey, Barratt and others, have created huge, homogeneous suburban housing developments in most British cities. At the same time, the complementary decisions by local authorities to zone land for residential use, to control the supply of land for housing and in other ways have had a very powerful influence on the supply, the location and the price of new housing.

Returning to Figure 4.1, infilling of pockets of land within the built-up area contributes far less quantitatively to a city's housing stock than new building on the periphery. This is because, for the most part, such pockets of land tend to be small. There are two major exceptions to this. One is the construction of public housing. Unlike most private housing development which characteristically takes place at the edge of the built-up area, public housing tends to occur in discrete nuclei. These may be either distributed throughout the built-up area of a city or even way beyond its boundaries as in the case of local authority 'overspill' schemes. In the private sector it is high-rise apartment blocks which most commonly occupy new sites within the built-up area, particularly in locations close to major transportation facilities such as urban freeway interchanges or mass transit stations.

Modifications to the existing housing stock: the filtering process

Since new housing construction adds such a small percentage increase to the aggregate housing stock, it is clear that the major source of housing supply at any single point in time arises from the *adaptation* of the *existing* stock. There are various ways in which housing may be adapted to affect the supply of housing units. The central section of Figure 4.1 identifies four ways: change in relative value, change in intensity of occupancy, change in tenancy and change in use. The first three are very closely related.

Probably the most important form of adjustment to the housing stock is the process of *filtering* which some would regard as the principal dynamic force in the housing market. Figure 4.5 is a highly diagrammatic and simplified representation of the filtering process in a hypothetical city. The most common initial assumption is that new housing (in the private sector) is generally constructed for higher-income households since these are most able to afford newly built single-family dwellings. A second assumption – Stage I in Figure 4.5 – is that housing quality improves with increasing distance from the city centre (this reflects the age-of-housing gradient noted earlier). The filtering process begins, therefore, with the construction of new housing, probably on the periphery of the city. Such housing, it is claimed, will be occupied by the higher-income groups (Stage II). As they move to the new houses, they leave behind vacancies which can be occupied by the next-lowest income group. These moves, in turn, create further vacancies which ripple down the income scale (Stages III, IV).

The Filtering Process

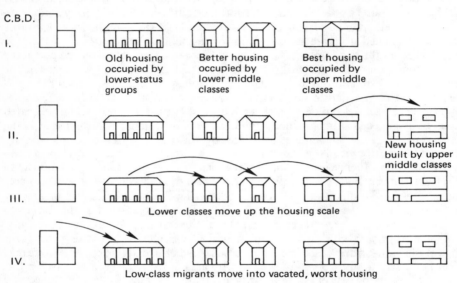

Figure 4.5   A simplified view of the filtering process

Source: R.J. Johnston (1971) *Urban Residential Patterns*, London: Bell & Hyman, figure III.8.

In practice, the filtering process is far more complicated than this simple example suggests. Not all new housing is constructed for the wealthy; not all new housing is constructed on the outer edges of cities. There is unlikely to be a straightforward adjustment process through the chain of vacancies. Quite apart from these and other complications – some of which we shall look at in subsequent sections of this chapter – filtering need not be a one-way process. It is usually regarded as a general decline in the relative value of a house so that it becomes accessible to a lower-income household. But the process also operates in the opposite direction. Low-income housing, especially that in certain kinds of location, may be taken up by higher-income households. Thus most large cities contain examples of what has come to be called *gentrification* – the upgrading of formerly artisan housing.

In the United States, for example, Georgetown in Washington DC and Greenwich Village in New York experienced substantial renovation in the 1960s. Berry (1980) points to the example of Capitol Hill in Washington as a more recent example:

Restoration on the Hill now covers 100 blocks of downtown Washington. Once a middle-class neighborhood of Victorian terraced houses, Capitol Hill fell into disrepair in the 1930s and 1940s. By 1950, when the first tentative signs of renovation appeared, the neighborhood contained some of Washington's worst slums. Renovation caught on in the neighborhood during the early 1960s. In areas of the Hill overtaken by restoration during the 1960s, housing rents and values rose more than twice as rapidly as in the District as a whole. A recent small scale survey of new home buyers on Capitol Hill found that 80 percent of home buyers are white. The average age of buyers was 35 years. Ninety percent received annual incomes of more than $20,000 and eight out of ten were buying their first home. This general profile is typical of home-buyers in neighborhoods being renovated around the country. By contrast, families leaving these renovated neighborhoods are very different, tending to be poor, tenants, and blacks or other minorities, or elderly.
Berry (1980), p.22.

In London, similarly, as Hamnett and Williams (1980) show, it is some of the centrally located areas of Georgian and Victorian terraced housing which have undergone considerable gentrification – areas like Chelsea, Kensington, Pimlico and, more recently, parts of Islington, Camden, Lambeth and Hammersmith. In some cases the process is one of extension of existing middle-class residential districts such as Hampstead, Highgate and Bloomsbury into adjacent areas. Often the process can be extremely rapid: formerly working-class streets in 'good' locations have been gentrified into middle-class streets in little more than a decade. The characteristics of the gentrifiers in London are much the same as in the Washington example quoted above: they are generally professional and managerial households with either very young or no children. In both cases the process reduces the housing stock – particularly rentable housing – available to low-income groups. Ironically, in the United Kingdom much of the renovation of property has been carried out using publicly funded improvement grants (Hamnett 1973).

Filtering, then, is a mechanism by which the supply characteristics of housing change within the existing housing stock. Another mechanism, which may be associated with filtering, is the conversion of single-family dwellings into multiple-family units. Again, this is especially characteristic of older housing in the inner areas of cities. Here, at least part of the housing stock tends to consist of large, or even very large, houses which have been vacated by their previous occupants. Conversion of such houses into apartments, bed-sit accommodation and so on has been a feature of the housing market for many years. One outcome of the increase in intensity of occupancy as several households occupy the space formerly occupied by a single household is an increase in the residential population density. Housing space near the city centre tends to be much smaller than housing space in the suburbs. The result is a widely observed regularity in the decline of residential population density with increasing distance from the city centre.

The combined operation of a number of elements – in particular, adaptation of existing housing, new construction and the replacement of obsolete structures – produces the prevailing pattern of housing supply. In any particular area, the supply of housing – the housing stock – is made up of dwellings of greatly varying ages, sizes, quality, and types of tenure; of private and public housing. Age, size, quality of housing tend to display a general spatial regularity with distance from the city centre. Some dwelling units are supplied in small, multi-occupancy lots in areas of low amenity near city centres often rented and of poor quality. Others are detached, self-contained with a spacious high-amenity suburban location generally owner-occupied. These, of course, represent just two sample points on a continuum of housing supply characteristics. Overall, a distinctive feature of the supply of housing is its wide spatial variety and tendency to occasional dramatic spatial change. This characteristic is also true of the supply situation over time. Housing production tends to move in distinct cycles – increasingly fuelled more by government attacks on the 'housing problem' than by the operation of the free market, although the precise nature of government involvement varies considerably between different countries. The declared objective of all national governments is to provide decent housing for its resident population. To see how the supply of housing relates to the demand for housing, we need to look at the workings of the *housing market*.

MATCHING DEMAND AND SUPPLY: THE ALLOCATION OF HOUSING OPPORTUNITY

A housing market, like other economic markets, is a set of arrangements for bringing together buyers and sellers for purposes of exchange.
Bourne (1976), p.113.

In a perfectly adjusting world, the demand for, and the supply of, housing would match; the housing market would tend towards a state of equilibrium or balance. But we do not live in such a world. Even if the *number* of available housing units were to exactly equal the *number* of households, this need not imply that all housing needs were met. As we have seen, housing is a highly complex commodity; a household's housing needs are both multidimensional and also variable over time as the household passes through the family life-cycle. Housing supply may be of the wrong size, the wrong type, be too expensive or be in the wrong place. It is no comfort to a family living in one city where its particular housing needs cannot be met to know that there is an abundance of such housing in another city several hundred miles away. So, to understand the residential base of modern industrial society, that is, to understand how housing needs are in fact met, we need to look in some detail at the structure and operation of the *housing market*.

One fact emerges very clearly. As in the case of labour markets there are many different housing markets. For example, housing markets can be identified at a variety of geographical scales – national, regional, local. For the individual house-hold it is the supply of housing available locally – say within the same urban area – which is of greatest importance. Certainly, some people do change their place of residence over considerable distances but all studies of residential mobility show that the vast majority of residential moves take place over very short distances. Even in the United States – the most geographically mobile of modern societies – some 40 percent of heads of households live within twenty-five miles of their birthplace and nearly two out of every three live within 100 miles of their place of birth. Figure 4.6 shows the distances moved by house purchasers in the United Kingdom and strongly confirms the view that most residential moves take place over extremely short

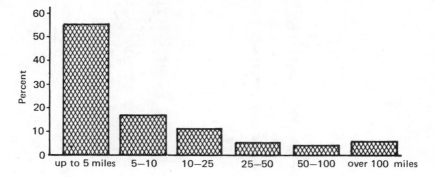

Figure 4.6   Distances moved by house purchasers in the United Kingdom

Source: Nationwide Building Society (1970) *Why do people move?* Bulletin 99, p.6.

distances. In looking at the housing market, therefore, we shall confine ourselves to the *intra-urban* scale.

There has been a marked shift of focus in geographical research on housing in recent years. In the 1960s, *individual choice* was the focus of attention, the residential location decision of the individual households was regarded as the key variable in explaining the spatial pattern of residential areas. In the 1970s, the research emphasis changed to a concentration on the *constraints* within which choices are made and, especially, to the ways in which *institutions* in the housing market operate to allocate households to housing. In fact, the two approaches need not be mutually exclusive as we shall see in the following discussion.

Residential choice

The framework on which studies of residential choice are most commonly based is shown in Figure 4.7. This decision-making model was introduced into the residential literature by Brown and Moore in the late 1960s. It was strongly influenced by the research into residential mobility carried out by Rossi in Philadelphia in the mid-1950s. Brown and Moore see the residential location decision as a two-part process:

1 the decision to seek a new dwelling;

2 the search for, and choice of, a new dwelling.

The distinction is an important one.

The decision to seek a new dwelling is seen as being the outcome of dissatisfaction with the household's existing dwelling. Figure 4.7 indicates that such dissatisfaction can be generated both internally and externally. The most important *internal* stresses seem to be related to changes in the family life-cycle which we discussed earlier, together with dissatisfaction with the quality of the dwelling in terms of the household's aspirations (the social status element). *External* stresses relate specifically to the characteristics of the neighbourhood. Again these may vary in their significance with both family life-cycle and social status considerations. Among the

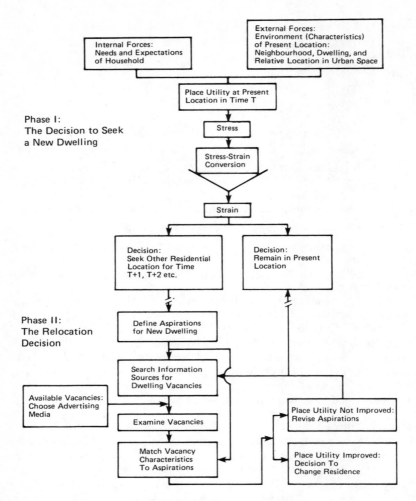

Figure 4.7   A model of the residential location decision process

Source: L.A. Brown & E.G. Moore (1970) The intra-urban migration process: a perspective, *Geografiska Annaler Series B* 52, figure 1.

neighbourhood attributes which are often cited as being conducive to household stress are aspects of the physical and social environment – for example, open space, noise, pollution, neighbours, access to facilities such as shops, schools, medical and other services.

In the residential choice model, therefore, the decision to seek a new dwelling is the result of these two related sets of forces. If one or the other, or both in combination, generate sufficient *stress* then, it is argued, the household will take one of two courses of action. One is to try to remove the stress without moving house. For example, if the problem is lack of space a common response is to build on extra rooms. The other action is to seek a new residence. It is at this point that the limitations of the residential location decision model became apparent. Most of the literature until recently has concentrated on those who move, especially those who move voluntarily. In doing so, the emphasis has been placed on freedom of choice. But for every voluntary mover there are both many more stayers, households which cannot move because of lack of resources, and also many forced movers (for example, because of termination of lease, demolition of the dwelling through urban renewal).

The residential location decision models thus emphasize the exercise of choice and preference by households. But

> preference is irrelevant unless seen within constraints of varying sever-ity. . . . How far are aspirations and needs at particular stages in the life cycle, or for particular life styles, in fact compelled by the distribution of resources and by people's recognition of this distribution and of their own social status . . . ? The stage in the life cycle and nature of life style may generate housing need, but the housing system does not, of course, distri-bute resources according to need. The housing situations and opportunities for families with similar requirements in terms of these factors do, indeed, vary greatly.
> *Duncan (1976), p.16.*

Thus the second part of the residential location decision model in Figure 4.7 – the choice of a new dwelling – is of much narrower application than the first part. All households are subject to varying degrees of stress in terms of their existing dwelling. In some cases, the level of stress may be intolerable. But only a proportion of households can actually exercise choice and move. We shall look more closely at these in a subsequent section of this chapter. But at this stage we need to turn to the *constraints* which operate in the housing market.

Constraints on residential choice: actors and institutions in the housing market

The housing market is made up of a variety of individuals, institutions and interest groups which interact in the process of housing allocation. They can be divided into two broad categories:

1 the occupiers of housing,

2 the housing market institutions.

Probably the most important distinction within the *occupiers* group is that based on *tenure*. At the most general level we can differentiate between owner-occupiers and tenant-occupiers. The two groups differ very considerably in their freedom of action. Various attempts have been made to produce a finer classification of occupiers which will reflect their relative access to housing resources. One of the most widely quoted schemes is that devised by Rex (1968), who identified seven *housing classes*:

1 Outright owners of large houses in desirable areas;

2 Mortgage payers who 'own' whole houses in desirable areas;

3 Council tenants in council-built houses;

4 Council tenants in slum houses awaiting demolition;

5 Tenants of private houseowners, usually in the inner ring;

6 Houseowners who must take in lodgers to meet loan repayments;

7 Lodgers in rooms.

A lower position in the housing class list implies reduced access to housing resources, whether these be in the private or the public housing sector. Rex's scheme was the result of his research in the inner area of Birmingham, England, and it is, to some degree, place- and time-specific. In different circumstances – say in the United States – some of Rex's housing class labels would be less appropriate. But the *concept* of housing class – of differences in the relative access of households to housing resources – is of general application, although the details may vary from place to place. Movement between some of the housing classes is very limited, as Figure 4.8 suggests for the British housing market. Although there is no complete correspondence between socio-economic status and household tenure, there are certainly clear tendencies for professional and managerial groups to own their own houses and for the extent of home-ownership to decline with movement down the socio-economic scale (Figure 4.9).

Movement within or between housing classes is mediated by the various *institutions* in the housing market. Indeed, it is probably more accurate to conceive of a number of different *housing submarkets*, entry to which is controlled by the institutions acting as *gatekeepers*. The major housing market institutions identified by Harvey (though not in order of importance) are:

1 real estate agents;

2 landlords;

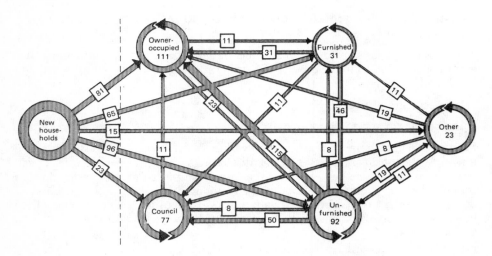

Figure 4.8　Household mobility between different types of tenure

Source: B.T. Robson (1975) *Urban Social Areas*, London: Oxford University Press, figure 3.1.

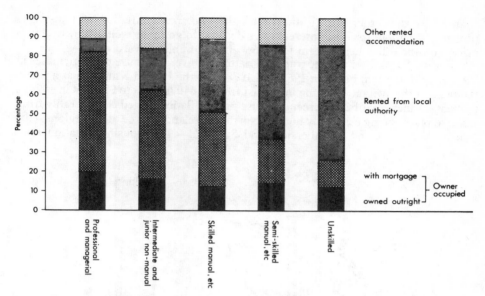

Figure 4.9 Tenure of households in Great Britain by socio-economic group, 1978

Source: based on Central Statistical Office, *Social Trends* 10 (1980), table 9.10. Crown Copyright.

3 developers;

4 financial institutions;

5 government institutions (both local and central/federal).

Precisely how these institutions behave in relation to households seeking a dwelling – and how households are able to behave in the complex housing market – can best be appreciated by looking separately at the private housing sector and the public housing sector. In so doing we can place the work on residential choice into a more realistic context.

Residential choice in the private sector

We noted earlier that there has been a marked trend towards owner-occupation of housing during the last few decades. It is reasonable to assume that, with certain exceptions, home-ownership is a primary goal of most households. Whether home-ownership can be achieved, or whether a family can move from one house to another, is very much determined by household *income*. As we showed in Chapter Three, the main source of household income is that earned by employment. Hence a person's position on the earnings tree or, more generally, his position in the labour market, is a critical factor in a household's ability to satisfy residential aspirations.

Investment in a house is a means of acquiring wealth and of offsetting inflation. However, the general inflationary trends which have characterized all industrial nations since the early 1970s have had a particularly serious effect on the price of housing. In the first place, the actual price of houses has escalated very markedly but, in addition, so has the cost of borrowing money to pay the price (the interest rate charged by the lending institutions). Of the two, price inflation of housing is probably the more serious. Interest rates do tend to go up as well as down; house prices, on the other hand, seem to follow an inexorable upward path.

Figure 4.10 shows the geographical pattern of average house price increases in the United Kingdom between 1969 and 1978. For the United Kingdom as a whole the price of the average dwelling increased from £4640 in 1969 to £15,594 in 1978; a percentage increase of 236 percent. House price inflation varied considerably from place to place, being especially high in Northern Ireland. Three other regions – the North, Yorkshire and Humberside, and Scotland – had housing inflation rates

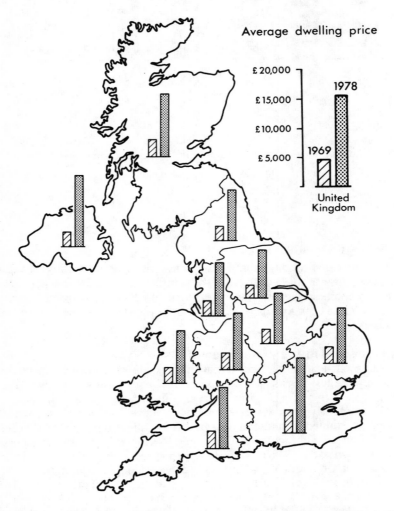

Figure 4.10   Regional variations in house price increases, United Kingdom, 1969–1978

Source: based on *Regional Statistics* (1980), 15, table 6.5.

substantially above the national average. Apart from Northern Ireland, the biggest absolute price increase was in the Southeast, where the average house price increased from £5897 to £18,981. Something of the spatial variation in the price of new housing in the United States is shown in Table 4.3, though the very broad regional definition obscures significant variation at a smaller geographical scale. Even so, considerable variation is evident. The price of a new one-family house in 1977 in the United States was 59.3 percent higher than in 1972; in the West the price was 86.4 percent higher.

Table 4.3 *House price inflation in the United States, 1965–1977:*
the price of new one-family houses
(1972 = 100)

Year	US	Northeast	North Central	South	West
1965	71.2	62.2	70.6	71.1	75.9
1968	80.3	75.8	82.4	79.0	81.7
1972	100.0	100.0	100.0	100.0	100.0
1974	119.1	118.3	115.8	115.2	126.3
1975	131.0	128.3	126.8	125.7	141.7
1976	142.0	133.5	138.1	134.6	157.3
1977	159.3	142.1	153.3	147.3	186.4

Source: *U.S. Statistical Abstract* (1978), table 1368

Access to home-ownership is thus very much a function of household income. However, only a small proportion of the population buys a house outright. Not only does this presuppose the possession of a large capital sum but also it may not be the most sensible way even if the capital is available. This is the case, for example, in such countries as the United Kingdom and the United States, where there are substantial tax benefits associated with taking out a mortgage to purchase a house, benefits which increase up the income scale because of the nature of the income tax system. The primary gatekeepers in this part of the private sector housing market are the financial institutions which provide mortgages – banks, savings and loan institutions and, in Britain, building societies. Although their precise rules may differ, the general criteria for eligibility for a mortgage are, first, the character of the borrower – especially his or her long-term credit-worthiness and possession of some capital for a down-payment. Most mortgages are for a part of the total house price so that an applicant has to find a down-payment or deposit. This may be a considerable sum to find, especially on older properties. As house prices have escalated in recent years, so too has the capital sum needed to get to the mortgage 'starting line'. This immediately cuts out a segment of the population which cannot raise the down-payment. But even for those who can find this sum, guarantee of a mortgage is not assured. The financial institutions are concerned not only with absolute levels of income but also with the stability of that income and the general credit-worthiness of the applicant (Boddy 1976). Hence, white-collar workers tend to be favoured more than blue-collar workers.

The second criterion which the mortgage institutions take into account is the type of property involved, including the neighbourhood in which it is located. As Boddy points out, lenders of funds are concerned with the future exchange value of the property which could be realized in the event of failure to keep up the mortgage repayments. Much old property, in particular, is regarded as offering potentially low exchange value. Now we have seen already that older housing tends to be concentrated in particular parts of the city according to the chronology of urban development. Certain parts of the city are also regarded as being socially or economically unstable or undesirable, or where the exchange value of property may not be maintained. Thus, there is generally a clear *spatial* unevenness or bias in the

Table 4.4   *Housing submarkets in Baltimore, 1970*

			Percentage transactions by source of funds						
area	Total houses sold	Sales per 100 properties	Cash	Private	Federal savings & loan	State savings & loan	Banks (including mortgage banks)	% sales insured by FHA	Average sales price $
Inner City	1,199	1.86	65.7	15.0	3.0	12.0	2.9	2.9	3,498
Ethnic	760	3.34	39.9	5.5	6.1	43.2	3.7	2.6	6,372
Hampden	99	2.40	40.4	8.1	18.2	26.3	7.0	14.1	7,059
West Baltimore	497	2.32	30.6	12.5	12.1	11.7	27.0	25.8	8,664
South Baltimore	322	3.16	28.3	7.4	22.7	13.4	19.3	22.7	8,751
High turnover	2,072	5.28	19.1	6.1	13.6	14.9	39.7	38.2	9,902
Middle income	1,077	3.15	20.8	4.4	29.8	17.0	19.2	17.17	12,760
Upper income	361	3.84	19.4	6.9	23.5	10.5	36.9	11.9	27,413

Source: D. Harvey & L. Chatterjee (1974) Absolute rent and the structuring of space by governmental and financial institutions, *Antipode*, 6, table 2(i)

allocation of mortgage funds. The practice of 'red-lining' undesirable areas, though frequently denied by mortgage institutions, certainly exists. As a result, certain localities – especially inner-city areas and concentrations of ethnic groups – tend to be starved of mortgage finance. Table 4.4 and Figure 4.11 illustrate this practice in the case of the City of Baltimore. The discrimination against inner-city, ethnic and lower-price housing areas is clearly revealed. In the inner city of Baltimore, for example, the low level of mortgage lending has as its counterpart a high percentage of cash sales.*

Owner-occupation is the largest segment of the private housing market overall, but for certain groups, and in certain locations the rented sector dominates. Renting tends to be characteristic of particular groups within the population. For some people, private renting is but a temporary halt on the road to owner-occupation. A

---

*On the basis of such evidence, Harvey argues that

banks and other financial institutions will avoid financing activities which yield very low rates of return. They also will tend to avoid financing those activities and developments which incur high risks and which involve them in numerous small-scale transactions within a highly disaggregated market situation. In such situations they may choose to work through an intermediary (such as a real estate corporation or a professional landlord) who will bear much of the risk and negotiate the numerous small-scale transactions needed. A natural outcome of this calculation is that financial institutions tend to avoid direct involvement with low income and old housing because these areas are dominated by high risks and low rates of return. It also happens that much of the old housing in which low income groups live is in areas of the city which could much more profitably be used for other uses and which, if developed, would in any case enhance the value of commercial interests in the CBD. . . . It should not be surprising, therefore, if private financial institutions tend to deny support to the housing market in certain parts of the city. It is therefore extremely difficult to get mortgage financing in many inner city areas . . . [this] . . . effectively kills the housing market in certain areas while it forces landlords to maximise income rather than to increase their wealth. As a consequence of this policy, the housing in such areas tends to deteriorate rapidly under market pressures, until such point as it becomes feasible to buy up the land and redevelop it. *Harvey (1972), p.45.*

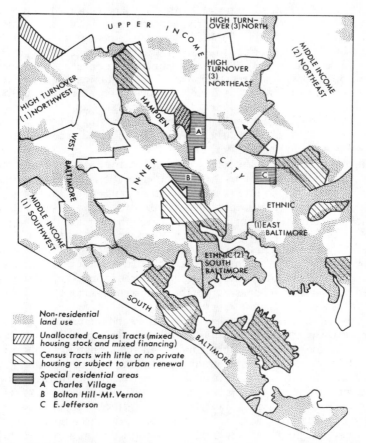

Figure 4.11   The spatial distribution of housing submarkets in Baltimore, 1970

Source: D. Harvey & L. Chatterjee (1974) Absolute rent and the structuring of space by governmental and financial institutions, *Antipode*, 6, figure 1.

glance back to Figure 4.8 shows that a large proportion of new households enter the housing market for the first time via the private rented sector and that, from there, the major flow is into owner-occupation. But in some cases the private rented sector is the only possible source of housing. One reason is that the 'entry requirements' are less stringent than those for owner-occupation. The gatekeeper is the landlord (frequently operating through the real-estate agent). In the more exclusive rented sector – for example, the expensive high-rise apartment blocks – occupancy is on a period leasehold basis and entry depends both on ability to pay the rent and on character references. Lower down the scale, however, the criterion is likely to be the ability to pay one week's or one month's rent in advance and little else.

The less stringent entry requirements to the private rented sector inevitably mean that some groups in society are more heavily concentrated within it. For example, in the United States as a whole, a much larger proportion of black households than white households are renters. In 1976, 56 percent of non-white household units were rented, compared with only 32 percent for white households. Another characteristic feature of the private rented sector is its high turnover rate. Thus Grigsby's (1963) study of the Philadelphia housing market revealed that annual turnover in the owner-occupied sector was only 6 percent; that in the rented sector was 40 percent. Boyce (1969) found similar differences in the case of Seattle where some 50 percent of the rented housing in a predominantly black area turned over each year, compared with only 7 percent of owner-occupied housing in the same area. He found that the same kind of differential also applied in middle- and high-value housing areas. Since the rental market tends to be concentrated in the central residential areas of cities rather than in the suburbs, the central areas tend to have high residential mobility rates.

Having outlined some of the constraints in the private sector housing market we can now return to the question of the residential location decision and Figure 4.7. The decision of whether to move or stay is, for many households, totally academic. A move to another house, or from the rented to the owner-occupied sector, is out of the question for all those who cannot meet the entry requirements of the housing finance market. Among those who can exercise a choice of whether to move or stay there is, again, great variation in their degree of freedom. Housing aspirations, therefore, are likely to be adjusted to a level which is attainable. Given these constraints, however, studies of the way choice of a new dwelling is exercised (Stage II in Figure 4.7) throw some interesting light on other aspects of the housing market and especially upon the influence of its existing spatial structure.

As in any decision-making process, *information* about alternatives is fundamentally important. Given a particular household's housing aspirations and its financial resources, how does it obtain information about the availability of housing of the right sort? First of all we need to emphasize that the type of housing opportunity varies very considerably within an urban area. As we have noted already (and as we shall see in more detail later in this chapter), there is a clear *geography* of residence in which particular housing types – in terms of age, quality, size, price, etc. – tend to occupy distinct geographical areas. In other words, there is a housing opportunity surface. The second point is that individuals seeking a dwelling are likely to be aware of only limited parts of that surface. Even attempts to extend such knowledge will fall short of complete knowledge.

The search for a suitable dwelling begins from the basic *spatial image* which the individual house-seeker has accumulated through direct and indirect experience. As with all images, it consists of both factual knowledge – what is where – and evaluative knowledge – the feelings, opinions, attitudes towards different neighbourhoods and areas. Some parts of the city are 'known' to be desirable, others are 'known' to be undesirable. In general, spatial knowledge is greatest in the area surrounding the individual's existing residence and around and between the other places with which interaction occurs most frequently. Workplace, regularly visited shopping centres, homes of friends and relatives are obvious examples. Starting with the assumption of a single-centred city, Adams (1969) has suggested that the *mental map* of the typical Midwestern city-dweller (Mr. X) tends to be wedge shaped (Figure 4.12):

> at the tip of the wedge is the downtown area (R₁). Near downtown is another zone that is known only from inferences made while passing through (R₂). Much of what Mr. X knows or thinks he knows about R₂ is based on observations made from the path taken to downtown. In R₃ is Mr. X's local neighbourhood. Ring R₄ forms a newer neighbourhood extending out to the suburbs and also known mainly by inference. Travel to and from suburban shopping centres, even if freeways are used, takes residents of R₃ past new houses, clean streets, low densities, and many trees. In R₃ is home. The image of R₂ produces a negative reaction in Mr. X, and he and his family would consider a move to R₄ as a step upward. But what about sectors S₂, S₃,

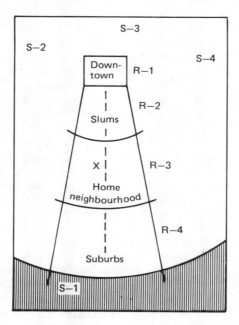

Figure 4.12   Perception of an urban area by a central-city resident

Source: J.S. Adams (1969) Directional bias in intra-urban migration, *Economic Geography*, 45, figure 3.

and S_4? To an external observer these sectors might be virtually identical to S_1. Such places, the author would argue, are irrelevant for Mr. X living in ring R_3 in sector S_1. The desirable areas in other sectors are fuzzy or absent from Mr. X's mental map. Thus, it is R_4 or stay put unless some drastic financial or domestic reverse such as death, divorce, bankruptcy, and so forth, forces relocation into R_2.
Adams (1969), p.305.

In fact, urban mental maps are far more complex than this hypothetical example suggests. We shall look at some of their characteristics and variability in Chapter 5. Whatever the detail of such variability and complexity, one point is abundantly clear when we consider residential search. Every individual begins such search from a position of variable knowledge (or ignorance) of, and attitudes towards, different parts of the urban area. Biases of distance and direction are prominent features. Almost certainly this pre-existing spatial image has a strong influence on the residential search process. Some areas are automatically excluded from consideration; others are simply not known about. In addition to such *spatial* bias there also appears to be bias (or selectivity) in the *information sources* which are used to identify specific housing opportunities.

Table 4.5 shows the information sources used by house-searchers in two different geographical areas: Philadelphia and Swansea. Broadly the sources fall into two groups: formal and informal. Newspapers and real-estate agents are formal sources, they are part of a process which aims to bring available housing to the attention of those searching for a residence. The informal channels are themselves of two kinds. On the one hand, there are the usual channels of social communication – family, friends, contacts at work. On the other, there is the process of 'looking around' for suitable housing. Table 4.5 suggests that informal sources tend to be more significant than formal sources of information. In the Philadelphia case (Table 4.5a), personal contact and 'windfall' (the acquisition of information without search; for example, an acquaintance might casually mention a vacancy) had a much higher index of effectiveness than the other sources, followed by 'walking or riding around'. Similarly, in Swansea 'family and friends' and 'looking around' ranked highly. In general, there seemed to be a considerable difference between high- and low-cost areas. In the high-cost area too, newspapers and estate agents were far more important sources of information than in the low-cost area. Thus higher socio-economic groups appeared to make greater use of real-estate agents and newspapers than those in lower-status groups, although this may be related to the type of property involved. Low-priced property may well be handled less often by estate agents or advertised in newspapers.

Although informal sources are especially important, the role of the real-estate agent should not be underestimated. Like other institutions in the housing market, the estate agent acts as a *gatekeeper* – primarily of information about housing opportunities but also, quite often, of sources of finance. It is also likely that the real-estate agent is a particularly important information source for households moving into the urban area from outside, say from another city some distance away. Palm (1976) carried out a detailed study of the information-providing role of real-estate agents in Minneapolis, and found that even in a fairly homogeneous, medium-sized metropolitan area there was no single information field of housing

Table 4.5 *Information sources employed in searching for a residence: examples from Philadelphia and Swansea*

(a) Philadelphia (1950s)

	Assessment ratings of information sources		
Information source	Coverage* (proportion using source)	Impact* (proportion effective use)	Index of effectiveness
Newspaper	63%	18%	0.29
Personal contact	62%	47%	0.76
Walking or riding around	57%	19%	0.33
Real-estate agents	50%	14%	0.28
Windfall	31%	25%	0.81

* 100% in this table is the 444 cases of recent movers.

The coverage of each channel was ascertained by asking the respondents questions concerning each of the channels along such lines as the following:
'Did you read newspaper ads?'
'Did you ask people you know?'
The 'impact' of the channels was obtained from answers to the following question:
'You told me what you did in looking for a place in general. Now would you tell me how you found this particular place?'

(b) Swansea (1970s)

	Rating of information sources									
	High-cost area					Low-cost area				
	5	4	3	2	1	5	4	3	2	1
Newspapers	18	9	21	12	40	11	7	19	19	44
Estate agents	32	9	15	9	35	11	19	4	15	51
Work contacts	6	9	24	15	46	11	4	4	26	55
Friends/family	32	15	9	12	32	37	11	0	11	41
Looking around	47	18	9	3	23	33	26	7	7	27
Normal trips	9	6	35	15	35	4	11	30	7	48

Scale from 5 (very important) to 1 (irrelevant). All figures are percentages.

Source: (a) P. Rossi (1955) *Why Families Move*, New York: Free Press, table 9.6; (b) D.T. Herbert (1973) The residential mobility process: Some empirical observations, *Area*, 5, table 1

opportunity. Even those real-estate agents who belonged to a city-wide co-operative listing service and who should, therefore, have provided the most complete, and least spatially biased, source of housing information gave prospective buyers an incomplete picture.

Most real-estate agents were found to cover only a limited segment of the total urban housing market: each had clearly identifiable territories. Not unrelated to this was the tendency for some agents to specialize in certain price brackets. Some catered to the high-income market exclusively, others dealt mainly in low-price property, some, of course, offered a range. Perhaps more significant, however, was the variation in agents' recommendation of residential neighbourhoods (according to the status of the family seeking a new dwelling) in relation to their own office locations and listings. Palm found a clear tendency for agents to over-recommend areas close to their offices. Since no financial gain was involved, she suggested that such bias reflected the agents' actual knowledge and opinions of various parts of the city, despite their involvement in the co-operative listing service.

Since both individual images of urban space and also the availability, use of, and information provided by different information sources is so clearly uneven, we should not be surprised to find biases in the ultimate choice of housing. This is reinforced by the time and cost constraints imposed on the search process itself. It is not uncommon for a residential mover to accept the first satisfactory opportunity to be found (Moore 1972). Even those indulging in a more extensive search find ways of limiting the number of alternatives to be considered. The most commonly suggested biases in the residential movement process are those of distance and direction. In the case of distance, we have already noted (Figure 4.6) the tendency for most moves to be short distance. But distance may be viewed in other than simple physical terms. Much will depend upon the existing spatial structure of different housing types within the urban housing market. If, for example, the high-value housing neighbourhoods are not spatially contiguous but scattered across the city, then relatively longer-distance moves geographically may be short-distance moves in terms of housing type and social status.

Table 4.6   *Residential movement in Seattle, 1962–1967*

Movement types	Housing area types (percent in each type)			
	Low value Negro	Low value White	Middle value	High value
Within same value area	58.2	24.0	3.0	17.0
To other areas in city	26.4	39.9	47.9	38.4
To 'suburbs'	3.0	13.4	15.7	14.5
To other cities	12.3	23.0	33.4	30.2
Total	99.9	100.3	100.0	100.0

Source: R.R. Boyce (1969) Residential mobility and its implications for urban spatial change, Reproduced by permission from *Proceedings of the Association of American Geographers*, 1, table 2.

Table 4.6 illustrates this point. As Boyce explains, the higher-value housing areas are geographically separated in Seattle, giving apparently longer-distance moves. Table 4.6 also shows vast differences in patterns of movement between different housing value types. In particular most movement in the low-value Negro areas is internal, a point we return to later. Overall, it would seem that within the constraints of the spatial structure of the housing market, distance moved is positively related to socio-economic status. In terms of direction of move it has been suggested by Adams (1969), Brown and Holmes (1971) and others that much residential movement may be sectorally biased and that this is related to the form of the individual's mental map (see Figure 4.12), but the evidence to support such a view is not too strong. Again, much depends on the spatial structure of the housing market in question.

Thus, even voluntary residential movement in the private housing market is constrained both by the resources available to the household and by the biased and incomplete nature of information about housing opportunities. These add to the imperfections of the housing market, helping to create what are, in effect, a series of separate submarkets. Overall, according to Adams and Gilder, in the United States at least,

> the best predictors of *where* and *what* families move to are income and race. Poorer and non-white households tend, more than others, to move shorter distances, locate in the central city, rent apartments, have fewer rooms and either pay lower rents or own cheaper houses.
> *Adams and Gilder (1976), p.183.*

Without any doubt, one of the major imperfections – or failures – in the housing market is that based on race (or nationality). Discrimination – either overt or covert – against certain minority groups in the private housing market is a marked and long-established feature of many societies, even those in which equality before the law is enshrined in the constitution. We noted earlier that in the United States, for example, a larger proportion of the black population tend to be renters rather than owners. Even among those who are owner-occupiers, however, there are severe institutional and spatial constraints on the type of housing available and on its geographical location. One of the most pronounced features of almost all large cities in North America and the United Kingdom is the existence of clearly defined areas in which the concentration of particular ethnic groups is extremely high. (Figures 4.13 and 4.14 show examples of such concentration in the United States and in Britain.) In each of the cities illustrated there is a very clear high level of concentration of ethnic groups in small restricted parts of the urban area. Where such concentrations are extreme, they are termed *ghettos*. We shall examine some of the processes underlying their geographical development when we discuss the geography of residence later in this chapter. For the moment our concern is with their role in the housing market.

In itself, the clustering of certain social groups in particular parts of an urban area does not necessarily imply discrimination. There are many good reasons for distinctive groups to reside close to each other. But where such clustering is either partially or totally enforced – where it is a function of *segregation* rather than *congregation* – then it suggests that the explanation lies in the operation of the housing market. It is often difficult to separate the influence of income from that of ethnicity.

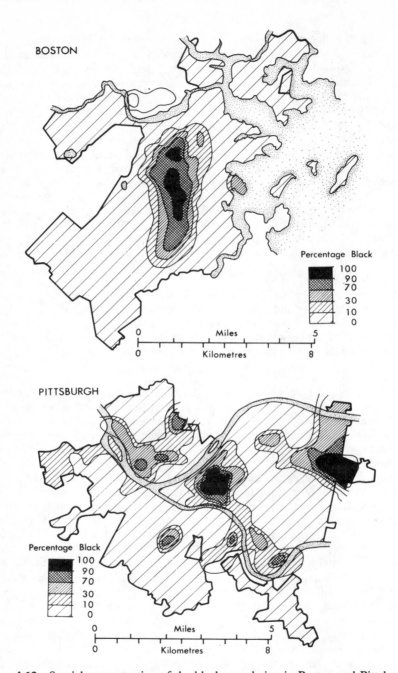

Figure 4.13 Spatial concentration of the black population in Boston and Pittsburgh

Source: R. Abler & J.S. Adams (1976) *A Comparative Atlas of America's Great Cities*, Washington DC: Association of American Geographers and The University of Minnesota Press, pp.25, 115.

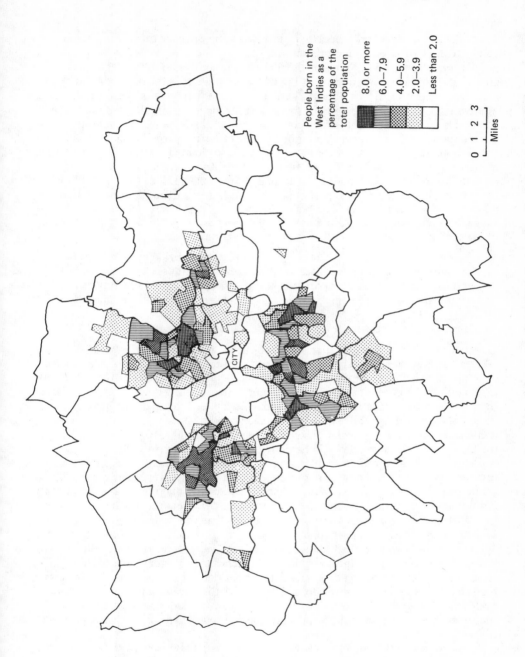

Figure 4.14   Spatial concentration of West Indian population in London, 1971

Source: J. Shepherd, J. Westaway & T. Lee (1974) *A Social Atlas of London*, Oxford: Clarendon Press, figure 4.2(a).

As we have seen, level and security of income is the primary qualifying element in entry to the owner-occupier market. In general, the income levels of the black population in the United States or the 'new' Commonwealth immigrants in Britain are significantly lower than those of the white population, a function very largely of their lowly position in the job market. This immediately puts these groups at a disadvantage in the private housing market. It means, for example, that only certain types of housing are available to them: generally old, substandard dwellings in the inner area. Often a mortgage cannot be obtained on such property; hence, as Table 4.4 demonstrated, cash sales are more prevalent, or loans raised at extremely high interest rates from other types of financial institution. Again as we saw earlier, renting is more prevalent among black than white households in the United States.

Much of the blame for perpetuating discrimination in the private housing market of the United States has been attributed to real-estate agents. It has been suggested that real-estate agents have deliberately encouraged the perpetuation of black segregated areas. Morrill, for example, claimed that

> segregation is maintained by the refusal of real estate brokers even to show, let alone sell, houses to negroes in white areas. Countless devices are used: quoting excessive prices, saying the house is already sold, demanding unfair down payments, removing 'for sale' signs, not keeping appointments and so on.
> *Morrill (1965), p.346.*

Commenting on racial segregation in the suburbs of American cities, Muller (1976) takes a broader view. He argues that in addition to real-estate agents, subdivision developers strive to maintain a homogeneous social composition of their developments by various types of restrictive covenants and screening devices. He also claims that, prior to the 1960s federal government policy 'encouraged and heavily subsidised policies creating white suburbs and black central cities by explicitly forbidding home construction loans which fostered racial integration' (Muller 1976, p.21). To the extent that discriminatory behaviour exists, its causes must lie in the deeper workings of society rather than in the behaviour of particular organizations or institutions. Certainly, concern about the effect of minority – especially non-white – groups on property values (a house, after all, is the only major capital asset of most families), or on cultural homogeneity, pervades many sections of the population.

Whatever the reasons, there is little doubt that the poor in general, and the non-white population in particular, are faced with barriers in the housing market which drastically restrict their choice of a place to live. The fact that old, dilapidated low-standard housing tends to be spatially clustered in particular parts of the city is a major reason for the observed short-distance residential movement of low-income households. Where this is reinforced by racial discrimination (or by voluntary preference for a particular ethnic area), the pattern of residential mobility may take the form shown in Figure 4.15 for a sample of movers within the black ghetto of Milwaukee.

Our emphasis throughout this section has been upon household choice and upon the constraints on the freedom of choice in acquiring the dwelling which operate in the private sector housing market. As we have seen, level and stability of income – credit-worthiness – are the major conditions of entry to the private sector housing market which is controlled and operated by a variety of institutions acting as gatekeepers. In the other segment of the housing market – the public sector – the constraints and opportunities are rather different.

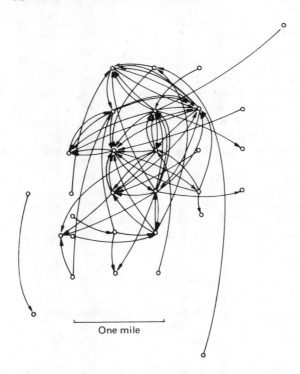

Figure 4.15   The short-distance movement of black households in Milwaukee, 1960–1962

Source: W.A.V. Clark (1972) Patterns of black intra-urban mobility and restricted relocation opportunities, in H.M. Rose & H. McConnell (eds) *Geography of the Ghetto*, Vol.2 of *Perspectives in Geography*, De Kalb, Illinois: Northern Illinois University Press, figure 1.

Housing allocation in the public sector

We noted earlier that the size of the public housing sector varies considerably between countries. In the United States, public housing represents less than 2 percent of the total housing stock; in the United Kingdom, almost one-third of the housing stock is public. These variations reflect differences in approach to the 'housing problem'. That there is a housing problem even today cannot be disputed. However difficult an estimation of general housing need may be, there seems to be a consensus that severe housing shortages exist and that demand far exceeds supply. In affluent societies many people are simply unaware of the appalling living conditions in which many people still have to live.* Whatever the definition applied to

---

*Downs, for example, has asserted that

> most Americans have no conception of the filth, degradation, squalor, overcrowding, and personal danger and insecurity which millions of inadequate housing units are causing in both our cities and rural areas. Thousands of infants are attacked by rats each year; hundreds die or

become mentally retarded from eating lead paint that falls off cracked walls; thousands more are ill because of unsanitary conditions resulting from jamming large families into a single room, continuing failure of landlords to repair plumbing or provide heat, and pitifully inadequate storage space. . . . These miserable conditions are not true of all inadequate housing units, but enough Americans are trapped in the hopeless desolation of such surroundings to constitute both a scandal and a serious economic and social drag in our affluent society. *Downs (1968), p.116.*

housing need, it would appear that some of the simplest of the complex bundle of housing requirements are being seriously undersupplied. Much is lost by turning to simple statistical counts of 'substandard' housing but Table 4.7 shows some of the relevant magnitudes for the United States. While considerable improvement has been made, the fact remains that some 7 million substandard units were in existence in the United States in 1970. The figures do not include problems of overcrowding. In 1970 in the United States, overcrowding (that is, all units with more than one occupant per room) would add a further 8 percent of all households and 5.2 million families to the housing problem. For the United Kingdom there is a similar problem of housing shortage. Measured by the substandard homes criterion there were in 1971 1.25 million unfit dwellings in England and Wales, accounting for 7 percent of the housing stock. For Scotland a further 190,000 dwellings were unfit, that is, 10 percent of its housing stock (Cherry 1974).

Table 4.7 *Substandard housing units in the United States*

	All housing units (millions)	Substandard units (millions)	Percent substandard
1950	46.1	17.0	36.9
1960	58.5	11.4	19.5
1970 (estimated)	69.5	6.9	9.9

Source: A. Downs (1968) Moving toward realistic housing goals, in K. Gordon (ed), *Agenda For The Nation*, Washington, DC: Brookings Institution, table 1

In many ways experiences in Britain and the United States with respect to the supply of housing have been very different since World War I. Britain has, in adopting a welfare state policy of intervention, sought both to adjust the housing market operation and, in many areas, to replace it wholly by state-sponsored programmes. The United States, on the other hand, has sought to avoid a large direct public role in housing and has promoted such policy as it has adopted through a battery of mortgage-guarantee schemes designed to adjust the resources with which the consumer bids on the 'open' housing market. In the United States, according to Henderson and Ledebur (1972), 'the focus of the federal public housing activity has been on providing adequate numbers and quality of residences for middle income people not low income families.' More recently, however, with the Model Cities programme and the 1968 Housing Act, there has been a shift of emphasis towards helping the urban poor. According to Rose, public housing in the United States serves to house blacks and elderly white poor in particular. He points out that by 1965 more than 51 percent of all public housing occupants were black and that during the 1960s support for public housing was basically aimed at satisfying the needs of the elderly.

Since the public housing sector is more important quantitatively in the United Kingdom, our discussion here concentrates on the British public housing sector. Our interest is in how the operation of this section of the housing market affects the choice – or rather the allocation – of households. In doing so we draw heavily on the work of Gray (1976).

> Two major sets of mechanisms exist. First, a number of procedures and rules are used to *select* those households which are allowed to move into council dwellings, and which therefore act to categorise households according to their *eligibility* to move. A second and related set of devices is used to *allocate* dwellings to households which have successfully passed through the first set, and these operate to assess a household's *suitability* for particular dwellings. From the household's point of view, whether it is offered a house and if so, what type of house it is depends on its power to exert administrative pressure on the housing department. However, the criteria of, and limits to, the power a household has to gain access to housing are necessarily defined solely in terms determined by the corporation and interpreted by officials. For example, an individual may consider that he has a right to, and is in need of, a council house, but will only be successful if his own assessment of need coincides with the official criteria of eligibility and suitability. Seen in this way, the local authority managers are the independent variable which determines a household's access to council housing. *Gray (1976), p.37.*

In terms of the *selection* of households Gray identifies three types of demand for public housing. The first type includes those people living in dwellings which are to be cleared as part of a slum clearance programme. We referred earlier to the massive clearance schemes which have taken place in British cities since World War II. For the most part these have been based on the view that government has a responsibility to remove the physical decay of residential areas, to rehouse people living in substandard or unfit dwellings. Much of the housing built to replace the slums has been in the form of high-rise apartment blocks. Indeed, for some time central government housing policy positively encouraged high-rise building. Some critics have argued that the initial impetus came from followers of the le Corbusiér school of architecture eager to create a brave new world of residential living. In the mid-1970s, however, a major reaction against high-rise public housing became evident. Few are now being built; several of those already built are being demolished, often at a cost greater than that of originally building them. Examples include high-rise blocks in Leeds and Birkenhead in England and in various United States cities – the most notorious being the Pruitt Igoe complex in St. Louis.

The second set of demands on public housing comes from households on the waiting list, that is, those wishing to move into public housing. Various eligibility criteria operate with some variation between different parts of the country. Basically, eligibility is according to *need*, but this is interpreted in various ways. Variables such as marital status, family size, state of existing dwelling, health of members of the family are important factors, as is the length of time the household has been on the local authority's housing list. Not surprisingly, there is much concern about individuals 'jumping the queue'. The widespread use of length of time on the housing list as an eligibility factor has been suggested as one reason for the relatively small proportion of non-white immigrants occupying public housing in the United Kingdom (Jones 1976). For example, 33 percent of the English population of seven inner-London boroughs in 1966 was in public housing compared with only 5 percent of the non-white population in those boroughs (Robson 1975). However, this does not necessarily imply discrimination by local authorities; it seems that the non-white population as a whole has a stronger preference for owner-occupation.

The third element in the demand for public housing comes from tenants already in council housing but who wish to transfer either to another dwelling within the same authority or to another area, perhaps in association with a change of employment. The major difference between households in the private sector who wish to move and those in the public sector wishing to move to another council dwelling is that the latter 'are only free to do so with the consent of their housing manager' (Bird 1976). Eligibility in this case seems to depend a good deal on the tenant's status.

Each of these three population groups seeking accommodation in public housing has different priorities in terms of allocation since demand almost always exceeds supply. In general, households living in Compulsory Purchase Areas have the highest priority, followed by existing local authority tenants and finally by households on the waiting list but outside these two categories. Allocation of housing to those households which qualify and get to the top of their list is according to the family's primary needs – number of children, age and health of tenants and so on. But there is also an undoubted tendency to evaluate tenants in terms of their 'quality' and to locate them accordingly. Hence both the quality of the property and the general nature of the housing area tend to be related quite closely to the authority's evaluation of the tenant. Jones (1976) quotes evidence which claims that non-white tenants on Greater London Council housing estates have tended to be disproportionately allocated to older and poorer-quality housing and also to be increasingly more concentrated in inner-London housing estates than in those farther out.

Although there are variations in practice from place to place it is clear that the rules and priorities operated by the gatekeepers – the local authorities and their officials – are the major influence on housing allocation both to, and within, the public housing sector. However,

> Of more importance than the management processes themselves are the variety of social and spatial consequences they have. Thus, both the life chances of various groups in the city and the socio-spatial structure of urban areas are influenced in major ways by the selection and allocation procedures employed by local authority managers. For some groups of households the result of the policies used by officials is to increase housing opportunity: for others they act to reduce the chance to be mobile or to move to particular sorts of dwelling area. Tenants with a low status are likely to be refused the opportunity to move within the local authority sector. For such households an alternative option is to move into the private sector. However, in a local and national context where the amount of private rented accommodation is shrinking and housing costs are relatively high,

and where it is increasingly difficult for potential first-time owners to break into the owner-occupied sector, there will be no real choice for many families but to remain in their present accommodation. . . . Low status tenants (who are often those in greatest need, such as one parent families, immigrants, and the unemployed) are often discriminated against when compared with high status 'deserving' tenants. Low status tenants are likely to be residentially immobile and become trapped in low status property. From this point of view, council housing policies often add to, rather than help solve, the problems experienced by relict social groups.
Gray (1976), pp.42–43.

The housing market: a summary

It should now be abundantly clear that the allocation of housing opportunity in modern industrial society is a highly complex process in which a variety of individuals, institutions and interest groups interact. Institutionally, the major actors are the financial institutions, landlords, real-estate agents and government. These act as gatekeepers to households wishing to enter, or move within, the housing market. In fact, as we have seen, it is more realistic to think in terms of a whole series of housing submarkets, differentiated in terms of different entry requirements. We can agree with Harvey (1972) that 'the key to the housing situation is finance'. At the aggregate level the total amount of money invested in the housing sector is a function of the relative rate of return on investment by private capital and of government policy towards the national housing stock in the public domain. From the viewpoint of the individual household, residential choice is heavily constrained. Stresses exerted by changes in the family life-cycle or by social aspirations may lead to the desire to move yet, for many, this is impossible. We need, therefore, to consider the stayers just as much as the movers. Again, it is finance which is a key variable influencing the degrees of residential freedom. The higher the household's income level, the easier it is to get a mortgage and the greater the range of choice of housing. As income declines, so the constraints on residential movement increase. Even where choice exists, however, the nature of the household's image of residential opportunities, the information sources used and the biases inherent in these sources effectively limit the distance and direction of residential movement. Where market imperfections operate very strongly, for example, among lowest-income groups and also among minority or ethnic groups, the range of choice is even more severely limited. Rather different rules operate in the public sector but, again, it is the controlling influence of the local authority gatekeepers which is the primary determinant of the allocation of housing.

THE GEOGRAPHY OF RESIDENCE

Having examined the operation of the housing market in some detail, we are now in a position to look at the geographical pattern of housing which both results from, and has an effect upon, this housing allocation process. The geographical pattern of residential areas is the result of the interaction between two elements in geographical space:

1 the housing stock and its varied characteristics;

2 the social composition of the residential population.

As we have seen, such interaction occurs through the mechanism of the housing market. But the spatial structure which results is not just the *output* or end point of the process, it is also an important *input* into a continuing dynamic process. The spatial patterning of housing opportunity – the clustering of certain types of housing, of certain types of household – in effect produces distinctive housing submarkets. These are highly significant in steering subsequent developments. Thus, the geography of housing and of the residential population is of more than merely academic interest. It is the tangible expression of the working out of social processes on the ground. To a very considerable extent it illustrates the operation of Hägerstrand's authority constraints (see Chapter One).

'Classical' models of urban residential structure

Attempts to unravel the complex relationship between such social processes and their geographical outcome in the form of residential differentiation have a lengthy history. For example, many contemporary observers of the nineteenth-century city in both North America and Europe commented on what they saw to be geographical regularities in the pattern of housing and of social groups. Early writers were particularly impressed with what they saw to be a *concentric* or *zonal* tendency. Engels was certainly of this view. He observed the central commercial district of Manchester as being 'abandoned by dwellers, and . . . lonely and deserted at night', but around this central core he noted a 'girdle' of working people's housing some one-and-a-half miles in radius beyond which lived the 'upper and middle bourgeoisie . . . in free, wholesome country air'. But the most systematic development of the concentric model of urban structure came in the 1920s with the Chicago School of Social Ecology led by Robert Park and E.W. Burgess.

Figure 4.16 shows Burgess' idealized view of the industrial city (a) applied to the particular case of Chicago (b). As the diagrams show, Burgess identified five concentric zones:

1 the central business district;

2 the zone in transition;

3 the zone of working men's homes;

4 the zone of 'better' residences;

5 the commuters' zone.

Burgess' view of the residential structure of the city was not simply a description of a static pattern. He saw it as being moulded and driven by principles derived from the natural sciences, especially ecology. The major processes, he believed, were those of *invasion* and *succession* operating from the centre outwards as the city expanded in size. As the wealthier members of the population moved farther out from the centre of the city to the developing suburbs and ex-urbs their places were taken by lower-status groups. The lowest status of all congregated in what Burgess termed the 'zone in transition'. In particular this was the 'port of entry' for most in-migrants to the United States, especially those belonging to minority and ethnic groups – first from Europe but subsequently from the southern states and from Central and South

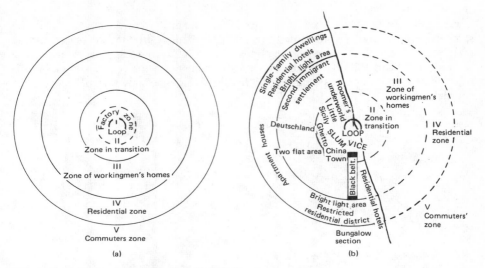

Figure 4.16   Burgess' idealized model of the city

Source; R.E. Park & E.W. Burgess (1925) *The City,* Chicago: University of Chicago Press, chart I and chart II. Reprinted by permission of The University of Chicago Press.

America. As particular immigrant groups became assimilated they would tend to move outwards, 'invading' the next zone.

Burgess' model was derived from his close observation of one city in particular, Chicago, although he stressed that he regarded it as an idealized model which could not be expected to apply in precise detail to any single city. The second major 'classical' model of urban residential structure, in contrast, was based on observations in 142 United States cities and was devised by the land economist Homer Hoyt in 1939. Hoyt carried out research on behalf of the Federal Housing Administration in order to identify areas of differing degrees of risk of mortgage-lending. On the basis of mapping the incidence of various criteria by individual city block – for example, age of housing, rent, owner-occupancy, structural condition, intensity of occupation, racial characteristics – Hoyt produced a series of maps showing the spatial pattern of rental areas (Figure 4.17). On the basis of these maps Hoyt suggested that

> rent areas in American cities tend to conform to a pattern of sectors rather than of concentric circles. The highest rent areas of a city tend to be located in one or more sectors of the city. There is a gradation of rentals downwards from these high rental areas in all directions. Intermediate rental areas, or those ranking next to the highest rental areas, adjoin the high rent area on one or more sides, and tend to be located in the same sectors as the high rental areas. Low rent areas occupy other entire sectors of the city from the centre to the periphery.
> *Hoyt (1939), p.76.*

Hoyt saw the sectorally distributed high-value residential areas of the city as being the major influence on the subsequent pattern of residential development. He argued that 'the high rent area . . . tends to pull the growth of the entire city in the same direction.' Figure 4.18 shows how the high-value residential areas in a sample of United States cities were seen by Hoyt as evolving in a clear sectoral pattern between 1930 and 1936. In Hoyt's view, major transportation routes were a significant element in this process, pulling high-value residences out towards more open countryside.

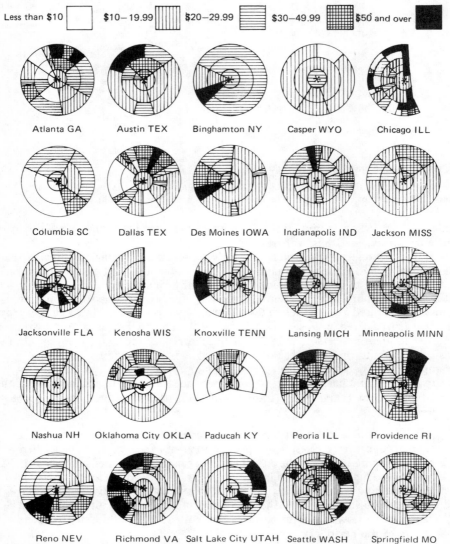

Figure 4.17   The idealized pattern of rental areas in thirty United States cities

Source: H. Hoyt (1939) *The Structure and Growth of Residential Neighbourhoods in American Cities,* Washington: Federal Housing Administration, figure 28.

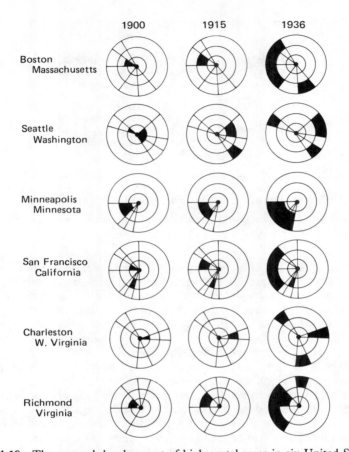

Figure 4.18 The sectoral development of high rental areas in six United States cities

Source: H. Hoyt (1939) *The Structure and Growth of Residential Neighbourhoods in American Cities,* Washington: Federal Housing Administration, figure 40.

Both Burgess and Hoyt assumed the existence of a single-centred urban area around which all other land uses were organized. In fact, a multicentred organization is more characteristic of large metropolitan areas. To that extent, the *multiple nuclei* model proposed by Harris and Ullman in the 1940s was a rather closer representation of reality than the concentric or sectoral models (Figure 4.19). Harris and Ullman suggested that high-status residential districts would tend to occupy locations away from the noxious influences of industry – pollution, railroad tracks and so on – and to prefer the higher land (where it existed). In contrast, the low-status residential areas tended to be juxtaposed with factories, warehouses, transportation facilities and other urban-industrial uses likely to produce an undesirable residential environment.

These three 'classical' models of urban residential structure exerted an enormous influence over subsequent studies, despite their obvious oversimplification. Except in very unusual circumstances, it is most likely that a city's residential

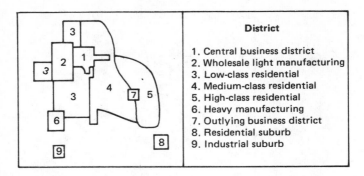

Figure 4.19   Harris and Ullman's multiple nuclei model of urban structure

Source: C.D. Harris & E.L. Ullman (1945) The nature of cities, *Annals of the American Academy of Political and Social Science*, 242, figure 5.

structure will be made up of a *combination* of concentric, sectoral and nuclear elements rather than any single one. Before exploring this idea more fully we need to look at an approach to urban residential – or more accurately social – structure which attempts to relate *social* patterns on the ground to the broader processes operating within society as a whole.

Social area analysis and related approaches

Social area analysis was introduced by Shevky and Bell in the 1950s as a theory of social differentiation which was then applied to the problem of relating variations in social space to variations in geographical space. Such geographical expressions of social processes were termed *social areas*. Shevky and Bell regarded the city as being inseparable from the society of which it is a part; its form and patterns of relationships could thus be regarded as reflecting larger-scale social processes. Shevky and Bell identified the major social process operating within Western urban-industrial society as one of *increasing scale of social organization* – a process which we have ourselves been emphasizing throughout this book. Table 4.8 summarizes both the characteristics of the social processes identified by Shevky and Bell and also the constructs which they derived to express these. As column 1 of Table 4.8 shows, increasing scale was seen to have three major aspects: change in the range and intensity of relations; differentiation of function; complexity of organization. Each of these three aspects could be identified by statistical data relating to the changing distribution of skills, the changing structure of productive activity and the changing composition of population (column 2). Shevky and Bell then suggested that each of the three tendencies in society could be regarded as constructs which, in turn, could be expressed as empirical indexes and used to explore the spatial structure of social areas. As column 4 of Table 4.8 shows, the three constructs of social area analysis are

1 *social rank (economic status)* – measured by such indicators as occupation, schooling, rent

2 *urbanization (family status)* – measured by fertility, percentage of women at work, single-family dwelling units

Table 4.8 *Social area analysis: steps in construct formation and index construction*

Postulates concerning industrial society (aspects of increasing scale) (1)	Statistics of trends (2)	Changes in the structure of a given social system (3)	Constructs (4)	Sample statistics (related to the constructs) (5)	Derived measures (from column 5) (6)	
Change in the range and intensity of relations	*Changing distribution of skills:* lessening importance of manual productive operations – growing importance of clerical, supervisory, management operations	Changes in the arrangement of occupations based on function	SOCIAL RANK (ECONOMIC STATUS)	Years of schooling, employment status, class of worker, major occupation group, value of home, rent by dwelling unit, plumbing and repair, persons per room, heating and refrigeration	Occupation, schooling, rent	Index I
Differentiation of function	*Changing structure of productive activity:* lessening importance of primary production – growing importance of relations centred in cities – lessening importance of the household as economic unit	Changes in the ways of living – movement of women into urban occupations – spread of alternative family patterns	FAMILY STATUS (URBANI-ZATION)	Age and sex, owner or tenant, house structure, persons in household	Fertility, women at work, single-family dwelling units	Index II
Complexity of organization	*Changing composition of population:* increasing movement – alterations in age and sex distribution – increasing diversity	Redistribution in space, changes in the proportion of supporting and dependent population, isolation and segregation of groups	SEGREGATION (ETHNIC STATUS)	Race and nativity, country of birth, citizenship	Racial and national groups in relative isolation	Index III

Source: E. Shevky & W. Bell (1955) *Social Area Analysis: Theory, Illustrative Applications and Computational Procedures*, Stanford: Stanford University Press, table II-1 © Board of Trustees, Leland Stanford Junior University.

3 *segregation* (ethnic status) – measured by incidence of racial and national groups in relative isolation.

Using data from the Census of Population for individual census tracts, scores can be calculated for each index in column 6 of Table 4.8 to establish the spatial pattern of social areas. Shevky's and Bell's own empirical work was done initially in Los Angeles and San Francisco, though subsequent researchers have produced social area analyses for a large number of other cities in different countries. Figures 4.20 and 4.21 are just two examples of attempts to identify social areas. Figure 4.20 shows the social areas of San Francisco in 1950 as identified by Shevky and Bell. In general, the highest-ranking areas in terms of social rank (Figure 4.20a) are located in the west and north with the lowest-status areas in the east next to the Bay. The pattern of family status (Figure 4.20b) shows highest-family status values (low urbanization scores) in the south and lowest-family status scores in the centre and north of San Francisco. The most highly segregated census tracts (Figure 4.20c) are concentrated in inner areas, particular to the northeast. The three separate constructs are mapped together in Figure 4.20d. Figure 4.21 is the social area map of Winnipeg produced by Herbert:

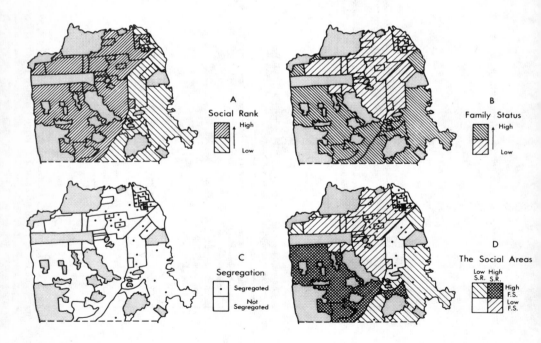

Figure 4.20   Social areas in San Francisco, 1950

Source: M.H. Yeates & B. Garner (1976) *The North American City*, New York: Harper & Row, figure 11.1. Reproduced by permission of Harper & Row Publishers, Inc.

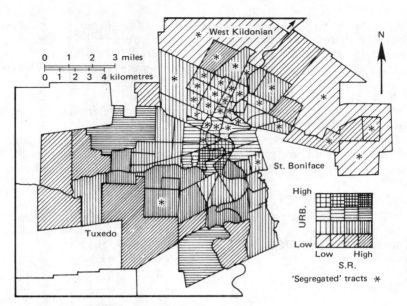

Figure 4.21   Social areas in Winnipeg, 1961

Source: D.T. Herbert (1972) *Urban Geography: A Social Perspective,* Newton Abbot: David & Charles, figure 41.

The southern and western parts of the city indicate the high prestige residential areas. The more central parts of the city and the northern and eastern districts, which include the central slums and tenaments and low cost suburbs, are characterised by low scores. Urbanisation scores distinguish between the central city districts of low family status and the outer suburbs of strong family life; segregation indices demarcate the Ukrainian districts extending north along Main Street.
Herbert (1972), pp.144, 146.

As with the classical models of residential structure before it, social area analysis has been subject to a good deal of criticism. Criticisms have focused on, for example, the validity of the underlying concepts, the nature of the constructs themselves and whether they are, in fact, independent of each other. More pertinent to our present discussion is the doubt cast on the link between the *social* theory and its *geographical* outcome in the form of social *areas*. There is no doubt a link between the two but it may be a good deal more complex than social area analysis suggests.

A further major criticism relates to the limited number and variety of statistical indicators used in the construction of the indexes and to the charge that 'what came out was predetermined by what went in'. Consequently, with the development of computer-aided data processing, attempts to identify patterns of social residential structure have come to incorporate a much larger number of statistical variables which are analysed in a multivariate fashion using factor analysis and principal components analysis in particular. These are statistical techniques designed to 'sort' a large number of variables into a smaller number of significant groups or clusters which effectively represent the major underlying characteristics or 'dimensions' of the total set of variables. When used to analyse social areas in cities, these multivariate techniques are generally grouped together under the term *factorial ecology*. The major difference between social area analysis and factorial ecology, therefore, is that in factorial ecology the dimensions or major patterns emerge from the empirical data, whereas in social area analysis the constructs are predetermined on the basis of certain theoretical assumptions.

A large number of factorial ecology studies have now been carried out for cities in a variety of economic and political contexts. Two of the best-documented studies are Murdie's study of Toronto and Rees' study of Chicago. Both Murdie and Rees

Table 4.9   *Major factors revealed in ecological studies of Toronto and Chicago*

(a) **Toronto, 1951 and 1961**
(No. of variables in the analysis: 86 for 1951, 78 for 1961)

Factor	Percent of total variance explained 1951	1961
1. Economic status	22.8	21.1
2. Family status	14.0	11.5
3. Ethnic status	13.1	
4. Italian ethnic status		15.6
5. Jewish ethnic status		7.7
6. Recent growth	8.7	6.9
7. Service employment – clerical employment	7.5	
8. Household characteristics	6.1	
9. Household and employment characteristics		12.2
% of total variance explained by the 'Social Area' factors (Economic status, Family status, Ethnic status)	49.9	55.9
% of total variance explained by six factors	72.2	75.0

(b) **Chicago, 1960**
(No. of variables in the analysis: 57)

Factors	Percent of total variance explained
1. Socio-economic status	17.8
2. Stage of the life-cycle	14.2
3. Race and resources	13.1
4. Immigrant and Catholic status	10.8
5. Population size and density	7.5
6. Jewish and Russian population	3.8
7. Housing built in 1940s, workers commute by car	3.0
8. Irish and Swedish population	2.6
9. Mobility	2.4
10. Other non-white populations, and Italians	2.1
% total variance explained	77.3

Source: (a) R.A. Murdie (1969) Factorial ecology of Metropolitan Toronto, 1951–1961, *University of Chicago, Department of Geography Research Paper*, 116, table 7; (b) P.H. Rees, The Factorial Ecology of Metropolitan Chicago (1968) master's thesis, University of Chicago

employ a large number of variables, as Table 4.9 shows. The table also shows those factors which contributed most to the statistical explanation of the variance in the social data. Although the larger number of factors 'explain' more of the total variance than the 'social area' factors alone, the fact remains that the constructs of social status, family status and ethnic status figure very prominently in both factorial ecology studies. Since these were not preprogrammed but arose out of the inter-relationships within the large data set, there is reason to see these analyses as confirmation of the importance of these three social dimensions. Indeed, the first two – social status and family status – figure prominently in virtually every multi-variate study of urban social structure carried out in urban-industrial societies. The third dimension – segregation – is far more important in the United States context than elsewhere. In other circumstances, different dimensions seem to add to the two basic ones. The most important one in British cities seems to be the existence of a public housing component.

The correspondence in many of the findings of the various multivariate studies have led to the suggestion that the three major social dimensions tend to be distri-buted spatially in regular patterns which recall some of the elements of the classical models. Figure 4.22 is Berry's and Rees' suggestion of an integrated spatial model of the urban residential area based on the city of Chicago. According to this model, socio-economic status tends to be distributed sectorally (Figure 4.22a), family status tends to be distributed concentrically (Figure 4.22b) whilst ethnic status is expressed spatially as nucleic areas of segregation (4.22c). Superimposing these three gives the composite pattern shown as Figure 4.22d, which suggests that the

> basic triad of spatially arranged social dimensions can be superimposed to
> form, at the intersections of sectors, zones and segregated areas, *communities*
> of similar social, family, and ethnic status.
> *Berry and Horton (1970), p.311.*

However, it is suggested that this idealized pattern may be distorted in a variety of ways, of which Figure 4.22 includes three possibilities. Figure 4.22e suggests that in the segregated areas the range of family status characteristics is present but in a compressed form. Figure 4.22f and g incorporate the effects of variations in the historical growth of the city, whereby ' "tearfaults" develop as the earliest zones of the city are outwardly displaced and cross sectoral boundaries'. Figure 4.22h and i incorporate outer industrial nodes. Other 'distortions' to this idealized model, local to particular contexts, can also be envisaged. In the United Kingdom, for example, the spatial distribution of public housing has a very marked impact, producing clusters of nuclei with particular socio-economic characteristics. As we saw in an earlier section, public housing is a major element of the housing situation in the United Kingdom. Given the kinds of allocation procedures which operate in the public sector and the higher propensity for some groups in the population to seek public housing, it is not surprising to find that a public housing component is a major dimension of the social geography of residential structures in United Kingdom cities. A further, though probably minor, distortion may be produced by the gentrification process, discussed earlier, whereby some low-income housing is taken over and renovated by middle- and upper-income groups.

Even allowing for local variation, the general persistence of the three basic dimensions of social status, family status and ethnic status suggest a certain stability

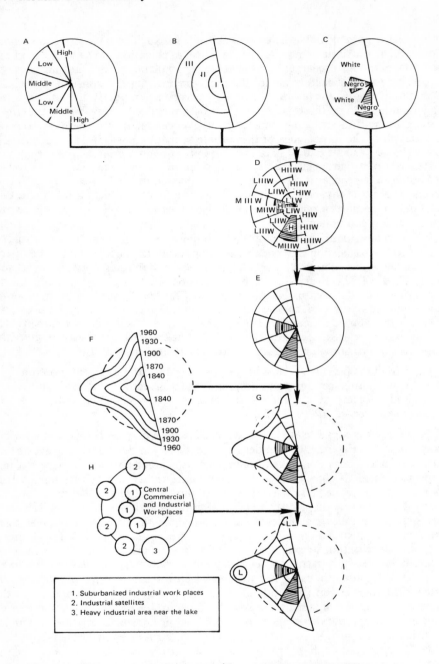

Figure 4.22   An integrated spatial model of a metropolitan residential structure

Source: B.J.L. Berry & P.H. Rees (1969) The factorial ecology of Calcutta, *American Journal of Sociology*, University of Chicago Press, 74, figure 13.

in the overall residential structure of urban areas. Since such constancy is maintained in the face of a continual movement of individual households, this would suggest that the forces operating in the housing market tend to encourage, or dictate, that people of similar status, of similar stage in the family life-cycle or of similar ethnic composition locate together in geographical space. As we saw in discussing social status and household needs earlier in this chapter, there are strong social drives which encourage people to seek to live near to others with whom they compare themselves.*

In some cases, such attempts to maintain residential homogeneity are reinforced by the actions of local governments. In the United States in particular, there has been much discussion of the practice of *exclusionary zoning*. Individual municipalities have the power to zone land for particular uses; they therefore have the power either to modify or to protect existing land uses within their boundaries. An increasingly common view of zoning, especially by surburban municipalities in the United States, is that it tends to be discriminatory in its effects. For example, it is possible for a municipality to influence the socio-economic structure of its residential population by insisting on a minimum plot size for new residences. Cox (1973) quotes the example of two counties adjacent to Cleveland, Ohio, one of which zoned two-thirds of the undeveloped land for single-family residences on plots of at least half an acre while the other zoned for minimum plots of one acre. Quite clearly, only people above a certain income level could afford to occupy such areas. Similarly, zoning for single-family dwellings rather than for multiperson residences, such as apartments, will influence an area's population structure. Although not designed as such, Soja (1971) argues that zoning in United States metropolitan areas is being used chiefly to protect suburban property owners. In effect it discriminates against certain socio-economic and racial groups by keeping house prices higher than they might otherwise be.

Ethnic residential segregation

The spatial segregation of ethnic groups, the third recurring element in the social structure of many residential areas, is perhaps one of the most persistent elements of all. Since it is also one of the most contentious issues and a focus of many social problems, it is worth examining in rather more detail. In particular, we need to look

---

*As Robson points out,

> social segregation can then be seen primarily as a way in which status distinctions in society are made clear and reinforced. In situations where status differences are very pronounced, residential segregation may be less necessary as a further means of pointing the distinctions as in the tendency for racial segregation to be less marked in southern than in northern American cities. Perhaps one can see something of the same in Britain in the tendency for social segregation to become more marked over time as social distinctions have become blurred. . . . Again, of course, the social and housing spaces interact to reinforce each other. If there is a belief that people prefer to live close to similar people, house builders will tend to build similarly priced housing in given areas, thus reinforcing the social segregation. . . . Interestingly, it appears to be status rather than simply income which determines such segregation. This is most plainly seen in studies which look at the location of the better paid manual and the lower paid white-collar groups. Despite their lower incomes, the white-collar families tend to live in 'better' areas. . . . The tendency for segregation by social status thus seems a well-established pattern in the creation of residential areas.
> *Robson (1975), pp.22, 23.*

at how the *geographical pattern* of such segregation evolves over time. Figure 4.23 provides the framework for our discussion. We can assume that the presence of an ethnic group in a city has originated through in-migration at some time in the past. Subsequent events – in particular the extent to which the group becomes assimilated into the host society – depend to a large extent upon the degree of distinctiveness of the ethnic group compared with the host society. Such distinctiveness may be perceived either internally or externally. Internally, the ethnic group may have a strong desire to maintain a separate cultural identity. Externally, the host society may regard the ethnic group as undesirably distinctive and resist its assimilation even where the ethnic group itself desires this. In either case, the spatial outcome will be the same: spatial concentration. On the other hand, where assimilation is easy the ethnic group is unlikely to be spatially concentrated at all. Our interest, therefore, is in those outcomes which produce the spatial concentration of ethnic groups. Boal divides such concentrations into three major categories: the colony, the enclave and the ghetto. The distinction between the ethnic colony on the one hand and the enclave/ghetto on the other is based upon differences in their time-duration. Colonies are short lived, enclaves and ghettos are more permanent. The enclave differs from the ghetto, according to Boal, in that the former is voluntary and the latter involuntary.

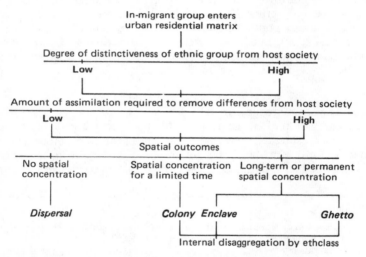

Figure 4.23   Ethnic groups, assimilation and residential spatial outcomes

Source: F.W. Boal (1976) Ethnic residential segregation, in D.T. Herbert & R.J. Johnston (eds) *Social Areas in Cities, Volume I: Spatial Processes and Form,* London: Wiley, figure 2.1.

The existence of residential concentrations of ethnic groups – colonies – seems to be an integral part of the process whereby new immigrant populations enter alien territory. Spatial clustering of new migrants may offer a number of advantages: security, shelter, common language and customs, help in finding employment, for example. It tends to be reinforced by the nature of the migration process itself – especially the chainlike characteristic whereby early settlers send back information to the home country or area and establish links which tend to steer subsequent migrants to the established areas of settlement. But even if there were no positive advantages from spatial concentration of new migrants, such concentration would almost certainly occur because of external pressures. Boal terms these *fabric* effects:

> a high proportion of in-migrants into cities tend, at least initially, to occupy a relatively unfavourable position in the economic structure of the particular society. For ethnic groups, the average household economic position may vary with time (social mobility) but some groups remain relatively disadvantaged for generations. Given relatively low economic position, a very considerable proportion of a particular city's housing stock is consequently unavailable to the in-migrant ethnics. Thus only the lowest cost (and frequently poorest quality) housing can be entered by these groups. . . . The poorest quality housing locations are almost invariably to be found in the innermost portion of cities, or where redevelopment is significant, in a ring immediately outside the expanding redevelopment zones.
> *Boal (1976), p.59.*

In the case of the development of nineteenth-century ethnic concentrations in United States cities, Ward (1971) also stresses the fact that the inner area at that time contained most of the employment opportunities open to the particular skills (or lack of skills) of the migrants. Ward suggests that the first generation of immigrant groups arriving in American cities in large numbers often provided almost the entire labour force of some activities located within the CBD.

In the case of most of the European immigrant groups in United States cities, however, the stage of very high residential segregation was ephemeral. As the immigrants became assimilated socially and economically, as their income levels and their aspiration levels rose, they began to move out of their ethnic colonies. Like much migration, this was often a selective process, members of the older generation remaining in the original area of settlement for some time. Along with the white population in general of North American cities, the assimilated ethnic groups tended to seek suburban residential locations and were succeeded in their original locations in the inner areas by a later immigrant group. On the whole, therefore, immigrant residential *colonies* tend to decline over time, having served as a *port of entry* for an ethnic group. The area itself, of course, may remain an ethnic area, though its ethnic composition may change as new migrant groups enter the places left behind by the earlier groups.

The distinction between enclave and ghetto – the two more permanent forms of ethnic residential concentration identified by Boal – is difficult to define in practice. Boal suggests that Jewish residential areas in North American cities may, today, be more enclave than ghetto (even though, of course, the term ghetto was originally applied to the legally segregated area of Jewish residents in European cities). Boal uses the example of Jewish residential areas in Winnipeg to illustrate his point (Figure 4.24). The original Jewish settlement was to be found in one or two clusters in the inner city. Over time, new, more suburban clusters were formed, the inner ones being abandoned. Boal suggests that these were enclaves rather than ghettos since a high degree of voluntary segregation was involved. Similar patterns are evident in most Western cities with large Jewish communities.

In modern Western society the clearest examples of *ghettos* involve the highly segregated black populations of the United States and the growing non-white – especially West Indian and Asian – immigrants of the United Kingdom. Although there may indeed be a degree of voluntary segregation involved, it is generally agreed that these groups are highly segregated *spatially* largely because of external forces, especially those of discrimination expressed through the operation of the housing market and the job market. Although the degree of concentration of West Indians and Asian groups may not yet be as high as that of black Americans, the spatial patterns and processes seem to be broadly similar in both cases.

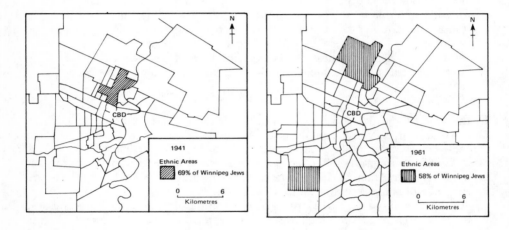

Figure 4.24   The ethnic enclave: Jews in Winnipeg

Source: F.W. Boal (1976) Ethnic residential segregation, in D.T. Herbert & R.J. Johnston (eds) *Social Areas in Cities, Volume I: Spatial Processes and Form*, London: Wiley, figure 2.3. Based upon L. Driedger & G. Church (1974) Residential segregation and institutional completeness: a comparison of ethnic minorities, *Canadian Review of Sociology and Anthropology*, 11, figures I and II.

Figure 4.25 shows the evolution of the spatial pattern of non-white immigrants in Birmingham, England, between 1961 and 1971. Jones (1979) describes the 1961 pattern (Figure 4.25a) – the 'pioneer stage' – as a classic concentric distribution some one to one-and-a-half kilometres outside the CBD, the concentric zone being inter- rupted only by the exclusive residential district of Edgbaston to the southwest of the city centre. The residential density of the non-white population was relatively low with only three areas of more than 300 persons per grid square. There was little non-white settlement outside the concentric zone. Figure 4.25b shows that by 1971 the concentric zone was both more extensive and rather more continuous. Not only had the zone spread outwards in a contiguous manner but also the settlement densities within the zone had increased considerably. Major concentrations of non-white population were present in Handsworth, in particular, but also in districts to the southeast of the city. In explaining this development, Jones agrees with Boal's concept of the 'fabric' effect

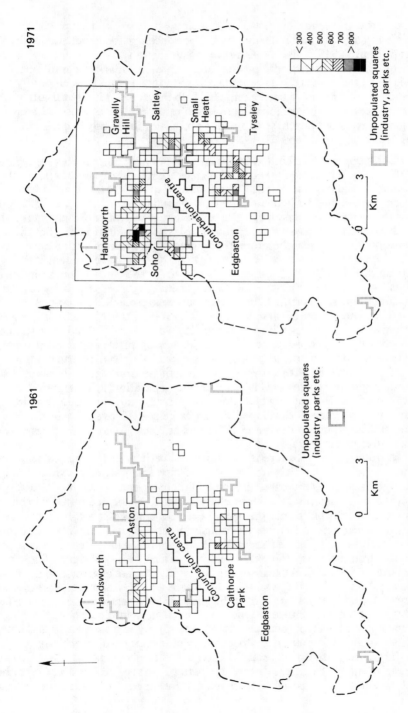

Figure 4.25 Geographical density of non-white immigrants in Birmingham, England, 1961 and 1971

Source: adapted from P.N. Jones (1979) Ethnic areas in British cities, in D.T. Herbert & D.M. Smith (eds) *Social Problems and the City: Geographical Perspectives*, London: Oxford University Press, figures 9.1 and 9.2.

whereby the influence of urban morphology is expressed through the accessibility of particular housing types. The concentric belt coincides with the zone of pre-1919 by-law housing, which although variable in detail . . . contains the lowest priced housing under present market conditions. Immigrants, faced with the disadvantages of low incomes and low eligibility for council housing, have been channeled into this zone. Initially this often meant poor rented accommodation in large, multi-occupied houses. Later this gave way to the purchase of smaller properties for family occupation. *Jones (1979), pp.165–166.*

The black population in United States cities is not only more highly segregated than any other group but also the segregated areas seem to be expanding rather than diminishing. Yet the large-scale black ghetto is a relatively recent phenomenon. In 1910, 73 percent of the United States Negro population was rural; by 1960, 73 percent of this population was urban. In particular, it was the northern industrial cities which experienced massive migration of black population from the South. It is since the turn of the century, therefore, that increases in black migration have led to ghetto development, and since 1920, in particular, such development has been especially rapid. Rose (1969) classified black ghettos in the United States into three generations based upon their stages of development (Figure 4.26). In 1920, there were only nine non-southern urban centres possessing black populations greater than 25,000, although three of these had more than 100,000. At this time, there were twice as many southern cities with more than 25,000 blacks (25,000 is regarded by Rose as a critical size). Rose suggests that cities having black populations greater than 25,000 in 1920 can be regarded as 'first-generation' or 'old' ghetto centres. As Figure 4.26 shows, seven of these were in the North-Central region. Between 1920 and 1950 new ghetto centres developed ('second-generation'). This period saw a massive exodus from the South which slowed down only during the Depression. A third generation of ghettos developed as the large-scale movement of the black population continued in the 1959s and 1960s and as blacks in northern cities moved to western cities in particular.

Within American cities there is, as suggested earlier, a close relationship between the location of black ghettos within the city and that of previous foreign immigrant ghettos. In every case, though, whether or not there has been a pre-existing ethnic concentration, the black ghetto tends to be located initially in one of the low-income sectors on the margin of the central business district. Its subsequent geographical development has been variously described as being predominantly concentric, sectoral or truncated-sectoral. Much would seem to depend upon particular local circumstances, for example, the pattern of availability of low-rent accommodation, the physical nature of the city itself, the rate of growth of the black population and its rent-paying abilities. These are all important contributory factors. Even though, in general, growth of the ghetto may be sectoral, there may in fact be more than one ghetto cluster. This can arise, for example, where the Negro demand for low-rent accommodation exceeds the supply in a single area and a new ghetto cluster may be formed in another low-income sector within the city. Consequently, the ghetto pattern in several old-established centres is polynuclear. Irregular topography may, of course, distort the pattern – especially as areas of rather higher elevation tend to be developed mainly for upper-income residents. San

Figure 4.26 The spatial and temporal evolution of a national ghetto system in the United States

Source: H.M. Rose (1969) Social processes in the city: race and urban residential choice, *Association of American Geographers, Commission on College Geography, Resource Paper 6,* figure 1.

Francisco (Figure 4.27) and Pittsburgh reflect this and both have a polynuclear ghetto pattern. Where the topography is relatively regular – as in Chicago, Detroit, Cleveland, for example – a more regular sectoral form is present.

Whatever the precise spatial form, a good deal of ghetto expansion seems to involve outward spread. Figure 4.28 shows the fairly regular development of the black residential area in Grand Rapids, Michigan. The mechanism of ghetto expansion involves a strong element of invasion and succession, though these are rather unfortunate terms (they derive, it may be recalled, from the ecological analogies of Park and Burgess). The key point about the ghetto system is its *duality*: not only are blacks excluded from white areas but also whites tend to be absent from black areas. This is shown particularly clearly in the different degrees of suburbanization of the black and white populations in the United States. Figure 4.29 shows white and black suburbanization trends between 1900 and 1970. It shows, as Muller (1976) has observed, that blacks have been largely denied entrance to the American suburbs. The detailed study by Rose (1976) of black suburbanization shows that the most active black suburban growth communities are, in fact, spatial extensions of central-city ghettos.

A key question is the point at which an area changes from being predominantly white to predominantly black. The entry of one black household into an area is unlikely to produce large-scale turnover of existing occupants. There appears to be a critical threshold, a significant percentage of black population, below which no great change occurs but above which accelerated outward movement takes place with little or no compensating inward movement of white population. This has been termed

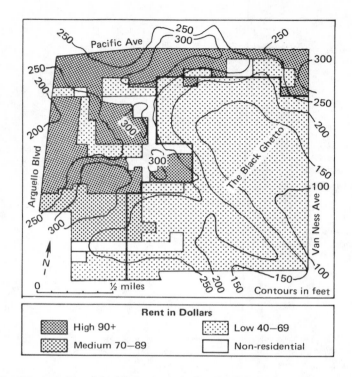

Figure 4.27 The location of the black ghetto in San Francisco in relation to topography and property values

Source: H.M. Rose (1969) Social processes in the city: race and urban residential choice, *Association of American Geographers, Commission on College Geography, Resource Paper 6,* figure 3.

the *tipping mechanism*, though it is unlikely that there is any unique tipping point applicable to all situations. Research in Philadelphia revealed that, when Negro penetration reached 30 percent of total households, demand for housing by the white population was between 85 and 94 percent below its former level, and that, even when there was only 5 percent Negro penetration, the demand for white housing was reduced by between 50 and 60 percent (Rapkin and Grigsby 1960). Morrill suggests that whites appear to be willing to accept between 5 and 25 percent Negro occupancy (with an average of about 10 percent) for a long time before beginning to abandon the neighbourhood, although this clearly varies according to the characteristics of the black population moving in, the proximity of the ghetto and the open-mindedness of the resident white population. But once the particular critical threshold is reached, residential change may be phenomenally rapid. Simmons points out, for example, that 'if whites panic, the turnover takes place rapidly, affecting as many as 75 percent of the dwellings in two or three years' (Simmons 1968, p. 634).

Thus, ethnic residential segregation is brought about by a set of highly complex forces. Certainly, housing market discrimination is important, but it is not the complete explanation. As Boal has pointed out, it provides no explanation for the segregation that exists *between* ethnic groups. Such internal segregation within

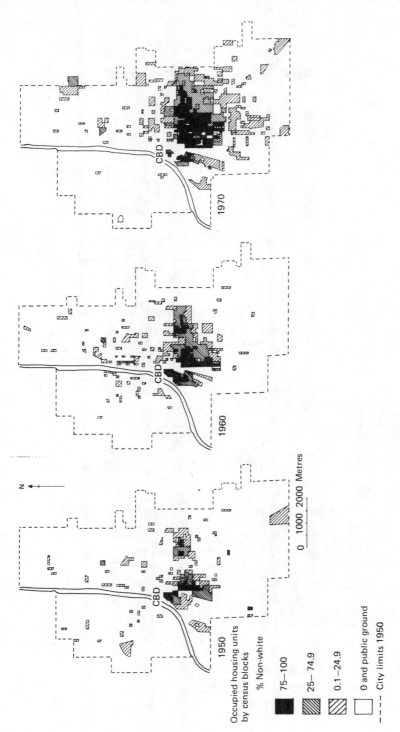

Figure 4.28 The geographical evolution of the black residential areas in Grand Rapids, Michigan, 1950–1970

Source: F. W. Boal (1976) Ethnic residential segregation, in D.T. Herbert & R.J. Johnston (eds) *Social Areas in Cities, Volume I: Spatial Processes and Form,* London: Wiley, figure 2.5.

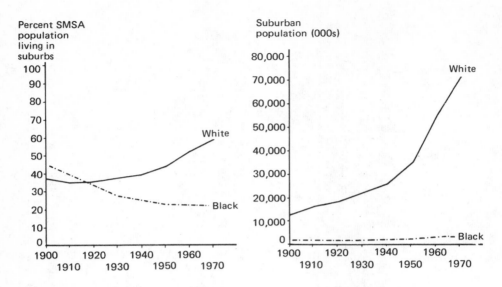

Figure 4.29   Black suburbanization trends in the United States, 1900–1970

Source: P.O. Muller (1976) The outer city: geographical consequences of the urbanization of the suburbs, *Association of American Geographers, Commission on College Geography, Resource Paper 75–2*, figure 8.

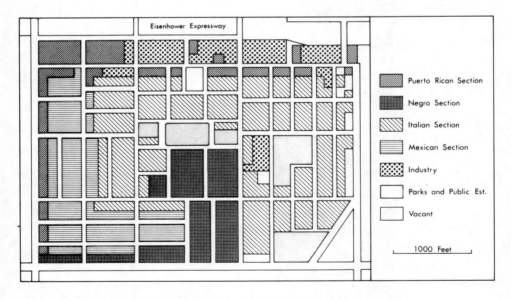

Figure 4.30   Internal segregation within the Addams district of Chicago

Source: G.D. Suttles (1968), *The Social Order of the Slum*, Chicago: The University of Chicago Press, map 2.

ethnic areas can be very marked indeed, as Figure 4.30 demonstrates. The map depicts the small district of Addams in the inner area of Chicago. Despite its small geographical extent, the area is shared by four ethnic groups: Puerto Ricans, Negros, Italians and Mexicans, each of which occupies clearly defined blocks. Similar internal clusterings of West Indian, Pakistani and Indian groups have been identified by Jones in his Birmingham study referred to earlier.

SOME IMPLICATIONS OF THE CHANGING RELATIONSHIP BETWEEN HOME AND WORK

We have stressed at several points in this, and the previous, chapter the very close relationship which exists between a person's place in the housing market and his or her position in the labour market. The two are intimately linked in a variety of ways. Perhaps most important of all is the influence of the income and occupational status derived from work on an individual's or a household's access to housing. The importance of an appropriate level and stability of income in ensuring entry to the private housing market in particular has been emphasized in this chapter. We have noted, too, that discrimination against minority groups in the housing market is compounded by the fact that members of such groups tend to occupy lowly positions in the labour market. They tend to be predominantly unskilled or semi-skilled, to earn low incomes. Many of them are firmly embedded in the secondary labour market. In effect, there is a basic *functional* relationship between the housing market and the labour market: the type and quality of housing occupied is greatly influenced by that household's position in the labour market.

There is also a very strong *geographical* relationship between the processes operating in the labour market and those operating in the housing market. In Chapter Three, for example, we showed that time-space constraints on individuals are important elements in the operation of local labour markets. The location of the home base is a fundamental determinant of access to jobs. This is particularly so for lower-income groups and those, such as married women, who can afford neither the money nor the time to travel long distances to work. Over time, of course, the geography both of jobs and of housing change. In recent years, such changes have become increasingly out of step with each other. In Robson's words,

> the job markets and the housing markets are being pulled apart and the very
> poor are caught in a trap in the central city.
> *Robson (1975), p. 49.*

In the early days of industrial and urban development, home and workplace were generally extremely close to each other. For all but the very small minority, the constraints on personal mobility and the lengthy hours of work necessitated the close geographical association between home and workplace. Such spatial symbiosis no longer exists to anything like the same extent. The *journey to work* has become a marked feature of everyday life, generating massive commuter flows as the geographical pattern of both jobs and residences has become more extensive and more segregated. As we observed in Chapter Three, there has been a substantial shift in the relative growth or decline of different occupations between central cities and suburbs. There has been an increase in all occupations in the suburbs but a major decline of certain occupational groups in the central cities. In particular, the number of blue-collar jobs – manufacturing operatives, craftsmen, labourers – and of sales workers has fallen dramatically in the inner areas. Such outward job shifts have been associated with the more rapid growth of manufacturing functions in the outer parts of metropolitan areas compared with administrative functions, many of which have remained in central-city locations. Overall, then, it has been blue-collar jobs, especially the unskilled jobs, which have become most suburbanized in recent years.

At the same time, the workings of the housing market have produced a major geographical resorting of the residential population. Suburbanization has been a socially selective process. In the United States in particular, but also elsewhere to varying degrees, the extent of residential segregation has become extremely marked, with the poor, and especially the black and other minority groups, effectively excluded from the suburbs. These are the groups with the most limited access to the housing market. These are the groups which can only find housing – whether rented or bought – in the older inner areas of cities. Apart from the occasional public housing development in the outer urban areas in such countries as the United Kingdom, such groups cannot find housing in the suburbs. Yet, as we have seen, more and more of the employment opportunities for such groups are in the suburbs.

The result is that, very often, the low-income worker has to make a longer and more costly journey to work than the high-income worker. This is a reversal of the traditional pattern in which the length of the journey to work tended to be positively related to social status. The low-status worker lived very close to his place of work, the professional or managerial worker living in the suburbs travelled greater distances back into the central city. As Wheeler has observed,

> The present trend, the reversal of the old association between distance travelled and social status, seems to point towards the time when the rich will live closest to their work and the poor the farthest – unless public policy intervenes to provide low cost homes in the suburbs.
> *Wheeler (1974), p. 46.*

The changing spatial distribution of homes and workplaces, together with the general increases in mobility which have occurred with the development of mass automobile-ownership, have led to very complex links emerging between home and workplace. Wheeler suggests that three categories of commuting are now characteristic of large urban areas. First is the traditional centripetal movement of suburban residents to jobs in the central city. Both individual and mass transport systems focus on the urban core. Second, there is 'reverse commuting', a phenomenon related to the suburbanization of jobs employing people who are residents of inner areas. Reverse commuting is far less well served by public transport so that inner-area residents whose jobs are in the suburbs must – at least in North America, though still rather less so elsewhere – possess or have access to an automobile.* Not surprisingly, in view of the developments we have been discussing, blue-collar workers are particularly heavily involved in reverse commuting. For example,

> In 1970, 19 per cent of Chicago's laborers worked in the suburbs compared to 7 per cent in 1960; 21 per cent of its craftsmen worked in the suburbs,

---

*The extent to which different social groups have access to personal transport is discussed in the next chapter.

compared to 10 per cent in 1960 and 22 per cent of its factory workers worked in the suburbs compared to 8 per cent in 1960.
De Vise (1976), p.351.

The third category of commuting – 'lateral commuting' – has developed along with the evolution of outlying clusters of employment opportunities such as industrial parks and estates. In this type of commuting, access to private transport is absolutely essential if jobs in these locations are to be reached. For those who cannot get housing close to such employment centres or do not have access to an automobile, such job opportunities are closed. Problems of physical accessibility between home and workplace, which are greatest for the poor and especially the ethnic groups in British and American cities, undoubtedly affect the employment prospects of these groups. Wheeler (1974), for example, quotes one estimate of the effects of residential segregation of blacks on their job opportunities which suggests that some 35,000 jobs in Chicago and 9000 jobs in Detroit in the early 1960s may have been lost to them.

But it would be incorrect to attribute all the unemployment and job problems of central-city residents to the influence of physical accessibility alone. The influence of other, more basic, factors is revealed in a study of job accessibility and underemployment in Atlanta carried out by Bederman and Adams. Their main conclusion was that variations in rates of unemployment in Atlanta could not be explained by variations in physical accessibility between home and workplace:

Atlanta's critically underemployed are mainly black female heads of families, and no matter where they live in the metropolitan area they have neither the skills to qualify them for most of the new jobs being created, nor the opportunity to acquire marketable skills.
Bederman and Adams (1974), p.386.

Thus, although many people may not be able to afford to travel to distant jobs, the more basic barrier to employment is that of levels of education and marketable skills.

A common response to problems of mismatch between home and work is to suggest that a person who cannot get a job within daily travelling distance of home should move to a new residential location where suitable jobs are available. This might be another part of the same city or a quite different city or region some considerable distance away. In other words, it could involve *residential migration*. This does, of course, happen. People do migrate at a variety of geographical scales though, as we pointed out earlier in this chapter, most residential moves take place over very short distances. Even so, long-distance migration, both intra- and internationally, is a significant feature of modern society, as it has been also in the past. Of course, by no means all migrations are related to the search for employment opportunities, though undoubtedly a substantial proportion is.* But, as should be clear from our discussion of the housing market in this chapter, moving house can be both difficult and costly.

---

*Historically, large-scale migrations have occurred for a great variety of reasons: political, religious and cultural factors being some of the most important. In recent years, with the introduction of retirement pensions and other benefits, migration of retired people to areas of amenable climate such as Florida, the Southwest United States and South and Southwest England has become common.

Employment-related residential mobility is of two basic types. One type involves the search both for a house and for employment in a new area. The other type occurs in the context of the internal labour market described in Chapter Three, where an employee is transferred to a different geographical location within the same company. From a housing point of view, this distinction is important. In both cases, of course, geographical distance is a very important variable. The greater the migration distance involved in a residential move, the greater the overall cost of movement is likely to be (defining 'cost' in the broadest terms to include not only economic but also social factors). The process of searching for satisfactory housing at a distance is complicated by the searcher's probable ignorance of the local housing market and his greater reliance on the formal institutions of the housing market, especially estate agents, than might be the case with short-distance moves. (Recall from Table 4.5 that informal information sources are generally more important in the short-distance residential location decision.) There may be a need to take temporary accommodation, perhaps splitting the family for a while, until satisfactory housing is found.

A person's tenure status is also important in long-distance residential moves. Theoretically, at least, it is easier to move within the rented sector than in the owner-occupied sector. A tenant has none of the complications of selling and buying houses, arranging mortgages and so on. In the private rented sector mobility is simpler, although there may be great variations from place to place in the availability of rented accommodation. In the United Kingdom there has been a substantial erosion of the stock of private rented dwellings. Mobility within the public housing sector, however, may be very different. Certainly this is the case in the United Kingdom where, as we have seen, the public sector is such a major element in the total housing stock. Mobility in the public housing sector in Britain is very limited, particularly over long distances, since eligibility for public housing depends primarily on position on a waiting list within the area itself. Various types of transfer system exist and, in a very few cases, local authorities have allocated some housing to newly arriving workers. But in general the frictions to residential mobility in the public housing sector are such as to greatly inhibit residential movement and, therefore, to greatly decrease the geographical mobility of labour.

The frictions to residential mobility in the owner-occupied sector are of a different kind. The existing house has to be sold and another in the new area purchased. But there are very substantial geographical differences in house prices. It is obviously more difficult to move up the house price gradient than to move down it. House prices tend to be highest where demand is greatest and this is likely to be where employment prospects are also high. One recent estimate put the difference in average house prices between Wales and Greater London at about £12,000. Thus a person moving from a low house-price area to a high price area either has to raise a substantially larger capital sum or, alternatively, try to find poorer accommodation. Geographical price differentials may not be the only problem, however. It may be difficult to sell a house, particularly where employment prospects are declining. The selling time may have to be extended or a lower price accepted. A high-cost bridging loan may have to be sought from a bank to cover the period when the mover has two mortgages to pay pending the sale of the original house. In each case, though, the effect is the same: the cost of moving is increased. But even if a house can be sold and another one bought without too much difficulty, the actual cost of moving is substantial when the fees charged by estate agents, solicitors and removal firms are added together.

However, some groups in the population are largely, or even totally, cushioned against the financial burdens of moving house to a different part of the country in association with a change of job. Many large organizations, both private and public, bear some or all of the 'dislocation' costs. This is the case, for example, where a key employee is transferred to a different geographical location within the same organization. Here, then, is a further distinguishing feature of the internal labour market. A common practice is for the firm to bear the actual costs of moving. Some firms also pay a 'resettlement' allowance, some compensate for the problem of moving to an area of higher house prices by a system of low-interest loans.

Quite clearly, therefore, residential mobility associated with a change of job is very much easier for some than for others. However, the social costs and benefits of a residential migration cannot be calculated so easily or expressed in financial terms. Much depends upon the extent of the individual's social integration at his existing location. Some people are heavily locked in to local family commitments, others may have a flourishing social life. In either case, a long-distance move disrupts these social relationships. Thus a combination of economic and social factors may inhibit residential and, therefore, employment mobility. The fact that people do move in spite of the frictions inherent in the workings of the housing market suggests very strong motivations. In particular, it suggests that many people see geographical mobility as a necessary prerequisite of economic and social advancement.

CONCLUSION

It should now be clear that the question of where people live in modern Western society is not a simple matter of individual household choice. The highly complex housing market offers choices within constraints of varying degrees of severity. For some households, especially those with high levels of income or social status, the constraints are relatively few and freedom of choice is great. For the very poor and for certain minority groups, the constraints are overwhelming and the opportunities of obtaining adequate housing severely limited. The majority of the population, of course, lies somewhere between these two extremes. The *geographical* pattern of residence, therefore, is the outcome of the ways in which the housing market operates, together with people's attempts to match their housing to their family life-cycle needs and to their social aspirations.

Timms summarizes the situation very concisely:

In practice, residential location is likely to be more affected by the constraints of the urban system than it is by the preferences and cognitive maps of urban dwellers. Residential mobility is frequently forced rather than voluntary, and the opportunities which are available are restricted by costs, by knowledge and by social access. There is, in general, a remarkable stability in the urban residential system. The preference maps of urban residents are themselves guided by their conceptions of the constraints and opportunities of the urban system. Migration and attempts to alter the local habitat take place in terms of the overall system of differentiation charac-

teristic of the community concerned. Whether by coercion or by choice, particular types of people are located in particular sorts of areas. The complex of individual preferences, housing needs and financial capabilities, existing housing supply, information flows and market manipulations leads to a sifting and sorting of the population into distinct residential clusters organized in terms of basic social differentials. The attractions and repulsions between groups, differences in life cycle and life style, and variations in housing ideology are translated into residential differentiation.
Timms (1976), pp.35–36.

The workings of the housing market and the spatial patterning of residential areas illustrate very clearly the operation of Hägerstrand's *authority constraints*. 'Gatekeepers' of various kinds control the individual's access to particular types of housing and thus to particular segments of geographical space. To a considerable degree, the main criterion for entry is income (and, therefore, for most people position in the labour market is a key determinant of position in the housing market). But other factors, particularly various forms of social and racial discrimination, are very significant – if often covert. Practices such as red-lining by housing finance institutions, discriminatory dealing by estate agents or by sellers, zoning ordinances by municipal authorities (especially in American metropolitan suburbs) are some of the ways in which authority constraints operate to maintain residential homogeneity.

In whatever way the housing market operates, the outcome, of course, is that the individual comes to occupy a particular location in geographical space. The home is the specific base around which its members' daily time-space prisms focus. It is the point from which people connect to sources of satisfaction of needs and wants. Hence, not only is the physical quality of the house itself important for individual and family well-being, but also its geographical location is a primary influence on the quality of life through its spatial relationship with the distribution of 'goods' and 'bads'. This is the issue which forms the basis of the next chapter.

Chapter Five

Access to 'goods', proximity to 'bads': geographical variations in well-being

WHAT DO WE MEAN BY 'WELL-BEING'?

A precise definition of the notion of 'well-being' is almost impossible to achieve. Quite clearly, well-being relates in some way to the extent to which individual needs and wants are satisfied. As we pointed out in Chapter One, needs and wants can be regarded as forming a hierarchy in which the most basic needs of physical survival have to be met first, but beyond which there is increasing discretion as to what constitutes wants and desires. We also pointed out that the satisfaction of needs and wants is based upon *relative*, and not absolute, criteria. People compare themselves with other people and, for the most part, the comparison is upwards rather than downwards, and with people in the same society not in other societies:

> The poor in the United States might be rich in India but they actually live in the United States and feel poor. The middle class may have fresh fruit and vegetables that the richest kings could not afford in the Middle Ages, but they feel deprived relative to the upper middle class, who can afford things they cannot afford. . . . There is no minimum standard of living that will make people content. Individual wants are not satiated as incomes rise, and individuals do not become more willing to transfer some of their resources to the poor as they grow richer. . . . Wants become necessities whenever most of the people in society believe that they are in fact necessities. *Thurow (1980), pp.18, 198.*

A further difficulty is that individual wants may conflict with those of other individuals; most actions, as we suggested in Chapter One, are interdependent. Effects 'spill over' to others. The value gained from possessing a particular good or from engaging in a particular action may be greatly reduced as large numbers of other people come to possess the same good or to partake in the same activity. Congestion and crowding, in the broadest sense, become important disutilities as does the 'pollution' of an individual's social or physical environment by the actions of others. Thus, in Hirsch's terms, an increasingly important aspect of well-being is 'the ability to stay ahead of the crowd'; relative position becomes an important key to individual well-being.

Very often monetary income is used as a measure of well-being. Insofar as this is an indication of individual market power to acquire certain goods (including a 'desirable' place to live) there is some merit in income as a measure. But monetary income is, in itself, an insufficient indicator of well-being. *Non*-material goods and bads are a significant component of well-being. Indeed, it seems that as monetary income increases the importance of non-material goods increases. A person struggling to get enough food to eat is unlikely to be much concerned with preserving beautiful landscapes or even with the cleanliness of the atmosphere. Concern with the 'environment' has developed largely in association with increasing affluence.

In the light of these, and other, complications it is hardly surprising that no single and simple definition of well-being has been devised. What is needed is a measure of *real income* which incorporates both monetary income and also all the other benefits and costs which accrue to individuals. Quite apart from the essentially relative nature of needs and wants, any measure of well-being must in some way reflect both the variety of elements involved and also their relative importance or weighting in the overall well-being 'package'. Numerous attempts have been made to identify the elements which contribute towards individual well-being.* Table 5.1 shows just a few of these. As the table shows, there are some differences in detail but there is also a considerable degree of consensus between each of the lists of criteria. Thus we can regard well-being as some composite measure of a variety of individual elements, the specific combination and weighting of each one varying according to the norms and standards existing in a particular society at a particular time.

GEOGRAPHY AND WELL-BEING: SOME BROAD RELATIONSHIPS

Each of the items shown in Table 5.1 is unevenly distributed among the population. One major dimension is that of social status; in general, people with high social status enjoy a high level of well-being, people of low social status – the poor, the discriminated against – suffer a low level of well-being. To a considerable extent social status and well-being go together. A second dimension along which well-being varies – the one which is of most interest to us – is geographical:†

> There is no such thing as being born equal. It depends upon whether the address is good or bad.
> *Higbee (1970), pp.109–110.*

A person's location in geographical space is itself an important influence on well-being since the geographical distribution of many of the aspects of well-being – of 'goods' and 'bads' – is extremely uneven. The specific location into which a person is born is a key factor in determining the range of opportunities available, the variety and quality of 'life-chances'. Of course, the social and the geographical dimensions are not totally independent of each other. As we suggested in Chapter One, it is often extremely difficult to disentangle one from the other. Since people of similar social status tend to live near to each other and since well-being varies according to social status, then we would also expect to find geographical variations in patterns of well-being. In some cases, therefore, such patterns simply reflect the spatial coincidence of social elements. In others, however, they reflect the specific influence of locational variables of which both distance and the locational strategies of public and private organizations are key elements. As Pahl has pointed out,

> territorial inequality is substantial . . . men with the same occupation, income and family characteristics have substantially different life chances in different localities. . . . The range of territorial inequality is probably greater in many instances than the range of inequality between certain positions in the occupational structure; moreover, the former inequalities are widening more rapidly than the latter.
> *Pahl (1971), pp.135-136.*

---

*Smith (1977, chapter 2) provides a detailed review of attempts to construct measures of well-being. He notes three main approaches: (1) those based on psychological and sociological theory; (2) those which ask people to evaluate their own state of well-being; (3) those which refer to 'expert opinion'.

---

†There is a rapidly growing literature on the geography of well-being. Important contributions have been made by Smith (1977, 1979), Cox (1973, 1979), Harvey (1973), Morrill and Wohlenberg (1971), Coates and Rawstron (1971), amongst others.

Table 5.1   *Some alternative definitions of individual well-being*

UN components of levels of living[1]	Drewnowski's level of living index[1]	OECD areas of social concern[1]
Health, including demographic conditions	Nutrition	Health
Food and nutrition	Clothing	Individual development through learning
Education, including literacy and skills	Shelter	Employment and quality of working life
Conditions of work	Health	Time and leisure
Employment situation	Education	Personal economic situation
Aggregate consumption and savings	Leisure	Physical environment
Transportation	Security	Social environment
Housing, including household facilities	Social environment	Personal safety and administration of justice
Clothing	Physical environment	Social opportunity and participation
Recreation and entertainment		Accessibility
Social security		
Human freedom		

Smith's criteria of social well-being in the United States[1]	Harvey's list of needs[2]	Hägerstrand's concept of 'livability'[3]
Income, wealth, employment	Food	Continuous access to:
Living environment	Housing	air
Health	Medical care	a dwelling
Education	Education	Access to food several times a day
Social order	Social and environ-mental service	Some daily and weekly recreation
Social belonging	Consumer goods	Play and training during early years
Recreation and leisure	Recreational opportunities	Security of work
	Neighbourhood amenities	Continuity of education at irregular intervals during career
	Transport facilities	Assistance at an advanced age
		Random access at all times to: transportation relevant information medical care

Sources: [1] United Nations (1954) *Report on International Definition and Measurement of Standards of Living*, New York.

[2] D. Harvey (1973) *Social Justice and the City*, London: Edward Arnold, p.102

[3] T. Hägerstrand (1970) What about people in regional science? *Papers of the Regional Science Association*, 24, p.19

Some general geographical variations in well-being

It is possible to examine the general geographical dimension of well-being in two main ways. One way is to analyse separately the geographical incidence of each of the elements listed in Table 5.1. But because some of the items are very closely associated to each other, a more useful approach is to attempt to produce a *composite measure of well-being* in which each individual item is represented. The most common method of doing this is to employ the statistical technique of principal components analysis in which the inter-relationships between many variables can be analysed simultaneously and these relationships summarized into a smaller number of basic components. Each component consists of those variables which 'cluster together', that is, are most alike in their distribution.*

Several geographers have used such an approach in attempting to identify geographical variation in well-being at a variety of spatial scales. David Smith, in particular, has been especially involved in such investigations. As Table 5.1 shows, Smith identified seven criteria of social well-being in the United States. Six of these criteria (recreation and leisure were excluded because of measurement difficulties) were examined in more detail using forty-seven variables. Table 5.2 lists these, together with the positive or negative direction of each variable. Applying principal components analysis to the inter-relationships between these forty-seven variables led Smith to identify two major components of social well-being:

Table 5.2 *Criteria of social well-being and the variables used in the analysis of interstate variations in well-being in the United States*

	Criteria and variables	Direction
I	**Income, wealth and employment**	
	Income and Wealth	
	1 Per capita annual income ($) 1968	+
	2 Families with annual income less than $3000 (%) 1959	−
	3 Total bank deposits per capita ($) 1968	+
	Employment Status	
	4 Public assistance recipients (% population) 1964	−
	5 Union members per 1000 non-agricultural employees 1966	+
	6 White-collar employees (% of total) 1960	+
	Income Supplements	
	7 Average monthly benefit for retired workers ($) 1968	+
	8 Average monthly AFDC payments per family ($) 1968	+
	9 Average monthly aid to the disabled ($) 1968	+
	10 Average monthly old age assistance ($) 1968	+
	11 Average weekly state unemployment benefit ($) 1968	+

*We have already encountered such multivariate techniques in our discussion of social areas in Chapter Four. In effect, such standard methods of collapsing large matrices of variables to more readily interpretable smaller ones represent an 'empirical search for regularity'. Of themselves, such methods reflect primarily the quality of the information employed, although they can be useful in testing concepts or as a help to formulating ideas about relationships. But no magic prescriptions emanate from them.

	Criteria and variables	Direction
II	**The Environment**	
	Housing	
	12 Median value of owner-occupied houses ($) 1960	+
	13 Houses dilapidated or lacking complete plumbing (%) 1960	−
	14 Index of home equipment (max.=600) 1960	+
III	**Health**	
	Physical Health	
	15 Households with poor diets (%) 1965	−
	16 Infant deaths per 10,000 live births 1967	−
	17 Tuberculosis deaths per million population 1967	−
	18 Hospital expenses per patient day ($) 1965	+
	Access to Medical Care	
	19 Hospital beds per 10,000 population 1967	+
	20 Physicians per 10,000 population 1967	+
	21 Dentists per 10,000 population 1967	+
	22 Persons covered by hospital health insurance (%) 1965	+
	Mental Health	
	23 Residents in mental hospitals, etc., per 100,000 population 1966	−
	24 Patient days in mental hospitals per 1000 population 1965	−
	25 Mental hospital expenditures per patient day ($) 1965	+
IV	**Education**	
	Achievement	
	26 Illiterates per 1000 population 1960	−
	27 Draftees failing armed service mental test (%) 1968	−
	Duration	
	28 Median school years completed (×10) 1960	+
	29 Persons attended college per 1000 population aged 25 or over, 1960	+
	Level of Service	
	30 Pupils per teacher 1968	−
	31 Public school expenditures per pupil ($) 1967	+
V	**Social Disorganization**	
	Personal Pathologies	
	32 Alcoholics per 10,000 adults 1970	−
	33 Narcotics addicts per 10,000 population 1970	−
	34 Gonorrhea cases per 100,000 population 1970	−
	35 Syphilis cases per million population 1970	−
	36 Suicides per million population 1967	−
	Family Breakdown	
	37 Divorces 1966 per 1000 marriages 1968	−
	38 Husband and wife households (% of total) 1968	+
	Crime and Safety	
	39 Crimes of violence per 100,000 population 1969	−
	40 Crimes against property per 10,000 population 1969	−
	41 Motor vehicle accident deaths per million population 1967	

VI   **Alienation and participation**

Democratic Participation

42 Eligible voters voting (%) 1964   +

43 Registered voters per 100 population of voting age 1968   +

Criminal Justice

44 Jail inmates not convicted (%) 1970   −

45 Population per lawyer 1966   −

Racial Segregation

46 Negroes in schools at least 95% Negro 1968   −

47 City residential segregation index (max. = 100) 1960   −

Note: Direction of measures – a plus sign means that high values are 'good' and low are 'bad'; a minus sign means the reverse.

Source: D.M. Smith (1973) *The Geography of Social Well-Being in the United States*, New York: McGraw Hill, table 7.1. With permission of McGraw Hill Book Company.

1 *A general socio-economic well-being component* was the dominant component, reflecting especially the income, income supplement, housing, health and education variables of Table 5.2. The interstate performance on this general component is mapped in Figure 5.1a. With the exception of Florida, the whole of the southeastern block of states had low scores on this component. At the state level these displayed

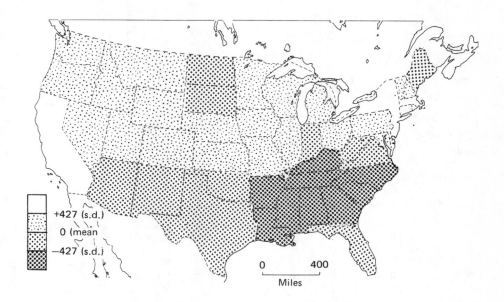

Figure 5.1   (a) General socio-economic well-being in the United States

Source: D.M. Smith (1973) *The Geography of Social Well-Being in the United States*, New York: McGraw Hill, figure 7.3. With permission of McGraw Hill Book Company.

the poorest levels of socio-economic well-being. At the other extreme, the highest levels of socio-economic well-being were found in New York state, Massachusetts, Connecticut and New Jersey in the Northeast and in California.

2 *A social pathology component* was made up primarily of such variables as crimes of violence, personal pathologies and alienation. Comparison of the state patterns on this component, shown in Figure 5.1b, reveal some very marked contrasts with the socio-economic component. Indeed, some states occupied completely opposite rankings on the two components. New York and California, in particular, ranked very high in terms of socio-economic well-being (ranks 1 and 4 respectively) but were in the two bottom positions on the social pathology component. As Smith points out, the extreme differences reflect the enormous social heterogeneity within some states, particularly those with very large metropolitan areas, such as New York City, Los Angeles, Baltimore and Chicago in particular. (The relationship between large cities and social well-being is discussed in more detail in subsequent sections of this chapter.)

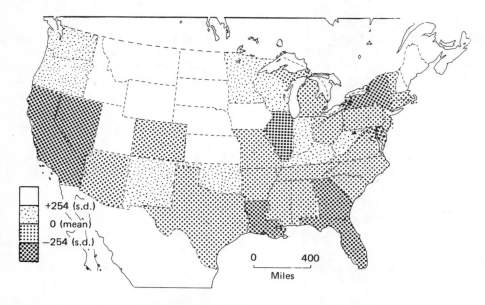

Figure 5.1   (b) The social pathology component in the United States

Source: D.M. Smith (1973) *The Geography of social well-being in the United States*, New York: McGraw Hill, figure 7.3. With permission of McGraw Hill Book Company.

A similar approach to the study of geographical variations in well-being in Britain has been utilized by Knox (1975). Table 5.3 and Figure 5.2 provide the details of his analysis of social well-being in England and Wales in 1971. In this case, twenty-nine variables were employed, many of which were similar to those used by Smith in his United States study, though variables dealing with income and crime in particular were not included. Figure 5.2 shows that highest levels of social well-being were found in the Southeast (excluding inner London) and in the Midlands. In general, the more peripheral parts of the country had lower levels of well-being. The lowest levels of all, however, were located in some of the inner-London boroughs. Of the twenty lowest-ranking areas, eleven were London boroughs. Very low scores were also registered in other older conurbations, particularly Liverpool, Manchester and Newcastle. Conversely, high levels of social well-being were found in the prosperous suburbs of outer London and the surrounding counties.

Table 5.3 *Variables used in the analysis of social well-being in England and Wales, 1971*

1	% households overcrowded (more than 1.0 persons per room)
2	% households without exclusive use of all three census amenities (hot water supply, fixed bath/ shower, inside flush toilet)
3	% households sharing a dwelling
4	% dwellings with only 1 or 2 rooms
5	% dwellings owner-occupied
6	% dwellings privately rented
7	New dwellings completed per 1000 households
8	Infant mortality rate
9	Local health services: expenditure per 1000 residential population
10	Average list size of principal general medical practitioners
11	% students in age group 15–19
12	Ratio of pupils to teachers in primary schools
13	% professional workers
14	% unemployed
15	Female activity rate
16	% persons aged 0–14
17	% persons of pensionable age
18	% households of only 1 or 2 persons
19	% population change per annum 1961–1971 due to migration
20	% poll in local elections
21	Households without a car
22	Index of rateable property values ($\frac{\text{product of 1d. rate}}{\text{total population}}$)
23	Public libraries: expenditure per 1000 residential population
24	Cinemas per 1000 resident population
25	Population per social worker
26	Police services: expenditure per 1000 residential population
27	Divorce rate
28	Illegitimacy rate
29	Child care referrals per 1000 population age 0–17

Source: B.E. Coates, R.J. Johnston & P.L. Knox (1977) *Geography and Inequality*, London: Oxford University Press, table 3.4.

Again, as in the United States, it is the influence of the major urban areas which does so much to modify the well-being surface. The broad regional division in well-being between the affluent South and the poorer North, so often remarked upon by countless observers, is far too simple a dichotomy, even though it does contain an element of truth. For the most part, broad regional data tend to obscure pronounced intraregional differences, combining, as they do, urban with rural, inner urban with suburban, rich with poor, to produce a meaningless regional average. There may, indeed, be 'two Britains' or 'two Americas' – North and South – but in neither case are they homogeneous entities separated unambiguously by simple lines on a map. Areas of affluence exist within the generally poorer regions; areas of poverty exist within the generally richer regions. In Figure 5.2, for example, places with really low levels of social well-being show up as 'holes' within the generally affluent surface. Most of these 'holes of deprivation' coincide with the

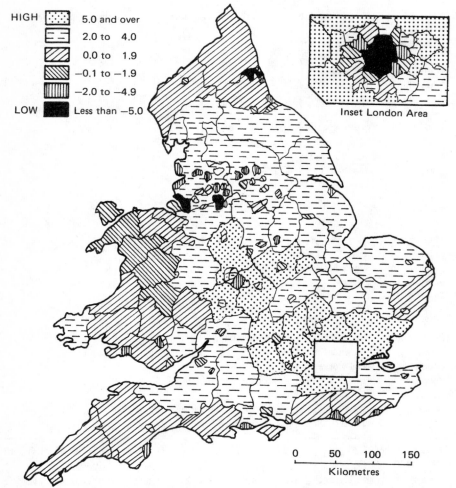

Figure 5.2   Social well-being in England and Wales, 1971: an index of level of living based on 29 variables

Source: B.E. Coates, R.J. Johnston & P.L. Knox (1977) *Geography and Inequality*, London: Oxford University Press, figure 3.7.

inner areas of the large metropolitan areas though others reflect rural poverty. In the United States, the same story can be told. Really low levels of well-being are found sitting cheek by jowl with very high levels of well-being in the major metropolitan areas, whether these are in the industrial North or the Deep South, in the Sunbelt cities or in the Midwest. Similarly, well-being is high in many prosperous rural counties but dreadfully low in others, particularly in the South and the Appalachians.

Interurban variations in well-being

Since the majority of the populations of modern Western societies live in urban areas, it is appropriate to consider a little more closely the extent to which well-being varies between one urban area and another. Again, it is Smith who has made some of the best-known attempts to measure interurban variations in general well-being using the same kind of multivariate analysis as in his state-level study. Table 5.4 lists the thirty-one variables used to identify intermetropolitan variations in well-being.

Table 5.4 *Variables used to measure social well-being in United States SMSAs with population greater than 250,000*

Criteria and Variables	Direction
Material Living Standards	
1 Annual income per capita ($) 1966	+
2 Annual incomes under $3000 (%) 1967	−
3 Annual incomes over $20,000 (%) 1967	+
4 Unemployment (% of total workforce) 1968	−
5 Average weekly earnings of production workers ($) 1968	+
6 Local property tax per capita ($) 1967	+
7 Median property value of FHA insured homes ($) 1967	+
8 Total bank deposits per capita ($) 1968	+
9 Total retail sales per capita 1963	+
10 Increase in retail sales (%) 1958–1963	+
Welfare	
11 Local welfare expenditures per capita ($) 1967	+
12 Social security recipients per 100,000 population 1968	+
13 Total social security payments per recipient ($) Dec. 1968	+
14 Average benefit for retired workers ($) Dec. 1968	+
15 Total anti-poverty funds per capita ($) 1968	+
16 Old age assistance per recipient ($) Feb. 1969	+
17 Families with dependent children assistance per family ($) Feb. 1969	+
Health	
18 Physicians per 100,000 population 1967	+
19 Hospital beds per 100,000 population 1967	+
20 Dentists per 100,000 population 1967	+
21 Local health and hospital expenditures per capita ($) 1967	+

Criteria and Variables	Direction
Education	
22 Median school years completed 1960	+
23 Pupils per teacher in public schools 1967–1968	−
24 Local education expenditures per capita ($) 1967	+
Social Order or Disorganization (Crime)	
25 Murder and manslaughter per 100,000 population 1968	−
26 Forcible rape per 100,000 population 1968	−
27 Robbery per 100,000 population 1968	−
28 Aggravated assault per 100,000 population 1968	−
29 Burglary per 100,000 population 1968	−
30 Larceny $50 and over per 100,000 population 1968	−
31 Auto theft per 100,000 population 1968	−

Source: D.M. Smith (1973) *The Geography of Social Well-Being in the United States*, New York: McGraw Hill, table 8.5. With permission of McGraw Hill Book Company.

It differs from Table 5.2 mainly in its lack of variables concerning social disorganization, alienation and participation. Figure 5.3 maps what Smith terms a general social indicator for each of 109 SMSAs of more than 250,000 population. A very clear regional picture is evident. All the SMSAs in the South recorded negative scores and there is a very marked difference between these and the positive scores of the northeastern SMSAs. With a few exceptions western SMSAs all had positive scores on the general social indicator. Further analysis of the variables into two components – one of *affluence*, the other of *crime* – revealed some interesting geographical variations between the metropolitan areas. Social well-being was especially low in the cities of the South. On the affluence component Smith attributes this to the existence of relatively large proportions of poor – mainly black – people in southern cities, together with a lower level of development of health, education and welfare services. The poor southern showing on the social pathology or crime component is suggested to be due to class and racial influences and a propensity towards violent behaviour in the South. In the northern cities, by contrast, it is suggested that, overall, the greater levels of affluence tend to offset the effects of pathological behaviour (particularly in the ghetto areas).

But it is the cities of the West which show the greatest differences between the affluence and pathology components:

> Western cities tend to show the extremes. The affluence associated with technologically-advanced industry is exemplified in the rapidly growing Californian metropolitan areas. But this strong performance on the affluence dimension appears to be achieved at the price of greater tensions than in cities in most other parts of the country and higher incidence of physical and mental stress-induced illness. Poor performance on the pathology dimension also reflects the instability of a population with many immigrants, some of whom are chicanos and blacks subject to the usual abuses and

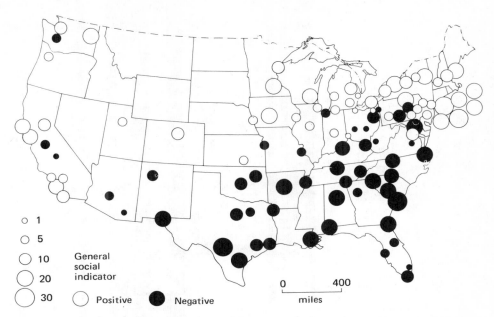

Figure 5.3   The geographical pattern of metropolitan social well-being in the United States

Source: D.M. Smith (1973) *The Geography of Social Well-Being in the United States*, New York: McGraw Hill, figure 8.2. With permission of McGraw Hill Book Company.

deprivation of racial minorities. The perpetuation of something of the hustling, anxiety and violence of the frontier days in this region of ethnic and socio-economic heterogeneity thus produces distinctive cities. With its extremes of conspicuous material affluence and untreated social degradation the urban West many still be considered 'wild'.
Smith (1973), p.119.

There is no comparable study of variations in interurban well-being in Britain, largely because comprehensive data are not published for urban areas. Such studies as have been carried out in recent years tend to emphasize the 'deprivation' end of the well-being scale, whereas the United States study discussed above covered the whole range, from affluence to poverty. The most comprehensive study of interurban variation in deprivation in Britain is that carried out by Sally Holtermann (1975). 'Deprivation' was defined by Holtermann using eighteen indicators. Eleven cover housing amenity, density and forms of tenure. Three economic variables relate to male and female unemployment levels and occupational classification (percent unskilled manual). The remainder take account of car-ownership, life-cycle needs (the elderly or families with small children) and race or immigrant status. Holtermann thus defines deprivation as a concept broader and more complex in scope than poverty, including elements not simply of money income but also of real income.

Table 5.5 shows variations in deprivation between the major British conurbations. In the case of each indicator the figure shows the conurbation's share of the worst 5 percent of Enumeration Districts. Although there is some variation in the

Table 5.5 *Geographical distribution of deprivation among British conurbations, selected indicators*

Conurbation	Percentage of worst 5% of enumeration districts													
	All EDs in Great Britain	Share or lack hot water	Lack bath	Lack inside W.C.	Households overcrowded > 1.5 ppr	Sharing dwelling	Lack exclusive use of all basic amenities	Males unemployed but seeking work or sick	Females unemployed but seeking work or sick	Households with no car	SEG 11 (unskilled manual)	Children 0–14	Pensioner households	New Commonwealth origin
London Group A*	8.6	27.7	15.3	7.0	21.8	55.7	21.7	2.9	6.3	12.9	9.9	3.5	4.3	39.9
London Group B*	10.4	3.9	1.9	2.1	5.5	17.6	1.9	1.9	1.9	0.4	3.2	3.3	3.3	16.7
Tyneside	2.0	2.7	3.7	6.0	1.3	0.3	4.2	6.7	2.9	7.2	4.4	1.9	1.4	0.1
West Yorkshire	4.3	1.7	2.4	3.6	3.0	0.9	2.6	4.2	3.5	8.6	3.9	3.3	5.3	6.7
Merseyside	2.7	5.2	5.3	6.8	1.5	1.1	5.4	9.0	6.2	5.0	6.0	3.4	0.9	0.1
S.E. Lancashire	5.8	4.8	7.4	13.6	1.9	1.5	9.6	6.1	5.4	8.9	8.1	4.3	3.8	4.7
West Midlands	4.8	7.5	4.0	6.2	5.6	2.3	4.7	2.8	3.8	2.9	4.1	5.5	1.4	15.3
Clydeside	4.3	15.5	16.9	5.9	37.3	0.4	13.5	23.1	13.7	25.7	11.7	12.8	4.3	0.8

* London A includes the inner boroughs; London B covers the remainder of the GLC area.
Source: S. Holtermann (1975) Areas of urban deprivation in Great Britain: An analysis of 1977 census data, *Social Trends*, 6, table 2. Crown Copyright.

performance of individual conurbations depending on the indicator examined, it is very clear that the Clydeside conurbation, centred on Glasgow, registers the highest deprivation percentages, together with inner London. In general, however, the conurbations as a whole contain a disproportionate share of the 'worst 5 percent EDs', primarily in their inner areas. In terms of 'multiple deprivation' the poor performance of the conurbations was found to be even more marked:

> The geographical distribution of E.D.s with more than one kind of depriva-
> tion is, if anything, even more dominated by the conurbations, especially
> Clydeside and inner London, than that of individual deprivations.
> *Holtermann (1975), p.40.*

Thus, Holtermann's study of deprivation is very much a catalogue of the older urban areas of Britain, whether in the North or the South. The other urban areas outside the conurbations, though containing 'pockets' of deprivation, are substantially better off on Holtermann's criteria.

Well-being and urban size
It is quite clear that there are substantial variations in social well-being between urban areas in both the United States and Britain. Some of this variation seems to be related to broader regional influences. In the United States, aggregate social well-being tends to be lower in southern cities than in northern cities; in Britain it is the northern cities which tend to be lower on the well-being scale than southern cities. But over and above such regional variations it is often argued that *city size* is a key influence on well-being. Increasingly, it seems, the big city is regarded as a 'bad' rather than as a 'good', as the locus of many of the serious problems facing modern society, particularly social and environmental problems. Something of this view-point is reflected in Figure 5.4 which portrays 'Urbanman' (a collective term for both male and female) equipped to deal with the many hazards which have come to be regarded as endemic to the big city. In fact, it is extremely difficult to separate out problems which occur *in* the city, and simply reflect the fact that a majority of the population live there, from problems which are intrinsically *of* the city in the sense that they are produced by urban processes. More specifically it is also very difficult to disentangle the influence of city size from other influences.*

Attitudes to living in large urban areas
A number of opinion surveys show a widespread disaffection with the large city. Table 5.6 shows that the overwhelming preference of a large sample of people in the United States was to live in a rural area or small town (53 percent) or a small urban place (33 percent). Only 13 percent of the sample would prefer to live in a large urban area. However, preference for such areas was considerably greater for respondents actually living in big cities than for those living in rural areas or small towns. Apart from existing place of residence, the biggest differences of opinion regarding large urban places were related to the colour, education and income of the respondents. Black respondents showed a much stronger preference for large urban areas than did

---

*Richardson (1973) provides a detailed analysis of the urban size issue. Hoch (1972) presents some empirical evidence relating to United States cities, some of which is summarized in Cox (1979). This section draws extensively on these sources.

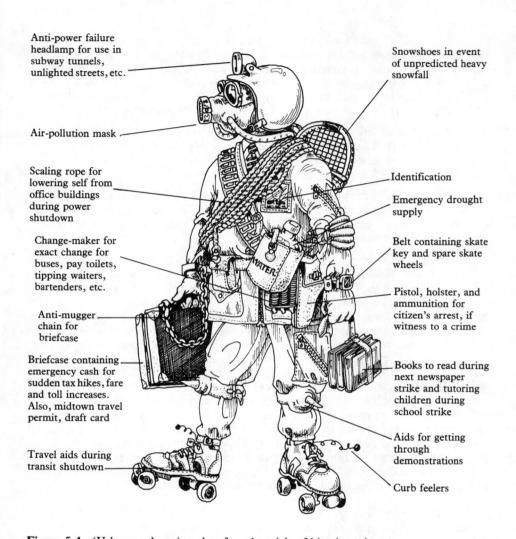

Anti-power failure headlamp for use in subway tunnels, unlighted streets, etc.

Air-pollution mask

Scaling rope for lowering self from office buildings during power shutdown

Change-maker for exact change for buses, pay toilets, tipping waiters, bartenders, etc.

Anti-mugger chain for briefcase

Briefcase containing emergency cash for sudden tax hikes, fare and toll increases. Also, midtown travel permit, draft card

Travel aids during transit shutdown

Snowshoes in event of unpredicted heavy snowfall

Identification

Emergency drought supply

Belt containing skate key and spare skate wheels

Pistol, holster, and ammunition for citizen's arrest, if witness to a crime

Books to read during next newspaper strike and tutoring children during school strike

Aids for getting through demonstrations

Curb feelers

Figure 5.4   'Urbanman' equipped to face the trials of big-city existence

Source: J. Helmer & N.A. Eddington (eds) *Urbanman: The Psychology of Urban Survival*, New York, p.ii. © by the Free Press, a division of Macmillan Publishing Co., Inc.

white (33 percent compared with 11 percent). Respondents who had completed a college education were more likely to prefer a large urban place than those with less formal education. Higher-income respondents – many of whom presumably also had a college education – showed a stronger preference for large urban areas than those in lower-income groups. A similar dislike for large cities and a preference for smaller places is evident in the preferences of a sample of university students drawn from various parts of Britain. One interesting feature of Table 5.7 is that London ranked high on both lists; that is, some people strongly preferred it, others strongly disliked it. Perhaps capital cities, being a rather special case, generate rather ambivalent attitudes towards their merits as places to live.

Table 5.6 *Residential preferences for urban and rural living in the United States*

	Rural or small town (%)	Small urban (%)	Large urban (%)	No opinion (%)	No.
United States	53	33	13	1	1708
Residence					
Rural or small town	88	10	2		473
Small urban	39	55	6		753
Large urban	34	26	39	2	478
Region					
Northeast	58	28	14		371
South	57	30	12		583
North-Central	46	37	17		480
West	50	38	12		274
Age					
Under 30 years	56	28	15		468
30 years and over	52	34	13	1	1219
Colour					
White	54	33	11		1362
Black	33	34	33		320
Education					
Less than high school	57	30	12	1	641
High school complete	54	32	13	1	542
Some college	47	38	14	1	300
College complete	40	38	22		206
Income					
Under $5000	57	32	10	1	402
$5000–9999	53	34	12		487
$10,000–14,999	45	29	11		344
$15,000 or more	45	34	21		255

Note: *Rural* or *small town* includes the farm, open country, or small town responses. *Small urban* represents small city or medium-size city and suburb. *Large urban* includes the large city and its suburbs.

Source: S.M. Maizie & S. Rawlings (1973) Public attitudes towards population issues, in S.M. Maizie (ed), *Population Distribution and Policy*, Washington DC: USGPO, p.605

Of course, such generally negative attitudes towards large cities are not necessarily reflected in actual decisions of where to live. As we saw in Chapter Two, there is some evidence of a relative shift of population away from large metropolitan areas and towards smaller urban places. In general, however, large cities still retain large populations. One reason, of course, is that, whilst employment opportunities remain in big cities, many people have little real choice other than to live where the jobs are. Changing job and changing home are, as we have emphasized, difficult and costly

Table 5.7   *Most-preferred and least-preferred urban areas in Britain*

	Most preferred			Least preferred	
Rank	Area	Weighted score*	Rank	Area	Weighted score*
1	Keswick	158	1	Birmingham	449
2	Ambleside	106	2	London	388
3	London	97	3	Liverpool	222
4	York	83	4	Manchester	220
5	Oxford	77	5	Wolverhampton	214
6	Chester	73	6	Newcastle	210
7	Penzance	66	7	Middlesbrough	98
8	Bath	58	8	Leeds	88
9	Bristol	56	9	Bradford	78
10	Plymouth	55	10	Wigan	75
10	Exeter	55	11	Cardiff	74
12	Tunbridge Wells	52	12	Hull	69
13	Stratford-upon-Avon	46	13	Warrington	68
13	Aberystwyth	46	14	Sheffield	65
15	Cambridge	40	15	Barrow	63
16	Windsor	39	15	Swansea	63
16	Norwich	39	17	Tynemouth	60
16	Hereford	39	18	Dartford	56
19	Torquay	38	19	Rochdale	51
20	Gloucester	36	20	Coventry	41
21	Cheltenham	35	20	Merthyr Tydfil	41
			22	Whitehaven	36
			23	Stoke-on-Trent	35
			23	Sunderland	35

* Respondents were asked to rank up to six areas in which they would most like to live and six in which they would least like to live. An inverse scoring system was used so that the first-ranked place on both scales scored 6 (most-liked and most-disliked) and the last-ranked place scored 1.

Source: P. Dicken & M.E. Robinson (1976) Place preferences and information, *University of Manchester School of Geography Research Paper*, 1, tables I and II

steps to take. More generally, Hoch sees the apparent paradox of people preferring to live in small towns with their actually living in large cities as a 'trade-off'. As he points out, 'other things being equal' people tend to prefer smaller places, but 'other things are not equal' and the income benefits of large cities keep people living there.

Costs and benefits of living in big cities

What, then, are the elements in this trade-off, what are the relative benefits and costs of big city living for the private individual?* The most often-quoted benefits and costs of living in large cities are:

Alleged benefits

Higher monetary incomes

More varied employment opportunities

More varied provision of private
and public goods and services

Alleged costs

Higher costs of living

Environmental pollution,
including congestion

Greater exposure to crime

Psycho-social stress

The problem, of course, lies in evaluating the benefits and costs of things which are not always directly comparable, of establishing a *net* well-being value. Many of the elements in the equation are either measured in non-comparable units or are difficult to measure at all. There is the additional complication that benefits and costs may affect different elements in the population in different ways. Big cities may be better for some groups and worse for others. The question of 'who benefits and who pays?' has to be asked. Unfortunately, our present state of knowledge is such that a clear, unequivocal answer cannot be given. What we can do, however, is look at the rather fragmentary evidence relating aspects of well-being to city size.

1 **Earnings and living costs** In the United States, at least, there is clear evidence that average earnings increase systematically with city size. Table 5.8 shows that in each major region of the United States the larger the SMSA the higher the level of earnings. For example, average hourly earnings in SMSAs with more than 1 million inhabitants were 34 percent higher than those in urban places smaller than 10,000

---

*Much of the literature on the benefits and costs of city size is concerned with their impact on business firms. In this chapter, we are concerned with their impact on individuals and social groups.

population and 42 percent higher than in rural areas. Although the absolute levels differed between regions, and between white and non-white male workers, the positive relationship between earnings and city size was extremely consistent. The figures in Table 5.8 are rather dated but a more recent estimate by Hoch (1972) for 1969 showed that the relationship between earnings and city size still held.

Table 5.8 *The relationship between city size and average earnings, United States, 1959 (dollars per hour)*

| | | Urban places | | Standard metropolitan statistical areas | | |
	Rural	Under 10,000	10,000– 99,999	Under 250,000	250,000– 499,999	500,000– 999,999	Over 1,000,000
Total	2.00	2.12	2.23	2.39	2.43	2.56	2.84
South	1.71	1.82	1.94	2.15	2.31	2.34	2.62
Non-South	2.22	2.30	2.39	2.54	2.50	2.67	2.87
Northeast	2.33	2.37	2.41	2.41	2.36	2.51	2.79
North-Central	2.11	2.22	2.33	2.61	2.61	2.79	2.90
West	2.36	2.43	2.50	2.65	2.62	2.71	2.98
White males	2.24	2.43	2.61	2.78	2.77	2.96	3.29
Non-white males	1.28	1.26	1.33	1.53	1.89	2.00	2.08

Source: V.R. Fuchs (1967) *Differentials in Hourly Earnings by Region and City Size, 1959*, New York: Columbia University Press, table 3

Average figures, of course, mask a great deal of variation. For example, it is often supposed that although incomes in general may be higher in large cities such places also house the majority of the poor population. Certainly very large numbers of poor people do live in large cities, often concentrated in the older inner areas, but it is not the case that most of the poor live in large urban areas. As Richardson points out,

The incidence of poverty is inversely associated with city scale. . . . The incidence of poverty (i.e. the proportion of population with incomes below the poverty line) is two-and-a-half times greater in non-metropolitan than in metropolitan areas. Two-thirds of the population live in metropolitan areas, but little more than half of the poor; for blacks the differential is even better. Of course, poverty is more prevalent among blacks (37 percent of the black population as opposed to 11 percent of the white), but this is heavily influenced by black rural poverty in the South. Urbanization has been a more powerful force in improving incomes and employment opportunities for blacks than for whites.
Richardson (1973), p.52.

Poverty in modern Western societies is much more widely spread geographically than is often supposed, even though specific, highly visible, concentrations do exist in the inner areas of large cities.

The importance of monetary income lies not in itself but in what a given amount can purchase. It may well be that monetary incomes in general are higher in larger cities than in small but that the cost of living is such as to negate the difference. Such data as are available at the urban scale suggest that the cost of living does increase with city size. Table 5.9 presents a cost of living index for urban centres of varying population sizes and by broad regional divisions. In each region the progression is clear: as city size increases so does the cost of living index. Living in big cities, on average, is more expensive than living in smaller cities. But, as Table 5.9 shows, there are even greater differences between regions, living costs in the South being substantially lower than elsewhere. It is extremely difficult to make comparisons between the kinds of monetary income figures shown in Table 5.8 and the cost of living index of Table 5.9 to calculate the net difference. Apart from the fact that the standard cost of living figures do not include the costs of such items as pollution, journey to work costs, congestion, crime and so on, there are obviously substantial differences in the pattern of consumer spending between different social groups. In addition, living costs vary substantially at different places *within* cities, particularly the very large ones. Allowing for such reservations, however, Richardson concludes that

> after deflation of . . . money incomes households remain much better off in
> real income terms in large metropolitan areas.
> *Richardson (1973), p.60.*

Table 5.9 *Relationship between cost of living and city size, by major region of the United States, 1966*

Size of urban place (000)	Cost of living index			
	Northeast	**North-Central**	**South**	**West**
5	0.935	0.923	0.875	0.930
50	0.970	0.954	0.894	0.960
125	0.987	0.968	0.903	0.978
250	0.999	0.979	0.910	0.990
375	1.007	0.986	0.914	0.997
750	1.021	0.999	0.921	1.011
1000	1.027	1.004	0.925	1.016
2000	1.042	1.018	0.933	1.031
5000	1.064	1.037	0.945	1.052

Source: I. Hoch (1972) Urban scale and environmental quality, in R.G. Ridker (ed), *Population, Resources, and the Environment*, US Commission on Population Growth and the American Future, Research Report III, Washington DC: USGPO, table 2

2   Variety of jobs, goods and services   One very clear and undisputed benefit of large cities is that they contain a significantly greater variety of employment opportunities, of consumer goods outlets and of services provided by private and public organizations. Diversity of employment opportunity is characteristic of the large urban area. No really large city is likely to be dominated by one single employer but a good many small towns are virtually one-company towns. Not only are there more employers in big cities but also the variety of occupations is greater. As we saw in Chapter Three, it is in the very large metropolitan areas that the higher-order occupations tend to be concentrated.

The relationship between city size and variety of goods and services outlets is one of the best-established regularities of the urban system. A great deal of the research activity of human geographers in the 1960s especially was devoted to verifying this relationship which was derived from the central-place theory of Walter Christaller and the more general location theory of August Lösch.* The underlying logic of the relationship is that places with large populations will be able to support the existence of more functions, and of more outlets providing these functions, than places with small populations. Every supplier of a good or service needs to be assured of a sufficient *threshold* of demand. Some goods and services, particularly those which are purchased relatively infrequently by individual consumers, have very high thresholds and, therefore, can be provided only in large population centres. A hierarchy of urban centres thus exists in which the variety of offerings increases systematically as city size increases. Figure 5.5 shows the kind of association between city size and number of consumer outlets which has been identified in so many circumstances that its general form can be regarded as typical. The same basic principle of varying theshold demand applies to non-material goods and services whether they are provided by private or public organizations. The number of doctors, dentists, hospitals, lawyers per head of population, the availability of libraries, theatres, museums, sports centres, all tend to vary closely with city size.

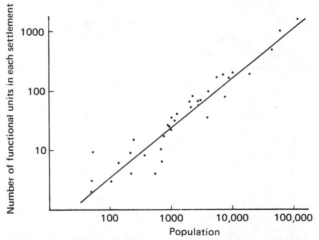

Figure 5.5   The relationship between the number of goods and services and settlement size

*For a detailed explanation of these theories and for empirical material relating to them, see Lloyd and Dicken (1977, chapters 2 and 3).

'How ya gonna keep 'em down on the farm after they've seen Paree' is a fair summary of the attractiveness of big cities compared with small towns and villages.

3   Social costs: pollution, crime On the other hand, big city living has a number of less tangible costs which may well contribute towards reductions in social well-being. In particular, big cities are regarded as generating major costs – social, physiological and even perhaps psychological – through environmental pollution, exposure to crime and a generally stressful psycho-social environment. Pollution is one of the most widely observed problems of urban as opposed to rural areas and of

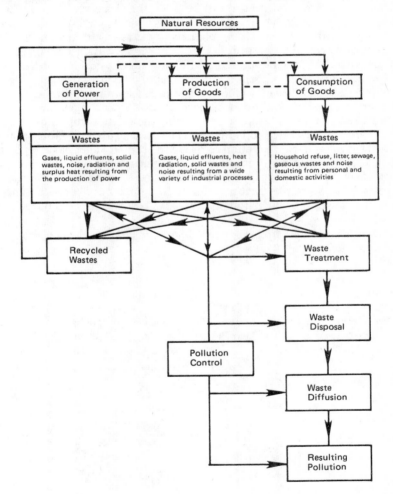

Figure 5.6   The pollution process

Source: C.M. Wood, N. Lee, J.A. Luker & P.J.W. Saunders (1974) *The Geography of Pollution: A Study of Greater Manchester,* Manchester: Manchester University Press, figure 1.

big cities as opposed to small towns. The pollution process, as Figure 5.6 shows, is a by-product of society's production and consumption processes, including the generation of power and energy. Where such processes are heavily concentrated in geographical space, as in large urban areas, we would expect to find major problems of pollution. Pollution of the atmosphere, of the human physical environment, together with noise, are the major problems in large urban centres. Here we focus particularly on atmospheric pollution.

Many of the worst excesses of atmospheric pollution by industry have been eradicated in recent decades through pollution control and through changed production technologies. Even so, the contrast between the clean, clear air of the countryside and the eye-smarting atmosphere of big cities is clear for all to see (and breathe). Again, although the precise relationship between city size and the various forms of atmospheric pollution is difficult to test (other variables involved include the specific industrial activities present, differences in physical layout and topography, differences in climate), there is a good deal of evidence to suggest that some relationship does exist. Table 5.10 shows how the concentration of three measures of pollution – total suspended particles, sulphur dioxide and nitrogen dioxide – varied with city size in the United States. In general, the relationship is quite regular, although there are certainly individual exceptions. As Cox (1979) has noted, the town which has the worst air pollution record in the United States has a population of only 11,000. A considerable proportion of the atmospheric pollution in big cities emanates, of course, from high levels of automobile use, as the notorious example of Los Angeles demonstrates. A further result of the dominance of private transport in cities is traffic congestion which both increases the cost and stress of intracity travel

Table 5.10 *The relationship between pollution concentration and city size in the United States, 1969–1970*

Size of urban area (population)	Concentration of			
	Total suspended particles	Sulphur dioxide	Nitrogen dioxide	Number of sites
Non-urban	25	10	33	5
Urban, less than 10,000	57	35	116	2
10,000	81	18	64	2
25,000	87	14	63	2
50,000	118	29	127	9
100,000	95	26	114	37
400,000	100	28	127	17
700,000	101	29	146	9
1,000,000	134	69	163	2
3,000,000	120	85	153	2

Source: I. Hoch (1972) Urban scale and environmental quality, in R.G. Ridker (ed) *Population, Resources, and the Environment*, US Commission on Population Growth and the American Future, Research Report III, Washington DC: USGPO, table 12

and further contributes to atmospheric pollution.

Quite apart from the unpleasantness created by atmospheric pollution, there is a clear link between its incidence and some types of physical illness. Standardized mortality rates for certain types of illness – particularly respiratory diseases and certain cancers – tend to be significantly higher in urban rather than in rural areas, as Figure 5.7 reveals. Of course, attributing particular illnesses and types of death to specific environmental influences is fraught with difficulty since so many intervening variables may be involved. Nevertheless, there can be little doubt that the concentrated atmospheric pollution of urban areas, and especially of big cities, is injurious to health and is, therefore, a major social cost. In fact, Hoch quotes evidence which suggests that major benefits – in both health and cost terms – would result from a 50 percent reduction in air pollution in major urban areas (Table 5.11). For example, more than $1 billion might be saved every year in the costs associated with all respiratory diseases. (Such costs include the direct costs of hospital and nursing home care and the services of medical staff, together with the indirect costs of foregone earnings.)

Just as there is evidence of a relationship between atmospheric pollution and city size, there is also a well-established association between the incidence of crime and city size. This does not necessarily mean that city size is the cause. Statistics of crime are generally poor and need to be treated with some caution. However, such data as do exist show a positive association between crime and city size. The larger the city, in general, the higher the crime rate (expressed as number of crimes per 100,000 population). This is especially true of major crimes as Table 5.12 and Figure 5.8 show for England and Wales and the United States respectively. In the case of England and Wales, for example, overall crime rates were 90.4 percent higher in cities over 400,000 population than in rural areas (in London they were 93.4 percent higher). For major crimes, however, the rate per 100,000 population was 168 percent higher in large cities than in rural areas and 207 percent higher in London than in rural areas.

Table 5.11 *Estimated effects of reducing air pollution in major urban areas by 50 percent*

Disease	Decline in incidence (percent)	Cost saving per year ($ millions)
Bronchitis	25–50	250–500
Lung cancer	25	33
All respiratory diseases	25	1222
Cardiovascular disease	10–20	468
All cancer	15	390

Source: I. Hoch (1972) Urban scale and environmental quality, in R.G. Ridker (ed) *Population, Resources, and the Environment*, US Commission on Population Growth and the American Future, Research Report III, Washington D.C., USGPO. p.256.

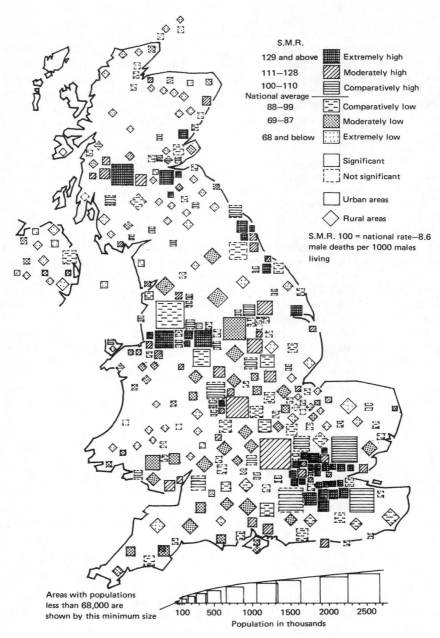

Figure 5.7   The pattern of standardized mortality rates for deaths from cancer of the trachea, lung and bronchus among males in the United Kingdom, 1959–1963

Source: G.M. Howe (1970), *National Atlas of Disease Mortality in the United Kingdom,* London: Nelson, on behalf of the Royal Geographical Society, p.110.

Table 5.12 *The relationship between crime rates and population size,
England and Wales, 1965*

Size class	Crimes per 100,000 population 1965	Major crimes per 100,000 population* 1965
London	3378	1565
Large cities (>400,000)	3327	1365
Large towns (200,000–400,000)	3333	867
Medium-sized towns (100,000–200,000)	2795	741
Small towns (<100,000)	2544	584
Rural areas	1747	510
England and Wales	2374	788

* Includes offences against the person, breaking offences and robbery, larceny.

Source: F.H. McLintock & N.H. Avison (1968) *Crime in England and Wales*, London: Heinemann

The implication of Figure 5.8 is that it is population density rather than
population alone that is the important variable. The rates of six major crimes in 86
United States cities ranging in size from 26,000 to more than 7 million population
show a clear increase as the 'total number of interaction opportunities per area'
increases. Such aggregate patterns obscure some significant intermetropolitan differences within the same size band:

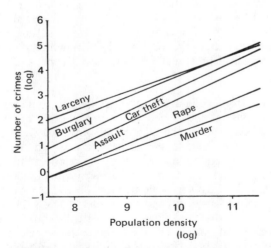

Figure 5.8   The relationship between population size and density and crime rates in United
States cities

Source: R.M. Haynes (1973) Crime rates and city size in America, *Area*, 5, figure 3.

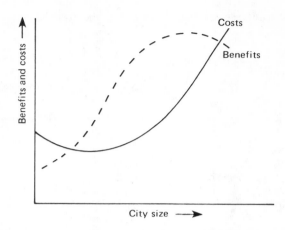

Figure 5.9   Hypothetical cost and benefit curves related to city size

> In the top tier, for instance, crime rates in Chicago are only about 55 percent
> of those prevailing in New York and Los Angeles; in the second size class
> the crime rate in Philadelphia is less than 40 percent of that in San Francisco
> and Detroit. Also, there are sizeable regional differences. Crime rates in
> Pennsylvania and New York state (apart from New York City) are very low,
> while crime rates in the Far West and Florida are consistently high . . . as
> far as serious crime is concerned, the rural crime rate is only a third of the
> national average.
> *Richardson (1973), p.100.*

Richardson goes on to observe that the social costs of higher crime rates in large cities
tend to vary between different groups within the population. He suggests that blacks
bear heavier costs than whites, that central-city residents suffer disproportionately
more than suburban residents. Indeed, middle-class white residents of big city
suburbs apparently face little greater risk of being a victim of crime than if they lived
in a smaller city.

4   Net well-being in large urban areas Quite evidently, some aspects of living in
big cities enhance individual and social well-being whereas other aspects detract
from such well-being. Ultimately, the issue is one of the *net* well-being accruing to
the individual, though, as we have suggested, it is very difficult to compare many of
the items in the well-being equation. In theory, the relationship between benefits
and costs on the one hand and city size on the other probably looks rather like the
pattern shown in Figure 5.9. As city size increases, benefits increase more rapidly
than costs initially but then flatten out and may even fall below the cost curve. But at
precisely what size of city costs exceed benefits is virtually impossible to determine.
The search for an optimal city size has proved to be extremely elusive. One reason is
that the relationship between benefits/costs and city size probably varies considerably between different groups within the population. Figure 5.10 illustrates this
possibility in very simple terms. Two *net well-being* curves are shown, one for
low-income groups and one for high-income groups. The optimal city size for the

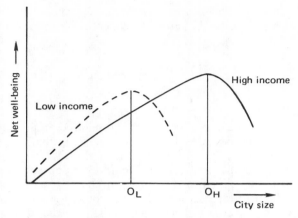

Figure 5.10 Hypothetical relationship between net well-being and city size for low-income and high-income groups

Source: K.R. Cox (1979) *Location and Public Problems*, Oxford: Basil Blackwell, figure 8.9.

low-income groups (O_L) is lower than that for high-income groups (O_H). Cox suggests several reasons for this:

> Lower income families in particular benefit from more competitive retailing and increasing competition among employers for labour. As cities grow in size, however, they are also the ones suffering most from growing crime levels, congestion, air pollution, and noise. The middle class, on the other hand is able to escape the problems – largely of the central city – by relocating to the suburbs. At the same time, residential segregation and jurisdictional fragmentation work to the benefit of the wealthier and to the disadvantage of the poorer. Those of higher income also benefit from the cultural amenities characteristic of large cities. The inflection . . . [of the net well-being curve] . . . , therefore, typically lies further to the right for the middle class than for the lower class. Cities optimally sized for the middle class are consequently too big for those of lower income.
> *Cox (1979), p.163.*

There is no doubt that very substantial *geographical* variations in well-being exist in modern Western societies. Both individual and composite indices point clearly to this, though the pattern we actually see is very much determined by the geographical scale or filter being used. The use of finer spatial filters makes us aware of variations in well-being which are not evident at coarser spatial scales. This begs the question as to what is the most appropriate scale to use in trying to examine geographical variations in well-being. The answer obviously depends upon the purposes involved. States, counties, cities are all appropriate for particular purposes, for indicating broad geographical variations. They show that where a person lives in a *general* sense is important. Which part of the country, whether in big city, small town or rural area are all significant influences. But from the viewpoint of the individual living out a daily life and attempting to satisfy needs, wants and aspirations, the most appropriate scale is a *local* one. How does the geographical distribution of 'goods' and 'bads' relate to the individual's *specific* location in geographical space: the home base? In other words, to what extent does a person's residential location provide access to 'goods' and proximity to 'bads'?*

ACCESS TO 'GOODS' AND PROXIMITY TO 'BADS': A CLOSER VIEW

A general framework

Our discussion of well-being at the local level is organized around the framework shown in Figure 5.11. This identifies the major components involved, together with the main links between them. Our basic assumption is that, at least in the short term, the individual's residential location is fixed. We have seen already how individuals come to occupy particular kinds of residential location. Thus the upper part of Figure 5.11 serves both to remind us of the main processes involved and also to emphasize the fundamental connections between the processes discussed in Chapters Three and Four and those which form the focus of this chapter. In particular, the specific geographical location which most people come to occupy is primarily the combined outcome of their position in both the labour market and, through the income which this generates, the housing market. There are, as we have seen, considerable variations between individuals in their degrees of freedom to choose a particular residential location. Changing where one lives is a costly, and for some a virtually impossible, operation. It is reasonable, therefore, to regard the home base as fixed, at least in the short term. The particular qualities of the dwelling itself obviously contribute towards its inhabitants' well-being. Housing quality, in particular its age, condition and level of basic amenities, has been seen to vary considerably from place to place. But it is the geographical *location* of the home base, and its influence on individual well-being, which is our major interest in this section.

The home base is the point from which people relate to the environment from which they must derive many of their basic needs and wants, both material and non-material. Thus, the quality of the environment in which the home base is located is a fundamental influence on well-being. Particularly important is the fact that sources of well-being (and of ill-being) are very unevenly distributed geographically. Hence, as Figure 5.11 suggests, an individual's well-being at a particular point in time and space is largely determined by his or her accessibility to 'goods' and proximity to 'bads'. Access to 'goods' – positive externalities – is closely related to the set of time-space constraints introduced in Chapter One. Such 'goods' are made up of salutary facilities,† both privately and publicly provided, and of other people through social relationships at the individual and community level. Proximity to 'bads' – negative externalities – results from the adjacent location both of noxious

---

*The distinction between accessibility and proximity in the context of well-being in an urban system was made by Harvey (1973, pp.56–57). On the one hand, accessibility to 'goods' has a price, on the other, proximity to 'bads' imposes a cost.

---

†*Salutary* facilities are those which make a positive contribution to well-being, *noxious* facilities are those which detract from well-being. See Reynolds and Honey (1978). Harvey (1972) defines noxious facilities as 'those things which nobody wants to be close to' (p.27). Thus, positive externalities are unpriced benefits while negative externalities are unpriced costs.

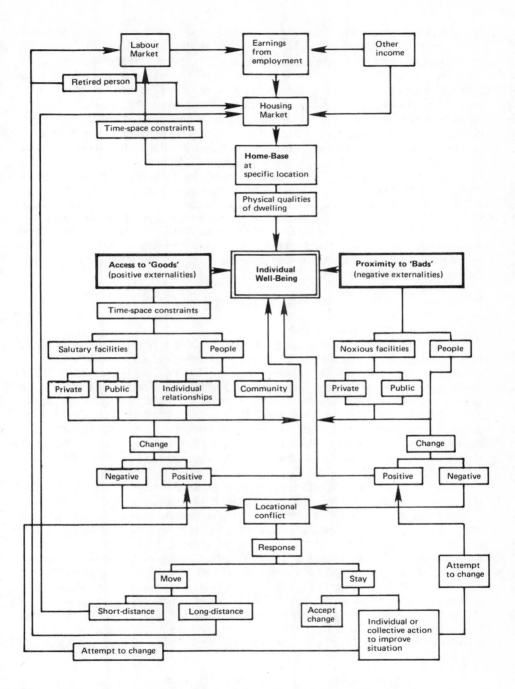

Figure 5.11   Access to 'goods' and proximity to 'bads': a general framework

facilities, again generated privately and publicly, and of people or groups regarded by the individual in question as being undesirable in some way.

Over time, of course, circumstances change. Individual needs and aspirations alter, for example, in association with progression through the life-cycle or with changes in social status. The quality of the local environment may also change as a result of decisions made by other people and, especially, by the private and public organizations which play such a dominant role in modern society. It may seem obvious that an improvement in some aspect of the local environment will increase individual well-being whilst a deterioration will decrease individual well-being. But as we shall see, things are not quite as simple at this. A change which increases the well-being of some people in a particular locality may decrease the well-being of others, and vice versa. Events which have a deleterious impact upon a locality in effect generate locational conflict. From an individual's point of view, such conflict may be resolved in two main ways. One is to move away, though, as we have seen, this may be difficult to achieve depending upon conditions in the relevant segment of the housing market. The other response is to stay and either accept the change fatalistically or to become involved in individual or collective attempts to alleviate the impact of the change.

Private and public provision of 'goods' and 'bads'

The increasing importance of public provision

In the kind of mixed economy characteristic of modern Western societies, both private and public organizations are involved in the provision of 'goods' and in the creation of 'bads'. Increasingly, as we saw in Chapter Two, governments have become more involved in providing goods and services on a collective basis. Public goods have increased in scope and variety. Much of the greatly increased size of the government sector (at all levels) results, in fact, from the increasing demand for public provision of goods and services. Some 50 percent of total central government expenditure in most Western societies is typically devoted to providing social and welfare 'goods', particularly income support programmes, health and education services and housing.

Much of this increased public expenditure takes the form of *transfer payments* to businesses and private individuals, often through the intermediary of lower levels of government. According to Thurow (1980), more than 10 percent of total United States GNP in 1978 'was devoted to taking income from one private individual and giving it to another private individual' (p.155). For some groups in the population – particularly the elderly, the sick and disabled, the unemployed – transfer payments raised out of taxation and paid as social security and related benefits may be the sole source of income. In the present context, however, we are concerned with public provision of goods and services rather than with direct income payments.

Decisions made by governments on the allocation of expenditure for the provision of goods and services are a major source of well-being for all members of the population and not only for the impoverished. As Teitz's well-known description states:

Modern urban man is born in a publicly financed hospital, receives his

education in a publicly supported school and university, spends a good part of his life traveling on publicly built transportation facilities, communicates through the post office or the quasi-public telephone system, drinks his public water, disposes of his garbage through the public removal system, reads his public library books, picnics in his public parks, is protected by his public police, fire, and health systems; eventually he dies, again in a hospital, and may even be buried in a public cemetery. Ideological conservatives notwithstanding, his everyday life is inextricably bound up with governmental decisions on these and numerous other local public services.
Teitz (1968), p.36.

A basic characteristic of modern societies is that the provision of such public goods (and also of private goods) is *geographically uneven*. In Chapter One we made an important distinction between two types of public good: pure and impure. A pure public good is one from which no individual within the area in question can be excluded. It is, therefore, equally available to all. But few, if any public goods are in fact pure. Even if the intention of the producer of the good or service is to provide it equally to all, the basic imperatives of geography make this difficult, if not impossible, to achieve in most cases. To understand why this is so we need to consider how geographical space modifies the availability, and thus the benefits and the costs, of public (and private) goods and services.

Externality gradients and externality fields

All localized public goods are 'impure' and the externality exists as a 'spatial field' of effects.
Harvey (1973), p.60.

Much of our present understanding of the relationship between the impurity of public goods and the influence of geographical space is derived from the work of Harvey (1973), together with that of Cox (1973) and, more recently, Smith (1977). The basic notion is very simple. Facilities, both public and private, have a specific geographical location. For the users of a particular facility, its benefits decline with increasing distance from the supply point. In other words the *price of accessibility* to the facility is determined by the distance separating the individual user's place of residence and the facility itself. Thus, users living close to a facility gain greater benefit from it than those living further away. At some distance away, the benefits disappear entirely because the price of accessibility is too high. To this extent, therefore, the good being supplied is *impure*; it is not equally available to all on the same terms. At the other extreme, noxious facilities impose *costs of proximity*, the costs being greatest for those people living closest to the facility. Again, distance alters these costs. The impact of noxious facilities lessens as distance from the source increases.

Figure 5.12 shows what such externality gradients and externality fields would look like in very simple circumstances. At any point away from the source of either the salutary or the noxious facility, its utility or disutility (U) is proportional to distance. In the terminology of Smith's diagram:

$$U_j = f(d_{ij})$$

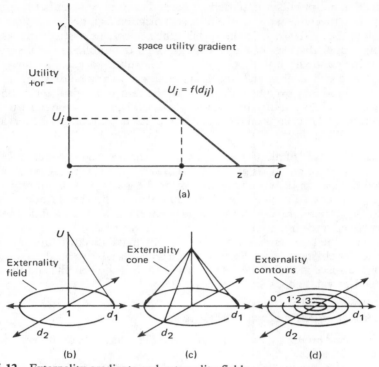

Figure 5.12   Externality gradients and externality fields

Source: D.M. Smith (1977) *Human Geography: A Welfare Approach*, London: Edward Arnold, figure 4.7.

where j is a point at some distance (d) from the source (i). Utility, or disutility, is greatest at i while the effects disappear at Z. Thus Figure 5.12a depicts the *externality gradient* emanating from the source of a salutary or a noxious facility. Both the intensity of the externality effect (the value of Y in Figure 5.12a) and the slope of the gradient will obviously vary considerably. Some facilities may have a very intensive but short-distance impact; others may exert their influence over very extensive geographical areas.

The other parts of Figure 5.12 demonstrate, again in very simplified terms, such spatial effects. If we assume that the effect spreads evenly outwards in all directions from the source (i), then an *externality field* can be envisaged (Figure 5.12b). With an even population distribution surrounding the source, it is possible to regard the externality effect as taking the form of a cone (Figure 5.12c), the total impact being proportional to the volume of the cone. In fact, of course, such even population density is unlikely. Finally, Figure 5.12d expresses the utility or disutility effect as a set of contours.

It is not difficult to think of examples to illustrate the general idea of externality gradients and fields. Nearness to good schools for parents with children, to hospitals, general medical services, to entertainment, recreational and cultural facilities, to friends and relatives (the nice ones) lowers the price of accessibility and, thus, increases the well-being of the users, while distance reduces well-being by raising the price of accessibility. It is even easier to think of examples of the spatial effects of noxious facilities and of people regarded as being undesirable. Air pollution, for instance, shows clear distance-decay patterns, although the spatial form may be somewhat irregular depending upon such factors as wind direction. Figure 5.13 shows contours of sulphur dioxide concentration in Greater Manchester. Intensity was greatest near the centre and generally declined with increasing distance outwards.

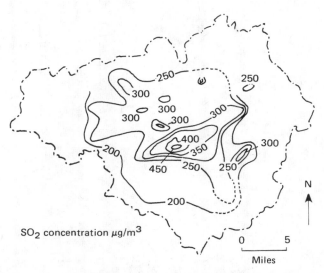

Figure 5.13   Contours of concentration of sulphur dioxide in Greater Manchester, winter 1963–1964

Source: C.M. Wood, N. Lee, J.A. Luker & P.J.W. Saunders (1974) *The Geography of Pollution: A Study of Greater Manchester,* Manchester: Manchester University Press, figure 15.

The noxious effects of large airports have generated a great deal of controversy in recent years as the volume of air traffic has increased. The construction of massive new airports, for example, at Tokyo, Montreal, Atlanta, Paris, the planned building of a third London airport and the major expansion of existing airports have all drawn attention to the problem of aircraft noise. The spatial pattern of this noxiant exhibits all the basic features of the externality field, as Figure 5.14 shows for the cases of Manchester and Boston airports. The 'footprint' imposed by aircraft noise varies in shape according to the alignment of runways and the take-off and landing patterns. But it shows a marked intensity gradient, as the noise contours of Figure 5.14 indicate. Noise is very severe in residential areas under the flight path, an external cost which is only partially compensated by sound-proofing and noise-abatement schemes. The area affected by the noise footprint has generally increased, as the Boston map shows, so that more and more people are affected by the negative externality effects of airports.

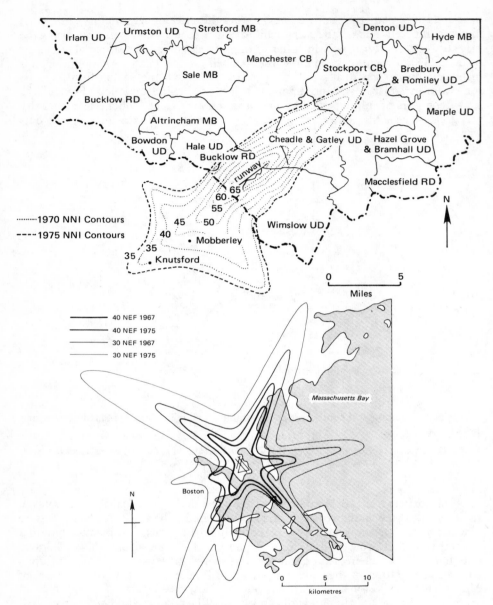

Figure 5.14 Negative externalities imposed by large airports:
Top: Manchester   Bottom: Boston (Logan)

Source: (a) C.M. Wood, N. Lee, J.A. Luker & P.J.W. Saunders (1974) *The Geography of Pollution: A Study of Greater Manchester*, Manchester: Manchester University Press, figure 29;
(b) G.M. Stevenson (1972) Noise and the urban environment, in T.R. Detwyler & M.G. Marcus (eds) *Urbanization and Environment: The Physical Geography of the City*, Belmont: Wadsworth, figures 8.11 and 8.12. By permission of Wadsworth Publishing Co.

So far we have discussed salutary and noxious facilities as though they were clearly separable. But relatively few facilities are either unequivocally good or unequivocally bad. The essence of the concept of externality effects is that a facility may generate *direct benefits* to its users but also *indirect costs* to others. The essence of the concept of externality fields is that such direct and indirect effects are inherently geographical. For example, air pollution is a 'bad' for those exposed to it, but the source of the pollution – say, an industrial plant – is a 'good' for its employees and for the purchasers of its products. A major airport is a 'bad' for those living very close to it and suffering its noise, but it is a 'good' for those who work there and for those who travel extensively, whether for business or pleasure. Thus, an airport is a 'bad' up to a certain distance and a 'good' beyond that distance. As Harvey points out, an airport is characteristic of many facilities which

> have a curious distribution of noxious effects . . . many facilities become noxious when they come too close – schools, bars, shops and the like. As a result there is often some ambiguity involved in the definition of noxious-ness. The degree of noxiousness changes with distance and it will also vary according to individual variations in the definition of noxiousness (proximity to a school may be annoying to some and not to others).
> *Harvey (1972), pp.27–28.*

Figure 5.15 shows a modification of Smith's externality gradient which Bale (1978) suggests reflects this 'dual' characteristic of most facilities. Instead of the single gradient of Figure 5.12, Figure 5.15 shows two gradients, one for the positive externality effect of a facility, the other for the negative externality effect of the *same* facility. Figure 5.15a depicts the kind of situation discussed above. Between *a*, the source of the facility, and *x* negative externalities exceed positive externalities. Beyond *x*, positive externalities are dominant, although negative effects are still experienced as far as *n*. Facilities such as airports, heavy industrial plants and football stadiums generate two externality fields, a negative field close to them and a positive field further away. But other possible relationships between positive and negative externality gradients can be envisaged. Figure 5.15b illustrates the situation in which, overall, positive benefits outweigh negative costs. A factory employing large numbers of people may be tolerated because of this. Conversely, Figure 5.15c shows negative costs completely outweighing positive benefits: noxious effects exceed salutary benefits. A nuclear power plant could be one example of this situation. Such a dual characteristic of facilities creates considerable complications:

> the direct impact field of a facility may be worth buying access to, but the indirect field (externality) may be worth paying to avoid. . . . Here the field effects counteract one another.
> *Dear (1974), p.50.*

Whatever the precise spatial form of externality gradients and externality fields, the fact remains that the *location* of both public and private facilities has important consequences for individual and social well-being. A major purpose of public facility provision is to redistribute resources, to provide 'goods' for people at large. Since both the direct and indirect effects of facilities vary geographically, it is obvious that the decisions made by public bodies to locate facilities in particular places have profound implications for the geography of well-being.

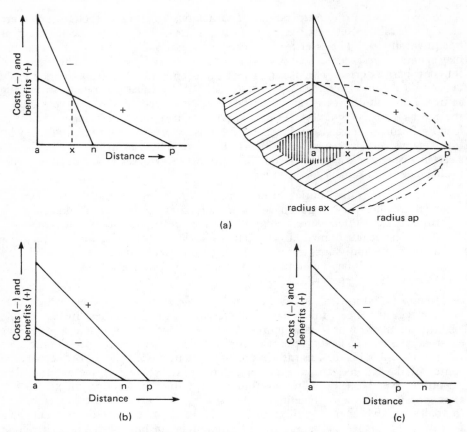

(a)

(b)

(c)

Figure 5.15 Positive and negative externality gradients for the same facility

Source: based on J. Bale (1978) Externality gradients, *Area*, 10, figure 1.

Changing geographical distribution of the supply points of goods and services

Over time, decisions are made both by public and private organizations to modify the geographical structure of their operations. Decisions are made to open new facilities, to modify the scale and functions of existing facilities and to close down others. We have already looked at this general process of re-organization in the context of changing employment opportunities in Chapter Three. Decisions to locate, relocate or close down facilities which provide goods and services obviously have important implications for individual and social well-being because they alter the spatial opportunity surface from which people have to satisfy their needs and wants. It is beyond our present scope to examine changes in detail for every type of facility which contributes towards well-being. We can merely indicate the major trends and provide some illustrations of their geographical outcomes. Two major trends in the provision of both public and private goods are clearly evident in modern Western societies. Both reflect the broad-scale changes discussed in Chapter Two.

First, there has been a pronounced tendency for the *scale* of individual facilities to become larger. Functions are being performed in larger and larger units. The usual justification for such increased *concentration* of activities into fewer and larger units is that they are more efficient. Economies of scale, it is argued, reduce the cost of providing goods and services; bigger is supposed to lead to better. This may well be the case, though it is by no means universally so. But bigger invariably does mean *fewer* and this, in turn, implies that individual supply points have to serve larger geographical areas, particularly where population densities are relatively low. This is the case, for example, in rural areas. The obvious corollary of such increased concentration is that individual users of the facility have to travel greater distances; the price of accessibility is increased. A key factor in the distributional effect of big, widely separated facilities is, therefore, the degree to which individuals are sufficiently mobile to use them. This is a topic we explore in some detail in a later section of this chapter.

The second general trend in the provision of public and private goods is closely related to the increased scale of facilities. Not only has the decline in the number of facilities been geographically uneven but also the location of new facilities has resulted in a changing geographical distribution of supply points. The evolving pattern has tended to increase provision in some types of area and reduce it in others. In general, two types of area have suffered in this process of spatial re-organization of goods and services. The number and variety of supply points has tended to decline in rural areas and small towns on the one hand and in the central cities of large metropolitan areas on the other. In other words, large urban areas have gained over small urban places and rural areas, as suggested earlier in our discussion of the well-being effects of city size. But many of these gains have been concentrated in the growing suburban areas, particularly in the United States, though perhaps less so in Europe. These two trends – an increased scale of facilities and the accompanying spatial re-organization of supply points – can be illustrated by looking at two types of facility: retail outlets and health-service provision.

1   Changes in retail opportunities   We saw in Chapter Two that many retail activities have become increasingly concentrated into fewer and larger units. The big department store, the hypermarket and massive discount store, the giant planned shopping centre have come to overshadow, and in some cases displace, the small store. Table 5.13 shows one example of this rationalization process. Tesco is one of the major food-retailing chains in Britain and is increasingly involved in hypermarket development. Tesco's policy has been similar to that of other big retailing corporations: to reduce its number of small stores and shift the emphasis to the very large outlet. Overall, Tesco increased its number of stores by 37.3 percent, but this overall increase involved a decline of nearly 50 percent in the smallest-size category. In 1966 stores of 2000 square feet represented 54.5 percent of all Tesco stores; by 1978 their share had fallen to 20.3 percent. The biggest growth rates were in stores of more than 10,000 square feet. In particular, Tesco had no stores larger than 20,000 square feet in 1966; by 1978 they had sixty-five.

In rural areas, the result of rationalization and re-organization processes in the retail sector has been the closure of many stores catering to the needs of the local population. In Britain, the number of shops in settlements smaller than 2500 population fell by 20 percent between 1950 and 1975. In the particular case of food

Table 5.13   *Changes in the size distribution of Tesco stores, 1966–1978*

	Gross floor area (ft^2)										
	2000		2000–4999		5000–9999		10,000–19,999		20,000		Total
	No.	%	No.	%	No.	%	No.	%	No.	%	No.	%
1966	270	54.5	131	26.5	63	12.7	31	6.3	0	–	495	100.0
1972	274	34.6	245	31.0	180	22.8	69	8.7	23	2·9	791	100.0
1978	138	20.3	204	30.0	171	25.1	102	15.0	65	9·6	680	100.0
Net change 1966–1978	−132	−48.9	+73	+55.7	+108	+171.4	+71	+229.0	+65	∞	+185	+37.3

Source: based on J.A. Dawson (1979) *The Marketing Environment*, London: Croom Helm, table 4.1

shops, a study of an area of rural Norfolk east of Norwich revealed that the number of village food shops fell from 132 in 1950 to 76 in 1966, a decline of 42 percent (Moseley 1979). The same general picture applies in the United States. The number of retail outlets serving local needs in villages and small towns has declined very markedly.

Within the large metropolitan areas of the United States in particular, the major change in the location of retail outlets has been the massive decline of the central area as a retail shopping centre and its displacement by the large planned shopping centre in the suburbs, strategically located to capture the motorized shopper. As Muller has pointed out,

> the expansion of postwar suburban retailing is really the story of the arrival and diffusion of the large shopping centre . . . once the break with down-town was made by 1960, the much larger scale regional centre quickly came to dominate suburban retailing.
> *Muller (1976), p.29.*

Accordingly, the number of retail establishments in the central business districts of metropolitan areas of the United States has declined dramatically. Between 1950 and 1967 this decline amounted to more than 25 percent in the largest metropolitan areas and almost 40 percent in the smaller metropolitan areas (Zimmer 1975). Table 5.14 shows the corresponding increased importance of the metropolitan suburbs as retailing centres.

One implication of these broad changes is that the prices of many retail goods tend to be higher in the poorer areas, both urban and rural. Most small food stores, for example, cannot compete in terms of price with the big supermarket chains (though they may offer various non-price advantages, such as more flexible opening hours). The other implication is that the declining number and changing geographical distribution of shops catering for people's basic needs, as well as for more discretionary goods, greatly alters the opportunity surface from which consumers are able to choose. For a number of groups in society, it effectively means a reduction in choice unless much longer journeys to shop can be made.

Table 5.14 *The increasing importance of
suburban retailing in the fifteen
largest SMSAs in the United States*

SMSA	Percent suburban share total SMSA retail sales	
	1963	1972
New York	32.9	N.A.
Los Angeles*	58.7	60.0
Chicago	43.1	56.8
Philadelphia	56.6	66.7
Detroit	57.3	74.1
San Francisco	52.0	63.3
Washington DC	57.9	76.3
Boston	68.8	76.3
Pittsburgh	65.9	77.0
St. Louis	62.5	77.2
Baltimore	41.9	61.5
Cleveland	45.2	69.0
Houston*	17.6	29.0
Minneapolis-St. Paul	38.5	62.9
Dallas*	28.8	58.6
Average	48.5	64.9

* Annexation of suburban territory since 1960.

Source: P.O. Muller (1976) The outer city: Geographical consequences
of the urbanization of the suburbs, *Association of American Geographers,
Commission on College Geography, Resource Paper* 75-2, table 3

2 Changes in the geography of health-care facilities The decisions of large retailing organizations to alter the scale and location of their operations, together with the associated decline of many smaller independent outlets, have important repercussions on individual and social well-being. This is possibly even more true of the changes which have been occurring in the geographical distribution of health-care facilities. Similar general trends are evident: the increasing scale of individual facilities, with a corresponding reduction in the number of outlets, and a spatial re-arrangement of the outlets themselves. In the United States, changes in many aspects of health care arise from similar forces as those operating in the retail sector. Health care in the United States is primarily a free-enterprise, market-oriented, 'fee-for-service' system. Monetary considerations, including the income of practitioners, play an extremely important role in determining the location of health-care facilities in the United States. In Britain, which has a predominantly public health service (though with a growing private sector), the forces for change are rather different. Nevertheless, some of the broad outcomes in the geographical pattern of facilities are similar in both countries.

In both countries, for example, there has been a general reduction in health care facilities in rural areas. In Britain this has resulted from the shift towards a group practice structure for doctors and other primary care facilities. Moseley (1979), for example, shows that in a part of rural Norfolk the number of individual doctor's surgeries declined from 115 in 1963 to 98 in 1975. Between 1961 and 1974, the number of village-based child health clinics declined from 97 to 62. A trend towards the concentration of hospital facilities into fewer, but larger, units is having a similar general effect. Rural areas of the United States have also witnessed major declines in the ratio of health-care facilities to population. Shannon and Dever (1974) provide a number of case studies to demonstrate this, of which Table 5.15 is one example.*
The more rural the county in Iowa, the greater the reduction in its ratio of physicians to population.

Table 5.15   *Change in the ratio of physicians to population in Iowa, 1910–1960*

Proportion of population that is rural in respective counties	Physicians per 100,000 population		
	1910	1960	Percent change 1910–1960
80% or more	148	53	−64.2
60–79%	168	63	−62.5
40–59%	154	82	−46.7
less than 40%	187	105	−43.9

Source: based on G.W. Shannon & G.E.A. Dever (1974) *Health Care Delivery: Spatial Perspectives*, New York: McGraw Hill, table 3.5. With permission of McGraw Hill Book Company, Inc.

Changes in the intrametropolitan location of health-care facilities in the United States show extremely close parallels with the changing geographical distribution of retail facilities discussed earlier. Indeed, several aspects of health-care – physicians, dentists, for example – are organized into the spatial hierarchy of retail centres and reflect a response to changing geographical patterns of the more affluent 'consumers'. As a result, there are enormous variations *within* metropolitan areas in the availability of health-care facilities. The poorer neighbourhoods, and especially the black neighbourhoods, tend to have far lower provision than the more affluent and the white neighbourhoods. In Chicago in 1960, for example, the average number of physicians in white census tracts was 5.31; in black census tracts it was 1.69. The equivalent figures for medical specialists were 2.89 and 0.53 respectively (Shannon and Dever 1974, p.62). Another study of health-care in Chicago by De Vise (1971)

---

*More generally, Shannon and Dever provide a very comprehensive survey of the geography of health-care in the United States at a variety of spatial scales.

revealed that the number of physicians in five inner communities declined from 475 to 76 between 1950 and 1970. Each of these communities was in the process of residential transition from middle-class white, to low-status black, communities. Similar intrametropolitan variations exist elsewhere. In Baltimore, for example, Harvey (1972) calculated that the ratio of people per physician ranged from 2700 people per physician in a low-income black area of the inner city to 620 people per physician in an upper-income white area.

Apart from individual details, however, the important general point is that the trends towards increasing concentration of private and public facilities into larger and fewer units together with the spatial re-organization of supply points substantially alter the opportunity characteristics of the social well-being surface. But in the case of *public* goods there is a further dimension to consider. Quite apart from variations in the specific (point) location of supply points, the quantity and quality of public goods and services also varies *territorially*. Some areas – states, counties, cities, districts – have a higher level of public provision than others. Because such inter-territorial variations can be so significant in their contribution to social well-being they merit separate attention.

Territorial variations in the provision of public goods
Territorial variations in the quantity and quality of public goods arise from differences in policies, revenues and expenditure between governments and other public agencies at various spatial scales. Public goods have to be paid for collectively. In general the revenue to pay for them is raised from the various forms of taxation levied on individuals and organizations at different jurisdictional levels. The problem is that the ability to pay varies very substantially between one jurisdiction and another. Very often the areas, and people, in greatest need of public goods and services have the least ability to pay for them. Hence, a major aim of public provision is to *redistribute* resources. In some cases – that of central cities and suburbs being the most obvious – the redistribution process seems to work the other way so that some citizens receive the benefits of public goods and services at a 'cut price'. It is not possible to examine all aspects of what is a massive and immensely complex topic. Instead we focus on just two aspects to demonstrate the existence of territorial variations in public provision. First we examine some examples of broad jurisdictional variations, second we discuss the problems of public provision between the central cities and suburbs of metropolitan areas.

1   **Broad geographical variations in public provision** The geographical scale and federal political structure of the United States help to produce very marked variations in public provision. At the *state* level, much of the variation arises from the precise combination of federal and state expenditure in particular states. In other words, much depends upon the scale of the *transfer payments* made by federal to state governments, together with the willingness and/or ability of individual states to contribute towards particular programmes. In general, the relative importance of federal funding in state (and local) revenues has been increasing. In 1955, for example, 10 percent of state and local revenues came from federal sources; by 1975 this share had doubled to almost 21 percent.

Interstate variations in the largest federal welfare programme – Aid to Families with Dependent Children (AFDC) – provide a good example of some of the influ-

ences involved. Although AFDC is a federal programme, there is enormous variation between states in its implementation and in the level of payments. Indeed,
Wohlenberg (1976) claims that the United States

> has not one but fifty-four different AFDC programs – one for each state,
> one for the District of Columbia, and one for each of three other territorial
> jurisdictions. Federal law allows the states a great deal of latitude in for-
> mulating their own public assistance programs based on certain federal
> regulations and guidelines.
> *Wohlenberg (1976), p.254.*

Figure 5.16 shows some of the resulting geographical variations in AFDC payments.
The map shows the largest amount paid for basic needs of a family of four in 1972.
Virtually all the southern states had very low AFDC grant levels, the exception being
Virginia. Apart from three New England states, most northern states had relatively
high payments. Even so, Wohlenberg found that many states paid maximum welfare
payments far below the official poverty line. Michigan and Alaska were the only
states in which AFDC clients could legally be paid benefits at the subsistence level.
In a mere twenty states benefits could be as high as 75 percent of subsistence level.

The reasons underlying such interstate differences are complex, though
Wohlenberg argues that differences in costs of living are not a sufficient explanation.
The size of the variation in benefits was very much greater than that in living costs.

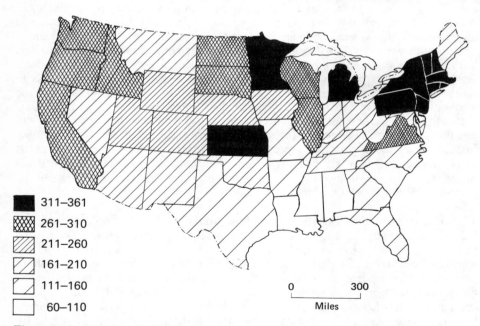

■	311–361
▨	261–310
▨	211–260
▨	161–210
◪	111–160
□	60–110

0   300
Miles

Figure 5.16 Variations in AFDC programme: largest amount paid for basic needs of a family
of four, July 1972

Source: E.H. Wohlenberg (1976) Interstate variations in AFDC programs, *Economic Geography*, 52,
figure 2.

Differences in each state's tax base certainly contribute. Richer states can afford to contribute more than poor states. Another reason for variations in AFDC programmes has been suggested by Johnston (1977). He looked at the political complexion of each state and claimed that those states

> where parties in power need to win votes from the poor to remain in power are . . . more generous in their benefits and in the levels of income allowed before benefits are withdrawn, more liberal in their acceptance of applications, and more effective in helping poor families.
> *Johnston (1977), p.350.*

Whatever the underlying reasons, it is clear that actual welfare benefits under the AFDC programme vary markedly by state. It is better to be poor in some states than in others. Similar geographical variations exist in state expenditures on education. Figure 5.17 shows state levels of public school expenditure per pupil in 1978. Twenty-seven states spent less than the national average of $1740. Most of the very low levels of pupil expenditure were in the southern states, though others such as Idaho, South Dakota and Utah also spent relatively low sums on education. Apart from Alaska, the highest pupil expenditures were in New York state, followed by New Jersey, Delaware, Massachusetts and Pennsylvania. Again, it would seem, differences in tax revenues between states may be an important, though not the sole, cause of such variations.

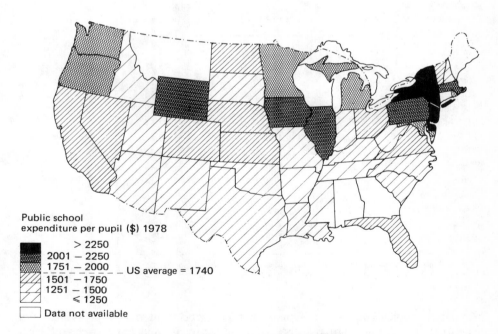

Figure 5.17   Variations in public school expenditure per pupil by state, 1978

Source: United States *Statistical Abstract* (1978), table 255.

Considerable geographical variations in public provision also exist in Britain despite a much greater degree of central government involvement. In the case of the health service, for example, there are very considerable differences between the regional health authorities in the resources available to their populations. Table 5.16 shows one aspect of this. The first column is a measure of the need of each area in relation to its population. The higher values (greater than 1.0) indicate greater need for health facilities. Apart from SW and SE Thames all the more 'needy' areas are in the North. This is reflected also in the second column of Table 5.15 which shows the deficit or excess of capital stock in each area based on an estimate of population need. As Smith comments,

> again, the disadvantaged RHAs tend to be concentrated in the north, with the South East relatively well-off. However, Merseyside is much better off than might be expected, and Wessex markedly worse off than other Southern regions. The resources needed to redress the disparities in regional levels of service provision are enormous.
> *Smith (1979), p.273.*

Table 5.16 *Regional variations in health-service need and provision in England*

Regional health authority	Index of need	Deficit or excess of capital stock (£ per capita)
Northern	1.02	−4.13
Yorkshire	1.03	−5.72
Trent	0.95	−7.72
East Anglia	0.94	+5.74
NW Thames	0.97	+16.28
NE Thames	1.00	+13.54
SE Thames	1.07	+0.84
SW Thames	1.09	+8.27
Wessex	0.98	−11.48
Oxford	0.88	+11.24
Southwestern	0.96	−1.16
West Midlands	0.95	−6.75
Mersey	1.04	+17.53
Northwestern	1.09	−16.54

Source: Sharing Resources for Health in England (1976). Crown Copyright

Similar examples could be drawn from other aspects of public provision. For example, there are substantial differences in educational provision between different parts of Britain. Table 5.17 shows two aspects of this: spending per pupil and pupil-teacher ratios. Only the upper and lower extremes are shown, but they indicate very wide variation. In primary schools the amount spent per pupil ranged from £206.84 to £125.30 in 1973–1974; in secondary schools the variation was even greater, from £344.56 in the Inner London Education Authority to £211.37 in Wigan. Wigan also fared badly in pupil-teacher terms, having the least favourable ratio of 20:2 compared with 12:7 in Bradford.

Table 5.17 *Variations in education provision in England and Wales*

Spending per pupil 1973–1974			
Highest spenders		**Lowest spenders**	
Primary			
	£		£
Cardiganshire	206.84	Cornwall	131.64
ILEA	201.22	Wakefield	131.52
Oxford	181.89	Bradford	130.46
Kingston upon Thames	178.63	Burnley	129.83
Hertfordshire	176.61	Southport	126.63
Newham	176.59	Blackpool	125.30
Secondary			
ILEA	344.56	Eastbourne	226.17
Bradford	323.41	Worcester	226.03
Southampton	319.27	Wakefield	224.42
Stoke-on-Trent	310.40	Bootle	220.82
Grimsby	308.94	Halifax	217.97
Norwich	307.64	Wigan	211.37
Pupil-teacher ratio			
Most favourable		**Least favourable**	
Secondary			
Bradford	12.7	Isle of Wight	19.1
Southampton	14.6	South Shields	19.1
Chester	14.6	Worcester	19.2
Richmond	15.3	Blackpool	19.2
Waltham Forest	15.4	Southend on Sea	19.3
Stoke-on-Trent	15.5	Wigan	20.2

Source: B.E. Coates, R.J. Johnston & P.L. Knox (1977) *Geography and Inequality*, London: Oxford University Press, table 6.3

2   City versus suburb: problems of spillover

Fiscal jurisdictions, to function efficiently, should be arranged such that those who benefit from particular services are also those who pay for them and who participate in the political process of making the relevant tax and expenditure decisions. If residents of jurisdiction X can tax those of jurisdiction Y to supply services useful to residents of X only, the decision process will be inefficient. Similarly, inefficiencies will result if residents of Y can gain benefits from services of X without compensating the residents of X (who pay for such services).
Musgrave (1974), pp.268–269.

Figure 5.18 shows diagrammatically how both costs and benefits may *spill over* from one jurisdiction to another. Only in Figure 5.18a are costs and benefits properly contained geographically. Figure 5.18c depicts the widely held view of the relationship between the central cities and the suburbs of large metropolitan areas. Quite obviously, *where* the boundaries are drawn between users of, and payers for, services will have a critical influence on the degree of spillover.

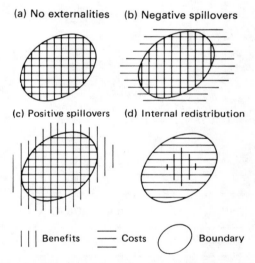

Figure 5.18   The spillover of costs and benefits across jurisdictional boundaries
Source: D.M. Smith (1977) *Human Geography: A Welfare Approach*, London: Edward Arnold, figure 5.5.

All large metropolitan areas in modern Western societies are made up of varying numbers of smaller-scale jurisdictions. In some cases, the degree of 'balkanization' can be extremely high:

molded by nineteenth century notions of the moral and ethical values of local autonomy and self-determination, much of the United States has become shattered like a pane of glass into a system of often competitive and mutually suspicious fragments. . . . Although the problems of local gov-

ernment fragmentation exist throughout the world, nowhere are their proportions and implications as great as they are in the United States. Both Chicago and New York, for example, are the focal points of an accretion of over a thousand local government units overlapping and intertwining in a multi-tiered (and multi-state) mosaic of political authorities.
Soja (1971), pp.45–46.

The 1974 local government reforms in England and Wales went some way towards rationalizing the geographical boundaries of metropolitan areas. Six metropolitan counties were created which were based upon amalgamations of pre-existing local authorities of differing levels. In the case of Greater Manchester, for example, a new metropolitan county was created consisting of ten new metropolitan districts formed through the amalgamation of eight county boroughs, fifteen municipal boroughs, forty-three urban districts and parts of two rural districts (Williams 1975).*

A major by-product of jurisdictional fragmentation within metropolitan areas is that it creates the kinds of conditions shown in Figure 5.18. Each jurisdiction is responsible for providing certain types of public service. Each area has to raise revenue to pay for those services. Most commonly, such revenue is raised through a property tax. Since different types of property generate different amounts of such tax, it is clear that the particular mix of properties in an area – factories, offices, shops, residences of different taxable values – will be a critical determinant of how much local revenue a local jurisdiction can raise. But jurisdictions also differ in terms of the demand for public services within their areas. The imbalance between demands for services and the financial ability to provide them is the crux of the interjurisdictional problem within metropolitan areas.

As we have seen at various points in this book, the relative mix of population and economic activities in different parts of the metropolitan area has been changing very markedly. For the most part, the internal political structure has not kept pace with these changes. Hence, most large metropolitan areas face major internal problems of financing public service provision. Most commonly, this is depicted as a simple clash between the central city on the one hand and the outer suburbs on the other. The near-bankruptcy of New York City in the mid-1970s was just one example of the financial problems facing very many older cities.

At the heart of the problem is the fact that the migration of both people and economic functions from central cities to suburbs has been *highly selective*. Higher-income groups, in particular, have moved out, leaving behind not only a large proportion of people on low incomes but also a large pool of individuals with heavy demands for public services – the elderly, the single-parent family, the unemployed. Not only has the local tax base been reduced by the exodus of higher-income groups and by industry, but also the smaller tax base has even greater demands placed upon it. Many of these demands are for particular social and welfare services.

But there are other services which the central cities are expected to provide which also benefit those suburbanites who travel into the city to work or for cultural,

---

*Such re-organization was not achieved without opposition. As Williams points out, almost half a million people expressed the wish to remain outside the new metropolitan county. This was especially true of some of the affluent areas of North Cheshire. Although many residents of these areas commute to work in Greater Manchester they wished to retain their non-metropolitan affiliation (and their Cheshire address!).

recreational and shopping purposes. The problem is that these non-city residents do not pay for them in full since the main basis of raising revenue is that of property. Suburban residents pay their property taxes to their suburban jurisdictions yet derive a good deal of benefit from central-city services for which they either pay nothing or which they get at a 'cut price'.* In addition,

> exacerbating the service-resource problem facing the central cities has been the fact that suburban population growth has not been matched by a proportional growth of suburban public services. The much larger impact of suburban population growth on central-city public services compared to its impact on suburban public services suggests that suburban residents may be unwilling to bear the costs of 'urban' services in their own area, and that they will continue to utilise central-city public facilities as long as doing so is less expensive than providing their own.
> *Berry and Kasarda (1977), p.226.*

Cox (1973) has attempted to quantify the fiscal disparities which exist between central cities and suburbs. He computed a *composite disparity index* to reflect both the differences in resources and in service burden between central cities and suburbs. Figure 5.19 shows that the biggest disparities were located in the older urban-industrial areas of the Northeast and Midwest.

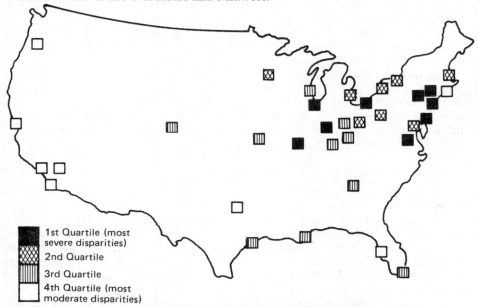

1st Quartile (most severe disparities)
2nd Quartile
3rd Quartile
4th Quartile (most moderate disparities)

Figure 5.19 The geography of the central-city/suburban fiscal disparity problem

Source: K.R. Cox (1973) *Conflict, Power and Politics in the City*, New York: McGraw Hill, figure 3.5. With permission of McGraw Hill Book Company.

*As Cox (1973) points out, suburban users of central-city businesses do pay indirectly insofar as the additional business they generate, for example, in central-city shops, restaurants, theatres and so on, will be reflected in the higher property taxes paid by the operators of those businesses.

Until relatively recently, most of the evidence of the disparities in finance and services between central cities and suburbs came from the United States. But it is now clear that similar problems exist in the United Kingdom. Eversley (1972), for example, has argued that declining populations in central-city local authorities have reduced the local revenue base and made local service provision more difficult. Table 5.18 shows just how far the urban cores of metropolitan areas in England and Wales fell behind in the growth of their rateable values between 1966 and 1971 compared with the outer areas. For each source of revenue – domestic, commercial and industrial – the relative position of the central cities worsened considerably.

Table 5.18 *Increases in rateable values for domestic, commercial and industrial uses within metropolitan areas in England and Wales, 1966–1971*

	Percentage increase 1966–1971		
	Domestic rateable value	Commercial rateable value	Industrial rateable value
Urban cores	9.2	11.7	4.0
Metropolitan rings	18.8	24.6	13.2
Outer metropolitan rings	21.3	16.3	16.2

Source: S. Kennett (1980) The inner city in the context of the urban system, *Social Science Research Council Inner City in Context Paper 7*, table 6.2

The case of Manchester illustrates the scale of the problem facing many old cities in Britain. In 1980, it was announced that Manchester was likely to have a financial deficit in both 1980–1981 and 1981–1982 of more than £20 million. The city displays most of the classic symptoms discussed in this section. Since 1951, its population has declined by almost one-third. At the same time its industrial base has shrunk dramatically. Between 1966 and 1975 alone, more than 111,000 manufacturing jobs were lost to the city. The age structure of the population has become increasingly elderly; the pressures to provide public and welfare services have increased to such a degree that spending on social services increased by 50 percent in 1979. Like many old cities, too, Manchester has a huge public housing sector to be financed and maintained. Some two-thirds of Manchester's total housing stock is publicly owned.

One result of the growing financial difficulties faced by central cities in both the United States and in Britain, therefore, has been a growing dependence on central government financial assistance. In the United States, for example, direct federal aid as a percentage of local revenue increased from an average of 1.1 percent in 1957 to 47.5 percent in 1978, for a sample of fifteen cities (Kirwan 1980). In the cases of Buffalo and Detroit, the federal proportion had reached more than 75 percent in 1978. In Britain, changes in the calculation of the Rate Support Grant first led to an increasing share going to the major cities, particularly London, at the expense of the shire counties.* In December 1980 the emphasis was reversed, favouring the shire counties once more.

---

*The aims of the RSG are to compensate local authorities for lack of resources; to provide extra resources to authorities with special needs; to relieve domestic ratepayers of the problem of excessive rate increases;

to make a general contribution to local government expenditure. For a detailed discussion of the complexities of RSG see Kennett (1980, paper 6).

The fragmentation of metropolitan areas into separate jurisdictions, together with the spillover of costs and benefits, produces major geographical differences in public service provision within metropolitan areas. In United States cities, such intrametropolitan inequalities are reinforced by the practice of exclusionary zoning (discussed in Chapter Four), whereby the socio-economic homogeneity of residential areas is further reinforced. The case of education provision illustrates the issue very clearly. Most of the school population in both the United States and the United Kingdom attend schools in the public sector. The most common basis for allocating pupils to schools is the neighbourhood or catchment area, although some local authorities claim to operate more flexible systems. Homogeneity of residential neighbourhoods, which is such a marked feature of the geography of residence, thus leads to socially homogeneous schools with relatively little social mixing. If school resources had to be provided entirely out of local revenue, the differences between schools in poor and rich areas would be immense. The involvement of federal and central government in contributing to local revenue reduces the disparity between local areas in resources devoted to education. Nevertheless, substantial disparities do exist between central-city and suburban areas.

Writing of the United States, Cox (1973) suggests four reasons for intrametropolitan disparities in education provision. First, he argues that the poorer, and especially the black, pupils of the central cities require a much greater investment of educational resources (both human and financial) than suburban pupils from less deprived backgrounds. Second, the costs of providing education tends to be greater in the central city. Land costs are higher but these are less important than the extra costs of inducing teachers to work in central-city schools. Costs of combating vandalism also add substantially to the central-city burden. A third reason relates to the maintenance and replacement problems created by the generally older capital stock of central-city schools. Fourthly, Cox points to the closure of central-city parochial (especially Roman Catholic) schools and the need to absorb extra pupils in the public sector.

Higbee paints a vivid picture of the kind of contrast that can exist between central-city and suburban school systems in the United States:

> The suburban community of Scarsdale in Westchester County has one of the finest public school systems in the United States. Scarsdale's wealth is generated in New York City. Of all high school graduates in Scarsdale, 99 percent go on to college. In East Harlem, New York City, less than 2 percent of the high school graduates even qualify for college entrance. . . .
> Scarsdale has achieved the future. New York City's East Harlem is a century behind time. It is not that the city's tax base fails to increase, it is that the city itself, which generates taxes for the Federal Government, is on the wrong tax base. It cannot catch the people who want good public schools. They leave each night on the commuter trains and over the federal interstate highways.
> *Higbee (1970), pp.105, 106.*

Although educational disparities between central city and suburbs in the United Kingdom may be less extreme than in the United States, there is no doubt that disparities do exist. Schools do reflect the nature of the neighbourhood in which they are located. Neighbourhoods do tend to be relatively homogeneous in socio-economic terms. Teachers do, with some exceptions, prefer to teach in suburban rather than in inner-city schools. The attempts to identify Educational Priority Areas, whatever their shortcomings, are evidence of the existence of pronounced spatial variations in education.

Territorial variations in the provision of public goods at the local scale add to the variations evident at the larger geographical scales of state or region. Together with the specific location of supply points of public and private goods and services, these produce very considerable variation in the opportunity surface facing individuals. A further element, however, is the extent to which individuals differ in their ability to make use of the facilities provided at different locations in geographical space. It is to this question of individual accessibility to 'goods', and to the influence of time-space constraints, that we now turn.

Individual accessibility to 'goods': time-space constraints

Each of us is faced with a geographically uneven surface of opportunities and resources from which we attempt to satisfy our needs and wants and to ensure our well-being. As we noted earlier, many facilities have become concentrated into larger, fewer and, thus, more widely scattered locations. Not only does the *quantity* of resources vary considerably from place to place but so also does their *quality*. Assuming that our residential location is fixed in the short term, then our ability to tap these geographically variable resources depends upon how accessible they are to us. Such accessibility may depend upon our degree of physical mobility but it may depend also upon whether we satisfy certain 'entry requirements'. In either case, it is the combined influence of the three sets of *time-space constraints*, discussed in Chapter One – capability, coupling, and authority constraints – which have a crucial influence upon our access to 'goods' and, hence, upon our level of well-being. The important point is that the supply points of such 'goods' must be accessible in both space *and* time; in other words they must be within the individual's *daily time-space prism*. It is not only the location in geographical space of goods and services which is important, but also the times when such facilities are available for use in relation to each individual's daily time-schedule.

Thus, the question of accessibility to 'goods' in modern societies is complex. Our starting point is the fact that the characteristic geographical separation between an individual's home base and the location of public and private facilities necessitates the making of *trips* to use such facilities.* The frequency with which trips have to be made varies for different types of activity. Figure 5.20 suggests that trip frequency is related to the essential or discretionary nature of the activity. Essential activities – work, education, convenience shopping – tend to require frequent (daily) trips. The exception, for most healthy people, is the need for medical treatment, which is essential but generally requires infrequent trips.

---

*In some cases, of course, goods and services are delivered and do not require personal travel. However, delivery seems to be increasingly less common for a wide variety of both private and public services. For example, milk delivery and home visits by doctors are less and less common in the United States.

Differential access to transport
The ability to engage in both the essential and discretionary activities shown in Figure 5.20 depends very largely on the individual's access to appropriate means of transport. As we saw in Chapter Two (Figure 2.33), one of the major characteristics of modern Western society has been the very rapid growth in automobile-ownership. But aggregate figures mask very significant differences between particular groups within the population. In 1971, for example, 22 percent of all families in United States metropolitan areas did not own a car. In the central cities, the car-less percentage was a good deal higher – some 32 percent of central-city families. Among certain social groups, car-ownership is even lower. Approximately 45 percent of Chicago's black population did not own a car in 1971. Car-ownership levels are lower in Britain than in the United States. Thus, in 1971, some 60 percent of households in the five provincial conurbations of Britain had no car (Moseley 1980). In London, car-ownership in the suburbs was of the order of 50 percent or more of households, compared with levels of 20 to 30 percent in the inner boroughs.

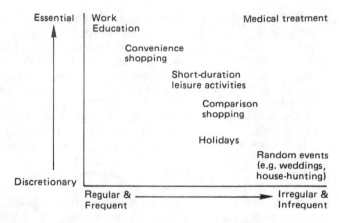

Figure 5.20   A classification of activities involving individual travel

Source: L.J. Wood & T.R. Lee (1980) Time-space convergence: reappraisal for an oil short future, *Area*, 12, figure 1.

One obvious influence on car-ownership is income. The costs of buying and running a car are extremely high and for some groups in the population such costs are prohibitive. Where car-ownership is unavoidable for the performance of the most basic activities – as in much of the United States and in many parts of rural Britain – economies have to be made on other items in the household budget. Apart from income, access to a car also varies very considerably by both sex and age, as Table 5.19 shows for five different types of geographical area in Britain. Quite clearly, the level of access to a car (and the possession of a licence to drive one) is much higher for men than for women in all geographical areas. In turn, elderly people of both sexes have substantially lower access to a car.

In considering variations in access to a car, it is important to distinguish between access at the household level on the one hand and at the individual level on the other.

Table 5.19 *Variation in access to a car by sex and age in five types of area in Britain*

	Household has:	Respondent has:	Village %	Small town %	New town %	City suburb %	Inner London %
Men (all ages)							
level 1	car	licence	67	70	64	54	40
level 2	car	no licence	6	7	3	1	7
level 3	no car	licence	8	7	10	10	9
level 4	no car	no licence	20	16	24	35	44
Women (all ages)							
level 1	car	licence	33	36	14	8	13
level 2	car	no licence	31	27	45	30	25
level 3	no car	licence	2	3	5	2	1
level 4	no car	no licence	34	34	37	60	61
Pensioners							
level 1	car	licence	24	13	18	3	4
level 2	car	no licence	18	13	6	3	4
level 3	no car	licence	–	3	6	3	–
level 4	no car	no licence	58	70	71	91	91

Source: reprinted from M. Hillman, I. Henderson & A. Whalley (1976) *Transport Realities and Planning Policy*, Report no. 567, London: Political and Economic Planning, now Policy Studies Institute, table 1.3.

A particular household may have a car but its use may be restricted to only one member of that household for most of the time. Generally, it is the male 'head of household' who uses the family car to commute to work. In such cases, the car used for commuting is unavailable for use by other members of the household for large portions of time. Hence, the ability of the car-less members of car-owning households to engage in activities outside the immediate neighbourhood is severely limited. Those who can drive may use the car during evenings and weekends; those who cannot drive are dependent on one who is willing to drive them to particular places. But many facilities are not open outside normal working hours. Here, then, is a prime example of the combined influence of time-space constraints operating to restrict individual choice.

The main alternative to private car travel (or bicycle) is, of course, public transport. But one of the by-products of increased private car-ownership has been a severe decline in the public transport system. As Figure 5.21 shows, the two curves of car-ownership and trips by public transport are diametrically opposed to each other. The process is a cumulative one (Figure 5.22): as car-ownership is seen to have greater utility or value to the individual, car-ownership rises. This has the combined effect of reducing the number of passengers on public transport (leading both to higher fares and to reduced frequency of service) and increasing traffic congestion.

As a result, the quality of public transport declines, the attractions of car-ownership increase further and the cumulative process is reinforced.

The uneven distribution of access to both private and public transport between different social groups means that certain segments of the population are, in effect,

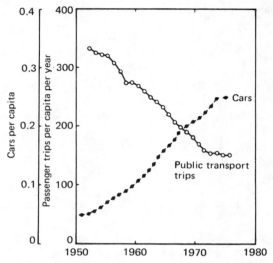

Figure 5.21   Trends in car-ownership and public transport passenger trips in Great Britain

Source: C.B. Mitchell (1976) *Some aspects of public passenger transport*, by permission of the Transport and Road Research Laboratory.

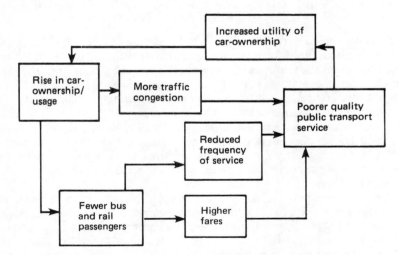

Figure 5.22   Decline in public transport as a cumulative process associated with increased car-ownership

Source: M.J. Moseley (1979) *Accessibility: The Rural Challenge*, London: Methuen, p.21.

on the margins of transport use and service: they are the 'transport poor'. As Figure 5.23 shows, the groups with least mobility in our society are the poor, the elderly, the handicapped and the young. To these should be added the female parent with young children who lacks access to a car and whose dual social role places particular demands upon her. Quite clearly, physical mobility is a vital ingredient of well-being since it helps to determine both the quantity and quality of resources available to individuals. The more mobile the individual, the greater the choices and the fewer the constraints. For large sections of the population, on the other hand, the constraints imposed by the lack of physical mobility reduce the daily time-space prism to a 'prison' of limited resources and opportunities (Peet 1975). Two examples can be used to illustrate the impact of time-space constraints on well-being. We begin by taking the case of the urban poor.

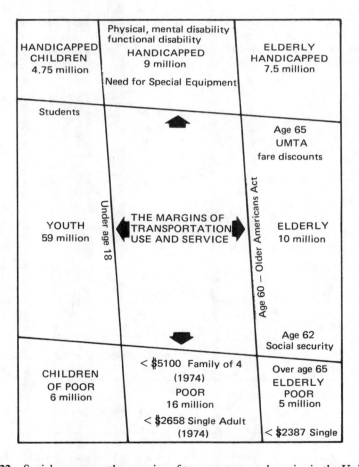

Figure 5.23   Social groups on the margins of transport use and service in the United States

Source: F.P. Stutz (1976) Social aspects of interaction and transportation, *Association of American Geographers, Commission on College Geography, Resource Paper 76-2,* figure 26.

Mobility problems of the urban poor

As we have seen, the combined operation of labour and housing markets has resulted in a concentration of the urban poor in the inner areas of large cities. Among this population, car-ownership levels are low (see Table 5.19) and public transport expenditures take up a substantial proportion of the household budget, especially where the employed members of the household have to travel lengthy distances to work. A substantial proportion of the inner-city population is 'service-dependent' so that travel to service facilities is especially important to the elderly, the handicapped and other service-dependent groups (Wolch 1979).

For the most part, the poor population of the inner areas is very limited in its geographical mobility. In the case of shopping trips, for example, lower-income groups tend both to shop more frequently and to patronize local stores. Figure 5.24 shows how the geographical extent both of actual shopping trips and of knowledge of shopping opportunities varies systematically with social class. The lower the socio-economic status of the shopper, the more limited the distance travelled to shop. Figure 5.24 also demonstrates that for each social class the spatial awareness of shopping opportunities is much greater than the area actually utilized. In the case of

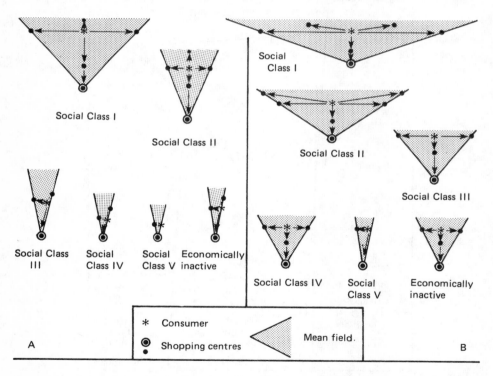

Figure 5.24   Variations in (a) the spatial extent of shopping behaviour and (b) of awareness of shopping opportunities by social class

Source: R.B. Potter (1977) Spatial patterns of consumer behaviour and perception in relation to the social class variable, *Area,* 9, figure 1.

the lowest social groups, therefore, it is obviously not merely ignorance of alternatives which explains the limited distance travelled to shop. Cost of travel, together with inadequacy of public transport, is a key factor. One result of the limited geographical extent of low-income shopping behaviour is that poor people often have to pay more for the items in their shopping baskets. As we noted earlier, the lower prices tend to be offered by the large supermarkets and other large retail chains which, especially in the United States, are located in the suburbs.

The spatial patterns of the use of medical facilities by the urban poor are less clearly localized. To some extent, patients do visit the nearest doctor, dentist or hospital. In some cases, the patient is allocated to a medical facility on the criterion of place of residence in the same way as pupils are allocated to schools on a neighbourhood catchment area basis. But in United States cities, in particular, the relationship between the use of medical facilities and distance from the user's place of residence is more complex. In many cases, authority constraints seem to be more important than capability (movement) constraints. Giggs summarizes the situation very concisely, pointing out that a variety of institutional influences affects the individual use of medical facilities. For example,

> Although Chicago had eighty hospitals in the late 1960s they were not equally accessible to all Chicagoans. Very few hospitals provided free (i.e. public) or subsidised services for poor persons. Others cater almost exclusively to minority groups in terms of occupations, age, race and religion (e.g. Roman Catholic and Jewish hospitals). In consequence, *there were significant intra-urban differentials in terms of both spatial and social access to necessary medical services. The medical travel patterns of most minority groups were therefore frequently more extended and directionally biased than those of the majority of Chicagoans. . . .* In the United States most patients . . . tend to go to the hospital to which their physician is affiliated. In many cases, this is not the nearest hospital that a patient could visit from home. . . . *Economic and social constraints frequently combine to provide a deleterious pattern of medical facility utilization among the poor, the aged, and minority groups.* These large disadvantaged groups tend to visit physicians much less frequently than higher-income white Americans. *Frequently they live in inner city neighbourhoods adjacent to large hospitals and specialist physician quarters. These facilities are, however, economically and socially inaccessible to them. The poor and non-white populations in many cities are obliged to undertake long, expensive, and time-consuming trips to distant hospitals.*
> Giggs (1979), pp.105, 107 (present authors' emphasis).

These comments help to put the importance of physical mobility constraints into a clearer perspective. Just as lack of physical mobility does not fully explain the incidence of unemployment among the inner-city population (see Chapters Three and Four), so, too, other constraints influence the use of health-care facilities. Indeed, Pahl has observed that

> the inequality of physical access is not as significant as the inequality of social access.
> Pahl (1979), p.35.

In fact, the two often reinforce each other, as is shown very clearly in the black ghettos of United States cities. Wheeler (1974) notes the paradoxical geographical position of urban blacks. They live close to the most accessible parts of the metro-politan area – the city centre – and yet they tend to be the least mobile of all groups in American society. Such relative immobility results from both physical and social constraints. Car-ownership is low among blacks and public transport in ghetto areas is extremely poor. There are physical barriers in the form of urban freeways, railroad tracks, industrial areas, for example, which tend to isolate ghetto areas from other parts of the city. Perhaps most significant of all is the *barrier of social distance* between the black population and the white. For all of these reasons, the interaction intensity of the black population tends to fall away very markedly at the edge of the ghetto, as Figure 5.25 suggests. Dependence on local facilities is thus a characteristic feature of the black ghetto population. Since the quality of facilities in ghetto areas is fre-quently substantially poorer than in the more prosperous white areas, the combined physical and social constraints on black mobility substantially reduce their levels of well-being.

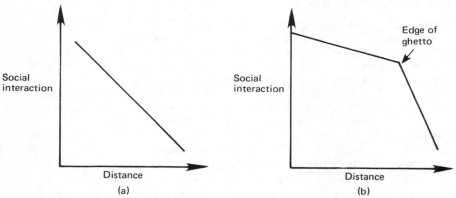

Figure 5.25   The effect of a ghetto boundary on the intensity of interaction

Source: J.O. Wheeler (1974) *The Urban Circulation Noose*, Belmont: Wadsworth, figure 4.2. By permis-sion of Wadsworth Publishing Company.

The compact, highly localized community is thus characteristic of low-income areas and, especially, of ethnic areas. Studies such as Young's and Wilmott's *Family and Kinship in East London* provide evidence of the very close, tight-knit com-munities which evolved in the low-income areas of London. Similar communities can be observed in all large cities, although the large-scale redevelopment of many slum housing areas was responsible for breaking up many of these communities as the population was dispersed. Where such communities exist, the meeting points are the doorstep, the street, the local pub or the church hall. Interactions tend to be short distance; 'neighbouring' is a prominent feature of social life.

In a similar way, the ethnic residential concentrations which we have seen to be such a prominent feature of the urban residential landscape generate very strong local communities. Indeed, those features which differentiate the ethnic group from the rest of society – language, culture, custom, as well as the cohesive effects of discrimination – produce particularly strong community links. Since most ethnic groups are both highly confined spatially into limited areas of the city and also limited to low-income occupations, the development of ethnic *place* communities tends to be very strong.

One outcome of this is the development of strong *territorial* identification. Two examples can be used to illustrate this. The first refers back to our discussion of ethnic segregation in Chapter Four and to Suttles' study of the Addams district of Chicago. Figure 4.30 showed the Addams district to be highly segregated internally between several ethnic groups. Suttles also shows how far local residents live their daily lives within assumed territorial divisions:

> There is the general assumption that boundaries exist and that the area included must 'belong' to someone. Thus the city is seen as something like an irregular lattice work from which a person's behaviour and appearance can be gauged, interpreted, and reacted to depending upon the section to which he belongs. . . . Each little section is taken to be a self-sufficient world where residents carry out almost all of their legitimate pursuits. *Suttles (1968), p.15.*

The second example of group territoriality with a strong place basis is drawn from Boal's work on the territorial effects of religious affiliation in Belfast, Northern Ireland. Figure 5.26 shows the very marked geographical separation of the Roman

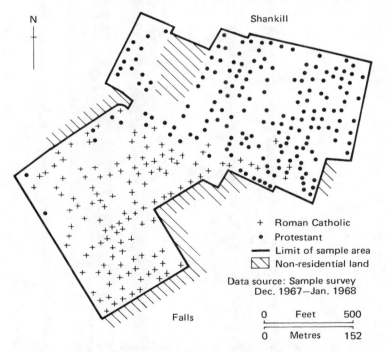

Figure 5.26   Residential segregation by religious affiliation in a part of Belfast

Source: F.W. Boal (1970) Social space in the Belfast urban area, in N. Stevens & R.A. Glasscock (eds) *Irish Geographical Studies*, Belfast: Queen's University, figure 6.

Catholic and Protestant groups in a part of west Belfast. The Shankill district is almost totally Protestant; the Falls district almost exclusively Roman Catholic. The dividing line between the two is extremely sharp and follows the line of Cupar Street. This territorial division is clearly reflected in the social trips of the two populations. Figure 5.27 shows that most visits by each religious group were confined to their 'own' territories Virtually nobody crossed the dividing line between the two com-

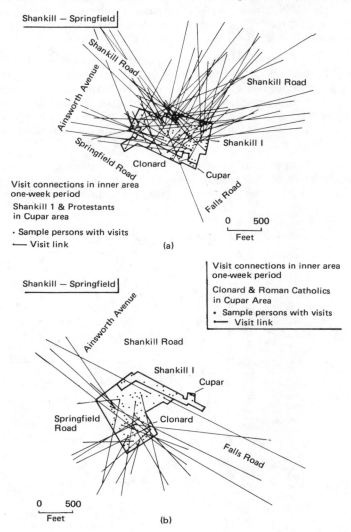

Figure 5.27   Religious territories in Belfast: restricted patterns of social visits: (a) Protestants, (b) Roman Catholics

Source: F.W. Boal (1969) Territoriality on the Shankill-Falls divide, *Belfast, Irish Geography*, 6, figures 10 and 11. By permission of *Irish Geography*.

munities. (It is worth pointing out that Boal's survey was carried out *before* the present disturbances began in 1969.)

The limited ability of the urban poor to participate in a variety of activities contributing towards their well-being is the result, very largely, of the combined operation of capability and authority constraints. The poor both have limited physical mobility and are also – particularly in the case of black and other racial groups – prevented from using certain facilities through a lack of appropriate entry requirements (including income). As a result, the daily time-space prism of low-income groups tends to be very restricted compared with those having higher incomes and greater access to personal transport.

These differences in the geographical scale at which low- and high-income groups operate are clearly reflected in their mental maps of the same metropolitan area. Figure 5.28, for example, is the composite mental map of Los Angeles held by white residents of an upper-class suburb, Westwood. It shows a very detailed knowledge of most of the metropolitan area, reflecting the residents' extensive geographical involvement. Figures 5.29 and 5.30 are in complete contrast to this. These are the mental maps of low-income residents of ethnic districts. Figure 5.29 shows the limited map of black residents of the Avalon district of Los Angeles. The features shown reflect the regular movements and interactions of the black population, in particular the north-south thoroughfare between Avalon (near Watts) and the downtown area. Figure 5.30 reflects an even more limited geographical pattern of behaviour. The Boyle Heights district is primarily a Spanish-speaking community. Its residents' view of Los Angeles is little more than a few city blocks. To the residents of this ethnic district, the city is, effectively, the local neighbourhood. As Orleans observes, these maps demonstrate the existence of different 'social worlds' which, though they may touch, rarely interpenetrate.

Restricted mobility of women with young children

Cutting across limitations of income, to some degree, are the constraints imposed by the *social role* of some groups in society. Women with young children, in particular, show especially clearly the impact of time-space constraints on accessibility to sources of well-being. In most families in Western urban-industrial society the socially derived role of the woman is essentially child-centred. She has the primary responsibility for bringing up, and caring for, the children. Tivers (1977) coined the term 'gender-role constraint' to describe this role. Operating through the triad of time-space constraints it produces very limited spatial mobility. Thus, women with young children generally have limited access to many sources of well-being. To illustrate this, we use two imaginary cases.

First, consider the case of the married woman with a husband in full-time employment and with two children, one at primary school, the other at nursery school. The family has one car but this is used by the husband to travel to work. As Figure 5.31 shows, the combination of capability and coupling constraints creates a particularly fragmented time-space prism for the wife. The outer bounds of the prism – her potential geographical scale of interaction – are set by her means of movement and by the times (and places) she has to spend in regular activities associated with her particular role. In Figure 5.31, there are four periods in the day when she has to be at home but her home-based activity is broken up by the need to travel to the two schools attended by the children and to shop.

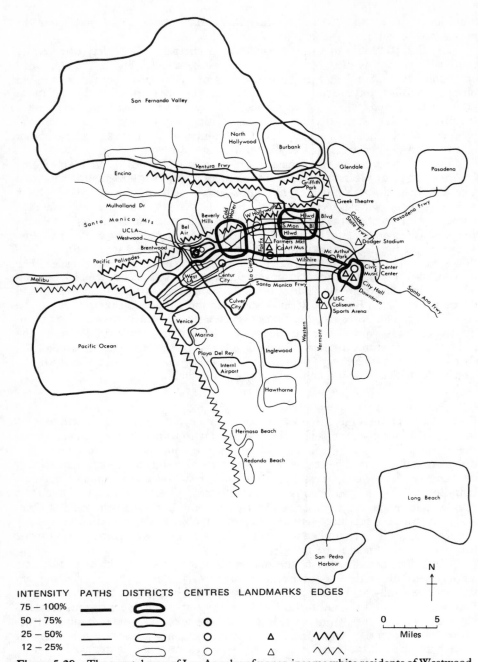

Figure 5.28   The mental map of Los Angeles of upper-income white residents of Westwood

Source: P. Orleans (1973) Differential cognition of urban residents: effects of social scale on mapping, in
R.M. Downs & D. Stea (eds) *Image and Environment,* London: Edward Arnold, figure 7.4.

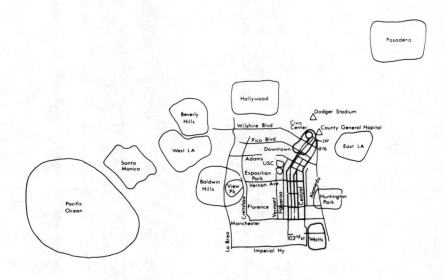

Figure 5.29   The mental map of Los Angeles of black residents of Avalon

Source: P. Orleans (1973) Differential cognition of urban residents: effects of social scale on mapping, in R.M. Downs & D. Stea (eds) *Image and Environment*, London: Edward Arnold, figure 7.2.

INTENSITY	PATHS	DISTRICTS	CENTRES	LANDMARKS	EDGES
75 – 100%					
50 – 75%	——			▲	
25 – 50%	——				
12 – 25%	——	⬭	○	△	

N

0   5
Miles

City Hall   Union Station
Brooklyn Ave
Downtown   1st st
Little Tokyo
6th st
Bus Depot

Figure 5.30   The mental map of Los Angeles of Spanish residents of Boyle Heights

Source: P. Orleans (1973) Differential cognition of urban residents: effects of social scale on mapping, in R.M. Downs & D. Stea (eds) *Image and Environment*, London: Edward Arnold, figure 7.3.

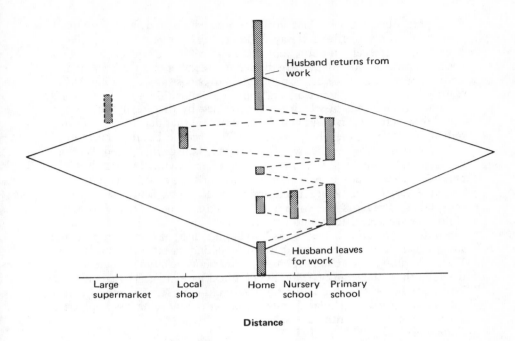

Figure 5.31   The daily time-space prism of a married woman with young children

After the husband leaves for work in the family car, the wife takes the older child to his primary school and on the way back home she delivers the younger child to nursery school. She then returns home to perform the domestic chores, including preparing lunch. After a relatively short time she has to collect both children from their respective schools and take them home for lunch. When lunch is over, the older child has to be taken back to primary school for the afternoon session. During this time, the wife and younger child do some essential shopping. However, scope for this activity is restricted by the need to get back in time to collect the older child from school. This restricts shopping opportunities to the small local store. The big supermarket, with its greater variety and lower prices, is beyond the woman's daily range.

It is clear from this imaginary case that the coupling constraints associated with the woman's social role, together with her lack of a car, greatly restrict the geographical scale at which she can operate. Possession of a car would obviously make a considerable difference, enabling an involvement in a wider range of activities. But the gender-role constraint would still exert an extremely powerful influence. The constraints are even greater for those women with young children who have to take paid employment outside the home in order to sustain the family. Figure 5.32 shows the case of an unmarried or divorced working mother. Palm and Pred describe her situation as follows:

Imagine Jane, an unmarried woman living with only her one child, age two, in an apartment building (A). Jane cannot leave her home before a certain

time, partly because her child must be dressed and fed, and principally because the only nearby full-day child-care service (D) does not begin operating until a certain hour. Jane must also return to her residence by a specified time in order to prepare dinner and feed her child at a reasonable hour. Let us say that she has two job offers to choose among (W_1 and W_2). Both jobs involve the same working hours and fall within her 'daily prism,' the outer dimensions of which are determined by the maximum average speed at which she can move and the assumption that her time is allocated only to travel. W_2 is the job she would prefer to accept, because it is more of a challenge and offers higher wages. However, Jane cannot accept W_2 both because she would get to work too late after leaving her child at the child-care centre and because after leaving work she could not get back to the child-care centre before its closing time. Not untypically, while W_1 is acceptable as regards the coupling constraints created by the available child-care service, it leaves no time for shopping or other errands unless Jane either can squeeze these tasks into her lunch-hour subprism (note the small prisms extending outward from the cylinders representing W_1 and W_2) or is willing to set back her child's dinner hour to a time which is likely to make the child cranky. This hypothetical case suggests that in some instances the best locations for full-day child-care services may be near spatially clustered workplaces, rather than at the more or less haphazard sites in or near residential areas.
Palm and Pred (1978), pp.103–104.

Palm and Pred provide several other examples to illustrate the situation of women in society. Each one demonstrates a varying degree of constraint on physical mobility and, hence, upon access to sources of well-being. Women with young children are particularly constrained in their range of choice, largely because they tend to have lower access to a car and also because of the various coupling constraints associated with children's needs. Where women with young children also have to take paid employment the constraints are particularly severe. Both the variety of employment opportunities and the general accessibility to 'goods' is severely restricted.

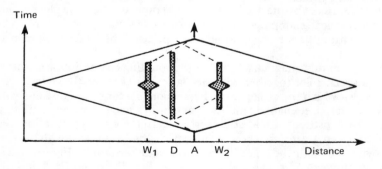

Figure 5.32   The daily time-space prism of an unmarried woman with young children

Source: R. Palm & A. Pred (1978) A time-geographic perspective on problems of inequality for women, in D. Lanegran & R. Palm (eds) *An Invitation to Geography*, 2nd edn, New York: McGraw Hill, figure 7.3.

The social and time-space constraints operating on women with children are reflected in much more limited geographical patterns of social relationships compared with those of their husbands. The male parent most likely spends five days out of seven at his place of work. He may develop social relationships with work colleagues which may also involve him in interest communities rather than place communities. As the geographical separation between home and workplace has increased, such a development is ever more likely. For the female parent, especially one with preschool children, the tie to the local neighbourhood is virtually total. Visits to local shops, to play groups, to neighbours with children of similar age form the bulk of her social network. Everitt's (1976) study of the spatial activity patterns of a sample of husbands and wives in Los Angeles bears this out. He found that 63 percent of the wives' activities occurred within five miles of home. The same percentage for the husbands' activities was not reached for almost nine miles. Not surprisingly, therefore, the husbands' mental maps of areas they knew well were far more extensive than those of the wives (Figure 5.33).

The urban poor and women with young children are just two examples of the variations which exist in the accessibility of different social groups to sources of

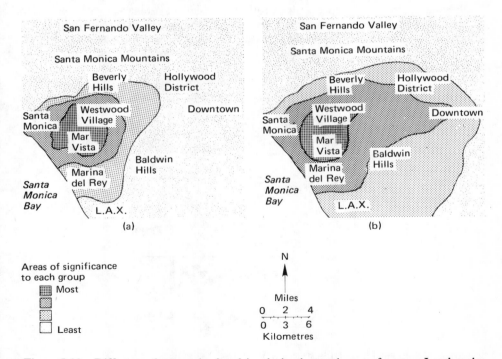

Figure 5.33   Differences between husbands' and wives' mental maps of western Los Angeles

Source: J.C. Everitt (1976) Community and propinquity in a city, *Annals of the Association of American Geographers*, 66, figures 4 and 5.

well-being. Accessibility to 'goods' varies substantially between individuals in modern society. In part, this reflects differences between people in their access to the means of travelling between home and the supply points of public and private goods. In effect, we can recognize a hierarchy of levels of accessibility to sources of well-being. Figure 5.34 shows three such levels. At the top-most level is the affluent 'jet-setter' who, either by virtue of wealth or skill (plus expense account), has the capacity to seek out sources of well-being on the widest possible geographical scale. He or she can operate across all the scales shown, from local to international. At the other end of the accessibility scale is the person with very low mobility, locked into highly localized geographical areas and dependent upon the quality of resources in that local area for his or her well-being. Between these two extremes lies a whole variety of individual experience.

Thus, although the *general* level of personal mobility is higher today than it has ever been, not all individuals have shared equally in this increase. Within our generally transport-rich society there is a substantial proportion of people who are *transport-poor*. Their problems are exacerbated by the growth of private, at the expense of public, transport. The difficulty is not simply one of cost, although spiralling transport costs are a major problem for many people. In many instances there may be a *lack of availability* of transport at the times when it is needed – for example, to get to shops or doctor's clinics during their opening hours and to get back home again. This is a particularly serious problem in rural areas where access to a car may be the only way of surviving, even though car-ownership is a heavy financial burden. (This is the major reason for a higher level of car-ownership in rural areas: the car is often the lifeline in the face of contracting public transport services.)

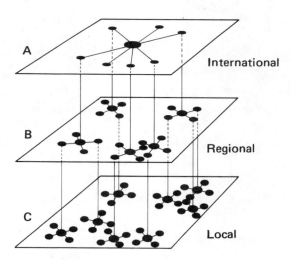

Figure 5.34   Levels of social interaction

Source: T. Hägerstrand (1967) A Monte Carlo simulation of diffusion, in W.L. Garrison & D.F. Marble (eds) *Quantitative Geography, Part 1: Economic and Cultural Topics,* Northwestern University Studies in Geography, 13, Northwestern University Press, figure 3.

However, it would be untrue to claim that all the variation in accessibility to 'goods' is caused by problems of physical mobility. The operation of various kinds of authority constraint is a powerful differentiating force. A person may live very close to a particular facility and yet be precluded from using it because he or she does not fulfil the 'entry requirements'. In many cases, this in effect means an inability to pay. But income may not be the only factor involved. Frequently there are more covert and subtle barriers to the use of facilities, particularly social and racial discrimination. Various 'screening' and 'filtering' devices are employed by groups in society to restrict entry. Whatever the individual detail, the result of the combined operation of capability, coupling and authority constraints, therefore, is very considerable variation in individual accessibility to goods. When, as is so often the case, the individual cannot move to a new residential location, his level of well-being is determined very largely by the quality of the local environment and its particular combination of 'goods' and 'bads'.

Response to change: locational conflict

The quality of a local environment rarely remains fixed for very long. Changes occur in the geographical distribution of 'goods' and 'bads' as both private and public organizations make locational decisions to open, close, expand or contract their operations in particular places. Since some places benefit and others suffer from such decisions, there is likely to be a *conflict* of interest, both between a local community and the decision-maker involved and also between one community and another, as each strives to attract the 'goods' and repel the 'bads'. We have already described the essential ingredients of such *locational* conflict. All facilities, whether salutary or noxious, create externality gradients and externality fields. As we showed in Figure 5.12, the impact of a facility is greatest at the source and declines with increasing distance away from that point. From a decision-maker's viewpoint,

> the noxious facility location decision requires a strategy for imposing a facility which reduces the locational satisfaction in one neighbourhood so that residents of other neighbourhoods in a jurisdiction may benefit . . . [on the other hand] . . . given the desirability of salutary facilities, the locational problem becomes one of denying competing sites.
> *Reynolds and Honey (1978), pp.144, 145.*

The problem is, of course, that many facilities generate effects which are good from one viewpoint but bad from another (Figure 5.15). For example, most people would agree that we need power stations to generate electricity but few would choose to locate one next door. All would agree that we need to find places to dump hazardous waste from industrial processes (assuming that such processes need to be used) – as long as the dump is not in *our* locality. Many people regard a new stretch of motorway as a 'good thing' – provided that it does not slice through *our* neighbourhood. Similarly, lots of people agree that there is some wasteful expenditure in the public sector and support measures to reduce it – as long as it does not result in the closure of *their* schools, *their* hospitals, *their* swimming pools, *their* libraries.

Hence, some degree of locational conflict is inherent in almost all public and private location decisions. Indeed, such spillovers are especially great in modern urban-industrial societies in which, as we pointed out earlier, 'everything effects everything else'. The relevant question at this point is how do people *respond* to such changes in their well-being. Obviously, much depends upon how serious the change is perceived to be. It also depends upon the extent to which people are prepared to join together with others in their locality to resist adverse changes in their local environment. Such willingness varies very considerably from place to place so that, in the case of noxious facilities,

> The decision maker is tempted to locate where resistance is low or, minimally, where resistance is less than elsewhere. . . . Locational costs would thus be concentrated in the few neighbourhoods receiving the facilities: likely, low income neighbourhoods with low levels of participation or political activity.
> *Reynolds and Honey (1978), p.144.*

To illustrate the kinds of response to locational conflict which individuals and groups may adopt let us take a hypothetical case: a plan by a local authority to build a motorway or freeway through part of a metropolitan area.*The new road would greatly improve the flow of traffic through a congested part of the city and, therefore, would benefit the users of the route – commuters, motorists travelling from one side of the city to the other, freight carriers and so on. It may even be possible to calculate some aggregate user benefit in monetary terms. On the other hand, the specific route chosen would involve the demolition of some residential property. It would also slice through some neighbourhoods, fragmenting them both physically and socially, creating noise and atmospheric pollution and lowering property values. Although some local residents might well benefit from using the road, most would not, particularly as it is a limited-access route. Assuming this kind of scenario, what alternative strategies do local residents have to a threat to their local environment which would materially reduce their well-being? Reference back to Figure 5.11 shows that there are two broad options available: *to move or to stay*.

The option to relocate – to move house to a different neighbourhood altogether – is perhaps the most obvious response. It is often pointed out that, in the United States especially, frequent residential change is endemic. People are said to move house with very great regularity. Several writers have argued that increasing numbers of Americans have fewer and fewer strong ties with particular places. Webber (1963, 1964), for example, suggested that the traditional community based on ties to a particular geographical locality was being superseded by the *non-place community*. More and more people, he argued, were involved in interest communities rather than in place communities and, as such, interacted over very extensive geographical ranges. To that degree, their involvement in happenings in particular places might well be lessened. In similar vein, Janowitz wrote of the emergence of the *community of limited liability* as an expression of a very loose allegiance to a particular place (Williams 1971). Williams goes on to observe that

> most urban dwellers vote by moving van, not by ballot box.
> *Williams (1971), p.35.*

---

*This is the kind of land-use conflict which has generated much attention. For detailed examples of this type and others the reader is referred to Wolpert, Mumphrey and Seley (1972), Cox (1978, part 2), Ley and Mercer (1980).

But, as we have observed at several points, not everybody has an equal propensity to relocate, whether over short or long distances. For those with the right credit-rating, access to mortgage funds or other keys to freedom in housing choice there would, perhaps, be little difficulty. For others, more constrained by their social and financial position, the freedom to make such a response might not exist. In another sense, those whose occupation constrains them to a particular location within the urban area might find themselves less free to respond or, at best, they might be faced with additional losses of income from the costs associated with commuting. Thus the relocation strategy can be highly socially selective in its availability to households.

The alternative to moving is to stay (Figure 5.11). But such a decision may be either involuntary or voluntary. It may reflect a fatalistic acceptance of the proposed urban motorway on the grounds that individuals cannot do much about 'it' anyway. But the alternative to 'stay and accept' is to 'stay and try to do something', a strategy which generally means some form of *collective* response. An increasingly common feature of modern life is the emergence of the local action group. In some cases, such groups may have a more or less permanent existence in keeping a watch on local matters. The residents' association is one example. It is the articulated expression of a place community concerned with its own backyard.

However, most action groups are formed for specific purposes, generally to fight some particular proposal (such as the urban motorway in our hypothetical example). They are *coalitions* rather than communities (Williams 1971). There is enormous variation in the propensity of neighbourhoods to create collective action groups. To some extent this variation is related to income differences between areas and, therefore, to such important assets as education, articulateness and professional skills. Table 5.20 shows a clear tendency for community involvement to be greater in higher- than in lower-income groups. In general, then, middle- and upper-income neighbourhoods are more likely to engage in effective collective organization to prevent the motorway from being built than are lower-income neighbourhoods. But there are exceptions. Strong local associations do exist in some low-income areas and are able to muster support to fight adverse changes. For the most part, though, organized opposition to adverse environmental change is likely to be less apparent and/or less effective in lower-income neighbourhoods. Hence the tendency noted above for noxious facilities to be concentrated in areas of low resistance.

Assuming that some form of local opposition is organized to fight the urban motorway proposals, what kinds of action can it engage in? Dear and Long (1978) have identified three possible strategies (other than relocation and resigned acceptance). The first of these – 'voice' – is the most common response. It involves such activities as collecting signatures for a petition, writing letters to and lobbying key people and organizations, organizing protest meetings. If a referendum were held, it would be the voice of the ballot box. A second strategy is 'formal participation', which involves participation in the planning process itself. Local information meetings to enable the airing of views and formal public inquiries are common examples. In a public inquiry, for example, local organizations have a forum in which to give evidence and to contest the need for the motorway or to argue the unsuitability of the proposed route. As Dear and Long point out, formal participation tends to be initiated by the planners of the change whereas 'voice' strategies are initiated by the local community itself. (Their other strategy – 'illegal action' – is more difficult to generalize.)

Table 5.20   *Relationship between income and propensity to engage in community activism*

Question:	'Have you ever worked with others in this community to solve any community problem?'
Income ($)	**% replying Yes**
less than 6000	14
6000–9999	17
10,000–14,999	25
15,000–24,999	39
More than 25,000	47

Question:	'Have you ever taken part in forming a new group or a new organization to try to solve a community problem?'
Income ($)	**% replying Yes**
less than 6000	10
6000–9999	10
10,000–14,999	13
15,000–24,999	19
More than 25,000	28

Source: K.R. Cox (1979) *Location and Public Problems*, Oxford: Blackwell, table 14.1

In the case of our hypothetical urban motorway, as in virtually all locational conflicts, there is a basic dilemma which exists whatever the form of local action. If a road (or an airport or a power station) is to be built at all, then it has to be located *somewhere*. Powerful local opposition may prevent its being located in neighbourhood A but that merely has the effect of shifting it to neighbourhood B. The residents of one neighbourhood have preserved their well-being but at the expense of residents of another. It is the classic zero-sum game: one side's winnings are the other side's losses. Thus, locational conflict raises very big issues of how decisions made for collective benefit are to be reconciled with the often inevitable costs which are imposed upon some members of society. In many cases, the conflict is resolved in such a way that the powerful win and the weak lose. In geographical terms, this has often meant the further deterioration of some neighbourhoods as they become the spoil heaps of other people's actions. At the extreme,

> The slum is the catch-all for the losers, and in the competitive struggle for the cities' goods the slum areas are also the losers in terms of schools, jobs, garbage collection, street lighting, libraries, social services and whatever else is communally available but always in short supply.
> *Sherrard (1968), p.1, quoted in Harvey (1973), p.79.*

DEPRIVED PLACES OR DEPRIVED PEOPLE?

Our basic theme in this chapter has been that a person's well-being is the outcome of two opposed elements: accessibility to 'goods' and proximity to 'bads'. Both 'goods' and 'bads' are provided in specific geographical locations and have particular externality fields in which the impact, whether positive or negative, generally declines with distance away from the source. The quantity and quality of sources of well-being vary substantially from place to place, both between and within individual territories and jurisdictions. People live in particular places and derive most of their needs and wants from their local environments. Their accessibility to the location of private and public goods is mediated through the interlocking set of time-space constraints. Over time, changes occur in the geographical distribution of goods and bads, changes which frequently generate locational conflict and force people to adjust either by moving to a new residential location or by some kind of collective response.

To a considerable degree, therefore, *where* one lives is an important influence on one's quality of life and on the opportunities available for enhancing personal well-being. But this does not necessarily mean that a particular geographical location is the sole *cause* of a particular level of well-being. For example, a poor family may live in a dilapidated street in a run-down area of a large city, a small town or a country village. However, the family's geographical location is not necessarily the *initial* cause of its poverty. The causal link may run the other way: the family's poverty may well be the cause of its occupying that particular geographical location. In particular, the family may live in that particular street because of its limited bargaining power in the housing market. But although geographical location, in this case, may not be the initial cause of the family's poverty, the very fact of living there is likely to *reinforce* the family's level of deprivation. Most likely, the quantity and quality of 'goods' within the family's reach in that locality will be poor. We mentioned this problem of isolating cause and effect – especially of identifying the contribution of geographical factors – in Chapter One. At this point, we return to it in the context of the bottom end of the well-being spectrum. Two questions are posed. First, to what extent is deprivation geographically concentrated into particular areas? Second, how far is deprivation essentially a place problem or a non-place (people) problem?

There is no doubt that we can identify certain geographical concentrations of deprivation. Most obviously, these occur in the *inner cities* of metropolitan areas. In the case of the United States, the *Comparative Atlas of America's Great Cities* (Abler and Adams 1976) contains numerous detailed maps to substantiate this. Here we present just two examples. Figure 5.35 maps the distribution of personal incomes within the Boston SMSA. The lighter shades dominated by eastern Boston represent the residences of individuals with less that $2500 annual income in 1970, a figure which by any standards brings them close to the poverty line. With progression up the income ladder the shadings darken to reach a peak in the T-shaped 'cocktail belt'. The stem runs from Brookline to Weston and the crossbar through the line of towns to the west of Route 128 – Lincoln, Weston, Wellesley and Dedham. Boston has retained the affluent in Beacon Hill and shows further signs of a return to the inner areas of some members of the affluent. These are particularly childless, professional couples seeking a town-house in a 'neighbourhood of character' close to their cultural haunts. Nevertheless, the inner-urban concentration of low incomes is clearly marked, as is the focus on the predominantly black neighbourhoods. In fact, almost 30 percent of Boston's poverty population is black, while Hispanics make up a further 6.3 percent.

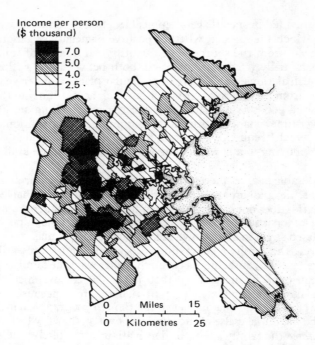

Figure 5.35   Personal income variation within Boston

Source: Reprinted with permission from J.S. Adams (ed) (1976) *Contemporary Metropolitan America, 1: Cities of the Nation's Historic Metropolitan Core*, Cambridge, Mass: Ballinger Publishing Co., figure 16.

New York-northern New Jersey, despite its well-known cluster of the affluent in mid-town Manhattan, has a clearly marked core of urban poverty households (Figure 5.36). While the peaks of suburban wealth appear in the outer reaches of the SMSA in areas such as Westchester, Northern Nassau and Passaic counties, the troughs of suburban poverty pervade Harlem, the Bronx, Queen's County and Newark and eastern New Jersey. One-quarter of all blacks and one-third of all Hispanics in the New York SMSA live below the poverty line.

To provide maps of income distribution in other American cities would be to repeat substantially the same theme – inner-area concentration of poverty – with only minor variations produced by particular local circumstances. Similarly, mapping many other distributions, for example, the location of the elderly, blacks, one-parent families, would show a close correspondence with patterns of low incomes. Similarly, the incidence of old housing, poor environmental conditions, higher levels of mortality and disease show the same spatial characteristic: a strong concentration in the low-income inner-city areas. Looked at through any lens, therefore, be it spatial or social, there are strong clusters of the poor within almost every American city.*

---

*Smith (1973, 1977, 1979) provides some detailed case studies of urban deprivation in United States cities.

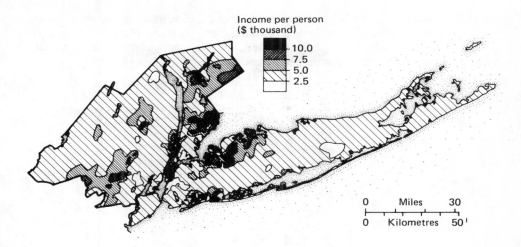

Figure 5.36   Personal income variation within New York–northern New Jersey

Source: R. Abler and J.S. Adams (1976) *A Comparative Atlas of America's Great Cities*, Washington DC: Association of American Geographers and The University of Minnesota Press, p.43.

The strongest spatial concentration of deprivation in American cities is to be found within the ethnic ghettos. As we saw in Chapter Four, the residential segregation of black people in particular, but also of other ethnic groups, is a pronounced feature of the American city. Ghetto areas share many common features with other areas of deprivation – low incomes, poor housing, inadequate services and so on. However, what marks the ghetto apart as something distinctive is its especially *restrictive* character. It is

> a region characterized by limited freedom – freedom in terms of the alternative choices and opportunities available to residents – alternatives, choices and opportunities in jobs, housing, education and health care and social interaction.
> *Henderson and Ledebur (1972), p.162.*

Henderson and Ledebur view the ghetto as being driven by a cumulative and circular causal mechanism of the kind often applied to regional development processes. In Figure 5.37 the process begins with *segregation* both economically and racially. The poor and the racial minorities become disenfranchised in the job, housing and consumer markets. The associated deterioration in the physical environment and the impact of changing conditions for the location of industry further accelerates decline through the *out-migration of white families and the suburbanization of industry*. The 'vicious circle of poverty' begins to become exaggerated for the segregated groups as a combination of low incomes, poor education opportunities, low labour productivity, unemployment and a deteriorating physical environment conspire to *reinforce the poverty condition*. Falling property values, the appearance of 'separate and unequal neighbourhoods', the declining tax-base following the loss of industrial enterprise give a further twist to the depressed physical appearance of the ghetto areas as property becomes blighted, crime and vandalism increase and the areas begin to acquire a 'hostile' image. Closing the circle is the return to the ghetto as a 'sink' for those who do not have the freedom either economically or in housing choice to escape its deteriorating living conditions.

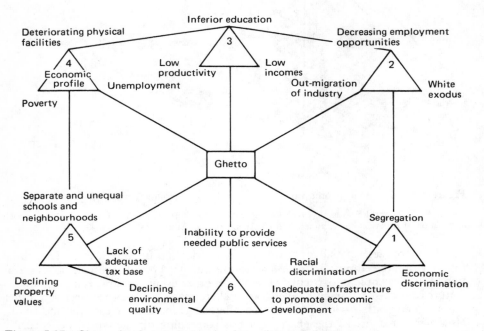

Figure 5.37 Ghetto development as a circular and cumulative process

Source: W.L. Henderson & L.C. Ledebur (1972) *Urban Economics: Processes and Problems*, New York: Wiley, figure 9.1.

In the context of our earlier discussion of externality patterns in the city, it is hard to think of a more consistently negative constellation of spillovers than those that exist in the poverty areas of the inner city. Physical blight, pollution, the intrusion of noisy highways and commuter rail-lines, high crime rates, inadequate public facilities, all conspire to provide substantial net reductions in real income among those with least freedom either to move away from them or to organize politically in such a way as to deflect their worst effects. For those with sufficient resources, movement away becomes imperative and this in itself becomes another turn of the screw in the reinforcement of the ghetto condition.

Hence, beyond a certain point the worsening of the ghetto syndrome becomes a product of the reasonable, rational and right-minded choices of individual residents. But the spillover effect of such choices, where no social bargains are made with those left behind, is to provide yet another empty property for the vandals and yet another source of fear and insecurity for those whose properties lie adjacent to it. The individual choices are thus essentially 'rational' – the problems lie in the nature of the social bargaining system and its 'one-way' nature along the class or status scale.

Though perhaps less extreme in intensity, geographical concentration of deprived people in inner cities is also characteristic of British cities.* We referred earlier to Holtermann's study of multiple deprivation in our discussion of well-being at the interurban scale. Holtermann concluded that

> on both single indicators and combinations of indicators it was found that the E.D.'s with extensive levels of deprivation generally occur within the conurbations, and that *the local authorities making up the central cores of the conurbations contain proportionately more of them than the rest of the conurbations. Severe deprivation is found both in the inner areas dominated by private rental accommodation, and on council estates, some in more peripheral locations.*
> Holtermann (1975), p.44 (present authors' emphasis).

However, Holtermann's study shows that deprivation is perhaps less strongly concentrated geographically than many have claimed. More specifically, Moseley argues that

> the very nature of the attempts to identify localized areas with severe social and economic problems, which were made in the early/mid 1970s, predetermined the emergence of certain *urban* areas as being most problematic. . . . Indeed our very mental image of poverty is an urban one – a picture of physical squalor – and this may be quite inadequate for a truly comprehensive view.
> Moseley (1980), p.6.

Moseley demonstrates that there may well be as many people suffering deprivation in rural areas as in the inner areas of cities,

> but *what* they are suffering may well be rather different and it is clear that the rural deprived suffer much less visibly than do their urban counterparts, both in the sense that numerically they constitute somewhat smaller proportions of their local population, and in the sense that they are geographically much more scattered.
> Moseley (1980), p.23.

Figure 5.38 shows that the outer rural areas and the inner-urban areas share some common problems which arise from the broad changes which we have been examining in this book. Both suffer from the changes which have been occurring in the demand for labour as economic circumstances change and as business corporations restructure their operations. Both suffer from problems associated with selective out-migration, with low levels of investment in public and private services and with housing markets which 'lock in' the poor to inadequate accommodation. The fact that these problems exist in both urban and rural areas and are generated by broad economic, political and social forces suggests that these are not specifically *place*

---

*The literature on the British inner-city problem has assumed avalanche proportions in the last few years. Kirby (1978) provides a concise but comprehensive summary of the issues. The Social Science Research Council Inner Cities Working Party (1980) has published a set of eleven reports which deal in detail with the social, economic and political facets of the inner-city problem. Jones (1979) has edited a series of individual essays exploring particular inner-city themes.

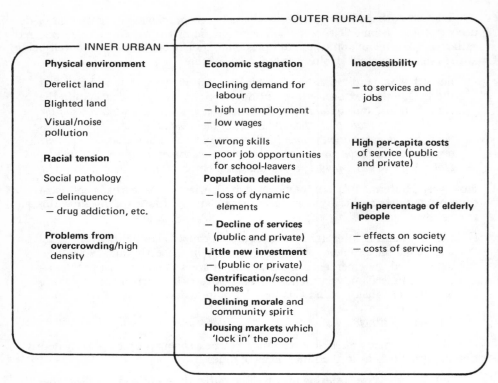

Figure 5.38 Overlapping sets of problems in urban and rural areas

Source: M.J. Moseley (1980) Rural development and its relevance to the inner city debate, *Social Science Research Council, Inner City in Context, Paper 9,* figure 5.

problems. Rather they are problems which particularly affect *people* in particularly vulnerable circumstances. For the most part these relate to inadequacies of skill and education, to inability to compete in the labour market. They relate also to circumstances of discrimination and of a lack of political clout. However, over and above the problems common to both urban and rural areas are some which are distinctive to one or the other. These are the problems which arise specifically from the characteristics of place and relate to the state of the physical environment in urban areas and the problems of inaccessibility in rural areas. They relate to problems of racial tension and overcrowding in urban areas and to the problems of the elderly in rural areas. Thus, although deprivation can be found in some specific geographical concentrations, particularly in inner cities, it is far less spatially concentrated than a focus on urban areas alone would suggest. Even in urban areas themselves, deprived people are not totally confined to the inner cities.

This does not mean, of course, that geographical location is unimportant to well-being. What it means is that it must be set within the broader context of the social, economic and political forces operating in society. More specifically, it means that policies which aim to alleviate the problems of the deprived members of society must recognize the subtlety of the situation. The problem with area-based policies, such as those associated with the Inner Cities Programme in the United Kingdom or the Model Cities Programmes in the United States, is that in focusing on particular *places* they do not necessarily solve the problems of the *people* living there.* They tend to concentrate on the physical environment – the bricks and mortar, the roads and the houses – on the assumption that improving people's living environment will solve their problems. They also, by definition, leave out those deprived people who live outside the designated areas. It is not that such schemes are unnecessary – they are very important – but they are not sufficient. They do not tackle the source of most deprived peoples' difficulties, which is their marginal position in both the labour and the housing markets. In particular, without access to the means of making a decent living or to appropriate support services, no amount of tinkering with the physical environment will solve the problem. To reiterate an example we have used already, simply providing cheap and efficient transport for inner-city residents to travel to work will not, in itself, solve their employment problem. To do this would involve retraining and re-educating for those jobs for which a demand exists.

Thus, the relationship between well-being and geography is highly complex. Where a person lives certainly has a profound influence on the quality of life he or she is able to lead, but the link between geography and well-being is less straightforward than is often supposed. On the other hand, to try to understand how and why peoples' life-chances vary without considering the geographical dimension is to consider only a part of the story. There is, indeed, a good deal of truth in the statement by Higbee with which we began an earlier section of this chapter:

> there is no such thing as being born equal. It depends upon whether the address is good or bad.
> *Higbee (1970), pp.109–110.*

---

*Eyles (1979) provides a useful review of area-based policies in British urban areas including Housing Action Areas, General Improvement Areas, Educational Priority Areas as well as those arising from the 1977 Inner Cities legislation.

Postscript

Where do we go from here?

Our aim in this book has been to provide a snapshot of contemporary living in modern Western society. Inevitably, we have been forced to simplify greatly what is a highly complex and dynamic picture. Our approach has been to identify what seem to us to be the dominant features of today's society at both the macro- and the micro-scales and to explore how these interact to produce a constellation of 'choices within constraints' which differ both between different groups in society and between different geographical locations. At the macro-scale, the dominant features explored in Chapter Two were the pervasiveness of the giant organization, with its massive bureaucracy, in both the private and the public spheres; the volatile nature of modern technology; and the changing scale and form of the urban environment in which the majority of us live.

These major dimensions interlock in complex and dynamic ways to influence the quality of people's lives. A major aim of this book has been to emphasize at least some of these basic connections. For most of us, access to many of the 'goods' and 'bads' of the world derives from how much disposable income we possess. This, in turn, reflects the kind of job we, or those on whom we depend, hold. Only a very small proportion of the population is able to live on the basis of accumulated wealth. A 'good job', therefore, is one of the keys to a 'good life', albeit not the only one. It is for this reason that we looked in some detail at the ways in which labour markets work in general and, more specifically, at how they operate to create geographical variations in job opportunities.

Housing of a size and quality appropriate to individual and family circumstances is one of the most basic of life's needs, but 'appropriate' housing is not equally available to all. The level, and especially the stability, of a person's income is the critical determinant of access to housing, particularly owner-occupation. Thus, the housing market and the labour market are very closely related, both functionally and geographically. Taken together, they represent the twin pivots of access to well-being in modern Western society for the majority of people. The resulting specific geographical location to which families are 'allocated' through the interaction of these two highly imperfect markets provides a dual key to well-being. The home base itself provides both accessibility to 'goods' and proximity to 'bads'. To a significant degree, this is reflected in housing valuation, ensuring that those with the greatest 'freedom' to choose by virtue of their income are offered the best choices. Indeed, the housing market becomes the prime means by which the 'goods' and 'bads', particularly of urban living, become distributed.

Implicit in the processes we have described is the *dual* role of geographical space. In the operation of labour and of housing markets, in the processes generating individual well-being, geographical space is both an input and an output. Distance and relative location, particularly their influence on the movement of materials, information and people, are the most obvious expression of the influence of geographical space upon economic, social and political processes. In turn, all such processes have a geographical output – a particular pattern of employment, housing, sources of 'goods' and 'bads' – which represents the physical surface of opportunities and constraints on which people live out their daily lives. As we have tried to show, this surface is both spatially uneven at any one point in time and also continually changing over time. For some, the processes of change may bring benefits, for others disadvantages. Faced with change or with the threat of change, 'ability to react' is critical to the prospects of maintaining life quality. Once again, such capabilities will tend to vary in accordance with social status.

A current preoccupation is the extent to which change is both more rapid and also less predictable than in the recent past. In drawing this book to a close, therefore, it is appropriate to pose the question 'where do we go from here?' and to look very briefly – and very broadly – at some general aspects of possible 'alternative futures'. Futurology is a big industry but one with an enormous diversity of products, ranging from dogmatic prediction at one end of the spectrum to wishful thinking at the other. Most commonly, however, the futures debate revolves around various alternative 'scenarios' of a possible future world. These scenarios are based upon whole series of assumptions, although these are not always made as explicit as they might be.

One of the most useful recent attempts to evaluate possible alternative world futures is that of the Science Policy Research Unit at the University of Sussex in England.* In our introductory chapter we noted two main problems facing all societies in their efforts to provide for their material needs: the problem of production itself and the problem of distributing the fruits of production among the members of society. This suggests that alternative futures need to be seen in terms of both of these basic dimensions and not only in terms of production. This, in effect, is what the SPRU does. They identify four possible profiles of the world's future:

1 A high-growth, more equal world

2 A low-growth, more equal world

3 A high-growth, less equal world

4 A low-growth, less equal world

From a moral standpoint, alternatives 3 and 4 can be discounted if we believe in the need to reduce the massive disparities in living standards which exist in today's world. Obviously, it would be easier to achieve a more equal world in circumstances of economic growth than in circumstances of economic stagnation.

Whether or not acceptable rates of economic growth can be achieved in the future is one of the main issues which divides the futurologists. The SPRU view is that such a growth rate can be achieved, despite the problems of food, energy and raw material supply. They do acknowledge, however, that the problem of energy

---

* A detailed analysis of the 'great debate' over alternative world futures together with the SPRU's own profiles of the future are presented in Freeman and Jahoda (1978). A less technical interpretation of this work is provided by Gribbin (1979).

supply is a particularly intractable one. An alternative view is pressed by writers such as Frank (1980) who regard the current tribulations of the world economy as indicative of the arrival of the 'crisis of capitalism'. Cataloguing the steady fall in the rate of company profit since the mid-1960s Frank sees the current trends as emerging from the need to recreate the reserve army of the unemployed and for capital and the state to collude in restructuring industry as a means of restoring profit. For those who espouse this viewpoint, the energy crisis is less significant than that which (inevitably in their view) derives from the political economy of capitalism.

Thus, although there are undoubtedly outer limits to the availability of key resources, constraints on achieving a more just distribution may well be primarily human rather than physical. To some extent, then, one answer to the question of 'where do we go from here?' is that we go where we collectively want to go assuming, of course, that the power exists to translate wants into achievements. However, simply to argue that the issue is merely one of collective will is to gloss over immense obstacles. As we observed in our discussion of locational conflict in Chapter Five, we may agree that a particular course of action is socially or economically desirable – as long as our own existing position is not adversely affected. It is very difficult to see how appropriate consensus can be reached in the face of the vetoing power of different interest groups, whether these are nation states or powerful groups within individual nations. This is the key issue explored in the United States context by Thurow in his book *The Zero Sum Society*.

Whichever general scenario evolves at the world scale in the coming decades, whether world economic growth is fast or slow, whether conscious attempts are made to reduce international disparities in material well-being, it seems certain that the lives and livelihoods of those of us living in Western urban-industrial societies will undergo considerable change. We have already seen in Chapter Three something of the shape of things to come in the world of work. In particular, manufacturing jobs are in steady decline – for men, for low-skilled operatives, for the residents of older cities and some previously powerful industrial regions. Hard-learned skills are becoming obsolete more quickly, a trend promoting a generally defensive attitude among labour unions dedicated to the preservation of their members' interests. The new, less demanding skills are being supplied most readily by an emergent female workforce, often in rural and suburban locations where the absence of union influence provides a growing attraction to companies. To this has been added the service boom in a 'positional economy' where demands for health, education and leisure services change the labour requirements of production. Again, this is a trend which, on the production side, has favoured well-educated professionals, the central regions, the wealthy suburbs and the metropolitan capitals. For those without access to the sector's well-paid white-collar jobs, admission fees and the activities of the gatekeepers also deny access to the desired services of the 'leisure society'.

Thus, for labour, both supply and demand conditions have been changing sharply in recent years. Vastly to oversimplify the outcome of a complex process, it can be suggested that we have been exchanging manufacturing jobs for service jobs, male jobs for female jobs and part-time jobs for full-time jobs. In all this, the allocation of the disbenefits has been to particular age and social groups and to particular locations, producing a disruptive 'stirring' to which some can respond and others cannot. The young are seeing opportunities to join the world of adult work shrinking before their eyes. The elderly are seeing a world of rapid urban change involving the breakdown of family and community ties, of inflation cutting into their fixed incomes and of a decline in essential services as public expenditures are cut. Within the occupational structure it has been the unskilled manual worker who has suffered most, now often dependent on his wife's part-time job for security. Spatially, it has been the traditional manufacturing region and the older industrial cities that have experienced the coldest wind of change. Project into them the young, the old, the black, the unskilled and the loading of the dice of life-chances becomes more readily apparent.

A major problem facing our society in the future, therefore, may well be the need to cope with permanently high levels of unemployment. Such levels are likely to vary substantially from place to place and between different social groups. An increasingly voiced view is that we need to redefine work in our society; to see it as not necessarily synonymous with employment in the formal, institutional economy but rather as tasks to be performed in the broadest sense. Pym, for example, argues that

> while the work to be done is limitless, the capacity of employment to undertake that work is not. . . . Many of the activities unsuited to employment are best undertaken by the *domestic economy* which covers the work of the self-employed, voluntary services, housewives and a host of home and community based activities.
> *Pym (1980), pp.224–225.*

His major point is that we are moving towards a dual economy in which the institutional economy is technologically intensive and employs fewer and fewer workers* while the domestic economy not only provides work for very large numbers of people but also is more satisfyingly integrated into the local community. Pym, like Gershuny, sees considerable evidence of the emergence of such a dual economy at the present time. However, it would be foolish to believe that such a change of emphasis from formal employment to informal work could be achieved easily. The social pressures to be formally employed and not unemployed are extremely powerful. Such deep-seated attitudes are likely to change only very slowly. Meanwhile, the shrinking of many types of employment, especially in manufacturing industry but also in some of the service occupations, will create very considerable individual distress and social tension.

Related to the question of the future of work in our society, but broader in scope, is the view that the whole *scale* of social and economic life needs to be changed if we are to cope with future problems, particularly those related to scarcity of energy and materials. This view is expressed most strongly in the work of E.F. Schumacher and the proponents of the 'small is beautiful' approach. Much of Schumacher's own work was concerned with urging appropriate technologies for Third World countries but his general approach has been adopted by a number of writers who regard our current scale of living and working as wasteful in economic, social and individual terms.

Schumacher's ideas have many critics on both theoretical and practical grounds,

---

* One estimate suggests that within the next thirty to fifty years the material needs of society could be produced by only about 10 percent of today's workforce working far fewer hours.

although few would argue that his ideas are totally irrelevant to our future. Indeed, the attempt to construct a scenario of Europe in the year 2000 by Hall and others leans heavily on Schumacher's general philosophy. They envisage the advanced industrial societies moving towards the re-organization of social and economic life into smaller-scale units which will be both conservative of energy and other materials and also based upon what Schumacher calls 'intermediate technologies'. They recognize, however, that such massive changes cannot occur over night. Indeed, they confess that they do not see how the changes will occur other than that recurring economic crises will stimulate a large-scale shift in values expressed through the political process.

Whether such a scenario comes about or not, change is bound to occur, and adjustment to change, whatever form it takes, will not be easy. For example, we are beginning to see the problems posed by our over-reliance on the private automobile as the dominant mode of transportation. In cities which have developed entirely in the automobile age – Los Angeles is the archetypal example – there is, at present, no alternative means of movement. More generally, we have emphasized the key role of specialization in the evolution of modern Western society but we may now be reaching the stage of *over*specialization in some respects. The problem with pervasive specialization is that it leads to a very high degree of interdependence, both functional and geographical. The problem with a high degree of interdependence is that it increases the degree of vulnerability to a breakdown or interruption in one part of the system. As Heilbroner points out,

> we are rich not as individuals but as members of a rich society, and our easy assumption of material sufficiency is actually only as reliable as the bonds that forge us into a social whole.
> *Heilbroner (1963), p.17.*

A feature of today's world, however, is that such interdependencies and, therefore, such vulnerabilities, operate on a *global* scale. The well-being of a family in inner city, suburb or small town does not depend simply on the quality of the local environment. Increasingly, it depends upon events occurring elsewhere, often many thousands of miles away. The quality of *our* lives thus cannot be considered separately from that of others. The quality of our future world depends upon our collective ability and desire to eradicate the severe inequalities which exist between different parts of the world as well as those which exist within the generally affluent urban-industrial societies. Indeed, it is the view of the Brandt Commission that the two are inextricably related. Thus, as we move into the uncharted waters of the 1980s it seems appropriate to end with some words of Willy Brandt in his introduction to the Commission's report:

> One should not give up the hope that problems created by men can also be solved by men.
> *Brandt (1980), p.10.*

Bibliography

ABLER, R. (1971) Distance, intercommunications and geography, *Proceedings of the Association of American Geographers*, 3, 1–4.

ABLER, R. (1975) Effects of space adjusting techologies on the human geography of the future. In R. Abler, D. Janelle, A. Philbrick, & J. Sommer (eds) *Human Geography in a Shrinking World*. North Scituate, Mass: Duxbury Press, chapter 3.

ABLER, R. (1975) Monoculture or miniculture? The impact of communications media on culture in space. In R. Abler, D. Janelle, A. Philbrick, & J. Sommer (eds) *Human Geography in a Shrinking World*. North Scituate, Mass: Duxbury Press, chapter 10.

ABLER, R. & J.S. ADAMS (1976) *A Comparative Atlas of America's Great Cities*. Washington DC: Association of American Geographers & University of Minnesota Press.

ADAMS, J.G.U. (1972) Life in a global village, *Environment and Planning*, 4, 381–394.

ADAMS, J.S. (1969) Directional bias in intra-urban migration, *Economic Geography*, 45, 302–323.

ADAMS, J.S. (1970) Residential structure of midwestern cities, *Annals of the Association of American Geographers*, 60, 37–62.

ADAMS, J.S. (ed) (1976) *Contemporary Metropolitan America, 1: Cities of the Nation's Historic Metropolitan Core*. Cambridge, Mass: Ballinger Publishing Co.

ADAMS, J.S. & K.A. GILDER (1976) Household location and the intra-urban migration. In D.T. Herbert & R.J. Johnston (eds) *Social Areas in Cities, Volume I: Spatial Processes and Form*. London: Wiley, pp.159–192.

AMBROSE, P. (1977) The determinants of urban land use change, *Open University Social Sciences Course D704, Section III, Unit 26*. Milton Keynes: Open University.

AMBROSE, P. & R. COLENUTT (1975) *The Property Machine*. Harmondsworth: Penguin.

ANDERSON, C.H. (1971) *Toward a New Sociology: A Critical Review*. Homewood, Illinois: Dorsey Press.

ARMSTRONG, R.B. (1972) *The Office Industry: Patterns of Growth*. Cambridge, Mass: MIT Press.

ARMSTRONG, R.B. (1979) National trends in office construction, employment and headquarters location in US metropolitan areas. In P.W. Daniels (ed.) *Spatial Patterns of Office Growth and Location*. Chichester: Wiley, chapter 3.

ATKINSON, A.B. (1975) *The Economics of Inequality*. London: Oxford University Press.

AVERITT, R.T. (1968) *The Dual Economy: The Dynamics of American Industry Structure*. New York: Norton.

BALE, J. (1978) Externality gradients, *Area*, 10, 334–336.

BARABBA, V.P. (1975) The national setting: regional shifts, metropolitan decline, and urban decay. In G. Sternlieb & J.W. Hughes (eds) *Post-Industrial America: Metropolitan Decline and Inter-Regional Job Shifts*. New Brunswick, NJ: Rutgers, pp.39–76.

BARBER, R.J. (1970) *The American Corporation*. London: MacGibbon and Kee.

BARNET, R.J. & R.E. MULLER (1975) *Global Reach: The Power of the Multinational Corporation.* London: Jonathan Cape.

BEDERMAN, S.H. & J.S. ADAMS (1974) Job accessibility and underemployment, *Annals of the Association of American Geographers,* 64, 378–386.

BELL, C. & H. NEWBY (1976) Community, communion, class and community action: the social sources of the new urban politics. In D.T. Herbert & R.J. Johnston (eds) *Social Areas in Cities, Volume II: Spatial Perspectives on Problems and Policies.* London: Wiley, pp.189–207.

BELL, D. (1974) *The Coming of Post-Industrial Society, A Venture in Social Forecasting.* London: Heinemann.

BERRY, B.J.L. (1970) The geography of the United States in the year 2000, *Transactions of the Institute of British Geographers,* 51, 21–53.

BERRY, B.J.L. (1972) Hierarchical diffusion: the basis of developmental filtering and spread in a system of growth centres. In N.M. Hansen (ed) *Growth Centres in Regional Economic Development.* New York: Free Press, pp.108–138.

BERRY, B.J.L. (1973) A paradigm for modern geography. In R.J. Chorley (ed) *Directions in Geography.* London: Methuen, chapter 1.

BERRY, B.J.L. (ed) (1976) *Urbanization and Counterurbanization.* Beverly Hills: Sage Publications.

BERRY, B.J.L. (1980) Inner city futures: an American dilemma revisited, *Transactions of the Institute of British Geographers, New Series,* 5, 1–28.

BERRY, B.J.L. & F.E. HORTON (eds) (1970) *Geographic Perspectives on Urban Systems.* Englewood Cliffs, NJ: Prentice Hall.

BERRY, B.J.L. & J.D. KASARDA (1977) *Contemporary Urban Ecology.* New York: Macmillan.

BERRY, B.J.L. & P.H. REES (1969) The factorial ecology of Calcutta, *American Journal of Sociology,* 74, 445–491.

BEYERS, W.B. (1979) Contemporary trends in the regional economic development of the United States, *Professional Geographer,* 31, 34–44.

BIRD, H. (1976) Residential mobility and preference patterns in the public sector of the housing market, *Transactions of the Institute of British Geographers, New Series,* 1, 20–33.

BLACKABY, F. (ed) (1979) *De-Industrialization.* London: Heinemann.

BOAL, F.W. (1969) Territoriality on the Shankill-Falls divide, Belfast, *Irish Geography,* 6, 30–50.

BOAL, F.W. (1970) Social space in the Belfast urban area. In N. Stevens & R. A. Glasscock (eds) *Irish Geographical Studies.* Belfast: Queen's University, pp.373–393.

BOAL, F.W. (1976) Ethnic residential segregation. In D.T. Herbert & R.J. Johnston (eds) *Social Areas in Cities, Volume I: Spatial Processes and Form.* London: Wiley, chapter 2.

BODDY, M.J. (1976) The structure of mortgage finance: building societies and the British social formation, *Transactions of the Institute of British Geographers, New Series,* 1, 58–71.

BOLLENS, J.C. & H.J. SCHMANDT (1975) *The Metropolis: Its People, Politics and Economic Life,* 3rd edn. New York: Harper & Row.

BORCHERT, J.R. (1978) Major control points in American economic geography, *Annals of the Association of American Geographers*, 68, 214–232.

BOULDING, K.E. (1953) Toward a general theory of growth, *Canadian Journal of Economics and Political Science*, 19, 326–340.

BOULDING, K.E. (1963) The death of the city: a frightened look at post-civilization. In O. Handlin & J. Burchard (eds) *The Historian and the City*. Cambridge, Mass: MIT Press, pp.133–145.

BOURNE, L.S. (ed) (1971) *Internal Structure of the City: Readings on Space and Environment*. New York: Oxford University Press.

BOURNE, L.S. (1976) Housing supply and housing market behaviour in residential development. In D.T. Herbert & R.J. Johnston (eds) *Social Areas in Cities, Volume I: Spatial Processes and Form*. London: Wiley, chapter 4.

BOURNE, L.S. (1976) Urban structure and land use decisions, *Annals of the Association of American Geographers*, 66, 531–547.

BOURNE, L.S. & M.I. LOGAN (1976) Changing urbanization patterns at the margin: the examples of Australia and Canada. In B.J.L. Berry (ed) *Urbanization and Counterurbanization*. Beverly Hills: Sage Publications, chapter 5.

BOURNE, L.S. & J.W. SIMMONS (eds) (1978) *Systems of Cities: Readings on Structure, Growth and Policy*. New York: Oxford University Press.

BOYCE, R.R. (1969) Residential mobility and its implications for urban spatial change, *Proceedings of the Association of American Geographers*, 1, 22–26. Reprinted in L.S. Bourne (ed) (1971) *Internal Structure of the City*. New York: Oxford University Press, pp.338–343.

BRANDT COMMISSION (1980) *North-South: A Programme for Survival*. Report of the Independent Commission on International Development Issues. London: Pan Books.

BRECKENFELD, G. (1972) 'Downtown' has fled to the suburbs, *Fortune*, October 1972, 80–87; 156; 158; 162.

BROOM, L. & P. SELZNICK (1975) *Sociology*, 5th edn. New York: Harper & Row.

BROWN, C.J.F. & T.D. SHERIFF (1979) De-industrialization: a background paper. In F. Blackaby (ed) *De-Industrialization*. London: Heinemann, chapter 10.

BROWN, L.A. & J. HOLMES (1971) Search behaviour in an intra-urban migration context: a spatial perspective, *Environment and Planning*, 3, 307–326.

BROWN, L.A. & E.G MOORE (1970) The intra-urban migration process: a perspective, *Geografiska Annaler*, Ser. B. 52, 1–13.

BRUNN, S.D. (1974) *Geography and Politics in America*. New York: Harper & Row.

CARLSTEIN, T., D.N. PARKES & N.J. THRIFT (1978) *Timing Space and Spacing Time*. London: Edward Arnold.

CARMICHAEL, C.L. (1978) Local labour market analysis: its importance and a possible approach, *Geoforum*, 9, 127–148.

CHANDLER, A.D. Jr. (1962) *Strategy and Structure: Chapters in the History of the Industrial Enterprise*. Cambridge, Mass: MIT Press.

CHECKOWAY, B. (1980) Large builders, federal housing programmes and postwar suburbanization, *International Journal of Urban and Regional Research*, 4, 21–45.

CHERRY, G.E. (1974) *Urban Planning Problems*. London: Leonard Hill.

CHESHIRE, P.C. (1979) Inner areas as spatial labour markets: a critique of the inner area studies, *Urban Studies*, 16, 29–44.

CHESTER, T.E. (1976) The public sector – its dimensions and dynamics, *National Westminster Bank Quarterly Review*, February 1976, 31–44.

CHISHOLM, M. (1975) *Human Geography: Evolution or Revolution?* Harmondsworth: Penguin.

CLARK, W.A.V. (1972) Patterns of black intra-urban mobility and restricted relocation opportunities. In H.M. Rose & H. McConnell (eds) *Perspectives in Geography, Volume 2: Geography of the Ghetto*. De Kalb, Illinois: Northern Illinois University Press, chapter 5.

CLEMENT, W. (1975) *The Canadian Corporate Elite*. Toronto: McClelland and Stewart.

COATES, B.E., R.J. JOHNSTON & P.L. KNOX (1977) *Geography and Inequality*. London: Oxford University Press.

COATES, B.E. & E.M. RAWSTRON (1971) *Regional Variations in Britain: Studies in Economic and Social Geography*. London: Batsford.

COHEN, Y.S. (1972) Diffusion of an innovation in an urban system: the spread of planned regional shopping centres in the United States, 1949–1968. *University of Chicago, Department of Geography Research Paper 140*.

COX, K.R. (1973) *Conflict, Power and Politics in the City*. New York: McGraw Hill.

COX, K.R. (ed) (1978) *Urbanization and Conflict in Market Societies*. London: Methuen.

COX, K.R. (1979) *Location and Public Problems*. Oxford: Blackwell.

COX, K.R. & D.R. REYNOLDS (1974) Locational approaches to power and conflict. In K.R. Cox, D.R. Reynolds & S. Rokkan (eds) *Locational Approaches to Power and Conflict*. Beverly Hills: Sage Publications, chapter 1.

DANIELS, P.W. (1975) *Office Location: An Urban and Regional Study*. London: Bell.

DANSON, M.W., W.F. LEVER & J.F. MALCOLM (1980) The inner city employment problem in Great Britain, 1952–1976: a shift-share approach, *Urban Studies*, 17, 193–210.

DAWSON, J.A. (1979) *The Marketing Environment*. London: Croom Helm.

DEAR, M.J. & J. LONG (1978) Community strategies in locational conflict. In K.R. Cox (ed) *Urbanization and Conflict in Market Societies*. London: Methuen, chapter 5.

DE VISE, P. (1971) Cook County Hospital: bulwark of Chicago's apartheid health system and prototype of the nation's public health hospitals, *Antipode*, 3, 9–20.

DE VISE, P. (1976) The suburbanization of jobs and minority employment, *Economic Geography*, 52, 348–362.

DICKEN, P. (1976) The multiplant business enterprise and geographical space: some issues in the study of external control and regional development, *Regional Studies*, 10, 401–412.

DICKEN, P. & M.E. ROBINSON (1976) Place preferences and information, *University of Manchester School of Geography Research Paper* 1.

DOERINGER, P.B. & M.J. PIORE (1970) *Internal Labour Markets and Manpower Analysis*. Lexington, Mass: D.C. Heath.

DOWNS, A. (1968) Moving towards realistic housing goals. In K. Gordon (ed) *Agenda for the Nation*. Washington DC: Brookings Institution, pp.141–178. Reprinted in A. Downs (1970) *Urban Problems and Prospects*. Chicago: Markham Publishing Co., pp.115–155.

DOXIADIS, C. (1969) The prospect of an international megalopolis. In M. Wade (ed) *The International Megalopolis*. Windsor: Univ. Windsor Press, pp.3–32.

DREWETT, R., J. GODDARD & N. SPENCE (1976) British cities: urban population and employment trends, 1951–1971, *Department of the Environment Research Report 10*. London: HMSO.

DREWETT, R., J. GODDARD & N. SPENCE (1976) Urban Britain: beyond containment. In B.J.L. Berry (ed) *Urbanization and Counterurbanization*. Beverly Hills: Sage Publications, chapter 3.

DRUCKER, P. (1969) *The Age of Discontinuity*. London: Pan Books.

DUNCAN, S.S. (1976) Research directions in social geography: housing opportunities and constraints, *Transactions of the Institute of British Geographers, New Series*, 1, 10–19.

ESTALL, R. (1976) *A Modern Geography of the United States*. Harmondsworth: Penguin.

EVERITT, J.C. (1976) Community and propinquity in a city, *Annals of the Association of American Geographers*, 66, 104–116.

EVERSLEY, D.E.C. (1972) Rising costs and static incomes: some economic consequences of regional planning in London, *Urban Studies* 9, 341–368.

EYLES, J. (1979) Area-based policies for the inner city: context, problems and prospects. In D.T. Herbert & D.M. Smith (eds) *Social Problems and the City: Geographical Perspectives*. London: Oxford University Press, chapter 12.

FIRN, J.R. (1975) External control and regional development: the case of Scotland, *Environment and Planning*, A, 7, 393–414.

FOOTE, N.N. & P.K. HATT (1953) Social mobility and economic enhancement, *American Economic Review, Papers and Proceedings*, 43, 364–378.

FOTHERGILL, S. & G. GUDGIN (1979) Regional employment change: a subregional explanation, *Progress in Planning*, 12, 3, 155–219.

FRANK, A.G. (1980) *Crisis in the World Economy*. London: Heinemann.

FREEMAN, C. (1974) *The Economics of Industrial Innovation*. Harmondsworth, Penguin.

FREEMAN, C. & M. JAHODA (eds) (1978) *World Futures: The Great Debate*. London: Martin Robertson.

FRIEDMAN, M. (1975) Unemployment versus inflation, *National Institute of Economic and Social Research. Occasional Papers*, 44.

FRIEDMANN, J. & J. MILLER (1965) The urban field, *Journal of the American Institute of Planners*, 31, 312–320.

FUCHS, V.R. (1967) *Differentials in Hourly Earnings by Region and City Size.* New York: Columbia Press.

FUCHS, V.R. (1968) *The Service Economy.* New York: Columbia University Press.

GALBRAITH, J.K. (1967) *The New Industrial State.* New York: Signet Books.

GALBRAITH, J.K. (1973) *Economics and the Public Purpose.* Harmondsworth: Penguin.

GERSHUNY, J.I. (1977) Post-industrial society: the myth of the service economy, *Futures,* 9, 103–114.

GERSHUNY, J.I. (1978) *After Industrial Society? The Emerging Self-Service Economy.* London: Macmillan.

GIGGS, J.A. (1979) Human health problems in urban areas. In D.T. Herbert & D.M. Smith (eds) *Social Problems and the City: Geographical Perspectives.* London: Oxford University Press, chapter 6.

GLEAVE, D. (1980) Labour supply and the matchmaking process, *Centre for Environmental Studies Working Note* 607.

GLEAVE, D. & M. CORDEY HAYES (1977) Migration dynamics and labour market turnover, *Progress in Planning,* 8, 1–86.

GODDARD, J.B. (1980) Industrial innovation and regional economic development in Britain, *Paper presented to the Commission on Industrial Systems, International Geographical Union Congress, Tokyo.*

GODDARD, J.B. & I.J. SMITH (1978) Changes in corporate control in the British urban system, 1972–1977, *Environment and Planning,* A, 10, 1073–1084.

GOTTMANN, J. (1961) *Megalopolis: The Urbanized Northeastern Seaboard of the United States.* Cambridge, Mass: MIT Press.

GOTTMANN, J. (1976) Megalopolitan systems around the world, *Ekistics,* 243, 109–113. Reprinted in L.S. Bourne & J.W. Simmons (eds) (1978) *Systems of Cities: Readings on Structure, Growth and Policy.* New York: Oxford University Press, pp.53–60.

GOULD, P.R. (1966) On mental maps, *Michigan Inter-University Community of Mathematical Geographers, Discussion Paper 9.*

GOULD, P.R. (1969) Methodological developments since the fifties, *Progress in Geography,* 1, 1–49.

GRAY, F. (1976) Selection and allocation in council housing, *Transactions of the Institute of British Geographers, New Series,* 1, 34–46.

GRIBBIN, J. (1979) *Future Worlds.* London: Sphere Books.

GRIGSBY, W.G. (1963) *Housing Markets and Public Policy.* Philadelphia: University of Pennsylvania Press.

GUDGIN, G., R. CRUM & S. BAILEY (1979) White-collar employment in UK manufacturing industry. In P.W. Daniels (ed) *Spatial Patterns of Office Growth and Location.* Chichester: Wiley, chapter 5.

HÄGERSTRAND, T. (1970) What about people in regional science? *Papers of the Regional Science Association,* 24, 7–21.

HÄGERSTRAND, T. (1973) The domain of human geography. In R.T. Chorley (ed) *Directions in Geography.* London: Methuen, pp.67–87.

HALL, E.T. (1966) *The Hidden Dimension*. New York: Doubleday.

HALL, P. (ed) (1978) *Europe 2000*. London: Duckworth.

HALL, P. et al. (1973) *The Containment of Urban England, Volume 1*. London: George Allen and Unwin.

HALL, P. & D. HAY (1980) *Growth Centres in the European Urban System*. London: Heinemann.

HAMNETT, C. (1973) Improvement grants as an indicator of gentrification in inner London, *Area*, 6, 159–160.

HAMNETT, C. & P.R. WILLIAMS (1980) Social change in London: a study of gentrification, *Urban Affairs Quarterly*, 15, 469–487.

HANSEN, N.M. (ed) (1974) *Public Policy and Regional Economic Development: The Experience of Nine Western Countries*. Cambridge, Mass: Ballinger.

HARRIS, C.D. & E.L. ULLMAN (1945) The nature of cities, *Annals of the American Academy of Political Science*, 242, 7–17.

HARVEY, D. (1972) Society, the city and the space-economy of urbanism, *Association of American Geographers, Commission on College Geography, Resource Paper 18*.

HARVEY, D. (1973) *Social Justice and the City*. London: Edward Arnold.

HARVEY, D. & L. CHATTERJEE (1974) Absolute rent and the structuring of space by governmental and financial institutions, *Antipode*, 6, 22–36.

HAYNES, R.M. (1973) Crime rates and city size in America, *Area*, 5, 162–165.

HEATON, T.B. & G.V. FUGUITT (1978) Nonmetropolitan industrial growth and population change, *Paper presented to the Annual Meeting of the Association of American Geographers*, New Orleans.

HEILBRONER, R. (1972) *The Economic Problem*. 3rd edn. Englewood Cliffs, NJ: Prentice Hall.

HEILBRONER, R. (1976) *Business Civilization in Decline*. London: Marion Boyars.

HELMER, J. & N.A. EDDINGTON (eds) (1973) *Urbanman: The Psychology of Urban Survival*. New York: Free Press.

HENDERSON, W.L. & L.C. LEDEBUR (1972) *Urban Economics: Processes and Problems*. New York: Wiley.

HENDERSON, W.O. & W.H. CHALONER (1958) *Frederick Engels' Condition of the Working Class in England*. Oxford: Basil Blackwell.

HENEMAN, H.G. & D. YODER (1965) *Labour Economics*. Cincinnati: South Western Publishing Co.

HERBERT, D.T. (1972) *Urban Geography: A Social Perspective*. Newton Abbot: David & Charles.

HERBERT, D.T. (1973) The residential mobility process: some empirical observations, *Area*, 5, 44–48.

HIGBEE, E. (1970) *A Question of Priorities: New Strategies for our Urbanized World*. New York: William Morrow & Co.

HILLMAN, M., I. HENDERSON & A. WHALLEY (1976) *Transport Realities and Planning Policy*. London: Political and Economic Planning.

HIRSCH, F. (1977) *Social Limits to Growth*. London: Routledge & Kegan Paul.

HOCH, I. (1972) Urban scale and environmental quality. In R.G. Ridker (ed) *Population, Resources, and the Environment*. U.S. Commission on Population Growth and the American Future, Research Report III. Washington DC: USGPO, chapter 9.

HOLT, C. (1970) Job search, Phillips' wage relation and union influence. In E.S. Phelps (ed) *Microeconomic Foundations of Employment and Inflation Theory*. New York: W. W. Norton.

HOLTERMANN, S. (1975) Areas of urban deprivation in Great Britain: an analysis of 1971 census data, *Social Trends*, 6, 33–47.

HOWE, G.M. (1970) *National Atlas of Disease Mortality in the United Kingdom*. London: Nelson.

HOYT, H. (1939) *The Structure and Growth of Residential Neighbourhoods in American Cities*. Washington: Federal Housing Administration.

HYMER, S. (1972) The multinational corporation and the law of uneven development. In J. Bhagwati (ed) *Economics and World Order*. New York: Collier-Macmillan, pp.113–140.

JAKLE, J.A., S. BRUNN & C.C. ROSEMAN (1967) *Human Spatial Behavior: A Social Geography*. North Scituate, Mass: Duxbury Press.

JANELLE, D.G. (1969) Spatial reorganization: a model and a concept, *Annals of the Association of American Geographers*, 59, 348–364.

JOHNSON, N. (1970) *How to Talk Back to Your Television Set*. New York: Bantam Books.

JOHNSTON, R.J. (1971). *Urban Residential Patterns*. London: Bell.

JOHNSTON, R.J. (1977) Political geography and welfare: observations on interstate variations in aid to families with dependent children programs, *Professional Geographer*, 29, 347–352.

JOHNSTON, R.J. (1979) *Geography and Geographers: Anglo-American Human Geography Since 1945*. London: Edward Arnold.

JONES, C. (ed) (1979) *Urban Deprivation and the Inner City*. London: Croom Helm.

JONES, P.N. (1976) Coloured minorities in Birmingham, England, *Annals of the Association of American Geographers*, 66, 89–103.

JONES, P.N. (1979) Ethnic areas in British cities. In D.T. Herbert & D.M. Smith (eds) *Social Problems and the City: Geographical Perspectives*. London: Oxford University Press, chapter 9.

KALDOR, N. (1976) Inflation and recession in the world economy, *Economic Journal*, 86, 703–714.

KASARDA, J. (1980) The implications of contemporary redistribution trends for national urban policy, *Social Science Quarterly* (December).

KEEBLE, D. (1976) *Industrial Location and Planning in the United Kingdom*. London: Methuen.

KEEBLE, D. (1980) Industrial decline, regional policy and the urban-rural manufacturing shift in the United Kingdom, *Environment and Planning*, A, 12, 945–962.

KENNETT, S. (1980) Local government problems: a context for inner areas, *Social Science Research Council, Inner City in Context Paper 6*.

KENNETT, S. (1980) The inner city in the context of the urban system, *Social Science Research Council, Inner City in Context Paper 7*.

KING, L.J. (1976) Alternatives to a positive economic geography, *Annals of the Association of American Geographers*, 66, 293–308.

KIRBY, A. (1978) *The Inner City: Causes and Effects*. Corbridge: Retailing and Planning Association.

KIRWAN, R. (1980) The inner city in the United States, *Social Science Research Council, Inner City in Context Paper 8*.

KNOX, P.L. (1975) *Social Well-Being: A Spatial Perspective*. London: Oxford University Press.

KRUMME, G. & R. HAYTER (1975) Implications of corporate strategies and product cycle adjustments for regional employment changes. In L. Collins & D.F. Walker (eds) *Locational Dynamics of Manufacturing Activity*. London: Wiley, chapter 12.

KUHN, A. (1966) *The Study of Society*. London: Associated Book Publishers.

LAMPARD, E. (1955) The history of cities in the economically advanced areas, *Economic Development and Cultural Change*, 3, 81–136.

LEE, R. (1976) Integration, spatial structure and the capitalist mode of production in the EEC. In R. Lee & P.E. Ogden (eds) *Economy and Society in the EEC*. Farnbrough: Saxon House, chapter 2.

LEE, R. (1979) The economic basis of social problems in the city. In D.T. Herbert & D.M. Smith (eds) *Social Problems and the City: Geographical Perspectives*. London: Oxford University Press, chapter 4.

LEVISON, A. (1974) *The Working Class Majority*. New York: Cowards, McCann & Geoghegan.

LEY, D. & J. MERCER (1980) Locational conflict and the politics of consumption, *Economic Geography*, 56, 89–109.

LEY, D. & M.S. SAMUELS (eds) (1978) *Humanistic Geography: Prospects and Problems*. London: Croom Helm.

LITHWICK, N.H. (1970) *Urban Canada: Problems and Prospects*. Ottawa: Government of Canada.

LLOYD, P.E. & P. DICKEN (1977) *Location in Space: A Theoretical Approach to Economic Geography*. 2nd edn. London: Harper & Row.

LLOYD, P.E. & P. DICKEN (1981) The components of change in metropolitan areas: events in their corporate context. In J.B. Goddard (ed) *Urban and Regional Perspectives on Contemporary Economic and Social Trends in Britain*. London: Methuen.

LOWE, J.C. & S. MORYADAS (1975) *The Geography of Movement*. Boston: Houghton Mifflin.

McLINTOCK, F.H. & N.H. AVISON (1968) *Crime in England and Wales*. London: Heinemann.

McLUHAN, M. (1964) *Understanding Media*. London: Routledge & Kegan Paul.

MAIZIE, S.M. & S. RAWLINGS (1973) Public attitudes towards population issues. In S.M. Maizie (ed) *Population Distribution and Policy*. Washington DC: USGPO, pp.599–630.

MALECKI, E.J. (1979) Locational trends in R & D by large US corporations, 1965–1977, *Economic Geography*, 55, 309–323.

MANNERS, G., D. KEEBLE, H.B. RODGERS & K. WARREN (1980) *Regional Development in Britain*, 2nd edn. Chichester: Wiley.

MASLOW, A.H. (1954) *Motivation and Personality*. New York: Harper & Row.

MASSEY, D. (1979) In what sense a regional problem? *Regional Studies*, 13, 233–243.

MASSEY, D. & R.A. MEEGAN (1978) Industrial restructuring versus the cities, *Urban Studies*, 15, 273–288.

MASSEY, D. & R.A. MEEGAN (1979) The geography of industrial reorganization, *Progress in Planning*, 10, 155–237.

MAYER, H.M. (1969) The spatial expression of urban growth, *Association of American Geographers, Commission on College Geography, Resource Paper 7*.

MICHELSON, W.H. (1970) *Man and his Urban Environment: A Sociological Approach*. Reading, Mass: Addison-Wesley.

MINTZ, M. & J.S. COHEN (1971) *America, Inc.* New York: Dial Press.

MOORE, B., J. RHODES & P. TYLER (1977) The impact of regional policy in the 1970s, *Centre for Environmental Studies Review*, 1, 67–77.

MOORE, E.G. (1972) Residential mobility in the city, *Association of American Geographers, Commission on College Geography Resource Paper, 13*.

MORGAN, B.S. (1976) The basis of family status segregation: a case study in Exeter, *Transactions of the Institute of British Geographers, New Series*, 1, 83–107.

MORRILL, R.L. (1965) The Negro ghetto: problems and alternatives, *Geographical Review*, 55, 339–361.

MORRILL, R.L. & E.H. WOHLENBERG (1971) *The Geography of Poverty in the United States*. New York: McGraw Hill.

MORRISON, P.A. (1975) The current demographic context of national growth and development, *Rand Corporation Publications, P-5514*, 3–13. Reprinted in L.S. Bourne & J.W. Simmons (eds) (1978) *Systems of Cities: Readings on Structure, Growth and Policy*. New York: Oxford University Press, pp.473–479.

MOSELEY, M.J. (1979) *Accessibility: The Rural Challenge*. London: Methuen.

MOSELEY, M.J. (1980) Rural development and its relevance to the inner city debate, *Social Science Research Council, Inner City in Conflict, Paper 9*.

MULLER, P.O. (1976) The outer city: geographical consequences of the urbanization of the suburbs, *Association of American Geographers, Commission on College Geography, Resource Paper 75—2*.

MUMFORD, L. (1934) *Technics and Civilization*. New York: Harcourt, Brace and World.

MURDIE, R.A. (1969) Factorial Ecology of Metropolitan Toronto, 1951–1961, *University of Chicago Dept. of Geography Research Paper*, 116.

MUSGRAVE, R.A. (1974) On social goods and social bads. In R. Marris (ed.) *The Corporate Society*. London: Macmillan, chapter 9.

NATIONAL COMMISSION ON TECHNOLOGY, AUTOMATION AND ECONOMIC PROGRESS (1966) *Technology and the American Economy, Volume II: The Employment Impact of Technological Change*. Washington DC: USGPO.

NORTON, R.D. & J. REES (1979) The product cycle and the spatial decentralization of American manufacturing, *Regional Studies*, 13, 141–151.

OECD (1978) *A Medium Term Strategy for Employment and Manpower*. Paris: OECD.

OECD (1979) *The Impact of the Newly Industrializing Countries*. Paris: OECD.

ORLEANS, P. (1973) Differential cognition of urban residents: effects of social scale on mapping. In R.M. Downs & D. Stea (eds) *Image and Environment*. London: Edward Arnold, chapter 7.

PACIONE, M. (1980) Differential quality of life in a metropolitan village, *Transactions of the Institute of British Geographers, New Series*, 5, 185–206.

PAHL, R.E. (1970) *Patterns of Urban Life*. London: Longman.

PAHL, R.E. (1971) Poverty and the urban system. In M. Chisholm & G. Manners (eds) *Spatial Policy Problems of the British Economy*. Cambridge: Cambridge University Press, pp.126–145.

PAHL, R.E. (1979) Socio-political factors in resource allocation. In D.T. Herbert & D.M. Smith (1979) *Social Problems and the City: Geographical Perspectives*. London: Oxford University Press, chapter 3.

PAHL, R.E. (1980) Employment, work and the domestic division of labour, *International Journal of Urban and Regional Research*, 4, 1–20.

PALM, R. (1976) Real estate agents and geographical information, *Geographical Review*, 66, 266–280.

PALM, R. & A. PRED (1978) A time-geographic perspective on problems of inequality for women. In D. Lanegran & R. Palm (eds) *An Invitation to Geography*, 2nd edn. New York: McGraw Hill, chapter 7.

PARK, R.E. & E.W. BURGESS (1925) *The City*. Chicago: University of Chicago Press.

PARKES, D.N. & N.J. THRIFT (1980) *Times, Spaces and Places: A Chronogeographic Perspective*. Chichester: John Wiley.

PEET, R. (1975) Inequality and poverty: a Marxist-geographic theory, *Annals of the Association of American Geographers*, 65, 564–571.

PEET, R. (ed) (1978) *Radical Geography*. London: Methuen.

PERRY, D.C. & A.J. WATKINS (1977) *The Rise of the Sun Belt Cities*. Beverly Hills: Sage Publications.

PHILLIPS, P.D. & S.D. BRUNN (1978) Slow growth: a new epoch of American metropolitan evolution, *Geographical Review*, 68, 274–292.

POTTER, R.B. (1977) Spatial patterns of consumer behaviour and perception in relation to the social class variable, *Area*, 9, 153–156.

PRAIS, S.J. (1976) *The Evolution of Giant Firms in Britain*. National Institute of Economic and Social Research, Economic and Social Studies, 30, Cambridge: Cambridge University Press.

PRED, A.R. (1975) On the spatial structure of organizations and the complexity of metropolitan interdependence, *Papers of the Regional Science Association*, 35, 115–142.

PRED, A.R. (1977) *City-Systems in Advanced Economies*. London: Hutchinson.

PYM, D. (1980) Towards the dual economy and emancipation from employment, *Futures*, 12, 223–237.

RAPKIN, C. & W.G. GRIGSBY (1960) *The Demand for Housing in Racially Mixed Areas*. Philadelphia: University of Pennsylvania Press.

REES, J. (1979) Technological change and regional shifts in American manufacturing, *Professional Geographer*, 31, 45–54.

REID, S.R. (1976) *The New Industrial Order: Concentration, Regulation and Public Policy*. New York: McGraw Hill.

REX, J. (1968) The sociology of a zone in transition. In R.E. Pahl (ed) *Readings in Urban Sociology*. Oxford: Pergamon, pp.211–231.

REYNOLDS, D.R. & R. HONEY (1978) Conflict in the location of salutary public facilities. In K.R. Cox (ed) *Urbanization and Conflict in Market Societies*. London: Methuen, chapter 7.

RICHARDSON, H.W. (1973) *The Economics of Urban Size*. Farnborough: Teakfield.

ROBSON, B.T. (1975) *Urban Social Areas*. London: Oxford University Press.

ROSE, H.M. (1969) Social processes in the city: race and urban residential choice, *Association of American Geographers, Commission on College Geography, Resource Paper, 6*.

ROSE, H.M. (1976) *Black Suburbanization*. Cambridge, Mass: Ballinger.

ROSSI, P. (1955) *Why Families Move: A Study in the Social Psychology of Urban Residential Mobility*. New York: Free Press.

SAMPSON, A. (1974) *The New Anatomy of Britain*. London: Hodder & Stoughton.

SCHAEFFER, K.H. & E. SCLAR (1975) *Access for All: Transportation and Urban Growth*. Harmondsworth: Penguin.

SCHELLING, T. (1974) On the ecology of micromotives. In R. Marris (ed) *The Corporate Society*. London: Macmillan, chapter 2.

SCHUMACHER, E.F. (1973) *Small is Beautiful*. London: Blond & Briggs.

SHANNON, G.W. & G.E.A. DEVER (1974) *Health Care Delivery: Spatial Perspectives*. New York: McGraw Hill.

SHEPHERD, J., J. WESTAWAY & T. LEE (1974) *A Social Atlas of London*. Oxford: Clarendon Press.

SHERRARD, T.D. (ed) (1968) *Social Welfare and Urban Problems*. New York: Columbia University Press.

SHEVKY, E. & W. BELL (1955) *Social Area Analysis: Theory, Illustrative Applications and Computational Procedures*. Stanford: Stanford University Press.

SIMMONS, J.W. (1968) Changing residence in the city: a review of intra-urban mobility, *Geographical Review*, 58, 622–651.

SIMON, H.A. (1960) *The New Science of Management Decision*. New York: Harper & Row.

SMITH, D.M. (1973) *The Geography of Social Well-Being in the United States*. New York: McGraw-Hill.

SMITH, D.M. (1977) *Human Geography: A Welfare Approach*. London: Edward Arnold.

SMITH, D.M. (1979) *Where the Grass is Greener: Living in an Unequal World*. Harmondsworth: Penguin.

S.S.R.C. INNER CITIES WORKING PARTY (1980) *The Inner City in Context*, Papers 1–11. London: SSRC.

SOJA, E.W. (1971) The Political Organization of Space, *Association of American Geographers, Commission on College Geography, Resource Paper,·8.*

STERNLIEB, G. & J.W. HUGHES (eds) (1975) *Post-Industrial America: Metropolitan Decline and Inter-Regional Job Shifts.* New Brunswick, N.J.: Rutgers.

STEVENSON, G.M. (1972) Noise and the urban environment. In T.R. Detwyler & M.G. Marcus (eds) *Urbanization and Environment: The Physical Geography of the City.* Belmont: Wadsworth Publishing Company, chapter 8.

STUTZ, F.P. (1976) Social aspects of interaction and transportation, *Association of American Geographers, Commission on College Geography, Resource Paper 76–2.*

SUTTLES, G.D. (1968) *The Social Order of the Slum.* Chicago: University of Chicago Press.

TAVISS, I. (1974) On contemporary social change. In R. Marris (ed) *The Corporate Society.* London: Macmillan, chapter 3.

TEITZ, M.B. (1968) Towards a theory of public facility location, *Papers of the Regional Science Association,* 21, 35–51.

THATCHER, A.R. (1979) Labour supply and employment trends. In F. Blackaby (ed) *De-Industrialization.* London: Heinemann, chapter 2.

THOMAS, H. (1978) Costing the value of ecological disasters, *Guardian,* 19 July 1978.

THRIFT, N.J. (1977) *An Introduction to Time Geography.* Norwich: Geo Abstracts Ltd.

THRIFT, N.J. (1979) Unemployment in the inner city: urban problem or structural imperative? A review of the British experience. In D.T. Herbert & R.J. Johnston (eds) *Geography and the urban environment, Volume 2.* Chichester: Wiley, chapter 5.

THUROW, L.C. (1980) *The Zero-Sum Society.* New York: Basic Books.

TIMMS, D.W.G. (1976) Social bases to urban areas. In D.T. Herbert & R.J. Johnston (eds) *Social Areas in Cities, Volume I: Spatial Processes and Form.* London: Wiley, chapter 1.

TIVERS, J. (1977) Constraints on spatial activity patterns: women with young children. *Department of Geography, King's College, London. Occasional Paper 6.*

TOFFLER, A. (1971) *Future Shock.* London: Pan Books.

TORNQUIST, G. (1968) Flows of information and the location of economic activities, *Lund Studies in Geography,* Series B.30.

TORNQUIST, G. (1973) Contact requirements and travel facilities: contact models of Sweden and regional development alternatives in the future. In A.R. Pred & G. Tornquist *Systems of Cities and Information Flows: Two Essays, Lund Studies in Geography,* Series B.38, pp.83–121.

TOWNSEND, A.R. (1977) The relationship of inner city problems to regional policy, *Regional Studies,* 11, 225–252.

ULLMAN, E. (1958) Regional development and the geography of concentration, *Papers and Proceedings of the Regional Science Association,* 4, 179–198.

UNITED NATIONS (1974) *Multinational Corporations in World Development.* New York: Praeger.

WARD, D. (1971) *Cities and Immigrants: A Geography of Change in Nineteenth Century America*. New York: Oxford University Press.

WARNER, W.L., D.B. UNWALLA & J.H. TRIMM (eds) (1967) *The Emergent American Society, Volume I: Large-Scale Organizations*. New Haven, Conn: Yale University Press.

WEBBER, M.M. (1963) Order in Diversity: Community without propinquity. In L. Wingo Jr. (ed) *Cities and Space*. Baltimore: Johns Hopkins Press, pp.22–54.

WEBBER, M.M. (1964) Urban place and the nonplace urban realm. In M.M. Webber, et al., *Explorations in Urban Structure*. Philadelphia: University of Philadelphia Press, pp.79–153.

WEIDENBAUM, M.L. (1969) *The Modern Public Sector: New Ways of Doing the Government's Business*. New York: Basic Books.

WESTAWAY, J. (1974) Contact potential and the occupational structure of the British urban system 1961–1966: an empirical study, *Regional Studies*, 8, 57–73.

WESTAWAY, J. (1974) The spatial hierarchy of business organizations and its implications for the British urban system, *Regional Studies*, 8, 145–155.

WHEELER, J.O. (1974) *The Urban Circulation Noose*. Belmont, Wadsworth Publishing Company.

WILLIAMS, G.W. (1975) *Metropolitan Manchester: A Social Atlas*. Mimeo.

WILLIAMS, O.P. (1971) *Metropolitan Political Analysis*. New York: Free Press.

WOHLENBERG, E.H. (1976) Interstate variations in AFDC programs, *Economic Geography*, 52, 254–266.

WOLCH, J.L. (1979) Residential location and the provision of human services: some directions for geographic research, *Professional Geographer*, 31, 271–277.

WOLPERT, J., A. MUMPHREY & J. SELEY (1972) Metropolitan neighbourhoods: participation and conflict over change, *Association of American Geographers, Commission on College Geography, Resource Paper 16*.

WOOD, C.M., N. LEE, J.A. LUKER & P.J.W. SAUNDERS (1974) *The Geography of Pollution: A Study of Greater Manchester*. Manchester: Manchester University Press.

WOOD, L.J. & T.R. LEE (1980) Time-space convergence: reappraisal for an oil short future, *Area*, 12, 217–222.

YEATES, M.H. (1975) *Main Street: Windsor to Quebec City*. Toronto: Macmillan.

YEATES, M.H. & B. GARNER (1976) *The North American City*, 2nd edn. New York: Harper & Row.

YOUNG, M. & P. WILMOTT (1957) *Family and Kinship in East London*. London: Routledge & Kegan Paul.

ZIMMER, B.G. (1975) The urban centrifugal drift. In A.H. Hawley & V.P. Rock (eds) *Metropolitan America in Contemporary Perspective*. Beverly Hills/London, Sage Publications, chapter 1.

Index